UNDER THE BO TREE

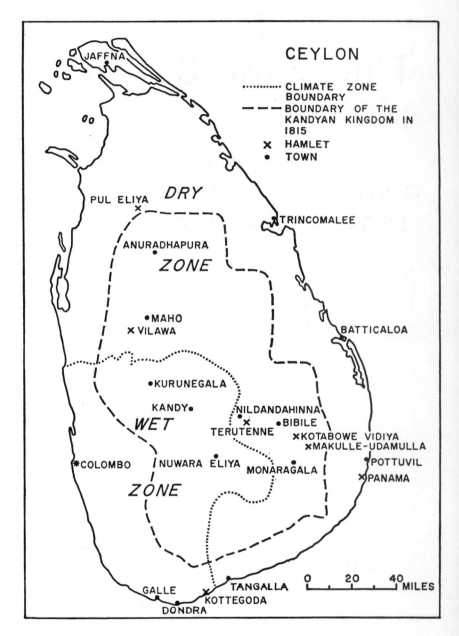

Map. 1. Ceylon.

Under the Bo Tree

STUDIES IN
CASTE, KINSHIP, AND MARRIAGE
IN THE INTERIOR OF CEYLON

Nur Yalman

UNIVERSITY OF CALIFORNIA PRESS

Berkeley, Los Angeles, London, 1971

University of California Press
Berkeley and Los Angeles, California

University of California Press, Ltd.
London, England

Copyright © 1967, by The Regents of the University of California
First Paperback Printing, 1971
ISBN: 0-520-02054-5

Library of Congress Catalog Card Number: 67-11939
Printed in the United States of America

TO MY FRIENDS IN CEYLON

Acknowledgments

I should like to record my gratitude here to my many friends in Ceylon who received me with kindness into their homes, and generously gave me their friendship and support. Among many who can hardly be repaid are Mrs. S. Fernando and Mr. D. B. Elapolla. Mr. M. Amarasuriya, the Bibile and Kotagama families, and Mr. and Mrs. Arulpragasim must also be mentioned. I want to thank, too, my lively colleagues Dr. S. J. Tambiah and Mr. I. Goonetilleke, who gave me their delightful companionship, shared with me their lives, and did me innumerable kindnesses. Professor R. Pieris' hospitality is also gratefully recalled.

Apart from friends in Peradeniya and Colombo, I must record my appreciation for the efficient Government Agent at Nuwara Eliya, and the District Revenue Officers of Walapane, Wellassa, and Panama in the period 1954–1956 for their constant assistance and unfailing interest in my work.

My debt to Mr. P. Cooray, Mr. W. M. K. Banda, and Mr. M. I. Yasin who acted as patient interpreters in different places is immense. I also cannot forget my hosts, the friendly, hospitable, sophisticated, and amusing villagers. Some of the happiest days of my life were spent among them.

I want to thank, too, Meyer Fortes, who started me in anthropology when he first took the Chair in Cambridge many years ago now and who has been a source of constant encouragement, and my friends and colleagues, Jack Goody, Frederik Barth, Jean La Fontaine, and Martin Southwold, without whose insight and assistance this work probably would never have got anywhere. My eminent teacher and thoughtful friend E. R. Leach in particular must be singled out. Our work in Ceylon partly coincided in time. I visited his village for a few days, saw his simple mode of life, his intense industry, and learned much about field work and anthropology from his example. We kept up a voluminous correspondence in Ceylon and although he is certainly not responsible for the many deficiencies in this work, the general approach owes a good deal to him.

The field work was supported from funds provided by the Wenner-

Gren Foundation and the University of Cambridge. This is gratefully acknowledged. In working on the material from Ceylon, I had the benefit of intellectual homes in Peterhouse, Cambridge, where I was a bye-fellow, at the Center for Advanced Study in the Behavioral Sciences at Stanford, and at the Department of Anthropology at the University of Chicago. The assistance and intellectual companionship of friends in all three places is gratefully recalled.

Mrs. G. Moran helped me at various stages of my work. Miss Beppie Anne Duker and Mrs. Shirley Taylor were patient and helpful editors. I am grateful to them. My wife's constant assistance is more than can be acknowledged.

The preparation of this work has been delayed by my military obligations and problems created by the coup d'état of 1960 in Turkey.

NUR YALMAN

Contents

BOOK ONE: *A Village in Ceylon*

PART I: *Orientation*   3

  1. Introduction   3
  2. The Kandyan Sinhalese   12

PART II: *Terutenne*   24

  3. A Village in the Highlands   24
  4. The Economy of the Dry Zone Village   36
  5. Caste   58

PART III: *Kinship and the Micro-Caste*   96

  6. The Constitution of the Nuclear Family   96
  7. Patterns of Inheritance and Descent   121
  8. The Marriage Alliance   150
  9. The Structure of the Micro-Caste   189

BOOK TWO: *Toward South India*

PART IV: *The Logic of Structure in Ceylon:*
From the Bilateral to the Patrilineal   227

  10. A Visit East: Uva Province   227
  11. More on Bilaterals: The Northwestern Province   247
  12. The Patrilineal Hypergamous Variant: The South Coast   271

PART V: *Logical Categories and Empirical Discoveries*   282

  13. The Tamil Moorish System: The Matrilocals   282
  14. The Articulation of Structures: Panama   310
  15. On the Eastern Littoral: The Matrilineal Hypergamous
      Variant   325

PART VI: *Variations on a Theme*   332

   16. The Cross-Cousin in South India   332

GLOSSARY   379
BIBLIOGRAPHY   387
INDEX   401

FIGURES

  1. Types of Dry Zone Villages   22
  2. The Potters of Terutenne   72
  3. Kinship Connections in Galpitiya   78–79
  4. Kinship Connections in Dunkalawatte   80
  5. Kinship Between Kinegolle–Galpitiya   84
  6. Kinship in Kinegolle   85
  7. Multiple Land Ownership   98
  8. Labor Arrangements in Multiple Land Ownership   99
  9. Types of Kandyan Dwellings   105
10. Mahapitiya and Elapita Gedara Households, Galpitiya   143
11. The Amunumulles   144
12. Field Corner House   145
13. Orange Tree House   148
14. The Interconnection and Lateral Extension of Claims for
    Cross-Cousin Marriage   154
15. The Factions in Terutenne   157
16. Interconnections of *Pavula* A, Helagama   192
17. Connections of *Pavula* A with Other *Pavula*   193
18. The Core of *Pavula* A   198
19. A Case of "Wrong" Marriage   214
20. More of a Case of "Wrong" Marriage   214
21. Bifurcate Merging   220
22. A Tank Village in the Maho Area   251
23. Kinship Connections in Vilawa   259
24. Sketch of the Main Field in Vilawa   260
25. Vilawa Landowners   261–262
26. Dowry Obligations in the Low Country   275
27. An Example of Muslim Property Rights   294
28. Marriage in Panama   313
29. A Sinhalese Family in Panama   320
30. A Tamil Family in Panama   320
31. Kinship Connections Between Figures 29 and 30   321
32. *Kudi* Cattle Brands, Panama   328

33. The Transformation of Models 334
34. MBD + ZD Marriage (Brahman) 351
35. FZD Marriage (Brahman) 353
36. Claims Between Brothers and Sisters 358
37. Patrilineal and Matrilineal Hypergamy 366
38. Matrilateral Cross-Cousin Marriage 369

TABLES

1. The Population of Ceylon 13
2. The Population of Terutenne 26
3. The Ownership of Paddy Lands in Terutenne 39
4. The Ownership of Paddy Lands in Makulle Watta and Vilawa 41
5. The Dispersal of Siblings 42
6. Occupational Groupings of Gainful Workers in Ceylon 43
7. Operations and Cost of Paddy Cultivation by Coolie Labor 45
8. The Shops of Terutenne 51
9. The Shops of Makulle Town in Wellassa 52
10. The Schoolteachers of Terutenne 55
11. Ownership of Rice Land Among Low Castes in Terutenne 64
12. Household Composition Among Tom-Tom Beaters of Terutenne 65
13. *Badde* Services (Tom-Tom Beaters) 67
14. *Henea* Services (Washermen) 68
15. *Achari* Services (Blacksmiths) 70
16. *Valan Karayo* Services (Potters) 72
17. Galpitiya: Population and Land Ownership 78
18. Dunkalawatte: Population and Land Ownership 81
19. Kinegolle: Population and Land Ownership 83
20. Some Terutenne Usages Between Speaker and Addressee of Different Castes 90
21. Commensal Units (*Ge*) per Dwelling in Terutenne 103
22. Dwellings in Terutenne with Single Cooking Units 115
23. Dwellings in Terutenne with Two Cooking Units 116
24. Dwellings in Terutenne with Three Cooking Units 117
25. Dwellings in Terutenne with Four or More Cooking Units 118
26. Adult High-Caste Population of Terutenne, by Origin 127
27. Natives of Terutenne: Locality of Marriage and Origin of Spouses 128
28. Settlers in Terutenne: Locality of Marriage and Origin of Spouses 129
29. Marriages and Separations in Terutenne 186

30. Children Living with Stepparents or Other Relatives in
Terutenne 187
31. Landholdings of *Pavula* in Helagama 201
32. The Population of Makulle Watta 230
33. Cooking Units in Udamulla and Vilawa 240–241
34. Locality of Marriage and Origin of Spouses, Udamulla and
Vilawa 242–244
35. The Stability of Marriage in Udamulla and Vilawa 245
36. The Population of Vilawa 249
37. Three Sinhalese Patterns of Kinship 280
38. Marriages in Kotabowe Vidiya 286
39. Membership of Households, Kotabowe Vidiya 298
40. Sinhalese–Muslim Tamil Ceremonial Customs 306–307
41. Names of Workers on Marakanda Mudalali's Lands, Panama 321

MAPS

1. Ceylon *frontispiece*
2. Walapane Division 25
3. Wekumbura Hamlet (with Baddegama) 27
4. Terutenne 38
5. Galpitiya 76
6. Dunkalawatte 80
7. Kinegolle 83
8. Helagama in Terutenne 191
9. Wellassa Division 229
10. Makulle Town in 1955 235
11. Wanni Hat Pattuva Region 248
12. Vilawa 258

A NOTE TO THE READER

Orthography in Sinhalese follows the general principles of Ryan, *Caste in Modern Ceylon* (1953).

For kinsmen, I have used the following system: F = father; M = mother; S = son; D = daughter; etc. But Z = sister: for example, FZD = father's sister's daughter.

Personal names are sometimes abbreviated. Chapter 5, pp. 91–92, may be consulted for their meaning.

Wherever the material discussed might be offensive to the persons concerned, fictional names have been utilized. The name "Terutenne" is fictional.

BOOK ONE:

A Village in Ceylon

PART I: ORIENTATION

1

Introduction

"The limits of my language mean the limits of my world.
Logic fills the world. The limits of the world are also its limits."
—L. Wittgenstein, *Tractatus Logico-Philosophicus,* ¶s 5.6

The process of learning to speak a language, either as a child or as an adult, is very different from that of analyzing its linguistic structure or grammar; and even when the structural analysis is completed, there still remains the question of translating messages from one language into another. The difficulties involved in this act of translation are obvious when one considers a subject such as poetry. If this is so in language, how much more difficult is the task of the ethnographer who undertakes to study the principles of social organization of a certain people and to relate his findings in another language to another audience. He may learn to live in the culture, and yet not understand its principles; or he may grasp the principles but be unable to see their interconnections or to explain them convincingly to others. Not only must the complexity of life in a strange environment be clearly understood in its basic principles, but in addition these must be accurately expressed in terms that have meaning in an entirely different world. Both processes are a search for forms. To succeed in this task without doing violence to the observed facts calls for sympathy, patience, and complete dedication. But this is not all. The account is worth little if it does not illuminate some aspect of human thought or behavior.

Ceylon is a highly sophisticated and complex island. The intellectual life of Colombo and Peradeniya is lively and important; its political repercussions can be felt around the world. But in this volume we leave all that aside, and concern ourselves almost entirely with the small, relatively isolated, traditional communities far from sophisticated centers. Why?

I am interested in the interconnections between certain categories of thought, certain patterns of behavior, and the principles of social

<u>organization</u>. That there is a general relationship here is hardly to be disputed, but the precise analysis of this connection is in practice very difficult. It is difficult enough to indicate it in terms of the ideas, the behavior, and the social background and position of the single individual; dealing with collective facts the problems multiply rapidly. It is important, therefore, to approach these questions in the context of as simple, traditional, and stable communities as possible. Only then can we discern how the patterns are rendered even more complex in the bazaars and the sophisticated towns of Ceylon.

Let me be quite clear here. <u>When we speak of social structure what we mean is that a large number of individuals regard the structure of their society in the same way and that they communicate and behave in an appropriate manner.</u> There are, of course, some individuals who do not accept this "collective picture," and outsiders who do not know or comprehend it at all. In other words, individuals are "tuned" to fulfill certain roles in the "structure." The structure, therefore, "exists" both outside as a collective fact, and in the "mind" of the individual. It is clear, also, that the relation of the "mind" to the "structure" is a two-way process.

These are some of the reasons why in simple communities the study of social structure may be related to the structure of thought. <u>I am</u>, therefore, <u>searching for a model that will explain the categories of thought, the patterned behavior of individuals, and the principles of social structure in small communities.</u> That there is such order is, I think, obvious: the mere fact that culture is used as a system of communication and that this can be learned even by the anthropologist means that it is coherent.

<u>This relationship between thought and behavior, the idea and the fact, "superstructure" and "infrastructure," is at the heart of much anthropological theorizing.</u> Nadel (1951b) tended to distinguish between "moral" and "statistical" structure: using some of Fortes' germinal work as an example (Fortes, 1949a), he observed that "structure" could be regarded merely as a statistical statement of regularities observed by the ethnographer. This use of "structure" could be contrasted with the extrapolations the people themselves make of how their system works—and how it "ought" to work. Thus Fortes in his Tallensi works had adopted the concept of "jural norms" as his material for the definition of "structure."

Leach's position, particularly exemplified in his work on the Kachin (1953), was that the people constructed "ideal models" of their system. Much of the politics in highland Burma could thus be seen as the manipulation of the contradictions in "ideal models."

Lévi-Strauss, who provided an important contribution to these issues in his paper on "Social Structure" (1953), resolved the question in a characteristically imaginative fashion. Replying to Maybury-Lewis' suggestion (1960) that it was possible to distinguish between patterns of thought and behavior, Lévi-Strauss (1960) defined "structure" as the "design" behind both thought and behavior—like the code or formula by means of which a lathe cuts material according to a predetermined pattern. Although Lévi-Strauss was writing here about principles that the anthropologist discovers behind the complicated data of behavior, the principles are not interpreted as existing outside the individual; rather, they are fundamental categories in the mind of every member of society. Such an approach is helpful in explaining the curious fact that "structures" reverberate through various levels of social life: principles found in kinship are repeated in caste concepts and, more subtly, as parts of religious ritual and belief.

Concepts such as "moral blueprints," models, and "principles" of organization make all comparisons between social systems and organic or natural systems somewhat irrelevant. Henri Bergson in *The Two Sources of Morality and Religion* (chap. 1) observes that societies often turn to nature or to a god to find a final justification, a divine anchorage, for a particular system: everything "conspires to make social order an imitation of the order observed in nature." But the analogies from chemistry or biology are simply confusing. It seems more fruitful to consider the example of linguistics and to regard order in social relations as an aspect of structure in a system of communication.

What appears to be highly thought provoking about social order is that, at least in traditional communities, it is consistent. It is a curious fact that when principles of social organization are discerned and formulated by the ethnographer, they become amenable to logical manipulation. It is always possible to say that, given such and such principles, certain further conclusions must necessarily follow. Indeed, not only can one return to the empirical data to see whether the logical operations are borne out, but also one can frequently dispute the facts themselves on the basis of such theorizing. Furthermore, just as the consistency within one society between the various levels of order in the family, in ritual, and in the economy is a legitimate sphere of inquiry, anthropologists find it possible to compare the logical implications of their constructs as between two or more societies. This is what Leach has called "Structural Implications" (1961a). In other words, he is thinking of "the 'function' of such rules in a mathematical sense"—for example (p. 61): "Given a rule such as that which defines [a special type of marriage] . . . and given various other common elements between society A and society B, can we infer, by logical arguments, that some other unknown characteristic 'X' must also be common to our two societies? And if we think we can do this, how far do empirical facts justify such a claim?"

It is, of course, the logical coherence of such interconnected principles that makes it possible for social anthropologists completely unfamiliar with the facts of a given society to dispute the formal analysis carried out by another anthropologist. If the general structure expounded is not internally consistent, and if it fails to explain all the facts, the analysis will be deemed erroneous.

Such a presumption of logical consistency, and, in the best works, the demonstration of systematic structures in traditional small-scale societies, is somewhat extraordinary. Lévi-Strauss, in *La Pensée sauvage* (1962), develops the thesis that the presence of this symmetry and order in almost every aspect of social life is related to certain properties of communication systems and that societies function systematically in this way because the human mind tends to order confusing experiences into cultural patterns.

One must not belabor the case for order and symmetry, however. Lévi-Strauss observes that systems exist in the flux of history. Events have a tendency to eat into orderly systems: there is always an antipathy between cosmos and chaos.

Some elements of society are more vulnerable than others. Political institutions, in particular, are susceptible to sudden alterations, if not destruction, and even the most highly organized political system can fall victim to events. Most of the structures concerned with the family and kin groups, on the other hand, appear to have greater stability and resistance to change. Owing perhaps to their generality in social systems, and perhaps also to their emotional roots, they tend to remain highly structured, consistent, and traditional. And since the same structure is repeated in many units in a society, the alteration or disappearance of a few has little or no effect on the structural form itself of the family organization in a culture. Thus there are good reasons to study the structure of kinship, especially when, as in Ceylon and South India, the task is made doubly interesting by evidences of a logical complexity in the structure.

I am concerned in this book to see how far such ideas on structure can be taken and still make sense. With this in mind, the first problem is to determine the principles of Sinhalese kinship structures. We must then deal with the logical operations that can be performed on these structures in order to transform them into other structures. These variations can be checked against the empirical evidence. Thus, after describing the structure of kin among Kandyan Sinhalese, I shall try to show first that the "logical structure" can be turned into either matrilineal-matrilocal or patrilineal-patrilocal structures without destroying its general form, and, second, that these alternative "models" are empirically to be found in various parts of both Ceylon and South India.

I am not attempting to establish a dialectic between thought and behavior, for I think that fundamentally the "structure" is behind both thought and behavior. But I am interested in the structural implications of the systems in a logical sense, and I shall attempt to test them against empirical evidence.

A conception of structure such as the one outlined above has important implications for the question of "change," and some brief consideration of the matter will be pertinent.

STRUCTURAL CHANGE IN TIME AND SPACE

There is a growing body of literature on "change"—most of it, unfortunately, marked more by a vague apprehension of a problem than by clarity of thought. Some kinds of change, such as the ebb and flow of missionary activity in Ceylon, are best left to historians who have the tools to place the events in their proper context and sequence. It is the problem of anthropologists to study *structural* change—that is, the alterations in those principles of the structure which we endeavor to lay bare in our monographs. There are, then, two stages to the problem: the discovery and formulation of the principles in any given structure, and the analysis of the rules of transformation whereby the elements of an existing structure can be altered to make way for another.

In this book I am directly concerned with the problem of structural change in both its stages. I describe one village in detail: what we see is both static and dynamic. It is as if the elements of a structure A which applies to the low castes and poorer people have been somehow slanted in one particular direction among the other residents to give rise to structure B. In the image of Leach (1961a), the "picture" of the structure on a sheet of rubber has been stretched without altering the picture unrecognizably. In so stretching, certain changes of course occur: in the village I study, the elements of the structure described for low castes are, for example, used differently by aristocrats and are taken in a patrilocal direction. In such a fashion structural change can begin to occur within one community; it does not mean that the picture will necessarily change further—but it may.

When we leave this village and go elsewhere in Ceylon, say the Low Country, we find that the rubber sheet is stretched even more. There are greater changes in the structure and we are faced with certain patrilineal descent groups. Or moving in the opposite direction, to the eastern areas, we find that a pull on the rubber sheet alters the structure again. We are now in matrilocal communities—and we also find matrilineal hypergamous castes who behave as the famous Nayar on the Malabar coast.

But are we still talking about the same structure? Obviously there has been a change, for in one sense, at least, the structure differs from what we were looking at earlier; but we can detect the similarity in principles and the underlying identity in the essentials of the structure. In Ceylon we are fortunate in being able to trace almost every step in the process whereby one structure is transformed into another. And even more, in a community like that of Panama, which has a bilingual population, we can see how the transformation is continuous. One structure does not clash with another but is merged and blended gradually. Indeed, certain communities are themselves clear examples of various compromises that are arrived at in this gradual process of transformation.

Note that we have moved in space and not in time. As Lévi-Strauss has observed, whereas history depicts societies in time, anthropology usually has to be content with depicting them in space. When laid out in the dimension of time, the continuity of a structure is seldom unclear, but when laid out in space, the sameness of the pattern becomes questionable and requires detailed demonstration. Fundamentally, however, the process is the same, for in both cases we must look out for changes in the essential principles of organization. In this comparative study of structures we are able to move not only in any direction in space, but also back and forth in time.

I think that the model suggested here has applications in South India. We can move only from the known to the unknown. The outlook exemplified in this book has made it possible at least to grapple with the extraordinarily complex profusion of castes, customs, and practices from this area, which is but a small part of India. I hope that the general layout of structural transformations depicted in the final chapter will be found useful in the structural analysis of South Indian materials.

In writing of logical symmetry, or structural principles, I do not want to minimize the tenacity of the emotional investment involved in any traditional structure.[1]

I recall a memorable example of such emotional roots. I was invited in 1955 to investigate some problem communities in the Gal Oya colonization scheme in eastern Ceylon. This scheme was an expensive but imaginative attempt by an eminent Prime Minister of Ceylon to breathe life into the backward Dry Zone. The economic pros and cons of the scheme need not concern us here. What is important is that the medicine men, the grass huts, the skimpy vegetable gardens, the

---

[1] See on this point some of the work done by the Tavistock Institute of Human Relations regarding the affective roots and therapeutic aspects of social structures: e.g., Jaques (1953), Menzies (1960).

stagnant pools of water, the malaria-breeding jungles were got rid of and in their place Gal Oya acquired a dam with a reservoir extending far into the dry jungles, modern roads, electricity, a carefully designed system of water lines, and new houses built upon a sensible plan. Most of the colonizers came from the lively and economically thriving Low Country, and they proved very successful on the virgin and fertile land. But the best sites in the colonization scheme were reserved for the people from the villages deep in the jungle, whose lands had been inundated by the waters of the new dam. They had vigorously opposed the construction of the dam, and as a measure of recompense were given choice sites, with new houses and generous credit. Despite every benefit, however, they continued to resist. They were unhappy with paddy cultivation and wanted to return to their old method of slash-and-burn cultivation. They did not like the complicated water lines and seemed unable to use them. Gradually, many began leaving the colony. Suicides were common, and those who stayed on looked as if they had lost the will to live. For them, the whole universe seemed to have caved in. Such is the tenacity of some of these traditional patterns. But this leads in the direction of fascinating but different problems that are beyond the scope of this work.

An approach to the study of structure as outlined in the previous pages has certain implications which lead in a different direction from the usual assumptions of functionalism. Even a cursory examination of South Indian and Ceylonese materials will show that anthropologists often write as if certain principles of marriage, for instance, can be explained in terms of the structure of groups, land tenure, and economic features within the confines of a particular community. In other words, they see the rules as having a specific utilitarian function, embedded in the special conditions of the location.

I suggest, on the contrary, that marriage rules as we find them in South India and Ceylon are not related to any particular economic or group features of special communities. In the first place we find the same rules in communities that exhibit every conceivable variation in ecology, economy, caste structure, lineage, and so on. Furthermore, they are embodied in a special systematic terminology. <u>Both observations suggest that the principles are a language of organization and exist in themselves</u>. In fact, I think it is the categories themselves, inherent in language, that determine marriage rules, and not exogamous lineages or the organization of kin that determines the terminology of kinship.

<u>It is in the nature of principles of social organization to be both specific and very general</u>. Thus, Leach (1961*b*) in an exhaustive work has described in minute detail how certain concepts of the Sinhalese

are manipulated to maximize certain special features of the ecology in one community in the North Central Province of Ceylon. In this book I shall take the reader in the opposite direction and show how the same general principles are used in widely different regions, even with widely different peoples.

The book is in three main sections. The first section (parts i and ii) provides a brief introduction to Ceylon and describes the parameters of a mountain village in the highlands, along with the historical and ecological background of Ceylon and the economy and caste structure of the community.

In the second section (parts iii, iv, and v), kinship and marriage are examined in detail—first in the mountain village (part iii), then, widening the scope (part iv), in three different Sinhalese villages, and next in comparison with communities showing matrilineal features (part v). The final section (part vi) compares conclusions drawn from the analysis of kinship structure in Ceylon with recent anthropological material from South India. By moving in this way from the particular to the general, it will, I think, be shown how the major theme of kinship is progressively and logically varied in different parts of Ceylon and South India. It is to be hoped that the work not only will throw some light on the ethnography of the area but also will demonstrate how principles of structure are themselves part of a symbolic language, with its differences of dialect.

Except where it is directly relevant, I have not been concerned with the highly important questions of religion and ritual among the Kandyan Sinhalese, since any approach through the social structure alone is of strictly limited use for an understanding either of Hinayana Buddhism or of folk Hinduism in Ceylon. These subjects are reserved for a later work on Sinhalese religious thought.

CONDITIONS OF FIELD WORK

The book is based on seventeen months of field work. I arrived in Colombo in August, 1954. As soon as I could put my camping kit together, I turned to the Kandyan highlands in the middle of the island and searched for a village which would be traditional, isolated, and fairly large. I found the village I was looking for in the distant Walapane division on the eastern approaches of the Kandyan highlands. This was Terutenne. I rented huts in different residential areas in the village and lived in very close contact with the villagers. Terutenne was an ancient village and had been noted for the insalubrity of its climate during the Kandyan period. It must have been a malaria-infested locality and was selected as a place of banishment by the kings "both on account of the remoteness of [its] situation, and frequently with a view of consigning the culprit to a lingering death" (D'Oyly, 1929, p. 59). I found it, fortunately, a delightful village, and I remained there till the end of the main harvest in June, 1955.

I had made excursions into the eastern parts of the north central provinces, and into the Bibile area, but after Terutenne I decided to settle down in Makulle Watta, about ten miles north of Monaragala. I lived in the house of a shopkeeper in this village and concentrated my attention on possible variations in the social structure between Makulle Watta and Terutenne, and on the shopkeepers of the business center of the village, Makulle "town."

Around September, 1955, I moved to a Muslim village in the Bibile area. This was Kotabowe Vidiya, also an ancient village with a famous regional cult and annual procession (*perahera*). I employed a Tamil interpreter in this community. The people knew and trusted him and were extremely friendly. We found a small hut and in the excitement of finding a different kinship arrangement, I did very intensive work. The thatch of my hut was pulled off by an elephant one night and I left for Panama.

It was in Makulle Watta that I had heard of the great celebration of *An keliya* and the Sinhalese–Tamil intermarriages of Panama. I used both Sinhalese and my Tamil interpreter and had a very rewarding period of work on the east coast. Panama provided me with the outer limits of the Sinhalese social system.

At the end of October, I left the Panama area and went to the Northwestern Province. This time I wanted to find out about the social system prevailing in economically more developed areas. The village of Vilawa in the Wanni Hatpattuva was near trade centers such as Maho and Kurunegala and was closely tied in to the economy of the island. Here I remained in the same house with a delightful polyandrous family until January, 1956.

2

The Kandyan Sinhalese

"I know no nation in the world do so exactly resemble the
Chingulays as the people of *Europe*."—Robert Knox, *An Historical Relation of Ceylon* (1681), p. 61

POPULATION

The ethnographer in Ceylon can barely refrain from plunging into the
legends of the island. The very names of Ceylon immediately evoke
them. The Sri Lanka of the Sinhalese was the Serendip of the Muslim
traders. In the west, Ceylon was known as Taprobane, and people in
the Middle Ages knew that Adam's Peak was somewhere in that
exotic place. The sacred mountain is still venerated by both Buddhists
and Muslims: to the Buddhists, it is the place where the Lord
Buddha first landed to plant his gigantic footprint on the rocks and
to claim the island for the doctrine, and the Muslims are certain that
Adam and Eve lived in Ceylon, and that Adam, too, first set foot in
the world in exactly the same place where the Lord Buddha landed
(Ludowyk, 1958).

The most numerous and important populations on Ceylon are
the Sinhalese—about 6 million—and the Tamils—about 2 million—
(see table 1). Within these two large categories, there are smaller
divisions, geographical as well as religious. The Sinhalese are mostly
Buddhists, but many in the maritime provinces have embraced Christianity. The Tamils, who comprise two major sections—the Indian
Tamils (usually workers on tea estates) and the Ceylon Tamils—are
further divided by their religions. They are mainly Hindu, but there
are many Christians as well, and some Muslims, who have their own
communal organization. All these divisions of Sinhalese and Tamils
are further broken up into a variety of castes.

For the most part, the Sinhalese and Tamil populations tend to
inhabit distinct areas of the island—the Tamils around the northern

TABLE I

The Population of Ceylon
(Based on the 1953 Census)

A. *Ethnic Groups*

Population	1953	Percent in Total Population
Low Country Sinhalese....	3,464,000	42.6
Kandyan Sinhalese........	2,157,000	26.7
Ceylon Tamils............	909,000	11.2
Indian Tamils............	984,000	12.2
Ceylon Moors............	468,000	5.8
Indian Moors............	6,000	0.1
Burghers, Eurasians.......	44,000	0.5
Malays..................	29,000	0.4
Europeans...............	6,000	0.1
Others..................	32,000	0.4
Total*...............	8,099,000	100.0%

B. *Religious Affiliation*

Religious Community	1953	Percent in Total Population
Buddhist................	5,317,000	64
Hindu..................	1,614,000	20
Christian†	715,000	9
Muslim.................	542,000	7
Others.................	11,000	0.1
Total.................	8,099,000	100.0%

* The population has been rising rapidly:

1827	889,584
1871	2,400,380
1901	3,565,954
1946	6,657,339
1953	8,099,000
1963 (last census)	10,625,000

† No breakdown in 1953 Census. Percentage in 1946 Census: 84% Catholic, 16% Protestant.

port of Jaffna, parts of the North Central Province, and on the east coast, and the Sinhalese in all other areas. Within the large towns, like Colombo, Kandy, Galle, and Anuradhapura, the population is mixed, but the different communities still maintain their separateness, and it is particularly in these towns that the Tamils and Sinhalese have recently fallen out over the national language issue, *Sinhala Pamanay*

(Sinhalese Only). The intense feeling has led to violent riots and finally to the murder of Prime Minister Bandaranaike by a Buddhist priest.

During the 150 years of British rule, when English was the official language of the island, many prominent families among both Sinhalese and Tamils accepted the English language as well as Christianity—to the extent that, among the rich families of Colombo, Sinhalese was relegated to the status of a "kitchen" language. After the granting of independence in 1947, Sinhalese nationalism surged forward. It is noteworthy that the symbols of nationalism which were adopted were precisely those indices that separated the Tamils from the Sinhalese—the Sinhalese language and Buddhism. The extremists, again mostly schoolteachers and priests, have been clamoring to make Sinhalese the only official language of the island.

The Sinhalese divide themselves into two main groups—the Kandyans, who regard themselves as "Up Country people" (*uda rata minissu*), and the "Low Country people" (*pahata rata minissu*). The distinction is mainly historical, the Kandyans being the inhabitants of the provinces that were successfully held by the Kandyan kings against the Portuguese and the Dutch and only capitulated to the British in 1815.

The Low Country Sinhalese live in the maritime provinces of southeastern Ceylon and have been under European influence since the first arrival of the Portuguese in 1505. The Portuguese were followed by the Dutch, who ruled the coastal area from 1658 to 1796 and who left, characteristically, a legacy of superb colonial architecture and the Roman Dutch Law. Foreign rule, a buoyant economy, and the existence of a large Christian, mostly Catholic, element in the coastal population have gradually strengthened the cultural differences between the two areas. Among the Kandyans, there are now idiosyncracies in the manner of speech, accent, and terminology that at once differentiate them from the Low Country people. In addition, in the Up Country, the presence of the ancient capital of Kandy, the famous temples, old and distinguished titles which are traced back to the Kandyan kingdom, and martial traditions render an unmistakable air of aristocratic superiority to the lordly families and to the region as a whole. Until recently, this aristocratic tone was preserved by the lack of intermarriage with the mixed peoples of the Low Country, but today new perspectives—the Low Country is wealthier and more sophisticated—have begun to erode this marriage barrier.

In the following pages, I shall outline the historical and ecological background of the communities with which we shall be concerned. It will be helpful to recall that the island is culturally very closely related to South India. Quite apart from the presence of Tamils, the social organization as well as the entire ideology of religion, even among the Buddhist Sinhalese, relates them to the mainland. Indeed, the great sophistication of Hinayana Buddhism, of which the Sinhalese are so justly proud, combined with the equally impressive caste system, makes Ceylon a valuable testing ground for all kinds of anthropological theories developed on the basis of South Indian evidence.

THE KANDYAN KINGDOM

Parts of Ceylon, like the rest of India, have apparently always had some form of government. Although the early history of the Sinhalese, like that of their island, is deep in legend,[1] it is known that in later centuries the Sinhalese-speaking peoples of Ceylon were united from time to time into kingdoms which kept up frequent wars against those which rose and fell on the mainland. The eleventh and twelfth centuries A.D. are filled with such martial activity (Sastri, 1955, pp. 180–208, *passim*) which was relieved now and again by carefully arranged marriages between the Tamil and Sinhalese ruling families.[2]

The archaeological evidence of the ancient cities of Anuradhapura and Polonnaruwa, in the heart of the Dry Zone, is so extensive that little doubt remains that these ancient kingdoms were very considerable states. In the luxuriant jungles around the two ancient cities, one finds ruined palaces, gigantic sacred mounds (*dagoba*), traces of what once were pleasure gardens, serene rock-hewn figures of the Buddha sitting under ancient trees, and elaborately laid out, vast irrigation systems. All this dates back to the time when Anuradhapura was a great Buddhist center. By the middle of the thirteenth century, however, the great cities had declined and the northern Dry Zone was left to the encroaching jungle.

In 1518, when the Portuguese established their fort in Colombo, the northernmost parts of the island were held by the Tamil kingdom of Jaffna and the main power in the Sinhalese areas was a kingdom hidden in the inaccessible regions of the central mountains called the "Five Counties Above the Mountains" (*Kanda Uda Pas Rata*). This is the domain that later became known as the Kandyan kingdom (R. Pieris, 1956, p. 5). We possess excellent accounts of this kingdom. There were reports by perceptive eyewitnesses, like Robert

---

[1] The Sinhalese language has North Indian affinities, and the epic of the great dynasty (*Mahavamsa*) also suggests a North Indian origin. Some scholars appear to be of two minds as to whether King Vijaya came from the northeast or northwest of India (Geiger, 1941).

[2] Sastri (1955), p. 182. For later marriages, up to the nineteenth century, see Percival (1803).

Knox,[3] who as privileged prisoners lived in the kingdom for many years, and also the accounts by British officers stationed on the island after the conquest. The most important of these latter was that of Sir John D'Oyly (1929), which deals with the elaborate feudal organization of the kingdom.

The political, social, and economic structure of the Kandyan kingdom rested on an elaborate system of land tenures. All the land was considered to belong ultimately to the king. On this principle, the king allowed aristocrats of the Radala subcaste to hold large estates, but the lords were expected to supply feudal services and payments as a token of their vassalage. The estates of the aristocrats were in turn held under fief by persons of other castes, again in return for hereditary services and payments. The tenants, in turn, could have subtenants of their own.

The same hereditary lords were also appointed by the king as provincial governors, and in their capacity as civil servants the lords appointed officials of lower ranks from the various castes. In lieu of salary, all officials received the right to the dues of various lands belonging to the king. In this fashion the pattern of feudal services (*rajakariya*, or king's duty), which were attached especially to the tenure of paddy lands, formed both the basis for the organization of the kingdom and the mainstay of the caste hierarchy.[4]

Caste services and land tenures were directly associated. All paddy lands had services and payments attached to them and elaborate registers of these tenurial obligations were kept in the districts. Persons who held the land were obliged to provide the services or dues formally attached to the property. Although free from duties such as tom-tom beating or laundering or pot-making, which the lower castes had to perform as part of their obligations, the higher castes were liable for payments and services in token of their allegiance to the particular lord whose lands they occupied.

The identity between birth status, landholding, and service obliga-

---

[3] Robert Knox's delightful book, *An Historical Relation of Ceylon* (1681), was probably one of the sources used by Defoe in writing *Robinson Crusoe*, though the main story is clearly derived from Captain Woodes Rogers' account of the rescue of Alexander Selkirk from the island of Juan Fernandez off the coast of Chile.

[4] D'Oyly (p. 45) gives some interesting details about land ownership: "The possession of land is the foundation of the king's right to the services and the contributions of the people and vice versa in general. Persons not possessing lands are liable to no regular service or duties. . . . Lands which properly subject the possessor to regular public services are low paddy lands which can be cultivated every year. . . . Four *lekam miti* or registers of persons liable to regular services are kept in the hands of the chiefs of the provinces of many departments to which they respectively belong. . . . No person retaining his land can, without the king's permission change his service, that is, abandon his proper department and service and resort to another."

tions was one of the important characteristics of the Kandyan kingdom.[5] Although individuals could change their villages or give up the
service by refusing to cultivate the land, the services that were attached
to the estate were immutable. The lands of the lower castes could not
be acquired by the high caste, since "the duty attaching to the land
could not be evaded by the transfer" (D'Oyly, 1929, p. 89).[6]

The possession of lands to which special privileges and duties were
attached was the material foundation for the hierarchy of castes. The
Kandyan Peasantry Commission, writing in 1951, states the point
cogently: "The mainstay of the caste system is stated to be the service
tenure system. Tenants have to perform services associated with certain
castes and so long as the service tenure system remained it was difficult
to eliminate the caste system fully. As a first step in the fight against
caste it is necessary to abolish the service tenures" (R.K.P.C., 1951, p.
108). But quite apart from the *rajakariya*, which immediately fixed
social position, the status of the various castes was also defined in
detail by elaborate sumptuary laws and complicated forms of speech
and etiquette.

The entire superstructure of caste and service was ceremonially
displayed at the annual "processions" (*perahera*) when in various
districts all caste groups passed in review, each one performing some
token service indicative of its position. The *perahera*, in one form
or another, still continues as an annual event in many parts of Ceylon.
The most interesting of these processions is probably that of Kataragama, which takes place in the dry season in the remote jungles of
Buttala (Yalman, 1964), but the main *perahera*, at Kandy, has now
become an excellent tourist attraction. Caste groups are paid for taking
part in the Kandy *perahera*, but the lower castes have lately been
complaining about "the degrading" nature of the ceremonial duties
that they are asked to perform by the temple authorities (R.K.P.C.,
1951, p. 108).

Service tenures were gradually abolished in Ceylon by various

---

[5] There are excellent accounts in Ryan (1953), Codrington (1938), and R. Pieris
(1956). As D'Oyly (1929, p. 66) observes, "It is impossible to define all the tenures
upon which Lands are held under a Ninde Proprietor, as these are different in
every village and as they rise from that of the Ooliyakkareya (whose condition appears to be little better than that of a slave) to that of a person who merely pays
homage, by appearing on particular seasons, or at Festivals with a few betel leaves,
which he presents to the Proprietor."

[6] "It is held that any land proprietor who has definitely sold his land, may re-
sume it at any time during his life, paying the amount which he has received and
the value of any improvement. . . . The reason for this custom is the respect and
attachment which belong to ancient family—rank and family estates—and the
importance ascribed to the preservation, as it is called, of name and estate, *nama
gama*—the name by which any person is distinguished and generally known being
that of the village in which his ancient or principal estates are situated." D'Oyly
(1929), p. 60.

British nineteenth-century enactments. The only estates where such tenures were retained were the lands that belonged to the temples. It would appear that the relations between the castes, which, in ordinary villages, can be put on a secular monetary basis—payment for services rendered—are seen as more binding (and thus less able to be legislated away) when the temple services for the propitiation of the Buddha and the deities are involved.[7]

The caste organization was admirably suited to the feudal structure and provided an effective economic and political framework, not only for the Kandyan kingdom but for similar South Indian kingdoms, to a degree not heretofore sufficiently emphasized. In the Kandyan kingdom, in the vicinity of the royal capital, there were many diverse castes, each with its special services and privileges; in the outlying districts of the realm, however, caste divisions were few and simple (Ryan, 1953). In the village, obviously, there was no need for the services of the watcher of the royal bath (*diyawadana nilame*) (D'Oyly, 1929, p. 132). Today, of course, caste precedence often gives rise to disputes which can never be finally settled, but in the ancient kingdom caste privileges were legally recognized and enforced.[8]

THE ECOLOGY OF THE DRY ZONE

The island of Ceylon is split sharply into two regions, the Dry and the Wet zones. When one climbs a vantage point like the top of the ancient rock palace of Sigiriya in the middle of the Dry Zone, one sees nothing but miles of dry scrub jungle stretching to the horizon. Here and there the jungle is dotted by small pools of water: these are the village irrigation reservoirs or "tanks." The southeastern parts of the island, in contrast, are covered by lush and verdant vegetation which hides the dense population.

The monsoons dominate the ecology of the island. The rains arrive with the northeast monsoons, about the middle of November, and are distributed over the whole island. Then follows an intermonsoon period from February to May, with only occasional showers, and the days (particularly in the Kandyan hills) are luminous and beautiful. In June and July the southwest monsoon brings the rains back, but though they water the southwesterly parts of the island only too well, the rest of Ceylon, including the Dry Zone, receives little rainfall at

---

[7] For excellent accounts of Sinhalese temple estates, called *devala gam* and *vihara gam,* see Hocart (1931), Ryan (1953, pp. 211ff.), and R. Pieris (1956, p. 74). A similar temple organization for South India is suggested by Sastri (1955, p. 312).

[8] For a concise account of the Kandyan state, see R. Pieris (1956). For land tenures see Leach (1961b) and Codrington (1938). For a comparison of the Kandyan state with pre-British Malabar, see Raja (1953, pp. 274ff.) and Schneider and Gough (1961).

this time. The time of the southwest monsoon is the dry season in the Dry Zone.

The rain reports of the Dry Zone do not show up the characteristics of the area. To one unfamiliar with the island, the 75 to 100 inches of rain in Walapane, and the 50 to 75 inches in Bintenne in the heart of the Dry Zone, would appear to leave little to be desired. But much of the rainfall is in fact condensed into the three months between November and January, when the villages are practically inundated. These months are then followed by long periods of drought which produce the peculiar ecological conditions of the region. Life is possible only where there is water, and this is the clue not merely to the distribution of the population but also to the organization of the villages (see Farmer, 1957).

The Dry Zone does not gradually yield to the Wet Zone as one travels southeast. It stops suddenly, and immediately the population becomes much denser. It would almost be possible for one walking along the southern coast road east of Tangalle or on the west coast north of Chilaw to walk out of the rain in the Wet Zone in fifteen minutes, and then turn back and watch the showers cutting across the country like dark curtains.

Economically, the Dry Zone is the most backward part of the island. It is populated by peasant farmers barely above a subsistence economy. Cash crops are few and far between. The Wet Zone, in contrast, is wealthy. Tea, rubber, and coconut are all profitably grown, and there is in addition a great variety of other minor crops (cacao, cinnamon, citronella, cardamom, and areca nuts). It is noteworthy that the economy of the island is almost entirely dependent on the first three crops. In 1953 the export of tea formed 56 percent, rubber and latex 23 percent, and coconut products 16 percent of the total exports of the island by value (*O.E.S.C.*, 1959, p. 25). This situation has not changed materially since that time.

Although much of the Kandyan country falls into the Dry Zone, an area around the central highlands west of Kandy and Nuwara Eliya does receive a high rainfall. This area, where tea is grown, is vital for Ceylon. But even though tea is the most profitable single crop of this region, it is of little direct significance to the Kandyan villagers who live near the tea estates. Below the hills where the tea estates are, in the bottom of the valleys are the small village rice fields. The villages and the estates exist almost in separate universes.

There is much agitation in Ceylon on the subject of tea estates. The extreme nationalists claim that the tea estates cover what used to be the highlands set aside for slash-and-burn cultivation of the traditional villages, and extremist politicians, of both Right and Left, harp on the complaint that after the arrival of the British these village

lands were taken away from the villagers by planters, who created
large estates, first for the cultivation of coffee and, when coffee failed
from 1868 onward, for the tea industry.[9] But even the extremists can
hardly ignore the fact that whereas slash-and-burn cultivation is extremely unproductive, as well as extravagantly wasteful of topsoil, the
revenue to the government from tea export duties alone formed 15
percent of the total revenue in 1953 (*O.E.S.C.*, 1959, p. 31).[10]

In contrast to the busy agricultural and industrial life elsewhere on
the island, most Dry Zone villagers live at the simplest level. When we
turn away from the economically developed parts of the island, the
Low Country and the tea estates, to the Dry Zone proper, we find ourselves in an area of small, traditional jungle villages.

In this region one factor alone—water—dictates the dispersal and
size of settlements. Life is made possible by two forms of cultivation:
rice on irrigable land (i.e., paddy cultivation), and shifting cultivation
in the dry jungles. The two types of agriculture are quite distinct.
Rice is an extremely thirsty crop and must stand in water throughout
almost the entire period of its growth. To ensure this, elaborate irrigation systems have been devised in the Dry Zone. The fields are laid out
in flat blocks with ridges around them to hold the water. In the plains
the blocks are fairly regular and the field is usually rectangular in
shape. In the highlands, the fields still have the blocks and the ridges,
but entire hillsides, often very steep, are terraced. A field rises in high,
narrow steps in steep places, but opens up and forms wider terraces
where the declination is less precipitous. The amount of human sweat
and toil that have gone into these elaborate rice fields is impressive,

---

[9] The Kandyan Peasantry Commission claims that communal village land was
turned into crown lands by the ordinance of 1840, for ulterior motives, and that a
channel was cleared for "the direct appropriation of village land." *R.K.P.C.* (1951),
pp. 71ff.

[10] The figure was 20 percent in 1950. The development of the estates has been
remarkable. The Kandyan Peasantry Commission, quoting Tennent (1859), says:
"The mountain ranges on all sides of Kandy became rapidly covered with planta-
tions. It was estimated that three million pounds were invested between 1837 and
1845. East India Company officers crowded to Ceylon to invest their savings." The
Report continues (p. 68): "In 1834 only forty-nine acres of crown land were sold.
From 1835 to 1838 the average annual sales increased to 6,412 acres. From 1840 to
1845 the acreage was 42,880 acres, the peak figure was reached in 1841 when 78,685
were sold. In 1848 the coffee extents went up to 60,000 acres, comprising 367 planta-
tions." The decline of coffee was fortunately matched by the rise of the tea industry. The story is much the same: "In 1873 there were only 250 acres under tea. . . .
By 1896 the area under tea had risen to 330,000 acres, and in 1900 to 392,000 acres,
and in 1903 to 406,000 acres. . . . In 1929 the area under tea was not less than
450,000 acres. Of this extent no less than 80 percent . . . was owned by British
companies while the remainder was owned by Ceylonese." (*R.K.P.C.*, p. 69.) Since
the granting of independence to Ceylon, however, the British companies have been
pulling their investments out of the island.

and an important result of these great investments is that both the fields and the settlements around them are always permanent.

Shifting cultivation stands in contrast to the picture. There is no permanence in the fields or in the settlements. The jungle is simply slashed down, allowed to dry, and then fired. When the rains come, the seeds are sown—without further preparing the soil—and in about four months the crop is gathered. The plot is then allowed to return to its former state. Such lands are brought back into cultivation, depending on the availability of highlands, in a cycle of four to twelve years. In the Wellassa area, where until recently jungles were more plentiful than anything else, the cycle of cultivation is still about twelve to sixteen years.

In Sinhalese, land is classified first into the two types that correspond to the two forms of cultivation. There is mudland (*mada idam*) —the low, irrigable lands—and there is highland (*goda idam*). More precisely, land can also be classified into rice lands (*kumbura*), gardens (*watte*, i.e., house sites planted with fruit trees and often referred to as *gedara watte*, "house garden"), and highlands (*hen*). I refer to highland in the text as chena, the Anglicized usage in Ceylon.

The *kumbura* are incomparably more valuable than the other lands.[11] The size of the rice fields is determined by the water supply. It is true that there are small communities, especially in the interior of the Wellassa, Uva, Bintenne, Buttala, and Walapane divisions, where the population depends upon chena only. But rice cultivation is considered to be much superior to shifting cultivation and most of the people of the Dry Zone prefer to live around paddy fields with reliable sources of water supply.

The agricultural settlements in the Dry Zone can in general be divided into four types. First (fig. 1A), there are the well-known tank villages of the northern plains. An excellent description of such a village is provided by Leach (1961b). These villages have a water reservoir; and the amount of water necessary for irrigation can be controlled by sluices and spills. The villagers, according to certain obligations inherent in their landholdings, work together to keep the reservoir, the bund, and the sluices in good repair. Houses are clustered around the *watte* on either side of the paddy field, and beyond the house gardens there are the chena highlands.

The second type of settlement (fig. 1B) occurs in the mountainous districts of the Central Province. Here, the people depend upon

---

[11] In 1955, in the village of Terutenne, *kumbura* was worth, according to its fertility, about 600–900 rupees an acre, chena about 15–20 rupees an acre, and *watte* (depending again upon its position in the village) about 50–100 rupees an acre.

② mountain streams, and there are no tanks, even though the streams, which run full during most of the rainy season, gradually dry to a mere trickle. Dams (*amunu*) are constructed across these streams and the water is channeled by irrigation lines (*ela*) to the terraced paddy

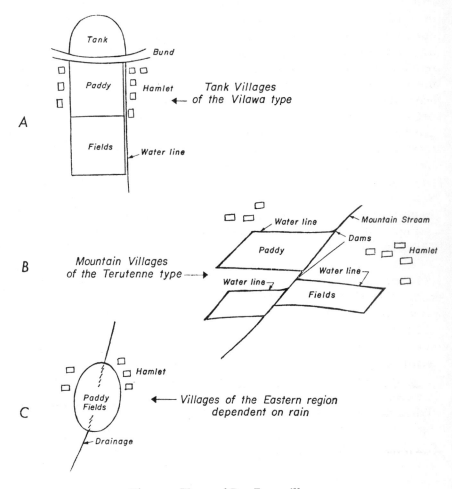

Figure 1. Types of Dry Zone villages.

fields. Despite the lack of control over the water supply in these areas, the fields and the settlements which depend upon them are large and usually more complicated than those to be found in the northern plains. The usual tank village in the plains may be anything from ten to about a hundred households, but in Walapane a village of two or three hundred households is not unusual.

③ A third type (fig. 1C) is that of the more backward parts of the eastern districts. In the large Uva Province, the water supply is even

more unreliable than in the rest of the Dry Zone, and many of the
fields have no artificial irrigation at all. They are laid out in depres-
sions in the ground and are entirely dependent upon the rainfall.
Such fields are referred to as *malan kumbura*.

The fourth type of settlement is that of the small chena communities which have no sort of irrigation at all. These communities are
usually extremely poor and, lacking rice fields, eke out their existence
by the cultivation of finger millet and vegetables. Often, also, they
resort to hunting like the ancient Veddas who are known to have
inhabited parts of the Uva Province until recently (Seligman and
Seligman, 1911). It is notable that the Sinhalese who live in established
paddy-cultivating villages consider these people to be wild, backward,
and dangerous. They will often refer to them simply as Veddas, even
though there are now no linguistic or other racial differences between
them. It is quite possible that some of these settlements on chena
lands may really be of Vedda origin, but even half a century ago the
Seligmans noted that it was extremely difficult to find true Veddas.
In my travels in the interior of the Uva Province, I did not come across
a single individual who could speak fluent Vedda. I was told by the
Sinhalese villagers, however, that some tiny communities of true
Veddas still existed in the Padiyatalawa region.[12]

In summary, these are the salient points of the ecology and economy
of the Dry Zone: Most of this region is settled by traditional villages
which depend mainly on a mixed rice and shifting cultivation subsistence economy, with the water supply determining the location of
the rice fields as well as the size and distribution of the settlements.
With the phenomenal rise in the population of Ceylon, the scarcity
of paddy land is being seriously felt in many districts. Where jungles
are still available, shifting cultivation provides a helpful alternative.
When no rice lands are available, the poorer villagers can and do turn
to their chena for a living.

---

[12] It should be mentioned that there are also Tamil-speaking people on the east
coast who are called Veddas by their fellow countrymen. Vakkarai, after the first
ferry on the Batticaloa–Trincomalee road, was pointed out to me as such a village.

PART II: TERUTENNE

3

A Village in the Highlands

"Ceylon, from whatever direction it is approached, unfolds a scene of lovelinesse and grandeur unsurpassed, if it be rivalled, by any land in the Universe."—Sir James Emerson Tennent, *Ceylon* (1859), I, 3

". . . nor will there easily be found in the whole universe an Island or Kingdom of that size in which are found the wealth and commodities of the Island of Ceylon."—F. de Queyroz, *The Temporal and Spiritual Conquest of Ceylon* (c. 1687; trans. 1930), pp. 70–71

"[The mountains] . . . are cool and pleasant, nevertheless it is a country better suited to wild animals than to men, and for this reason it is the usual exile of the criminals of Candea, who may escape death, but disease never."—*ibid.*, p. 63

It is always easy for an ethnographer to assume a greater uniformity in behavior than is warranted. That simplifies the complex picture of everyday life, takes care of the aberrant individuals, and presents an outline that is easy to communicate. But it also submerges the detailed evidence for emergent new patterns which may come to the surface at a later time or in a different place. Such small but cumulative differences in behavior may end up as variant structures among different classes within the same community or indeed may give rise to entirely new structures in different regions. For this reason, in parts ii and iii a detailed study of caste and kinship in one community is undertaken. This provides the firm ethnographic background for the analysis of structural differences from region to region in Ceylon in book two.

A DESCRIPTION OF THE COMMUNITY

Terutenne is a hill village of some 1,200 persons located in one of the most isolated and neglected parts of the central provinces. It is

situated in the division of Walapane (map 2), notable for its high
mountains, deep, precipitous valleys, and wild scenery. Most of this
division falls into the Dry Zone, but parts of it in the higher
altitudes are sufficiently well watered for a few tea estates to flourish.

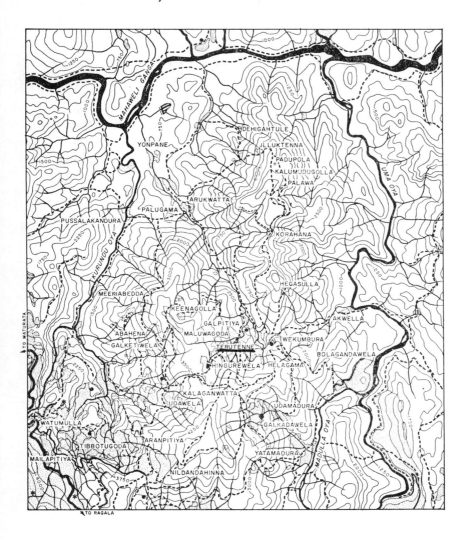

Map. 2. Walapane Division.

The village is approached by a four-hour walk from the bazaar of Nildandahinna, a small cluster of shops and stalls which are mainly memorable for their penetrating smell of dried fish. The path to Terutenne runs over the crest of high hills with excellent views into the settlements in the valleys on either side. Nearer the village one arrives at a high vantage point from which the layout of the residential areas, the fields, and temples may be observed.

The center of the valley, which near Terutenne fans out around another mountain, consists of the irrigated rice fields which come up to the edge of hamlets and fall away into the distance. The hamlets are placed around the fields just above the water lines. Further up, surrounding the village, are the treeless highlands covered with shrubs used for slash-and-burn cultivation. If one arrives at the end of the dry season, as I did, one can also see the charred black earth covered with fire-hardened spikes in patches where the chena fields have been fired and prepared for the rains.

I arrived in Terutenne in September, 1954, and through the hospitality of the local apothecary, the only Tamil in the village, was given quarters in the local dispensary. This was the base from which I started my survey.

TABLE 2

The Population of Terutenne

Hamlets	Males	Females	Total	Houses*
Wekumbura (excluding low castes)....	165	174	339	61
Helagama.........................	109	114	223	38
Galpitiya........................	74	67	141	21
Hegasulla........................	27	22	49	7
Enduruwatte......................	26	16	42	12
Hinguruwela.....................	26	27	53	10
Liyangahapitiya..................	24	16	40	8
Dunkalawatte....................	26	24	50	13
Kinegolle........................	14	18	32	4
Heneagama (Washermen).........	15	15	30	7
Valan Karayo (Potters)†..........	22	17	39	3
Kammal Karayo (Blacksmiths)†.....	12	7	19	3
Baddegama (Tom-Tom Beaters, plus 3 houses Galpitiya and 1 Helagama)	78	68	146	27
Total.......................	618	585	1,203	214

Total low-caste population, 234 (136 below age 20; 98 above age 20)
Total Goyigama population, 969 (550 below age 20; 419 above age 20)

* Each discrete dwelling is counted separately.
† Low-caste persons of Wekumbura, living slightly separate from the rest of the hamlet.

After a few days in the village it was clear to me that caste considerations were important in the dispersal of the dwellings. A part of the village was separated by a water line and was referred to as a Tom-Tom Beater "Village" (Baddegama). This hamlet was a distinct community with a population of about 146. It had a sacred Bo tree in the middle, and it appeared later that according to the traditional land tenure arrangements, these Tom-Tom Beaters used to cultivate separate paddy lands near their own hamlet. In 1955, few of them owned any land and they did sharecropping on the lands of landlords of various castes; some continued to perform the traditional occupation of their caste in the Buddhist temple of the largest hamlet, called Wekumbura. Wekumbura, where the apothecary and the rest

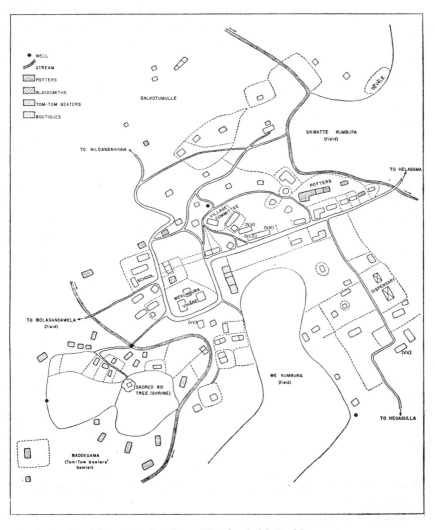

Map 3. Wekumbura Hamlet (with Baddegama).

of the village notables lived, consisted mostly of the high Cultivators
caste (Goyigama), though some Potters (Valan Karayo), and some
wealthy people of the Blacksmith (Achari) caste lived in separate
compounds of their own. They were in close contiguity with the high
caste.

Apart from the divisions between the castes, Terutenne was physically divided into two sections, *egoda gama* and *megoda gama*, meaning "that side village" and "this side village." The stream called "the
stream of merit" (*pinarawa*) which passed near the village shrine
(*devale*) was considered more or less the boundary between the two
sections. The main hamlets of Wekumbura and Helagama, and several
smaller hamlets including Hegasulla and Baddegama, were on one
side, and Galpitiya, Kinegolle, Dunkalawatte, Heneagama were on the
other side (see map 3 and table 2). This division, though not in itself
considered important, corresponded to the division of the village for
the purposes of the postharvest "game of the gods" (*An keliya*: hook
or horn play). In this "game," the village was divided into two teams,
Uda Pila and *Yata Pila* (Upper Side and Lower Side), the lower side
representing the goddess Pattini and the upper side her consort
Palanga. The game consisted of locking the ritual horns of the teams
together and having a tug-of-war to see which horn would break. It
was considered more auspicious if Pattini broke the horn of her consort. *An keliya,* which I have described elsewhere (1966), would im-
part health and fertility to the fields, animals, and human beings of
the village.

One of the hamlets, Galpitiya (see Yalman, 1960) and two other
small ones, Liyangahapitiya and Dunkalawatte, were of Cultivator
caste but were considered to be of lower status than the rest of this
caste. Some persons interpreted the low standing of these hamlets in
terms of the dual division in the village established for the *An keliya*
ritual. They would say that the village was simply divided into two
moieties and that no intermarriage was permissible across this division.
There was, however, no unanimity of opinion on this subject, and the
whole question of the curious ritual was more often than not dismissed
as a game of little immediate significance.

Within the hamlets, certain houses were referred to by the same
name, and paternal, maternal, and affinal kinsmen seemed to live
more or less all together. There was no great difficulty in changing
residences. If people quarreled they would simply build a hut in one
of the other hamlets near some other kinsman and move. They would
still work in the same fields at the center of the ring of hamlets.

There was no special feeling of unity in the caste sections or in the
hamlets. This was particularly true of the large Cultivator caste, which
numbered nearly 1,000 persons. The low castes did occasionally act

in somewhat greater unison than the upper castes. The Washermen—
who lived near Galpitiya—with a population of 30, the Potters with
a population of 40, and the Blacksmiths with a population of about
20 were in fact single kin groups. The Tom-Tom Beaters, numbering
about 150, were torn by internal strife, but even they had cooperated
to the extent of forming a Tom-Tom Beaters' Welfare Society. I
suspect, however, that this society was established more in the hope
that it would be eligible for government grants than from any genuine
esprit de corps.

Some unity was evident in Terutenne at the time of the annual
village rituals at the Buddhist temples (*vihara*) or at the temple of the
Hindu deities (*devale*). In the course of these ceremonies the various
castes were given special ritual duties in keeping with their traditional calling. The rituals were carried out to celebrate the most important occasions during the year—the birthday of the Buddha, the
Sinhalese New Year, the commencement and the end of the *Vas*
season when Buddhist priests were in retirement, and at the end of
the dry season, in August and September, to pray for rain, fertility,
and good times in the coming year. Of these rituals the most elaborate
ones were the fertility rituals (like *An keliya* or *Gam Maduva*) directed to the local Hindu pantheon.

This description of the general outlines of the village community
fits the traditional historical picture of the Sinhalese village rather
closely. A village is spoken of as a *gama* in Sinhalese. But the same
word can be used both for a village and for a hamlet; it may also
simply refer to the estate or landholding of one person. A landlord
is a *gam kariya*. These extensions appear to be similar in Sanskrit and
Pali as well (see de Lanerolle, 1938, p. 211; Codrington, 1938, pp.
1ff). The important point is that *gama,* which carries the connotation
of an "estate," in keeping with the feudal history of the Kandyan
highlands, does not have any implication of consanguinity. Dumont
has expressed the essential nature of these local residential groups
very succinctly (1957a, p. 49): "En somme elle apparaît comme une
communauté de nature surtout pratique, traversée par un triple
principe de division: caste, territoire et parenté. Elle n'est pas conçue
comme une totalité, mais seulement comme un fragment." I consider
this observation to be important in view of the undue emphasis that
most anthropologists have placed on the Indian village as an isolated
unit.

ADMINISTRATION AND NOTABLES

Let us turn now to the development of the administrative structure of
Terutenne. During the British colonial period, an excellent Civil
Service was built up in Ceylon. One feature of this was the system of

Government Agents appointed to the different provinces of the island. For the most part, these agents were men of exceptional talent and ability, and much of our knowledge of the remote parts of the island in the nineteenth century comes from their minutes, reports, and diaries.

Directly responsible to the Government Agents were the District Revenue Officers, of whom there were four or five in each province. As their name implies, they were originally responsible for the collection of taxes, but when the grain tithe was abolished at the turn of the century their functions became purely administrative. In the more isolated parts of the island, District Revenue Officers were appointed to the districts only very gradually. In many places the local Kandyan lords were simply confirmed in their hereditary positions. Where this happened the institutions of the Kandyan kingdom were kept intact, at least in form, though they were tightened by the central administration. Recently the tendency has been to supersede these old arrangements by the appointment of civil servants and bureaucrats at all levels of the administration, and this process has been accelerated since independence.

Under the present system, depending on the locality, each District Revenue Officer is responsible for some twenty-five to thirty villages. In the village itself, the administration is represented by the Village Headman, who is appointed from among the respectable and influential persons in the community by the Government Agent on the recommendation of the District Revenue Officer. In Walapane in 1955 an intermediate level of administration between the District Revenue Officer and the Village Headman had been retained. The four *palata* (sections) of Walapane had one *Korale* (Chief Headman) each.[1] The District Revenue Officer of Walapane lived in the bazaar of Nildandahinna and rarely came into the distant villages such as Terutenne. The *Korale* who lived in the neighboring village of Udamadura was a frequent visitor and knew the village quite intimately.

---

[1] These Chief Headmen claimed ancient aristocratic (*Radala*) status, but it is intriguing to note that although *Korale* was a Kandyan title associated with a feudal estate, Walapane did not have this office during the time of the Kandyan kings. It was an office which was established there, under the ancient title, by the British for administrative purposes. The villagers had the tradition that Walapane had been under the jurisdiction of a *mohottala* who lived in Terutenne. In 1955 I came across the descendants of this person (Amunumulle Mohottala) in the village. They were poor, and had intermarried with low-status people. In contrast to the generally accepted aristocratic claims of the *Korale*, the Amunumulle Mohottalas' claims to high status were the butt of jokes and lighthearted ridicule. Their claims were not greatly exaggerated, however: the existence of the *mohottala* is confirmed by D'Oyly 1929, p. 7), and Amunumulle Mohottala is mentioned specifically by name in the Grain Tithe Registers of Terutenne for 1857 in the Nuwara Eliya government offices (*Kachcheri*).

The Village Headman in a Kandyan village is often an influential person. He received a salary of about 125 rupees a month (in 1955), depending on seniority. In Walapane the Village Headman's area was known as a *wasama,* and since the villages were large, there was usually only one village in the *wasama.* In the case of the headman of Terutenne, the *wasama* (known as the *Bolagandawela Wasama*) included some further villages ten miles away, deep in the jungle, like Arukwatta and Korahana. The substantial amount of government financial assistance to the villages, which passed through the Village Headman's hands, made it possible for him to influence the fortunes of humble families very considerably.

Apart from the Village Headman, who is directly responsible to the government, there are also Irrigation Headmen and important Village Committees in Kandyan villages. The Irrigation Headmen (*Vala Vidane*) were individually elected by the landholders for six different groups of paddy fields in Terutenne (see map 4, chap. 4). These elections were then approved by the District Revenue Officer, and the Headmen chose one among themselves to be chief *Vala Vidane.* In Terutenne the chief *Vala Vidane* (T. P. R. Nissanka) was the brother-in-law of the Village Headman and at the same time the chairman of the Village Committee and one of the richest men in the area. Hence one family was placed fairly securely at the controls. The other Irrigation Headmen were poor and uninfluential. The task of these officers is to supervise and coordinate the cultivation of paddy. They receive no salary from the government but are expected to be remunerated by the cultivators at the end of each harvest by the payment in kind of a set amount of paddy.

In rural areas a major focus of political action and factional dispute is the Village Committee. In the division of Walapane, each district had its own committee. Terutenne's district, Meda Palata, was divided into twelve "seats" for election purposes, and three of these belonged to Terutenne. These three seats, for the residential areas of Wekumbura, Helagama, and Galpitiya, were filled by separate elections. In 1955, the member for Wekumbura was T. P. R. Nissanka, who was also the chairman of the Village Committee and the chief Irrigation Headman as well as the brother-in-law of the Village Headman. The interests of Nissanka and his brother-in-law were so close that they lived, indeed, in the same dwelling in Wekumbura and it was regarded as the political center of Terutenne. Since one of the important functions of the Village Committee is to administer the generous government grants for village improvements,[2] the elected members, who

---

[2] In 1947–1948 the Meda Palata Village Committee received 3,500 rupees; in 1948–1949, 10,000 rupees; and in 1949–1950, 6,000 rupees. See *R.K.P.C.* (1951), p. 424.

served without salary, were thought to be in an admirable position to
enrich themselves by receiving bribes from contractors and other
businessmen. Not surprisingly, these posts were greatly coveted.

There was another similar organization called the Rural Development Society, whose function seemed to be that of receiving government grants. In this case the elections were open to its members only,
and there were four posts—president, vice-president, secretary, and
treasurer—which were also coveted. The official aim of this society
was the construction by communal labor of new houses, schools, and
latrines. Its activities were received with much mirth and amusement
by the villagers, who took a completely hypocritical attitude toward
these odd preoccupations of their government. They willingly accepted money for latrines which they dug themselves and then used
for storing grain. The Tom-Tom Beaters' Welfare Society attempted
somewhat unsuccessfully to emulate the other two societies and get
nearer the supply of government money.

In addition to the officers of these societies, the rest of the ruling
branch, so to speak, of Terutenne consisted of the three schoolteachers
and the retired headmaster of the local school. These were not necessarily men of local influence, but with their salaries they could buy
land and achieve standing in the village if they chose to do so. Teachers were accorded great prestige in all Kandyan villages. In general
they were ambitious, energetic, and intelligent men who spoke eloquent Sinhalese and were well informed on national political affairs.
In fact, the popularity of the "Sinhalese Only" (*Sinhala Pamanay*)
movement in the villages was largely due to the propaganda of the
Sinhalese schoolteachers. It is notable how frequently small things
can affect national issues. The Sinhalese schoolteachers had a permanent grudge because they were not paid as well as the schoolteachers
who taught English. Hence, in reaction to the teachers of English
the Sinhalese teachers tended to be extreme nationalists and had an
intense dislike of the Westernized upper classes in Colombo and
Kandy.

A second group of important personages were the shopkeepers.
There were about twelve shops in Terutenne in 1955, having a total
invested capital of about 10,000 rupees. As we shall see in the following chapter, the importance of shops in the village economy cannot be
overestimated.

In addition to these persons who were looked up to, there were
other special persons of more humble status, regarded by the common
villager as persons he could associate with on equal terms. These were
astrologers (*sastra karaya*), the native physicians (*veda mahatmaya*),
and devil dancers (*yakka vedarala*), all with specific functions. The
astrologer drew up horoscopes and diagnosed certain illnesses which

were related to the planetary deities. He could foretell the future and give advice on new enterprises. The native physicians provided medicines against disease for a small fee. The devil dancers, too, had their own special techniques for dealing with illnesses, the causes of which were attributed to male or female demons (*yakka, yakkini*). Many of these healing rituals consisted of dancing and drumming and periods of possession (see Wirz, 1954a; Yalman, 1964).

Apart from caste distinctions, about which much will be said later, these were the main occupational divisions and the most important persons in Terutenne. The rest of the population was simply engaged in agriculture. The main focus of village factions, as opposed to private disputes over land or, more rarely, women, centered around the positions of power and influence, the village Headmanship and the committees of Terutenne.

RELIGIOUS INSTITUTIONS

In 1955, even with the suggestive persistence of some Catholic-sounding Portuguese names (such as Eva Francea Perera), Terutenne was an all-Buddhist community. The only exceptions were the apothecary (a Hindu Tamil) and the anthropologist. There were two Buddhist temples (*vihara*) and two shrines (a *devale* and a *kovil*) for the village. The *devale*, on the stream, was normally associated with the goddess Pattini, and the other shrine—far from the village in the jungles of Ekkassa—was dedicated to fourteen deities who were at times spoken of as one person, *Ekkassa devaya*. The Buddhist temples belonged to the two different sects that exist in Ceylon: the temple in the large hamlet (Wekumbura) belonged to the *Amarapura* order; the other temple near Galpitiya, called Maluvegoda, belonged to the monks of the Siamese order. These sectarian cleavages which divide the monks (*Sangha*) do not penetrate into the laity. The sects of the *Sangha* are differentiated on doctrinal points. The Siamese order (*Siam Nikaya*) allegedly did not accept members of the low castes. The Amarapura were organized in reaction to this, to accept low castes into the priesthood (see Ryan, 1953, pp. 39f.). The doctrinal differences are shown up symbolically by other indices. Siam Nikaya shave their eyebrows as well as the rest of their bodies. They do not cover their right shoulders with their saffron robes. The Amarapura, in contrast, do not shave their eyebrows, and their saffron robes, of a deeper orange than those of the Siam Nikaya, cover both shoulders.

The Buddhist temples are owned by the Orders, and the head monks of the region (*nayaka thero*) are charged with the ordination and appointment of incumbents to the local *vihara*. But the community may always build and dedicate a temple and choose an in-

cumbent itself if it wishes to do so. The Buddhist monks do not play
an intimate part in the social life of the village. According to the
teaching of the Buddha, they turn away from attachments to this
world. They shed their kinship and other social connections when
they are ordained and are henceforth treated as holy beings. Hence
they are cut off from all matters and activities which might taint
their purity. They cannot have sexual intercourse, or any connection
with women. Since hair is considered to be polluting, they shave their
entire body. They are not allowed to eat solid food after midday—a
rule which may be associated with keeping the insides of the body
clean (i.e., without feces). They are not permitted to watch the rituals
of the gods and goddesses which take place at the *devale,* since these
are characterized as the "play of the gods" and as fertility rites have
certain sexual undertones.[3]

From another point of view the Buddhist monks (referred to as
Bhikku, meaning "beggar") are associated with the "other world."
This is borne out in part by the emphasis placed on the contempla-
tion of death in Buddhism (Yalman, 1962a). The *Bhikku* turns away
from the world because in the face of death all desires and attachments in this world lose their importance. Also, it is only at the time
of death that the monk has anything significant to do with the ordinary person. The funeral rites are conducted by them. It is thought
proper that their garments (*siura*) should be stitched from pieces of
cloth left for them at the graveyards after funeral rites which they
may find in the course of their wanderings.

The *vihara* and the *devale* stand in a significant sense in contrast to
each other. The annual events of High Buddhism—the birthday of
the Buddha, the Buddhist New Year, and the special period of seclusion of the priests (*Vas*) are all celebrated at the *vihara.* They are
directed to the eternal goal of reaching Nirvana, after the contradictions of life and death, health and disease, joy and sorrow, success and
failure, fertility and barrenness, purity and pollution are at last resolved. But the *devale* is the specific site of health and fertility rites
which take place mainly at the end of the dry season. While the
Buddha and his Bhikku are concerned with eternity, the deities of the
devale provide or withhold the good things of this life. As my informants put it: the *vihara* is a place of "worship" (*vandinava*) but
one goes to the *devale* to "demand" (*illasitima*) or "beg" (*nyaknya
kirima*) for assistance or objects one needs in this existence.

Just as the *vihara* and *devale* are contrasted, their functionaries, the
Bhikku and the *Kapurala* (the "priest" of the *devale*), also stand opposed to each other. We have mentioned that the *Bhikku* is celibate,

---

[3] *Keliya,* "play," is also said to be sex play (e.g., *rata keliya*). Some of the games
of the deities are also spoken of in the same terms (*An keliya*).

has no kinship with human beings, and shaves his hair. The *Kapurala,* on the other hand, must wear his hair long; he may also marry and raise a family. He is an ordinary member of the Cultivators caste, and though in large towns he may be a permanent incumbent in a large *devale,* he acts as a *Kapurala* in the villages only on special occasions when the shrine is activated. His status as a *Kapurala* in his ordinary life is indicated by special food taboos he imposes upon himself. I was fortunate enough to have a cook who turned out to be one of the most highly powered *Kapurala* of the district. He was completely unassuming and even humble in his day-to-day behavior, but he would be strikingly transformed during the rites when he handled the symbols of the deity and went into trance states (*mayang*): he would then become an impressive figure, swinging his long black hair around his head, standing erect and speaking with a firm voice when the deity entered him. On one occasion he asked me whether he could eat some of the hare he had cooked for me. I urged him to do so; but I was later dismayed to find that we had broken one of his food taboos and he was quite sick for many days afterwards.

Whereas the *Bhikku* divests himself of symbols of sexuality to approach the Buddha and Nirvana, the *Kapurala*—who also has to observe abstinence before his rituals—wears a distinctive dress when he performs his rituals and enters into trances. He covers his breasts with crossed white sashes and wears a skirtlike undergarment. His costume seems appropriate for his role as a mediator, first, between the world of men and the world of gods, and, second, between male and female gods, for in the annual fertility rites it is the *Kapurala* who brings the symbols of the male and female deity to each other (Yalman, 1964).[4]

Since theoretically the *Bhikku* do not have worldly interests, the secular affairs of the *vihara* are handled by special lay Benefactors' Societies (*Dayakaya Samitiya*). These have permanent administrative officers (president, vice-president, and so on) and organize the repairs to the temple, the provision of food for the priest during the season of his seclusion, and collection of dues from the members of the society for diverse religious activities. They also used to organize the annual *vihara* rituals and occasional meetings for preaching (*bana*) and ceremonial chanting (*pirit*), to which are invited priests of the same order from other *vihara* in the district. In 1955, the secretary of one of the societies in Terutenne was a young Washerman who was elected to his post by a high-caste Cultivator majority. He was certainly a person of excellent character—pious, well-read, and exceptionally intelligent —and his special qualities were recognized by this honor.

---

[4] The well-known Sinhalese marriage broker who brings men and women together is also called *kapurala.*

4

*The Economy of
the Dry Zone Village*

"It is evident from this sketch of their agriculture that the lands
of Ceylon do not produce a crop at all equal to what by proper
cultivation they might be made to bear."—Robert Percival,
An Account of the Island of Ceylon, (1803), p. 192

THE OWNERSHIP OF LAND

What are the sources of income in Terutenne? How is wealth distributed in the community? What is the extent and the effects of
money economy? Is money a source of instability or change, or both,
in the village social structure? The answers to these questions are
basic for an understanding of the economic foundations of the Sinhalese village and for the analysis of social change in small traditional
communities.[1]

The villages of the Dry Zone are sufficiently simple in their economy
for the sources of income and wealth to be easily catalogued. The
main source of income and index of wealth in most Dry Zone villages
is land. The second source of income in most villages is the small
village shop which sells the foodstuffs and clothes on which most of
the cash income of the villager is spent. Third, there are the salaries
of civil servants, the Headman, schoolteachers and the like, as well
as the income that the villagers receive from the considerable cash
aid which the government channels into rural Ceylon by various
agencies. Fourth, the village industries, that is, the productive efforts
of the various low-caste potters, blacksmiths, and jaggery makers,
may be listed. Of this type of services in the villages only carpentry
and tailoring are not associated with caste traditions in Ceylon.

---

[1] The various figures that appear in the text are based on detailed surveys made
in the villages and crosschecked with the Village and Irrigation Headmen.

Transport service either with bullock carts (*tavalam*) or, in villages nearer the roads, with truck and bus could also be included in this category. Fifth, the efforts of the various "professionals"—the medicine men, astrologers, and devil dancers, may be mentioned.

We have noted that whereas chena cultivation could be undertaken by anyone in this region, the irrigated rice lands were restricted in size and owned in small plots by individuals or groups of individuals. All lands could be bought and sold, though most ancient families would be unwilling to lose possession of their lands.

The rice fields of Terutenne are irrigated by an elaborate system of water channels tapping the various mountain streams (see map 4). The small dams constructed across the streams are called *amunu* and each section of the field watered from one *amunu* is separately named.[2] These field sections are unequal in size and follow the contours of the hills; the level areas are more fertile than the steeply terraced parts. The extent to which the size of the rice fields is fixed by its water supply may be gathered from the following example. In Terutenne I had access to records of land tenure (Grain Tithe Registers in the Nuwara Eliya government offices) which were kept for the region of Walapane from 1857 onward.[3] From the 1895 records, it was possible to work out the size of a field referred to as Egodawela in Terutenne; it turned out to be 51 *pale* and 6 *kuruni*. In 1955 the same field was reckoned by the villagers to be 52 *pale*. (The difference, a matter of 4 *kuruni*, was probably due to a mistake in reckoning and is negligible.) Since the supply of water and the techniques of irrigation had not altered, the size of the valuable field had evidently not changed.

Rice lands are one of the chief indices of wealth in the community. It is true that some capital goes into trading ventures, and some of it is spent on weddings and other forms of conspicuous consumption, but the shrewd person with means always acquires land if possible. The psychology of this attitude is significant. In the villages it was felt that no other undertaking could compare to the acquisition of rice land, in terms of productivity and prestige. All other investments

---

[2] I use Sinhalese measurements when referring to rice land: 4 *kuruni* = 1 *timbay*; 10 *kuruni* = 1 *pale*; 4 *pale* = 1 *amunam*. These measurements are actually baskets of different sizes, used to measure various quantities of rice. When used in connection with land, they indicate the extent of land that can be sown with a certain quantity of seed. The acreage of land corresponding to, say, one *pale* basket of seed may be slightly larger on steep slopes than on level ones. Two *pale* of land are more or less equivalent to one acre.

[3] The government had added to the total extent of rice land available in Terutenne by providing the irrigation for a new fertile field in the south called Bolagandawela. This field is watered by the Uma Oya River and some of the villagers in neighboring communities—for example, Udamadura—also own and cultivate lands in it.

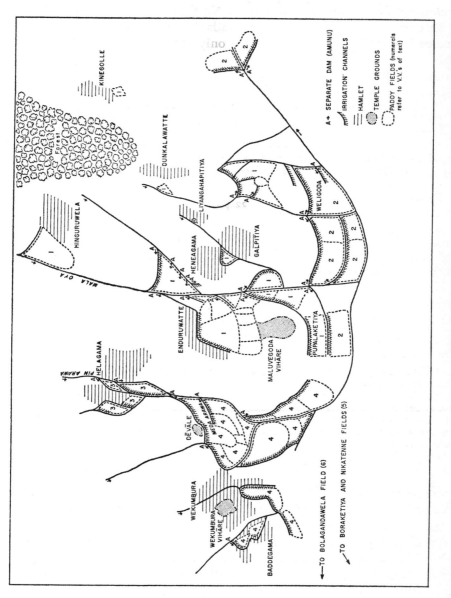

Map 4. Terutenne.

were considered risky, and unless one succeeded in becoming very rich they did not enhance one's social position.

I found the ownership of paddy lands in Terutenne restricted to a relatively small number of landlords. No single landlord controlled a particularly large extent of the available paddy fields, but, as a perusal of table 3 will demonstrate, only 182 persons out of a total

TABLE 3

*The Ownership of Paddy Lands in Terutenne**

Size of Holding (in *pale*)	Landholders: Number and Percentage of Adult Population†		Total Holdings (in *pale*) and Percentage of Total Area	
1 or less..............	64 ⎫	22.4%	51.5 ⎫	24.0%
1–2.................	48 ⎭		90 ⎭	
2–3.................	20 ⎫		55 ⎫	
3–4.................	17 ⎪		63.5 ⎪	
4–5.................	9 ⎬	10.8%	41 ⎬	35.2%
5–6.................	5 ⎪		29 ⎪	
6–7.................	3 ⎭		20 ⎭	
7–10................	5 ⎫	3.2%	40.5 ⎫	40.8%
10–27.5.............	11 ⎭		201.5 ⎭	
Total	182	36.4%	592	100.0%

* Total adult population: 517; total population: 1,203; *pale* per adult: 1.18; *pale* per head (total population): 0.50.

† It is not easy to disentangle the number of holders when some land is held in undivided ownership. For these purposes, I have worked out the size of the claims of the oldest members; if the father is dead, then each sibling with a claim is marked as a separate "holder." Obviously, therefore, some who appear to have no land will inherit later, but conversely, note that the population percentages do not include persons under twenty.

population of 1,203 held any paddy lands at all. To put it in more realistic terms, let us simply consider the adults. If we arbitrarily regard all those above the age of twenty as adult (even though many who are younger already have children), one gets the following figures: Only 182 persons (36.4 percent) out of a total adult population of 517 (100 percent) hold any rice lands at all. And among these 182 land-lords just 16 persons (i.e., 3.2 percent of adults) hold between them 40.8 percent of all the available rice lands in Terutenne.[4]

With the evidence in table 3, the gross figure of paddy per head of the total population is 0.50 *pale*. The impressive personal achieve-

---

[4] Compare Farmer (1957), pp. 60–61.

ments of some of the rich individuals in the village must be seen
against this figure. The chairman of the Village Committee had himself bought most of his holding of 27.5 *pale*. The fact that he was the
brother-in-law of the Village Headman, Agalakumbura, who had been
administering the village for nearly twenty years, had evidently not
hindered his own activities. The Village Headman had collected 21.5
pale, and the kin group of the Chairman and the Headman was one
of the wealthiest in the community. The leader of an opposing faction, an old astrologer and retired schoolteacher who had embraced
Buddhism after giving up Christianity, held 24 *pale* in Terutenne; he
was supported by another retired schoolteacher with 12.4 *pale* as well
as by the single Blacksmith family of Terutenne (20 *pale*), and the
heterogeneous "opposition" had no difficulty holding their own against
the "party in power."

The figures relating to the holding of landlords cannot be simply
turned around to work out the figures of the landless, for the percentages do not include exact details of the dependents of these landlords.
Some who appear landless will inherit later, but even with these
reservations it is clear that there is a large body of persons in the village who do not own rice lands. The alternative for them is to live off
slash-and-burn cultivation. If they prefer rice cultivation they may
work as laborers for a daily wage on the lands of others, or they may
attempt to cultivate some land on a sharecropping basis.

I shall discuss the other two Sinhalese villages, Makulle Watta and
Vilawa, later (see chaps. 10 and 11), but here a brief comparison with
Terutenne is instructive. The amount of rice land per adult in Terutenne is 1.18 *pale* (table 3). This compares with 1.77 in Makulle Watta
and 1.38 in Vilawa (table 4). I reckoned in Ceylon that an average
nuclear family[5] would need about 2 *pale* of land simply to survive.[6]
It should be obvious that the pressure on rice lands has reached its
absolute limits in the Dry Zone. For many persons in these traditional
villages who do not own rice lands, the only safety valve is chena
cultivation. Even if the income from rice lands in the villages were
evenly distributed—which it is not—there would still be good reason
for the cultivation of chena. This is true today, and, given the high
birth rate, serious consequences are likely to follow unless the

---

[5] I define a "nuclear family" as a couple with their unmarried children who form
a single cooking unit, that is, a *ge* in Sinhalese, which is usually about five persons.

[6] I arrive at this figure in the following manner: Let us assume that the family
needs 24 "measures" of rice per month for its basic food supply, at a conservative
estimate; a rice income of 18 *pale* per annum (unhusked) would thus suffice to keep
the family above starvation line. Assuming the yield to be about tenfold for an
ordinary field in Terutenne (slightly higher in Vilawa and slightly lower in Makulle Watta), that would mean cultivating 2 *pale* of paddy (yield, 20 *pale* of rice;
2 set aside for seed).

acreage under rice and productivity is sharply increased, or other opportunities for employment are found.[7]

It is also interesting to compare the landholding figures of the villages in terms of those with and without land. The percentages of landholders among the adult population in the villages are as follows: Terutenne, 36.4 percent; Makulle Watta, 25.3 percent; Vilawa, 44.3

TABLE 4

The Ownership of Paddy Lands in Makulle Watta* and Vilawa†

Size of Holding (in *pale*)	Landholders: Number and Percentage of Adult Population‡		Total Holdings (in *pale*) and Percentage of Total Area	
Makulle Watta:				
0–2	38	11.2%	41	6.4%
2–7	21	6.2%	87.5	15.4%
7 or more	27	7.9%	462	78.2%
Total	86	25.3%	590.5	100.0%
Vilawa:				
0–2	41	22.1%	46.3	18.2%
2–7	35	18.9%	133.4	51.9%
7 or more	6	3.3%	76.8	29.9%
Total	82	44.3%	256.5	100.0%

* Total adult population: 388 (estimated to be 45.5% of total population); total population: 743; *pale* per adult: 1.77.

† Total adult population: 185 (estimated to be 48.7% of total population); total population: 380; *pale* per adult: 1.38.

‡ It is difficult to compute the number of "holders" when some land is held in the form of "joint estates." For these purposes, I have worked out the size of the claims of the oldest members; if the father is dead, then each sibling with a claim is marked as a separate "holder." Obviously, some who appear to have no land will inherit later, but conversely, note that the figures of persons under twenty have been excluded from population percentages above.

percent. These percentages accord well with the ecology of the villages. Makulle Watta, with the fewest landholders, is situated in the wild and underpopulated Wellassa district; the water supply there is limited, but there are large areas for chena cultivation. In fact the chena cycle in the division is about twelve to sixteen years, compared

[7] Vittachi (1958) suggests that one of the main reasons for the fierce Sinhalese–Tamil riots in the Dry Zone, especially in the regions near colonization schemes, was the anger of the Sinhalese landless laborers at having Tamils settled on rice lands which they thought should be turned over to them.

to four to six years in Terutenne. Vilawa, on the other hand, is in the thickly populated Wanni Hatpattuva division. The water supply is favorable, but there are hardly any chena to speak of. Hence, although the figures suggest a more even distribution of rice land in Vilawa the lack of chena in this area should be taken into account.

In terms of the concentration of paddy land in the hands of the larger landlords (those who own more than 7 *pale* of rice land) the figures are as follows: in Terutenne 3.2 percent of all adults (those over twenty) held 40.8 percent of all rice lands; in Makulle Watta 7.9 percent held 78.2 percent; and in Vilawa 3.3 percent held 29.9 percent. In Makulle Watta, a few shopkeepers have acquired most of the rice land, but in Vilawa the distribution is more equitable. In both villages, however, the availability of chena lands remains a crucial factor.

It was my impression, taking both the extent of rice lands and the possibilities of chena into consideration, that Terutenne was worst off in absolute terms among these villages, and that Vilawa was probably in the most favorable economic circumstances. The statistics for the movement of persons in and out of these three villages supported this impression (see table 5). It should be noted, however, that the excep-

TABLE 5

The Dispersal of Siblings*

Status	Terutenne				Udamulla †				Vilawa			
	Men	%	Women	%	Men	%	Women	%	Men	%	Women	%
Married, still in village........	93	43	86	38	30	63.9	25	64	27	50	17	25.7
Unmarried, still in village.......	55	25	38	16.9	10	21.3	1	2.5	17	31.4	15	22.7
Gone out in marriage.......	8	3.7	78	34.5	3	6.3	13	33.3	6	11.1	34	51.5
Gone out to bazaars or colonization schemes........	55	25	24	10.6	3	6.3	—	—	3	5.5	—	—
Buddhist Monks...	6	2.9	—	—	1	2.1	—	—	1	1.8	—	—
Total........	217		226		47		39		54		66	

* Based on a study of sibling groups: 89 groups in Terutenne, 28 in Udamulla, and 29 in Vilawa.
† Udamulla is a hamlet in Makulle Watta (see chap. 10).

tionally high figures for emigration from Terutenne (25 percent for men and 10 percent for women) are partly related to the proximity of tea estates and of urban centers like Nuwara Eliya. Some of the people of Terutenne had also joined the colonization schemes such as Hinguragoda.

Two important conclusions emerge from this discussion. First of all, since the villagers already live at a critically low level, with barely enough food to go around, the amount that can be "saved" in economic terms for investment or for barter, so as to diversify the diet or even provide simple comforts, is strictly limited. It is probably too much to expect the peasants of the Dry Zone to contribute to the economic development of Ceylon by their savings. (For their relative numerical strength in the labor supply of Ceylon, see table 6.) More

TABLE 6

Occupational Grouping of Gainful Workers in Ceylon
(based on 1946 Census)

	Number (1,000's)		%
Agriculture....................	1,339.1		51.3
Village products............................	14.7*	⎫	
Plantations................................	28.9	⎬ 52.8	
Others....................................	9.2	⎭	
Forestry and fishing.............	42.3		1.6
Industry and mining............	286.5		11.0
Trade, transport, banking, etc.....	552.5†		21.1
Professions and public and domestic services............	390.9		15.0
Total......................	2,611.3		100.0

* Dubious figure, but note that only those classified as "gainfully employed" are indicated.

† This figure includes 270,000 occasional laborers.

significantly, it is quite apparent that there is a great possibility of raising levels of agricultural productivity. By any standards, a mere tenfold return on seed sown is extremely low, and even the highest I have come across in any Dry Zone village—about fiftyfold return in two harvests—is still very low by Japanese standards. There is here a real opportunity for vigorous development with appropriate fertilizers and more efficient techniques (I.B.R.D., 1953, pp. 287ff.). It is evident, of course, that it would be senseless to try to introduce wholesale methods that have worked successfully in other countries and climates, and one should pay heed to such claims by the villagers that the transplanting of rice seedlings, a method that gives excellent returns in Japan, will not work in the mountain areas of the Dry Zone: the topsoil, they argue, is too thin and the stones make transplanting arduous. These arguments may be mere rationalizations growing from a reluctance to change, but they cannot be disregarded.[8]

FORMS OF AGRICULTURE

The Cultivation of Paddy

There are three possible methods of cultivation for the owner of rice land. He may work the land himself with the assistance of his sons and sons-in-law. If he decides on this course, additional labor will be necessary during the plowing-sowing season, and later in the reaping-threshing stage. He may engage coolie labor at a daily wage of two and a half rupees without food (or two rupees with a midday meal and tea), or he may try one of the traditional labor exchange methods.[9]

The second method is to employ coolie labor for the entire cultivation cycle. The cost of this undertaking is calculated in table 7. This method is, of course, open only to those with ready cash, and only large landlords will attempt it. If a person works mainly alone but has some help from his sons and in-laws, he can cultivate five *pale*. Without any help at all, a man cannot hope to cultivate more than three *pale*. Using coolie labor, the large landlords can of course cultivate all their holdings.

The third method is to rent out the land on an annual sharecropping basis called *ande*. Here again, the arrangements are traditional. In Terutenne the *ande* agreements followed several different patterns, in which four factors of production were considered: land, labor, seed, and buffaloes. In one version of *ande,* the landlord provided the land, the worker offered his labor, and the cost of the seed and buffaloes was shared between them. At the end of the harvest the landlord and worker split the crop fifty-fifty. Sometimes, however, the landlord provided all the seed and all the buffaloes, in which case the worker reimbursed the landlord for his share of buffalo expenses after the harvest.[10] Seed paddy was treated somewhat differently. The worker was considered to have borrowed his share from the landlord and had

---

[8] The government of Ceylon has agricultural offices in some villages to give advice to the peasants. There are also model agricultural farms in various parts of the island. But it is clear that these officers have little or no influence in most traditional villages, and a much more aggressive and vigorous productivity campaign is called for.

[9] The most usual form of labor exchange is *attang*, a reciprocal arrangement whereby obligations are carefully reckoned in precise terms. There are other forms of reciprocal labor, like *kayya*, where large numbers of people, usually women, are collected for the finger millet harvest, but the reciprocities are not so closely calculated in *kayya* as in *attang*.

[10] In 1955 this was calculated at five rupees per pair of buffalo per day, or one bushel per paddy, if paid after the harvest (worth Rs. 6–12, depending on the season).

TABLE 7

Operations and Cost of Paddy Cultivation by Coolie Labor*
(Cultivation of 1 amunam, in rupees based on a wage of: Rs. 2 per day)†

	Terutenne	Makulle Watta
Initial plowing		
(to complete in one day 9 men needed; usual procedure 2 or 3 men 4 or 5 days)........	18	20
Buffaloes		
(4 pairs at Rs. 5 a pair per day)................	20	20
Preparation of the field		
Terutenne:		
Digging (*kotanta*), making ridges, etc. (20 man-days; usual procedure 2–4 men 5–10 days).....................	40	
Final preparation: smoothing and sowing (*vapuranta*) (15 man-days).........................	30	
Makulle Watta:		
Digging, "mudding," etc. (*kotanta, madavanta, vakkara bandinta*) (12 man-days; usual procedure 2–4 men 3–6 days).....................		25
Making ridges (*niyara kotanta*), preparing for sowing, sowing (*vapuranta*) (2–4 men 2–4 days).....................		15
Harvesting		
Preparation of threshing floor (*kammata*).........	16	16
Reaping (*kapanta*)............................	5	5
Transport to threshing floor (*goda karanta*).......	8	8
Threshing (*kola paganava*)......................	4	4
Total labor cost........................	141	113
Seed cost (4 *pale*)........................	40	40
Grand Total.........................	181	153

* These are two fairly generous assessments by informants in Terutenne and Makulle Watta. The latter is in the nature of an ideal, for it is rare for the fields to be plowed in that region. (Note the difference in cost of cultivation.) The fields are merely "mudded" (*madavala*) by making buffaloes walk over them. The yields are therefore correspondingly lower in general. Without plowing they are claimed to be 5–8 to the *pale* sown in Makulle Watta; 6–16 (depending on the location of the field) in Terutenne with plowing. In Vilawa, where the fields are carefully plowed two or three times, and two crops are grown (*Maha* and *Yala*), the yields may be as high as 24–32 fold during the main cultivation season (*Maha*).

Confining oneself to Terutenne and taking 12 as the yield, the return would be about 48 *pale* to the *amunam*. The cash value of this, during 1954–1955, would have been about Rs. 480. The argument for a landlord not to give his fields out on *ande* but to work them on coolie labor is decisive, particularly on those fields where the yield is much higher than 12. If the large landlords do have some of their lands on *ande*, it is because these workers provide them with a standing group of supporters in the village.

† Coolie wages, if food and drink are provided once a day: morning only (*varuvak*); Rs. 1; whole day (*davas*), Rs. 2.

to repay it after the harvest with 50 percent interest. It will be observed that with the price of a bushel of paddy running at about Rs. 10 in 1955, it was in the landlord's interest to cultivate his land by coolie labor rather than by *ande*. Even so, much land was worked under *ande*. There were two reasons for this. In the first place, close kinsmen used *ande* among themselves. (We must except fathers, sons, sons-in-law, full brothers, and brothers-in-law, for they may lend rice land to one another, if they are on good terms, without formal arrangements.) Second, large landlords often preferred to give the land on *ande,* on a fairly permanent basis, so as to acquire supporters in village intrigues and elections. Thus the retired schoolteacher of Christian origin whom I mentioned earlier as one of the large landlords in Terutenne, gave out most of his lands on *ande*. Being a stranger from the Low Country, he had to be particularly careful to maintain good relations in the village, even though his sister was married in the Hegasulla hamlet.

It will be seen that paddy cultivation rests on complicated arrangements involving a great deal of cooperation among persons who are not necessarily kinsmen. The important point for purposes of kinship analysis is that the income (paddy or cash) of individuals who own or cultivate paddy land is private and personal. Moreover, even young men who do not own paddy lands can have income by working as coolie labor or for *ande*.

Chena Cultivation

In contrast to the complicated arrangements of paddy, chena or slash-and-burn cultivation is a simple matter. In 1955 most of the chena lands of Terutenne were Crown land and could be worked on annual permits from the District Revenue Officer, easily obtained at a rental of one rupee per acre. The Crown Survey had also allowed some private claims on chena lands near the village.

Chena is normally worked by slash-and-burn cultivation from September, when the jungle that has been felled is burned, to February, when the last harvest is reaped. This cultivation is always undertaken by nuclear families. After the ground has been cleared a hut is constructed in the middle of the plot and the family may live a migratory life, partly in the highlands and partly in the village. So long as it has a permit, any nuclear family may undertake shifting cultivation anywhere in the jungle. Usually a number of such nuclear families—sometimes as many as forty or more—get together and work on one hillside, but each man is considered to own, for the cultivation season, whatever section of jungle he himself clears—usually one or two acres. Before the sowing, the entire community fences itself in to protect the plots from marauding cattle and pigs; once the harvest is completed, the land is allowed to revert to jungle. The cultivation cycle in Terutenne was between four to six years.

The chena community may be drawn from members of any of the hamlets in the village, but seldom do people of different villages join together in a chena community, although with kinship connections this might be thought likely. The larger hamlets of Terutenne usually formed several such chena communities and went to different highlands every year. Members of various castes could mix together in the highlands, but the Tom-Tom Beaters normally went off to a separate chena community all by themselves. For the purposes of land tenure, the significance of chena cultivation lies in the fact that there are no permanent rights on the land, the plot can be cultivated by any one man and his wife, and nuclear families can subsist by their own labor, working nothing but chena.

Strong exception has been taken to this form of cultivation by the Ceylon government, on the grounds that shifting cultivation tends to hasten land erosion by eliminating secondary jungle growth. This criticism is sound enough, but it is difficult to see how these practices can be stopped by legal action when no alternative sources of livelihood are provided for the large numbers of landless peasants in the interior villages of Ceylon. Given the increasing pressure on the land, it should be obvious that chena will be cultivated in the Dry Zone with or without the approval of the government.

Garden Lands

The garden lands (watte) of the village are used as house sites in the hamlets. These are pleasant compounds shaded by large fruit-bearing trees—usually jack (a kind of bread-fruit), coconut, and bread-fruit. The fruit of such trees makes an important contribution to the diet of the villager, and it is seldom marketed outside the village. Plantains, however, and, in the eastern parts of the Dry Zone, citrus fruits are an exception, and many villages make gratifying profits on their fruit gardens.

Not surprisingly, the watte trees are jealously guarded, and claims may be extended not only to single jack and coconut trees but even to shares of their fruit. Trees may be held in common between siblings and their produce may be taken in annual rotation. My interpreter in Terutenne owned a share of two coconut trees in the village of his mother, fifteen miles away. Such fragmented shares are often of negligible economic value, as in this case, but claims would be remembered since they could represent potential titles to a portion of an estate on which other kinsmen live.

Cash Crops

Apart from their fruit trees, most of the villagers did grow some cash crops for an additional source of income. In the Walapane region the most important of these crops were vegetables—peppers, beans, okra, and the like—which were either taken to the weekly market in Harasbedda or sold to vendors who distributed them as far away as Nuwara Eliya or Kandy. Inadequate irrigation made the growing of vegetables difficult and risky, and since the market was less sure than the rice market, no one attempted to grow vegetables on rice lands. In the dry season, when the fields were not under rice, some vegetables could be substituted, but the total amount was strictly limited by the lack of water. In areas nearer the town centers such as Nuwara Eliya, rice lands had been converted into vegetable gardens; it seemed clear that with a steady demand from organized markets and improved transport facilities there would be no insurmountable traditional hindrances to the cultivation of cash crops.

One particular crop which the villagers were fond of growing on their chena was *ganja.* This is a mild narcotic and fetches very high prices in the town markets. There were a certain number of *ganja* addicts in the villages as well. The government kept a watchful eye, on *ganja* cultivation, but officials could be bribed, and in any case the distant *ganja* plots in these deep jungles and inaccessible highlands could hardly be kept under close surveillance. It seems likely, in fact, that many of the distant jungle communities which appear to subsist on nothing in the heart of wilderness produce *ganja* for commercial purposes. I had the impression that *ganja* cultivation formed a good part of the income of the isolated jungle villages with no rice lands, in the Walapane, Bintenne, Wellassa, and Buttala areas.

Another crop which the villagers of Terutenne experimented with was tobacco. Some of the chena highlands were covered with this crop, but the cash returns appeared to be very poor. Persons with ready capital to invest in tobacco "barns" where the leaf was cured skimmed off most of the profits.[11]

In all these cases, it seemed to me that the villagers were not without the spirit to indulge in productive enterprises, but their initiative was dampened by circumstances—lack of transport, the unsteady nature of the demand for their products, and, most important of all, lack of capital. The poorer villagers could not be expected to risk what little they had in uncertain investments. Those who had the ready cash and were willing to take considerable risks usually found

---

[11] In 1955 the villagers sold the uncured leaf for 15 cents a pound (100 cents to a rupee). When cured, the price was about Rs. 2.50.

that shopkeeping and transport brought the best returns and therefore tended to invest in these areas if they did not buy rice lands.

THE MONEY ECONOMY

Shops

The ubiquitous village shop is one of the striking features of the Ceylonese landscape. These small trading enterprises are the channels which bring the money economy into even the most isolated villages of the Dry Zone. The products they sell range from cigarettes, small cigars, matches, a variety of condiments—chilies, onions, tomatoes and potatoes, dry fish from the Maldive Islands—to Japanese sardines, tinned milk from Europe, and the various sarongs and cloths which the Sinhalese villagers are fond of wearing.

The technique of shopkeeping is a subtle art. The efficient shopkeeper must bear three aims in mind: (a) as much as possible must be sold at the highest possible prices; (b) as much as possible must be given out in credit; and (c) in the process the firm must continue to exist. This last aim is not altogether easy to achieve and the rate of liquidation in these enterprises is extremely high. In all the villages I knew there were many bankrupt shops; indeed, bankruptcy was so universal a phenomenon that the word "bankrop" had been taken over into village Sinhalese and was widely used.

The successful shopkeeper is one who can go to the brink of "bankrop" and somehow pull off his deals, gather his credits, and make some profits. The extension of credit by the shopkeepers is an important factor in the success of the enterprise. It does not matter particularly if the shopkeeper charges high prices so long as he is prepared to extend credit for an undefined period, which may well last until the harvest.

Quick cash transactions are not to the liking of the villagers or—within reasonable limits—of the shopkeepers. The "credit connection" is to the advantage of both. From the point of view of the customers, shops that extend easy credit are naturally to be favored. At the same time, long-standing "credit connections" with particular customers mean for the shopkeeper that such customers will find it difficult to do business elsewhere. In these small villages nothing can be kept secret for very long: everyone usually knows where people trade, and if changes are made without good reason both credit and cordial relations at the first shop come to an end and the creditor will forthwith demand the money due him. Customers who accept credit are expected to be loyal in return.

I was friendly with a number of shopkeepers and found them to be, on the whole, the most enterprising and ambitious—and among the most intelligent—persons in the community. The successful shops were also the center of the social life of the village—full of villagers at all times of the day and night, who were served tea and betel by the shopkeepers or their assistants. The popularity of the boutique as a meeting place and center of gossip also enhanced trade.[12]

The enterprising shopkeeper had to be careful, of course, of extending too much credit, for he might find it increasingly difficult to keep his shop well stocked. To knowing customers, a near-empty shop is a sure sign that an enterprise is tottering; they cleverly take their "credit connections" elsewhere, and it becomes more and more difficult for the shopkeeper to collect his debts and build up his stocks. The collection may take many years, and in the process he may lose all his good will in the village. He may suffer in other ways as well, for the shopkeeper is himself usually indebted to other shopkeepers in the trade centers in the vicinity of the village.[13] These shopkeepers are in turn dependent on bigger businessmen (*bisniss kariyo*) in the towns, and so it goes all the way down to Colombo. There are good reasons for this efflorescence of intermediaries. Transport is a very rewarding business and the intermediaries who transport goods short distances between villages and trading centers and between such centers and towns reap excellent profits. But since it is impossible to do any business at the village level without an intimate knowledge of the community, neither the traders in the bazaars nor the formal government agencies (which demand more definite sureties than the villagers can provide) can bypass the village shopkeepers. Credit can be safely extended only to persons well known to the creditor, and a good shopkeeper, who is able to tell the "bad hats" from the good risks, is a necessary part of the whole chain.

The variable fortunes of "business" can best be shown by a description of the shops in Terutenne. In 1955 there were twelve shops in the village, with a total invested capital estimated at about Rs. 10,000 (see table 8). There were also six recently "bankrop" ones whose owners were trying rather unsuccessfully, to collect their credits. Not one of these twelve shops was more than ten years old; most of them were less than five. This is not to imply that there had been a recent flowering of trade prospects: the war period is said to have been much more profitable. Even in 1893, according to Le Mesurier (1898, pp.

---

[12] In Terutenne one of the entrepreneurs I knew was called Dharmadasa. He had started his shop in 1952. In 1955 he had about 400 rupees invested in merchandise alone, and in the three years he had succeeded in buying about 10.5 *pale* of rice land in Terutenne. By this time he had a total of Rs. 917.06 out on credit to 44 persons in Terutenne, the oldest account dating from the beginnings of the enterprise.

[13] The trade centers for the villages mentioned in this book are Nildandahinna for Terutenne, Monaragala for Makulle Watta, Maho for Vilawa.

266ff.) there were three shops in Terutenne. The short histories simply mean that shops come and go rather quickly.

The shopkeepers are fully aware of the risky nature of their enterprises, and for this reason many of them have a consistent policy of buying land as soon as it comes on the market. They are in an excellent position to acquire land—always a sensitive matter in peasant communities—not only because they are the only people in the village

TABLE 8

The Shops of Terutenne*

Name of Shopkeeper	Estimated Capital (in rupees)	Years in Business	Land Acquired (in *pale*)
Wekumbura:			
Ranbanda....................	4,000	4	4
Wegolle (former Village Headman of Arukwatte village)....................	1,000	3	11.5
Gallinde Tikiribanda..........	400	6	4.5
T. G. Kiribanda..............	300	2	—
K. G. Sudumenika (woman)...	600	10	4
H. P. B. Banda..............	100	6	—
Ukwatte Pbanda..............	60	4	I
Dharmadasa.................	400	3	10.5
Jayasekera..................	500	10	6.5
Helagama:			
Wegolle schoolteacher.........	100	2	5.5
Galpitiya:			
Elapita Kiribanda............	100	I	—
Kirihenea and Washerman partner....................	100	I	—

* Recently bankrupt: K. M. P. (who had acquired 2 *pale*), T. P. R. Nissanka (the Village Committee Chairman and the chief *Vala Vidane*, who had acquired 27.5 *pale*), John, Elapita Appuhami, and Nandina (a Tom-Tom Beater).

who can pay spot cash to clinch a sale with a wavering villager but also because they can cajole their debtors to mortgage and eventually sell their lands in return for what they owe the shopkeeper. One of the familiar complaints of the villagers in Terutenne was that the shopkeepers had tricked innocent people into selling their ancestral lands. The picture of the land-grabbing shopkeepers was more true in Makulle Watta than in Terutenne, as a comparison of tables 8 and 9 will show. In those distant regions of the Wellassa division some shopkeepers had amassed considerable fortunes by the trade and trans-

port of oranges, and had bought up most of the paddy lands of the
village.

It is unfair to the shopkeepers, however, to dismiss them all as land-
grabbers who cleverly plot to acquire land. The land comes onto the
market in consequence of clear economic difficulties which plague the
Dry Zone. Many of these are intricately bound up with customs and

TABLE 9

The Shops of Makulle Town in Wellassa*

	Estimated Capital (in rupees)	Years in Business	Land Acquired (in *pale*)	Caste
Name of Shopkeeper†				
1. Podi Appuhami..........	200	10	—	Goyigama
2. Hanthiyawa Punchibanda.	150	2	—	Goyigama
3. Hendi Sinyo.............	300	12	—	Halagama
4. S. U. Jayawardene........	5,000	20	13	Durava
5. M. Silva................	300	5	—	Karava
6. Ahangama..............	250	4	—	Durava
7. Jayasehera.............	3,000	3	—	Karava
8. Bentis‡.................	6,000	15	121.5	Durava
9. Batticaloa Muslims........	3,000	10	—	
10. Dodang Mudalali (operated busses and trucks).........	10,000	10	11.5	Goyigama
11. Saoris Jayawardene.......	600	15	37.5	Durava
12. M. Dissanayika..........	300	6	16	Goyigama
Udamulla Hamlet*				
1. Silva....................	200	4	—	Durava
2. Tengelwatte.............	100	3	2	Goyigama
3. William Sinyo............	2,000	3	14	Durava

    * I use Makulle Watta, except when specified, as a convenient term to refer to some
hamlets around one large paddy field (Maha Gandena, Makulle Watta, Udamulla,
and the shop area, Makulle Town). See chap. 10.
    † The numbers refer to the locations of shops on map 10, chap. 10.
    ‡ Bentis alone held nearly one-fifth of all irrigable paddy land in the village.

habits. Land will come up for sale because there are too many claimants on a particular estate and the shareholders prefer to sell the
property and divide the profits; or a family may be in debt because
there has been too great an outlay on wedding celebrations or high
dowries have been given to the daughters. Cash may be needed for
medical bills (the villagers at times take their sick to doctors in Kandy
and Nuwara Eliya), or for litigation, especially for land disputes, or
even for gambling debts (see Bailey, 1958, chap. 4, *passim*).

There are certain implications which follow from this account of the role of shops in the economy of the Dry Zone village. Most importantly, in the traditional village, shops introduce an element of instability into the system. Individuals and families may become rich through trade and intermarry with rich and respectable families. Many instances of this kind will be described in the following chapters. Alternatively, and more rarely, unwise investments in shops may lead to the impoverishment of formerly rich persons. The sale of land, meaning changes in the land ownership pattern of the traditional village, is also a factor of instability in the system.

The shops also, of course, have a profound influence on the social life of the village. The shopkeepers are regarded as worldly and sophisticated men who are intimately acquainted with the distant life of towns, and they are often accepted as leaders and looked up to by the villagers. The sophistication carries the implication, at the same time, that monetary matters are to be kept distinct from kinship and should be treated in an unsentimental fashion. This is probably the most unpleasant aspect of shopkeeping for the villagers. In small Sinhalese villages, kinship obligations are given great attention. The kin group is a mutual insurance association: the members aid each other in times of difficulty. The shopkeeper who starts his enterprise in his own village soon finds himself faced with impossible demands from his kinsmen. But if he wishes to stay in business, he must disregard the claims for special credits from his close kinsmen, for the final goal of these persistent kinship claims is to erode the kinsman who has become relatively wealthy down to the level of the rest of the family. Unfortunately for the shopkeeper, if he resists the claims, the kin group becomes poisoned with ill-feeling.

Given this categorical antithesis between shopkeeping and kinship obligations, it is not surprising to find that in most villages where there are a number of shops, they tend to be clustered around a central area more or less set off from the residential sections. It is as if the kinship areas were being isolated from the areas of economic competition and impersonal values. In the village of Makulle Watta, the process had been carried to its extreme and the twelve shops were distinctly separate, a "town," as it were, referred to as Makulle *tauma*.

The shopkeepers realized that the most effective way of separating the areas of kinship and business was to be a shopkeeper in a community where one did not have kinship connections. It is certainly noteworthy that the Muslims and the Sinhalese of the Low Country—often of the Karava (Fisher) caste—were the most successful shopkeepers of the Kandyan area. Naturally, their lack of kinship connections in the Dry Zone was not the most important reason why they appeared to predominate among the business people in these regions.[14] The more important reason probably was that Low Country people were directly involved in a more developed money economy than the Dry Zone villagers. The Fishers had always sold their catch for money, and were familiar with trade. Hence, it was natural for Low Country people of this sort with an adventurous vein to seek their fortunes in the distant Dry Zone where their limited capital would take them a long way.

Salaries and Other Incomes

A major source of money in Kandyan villages was salaries paid by the government for various services. It is difficult to overestimate the immediate effect on a person's position in society of these modest but assured incomes. In a community largely based on a subsistence economy without much access to cash income, those who could get near the fountainhead of even limited liquid assets found themselves in an extremely advantageous position. Not only did they live better than the rest of the villagers, but by giving credits, receiving mortgages, then waiting and eventually buying the property of villagers who had got into difficulties, they were also able to acquire much land.

I have already mentioned the Village Headman who received an income of 125 rupees. An even more important group of salaried persons was the schoolteachers. Ceylon, which has a fairly advanced state school system, is fortunate in having schools near some of even the most isolated villages. Schools play an important part in the life of the community and are admired by the villagers.[15] The villagers recognize full well the value of an education, because those who learn how to read and write have some chance—admittedly not a very great one with rapidly rising unemployment—of receiving a clerkship in a government office. Terutenne had a large school with a headmaster and three teachers, all rather young. There were also two retired teachers, one of them the astrologer previously mentioned, who received government pensions. It is noteworthy that the two retired teachers were among the biggest landlords in Terutenne. The headmaster was also doing well, and one of the young schoolteachers was going in the same direction (see table 10).

---

[14] Another striking example of the predominance of one caste in the same occupation is that of the moneylenders in Colombo and Kandy, many of whom are huge Pathans with enormous moustaches and turbans. They are usually referred to as Afghans. Of course their physical size is a crucial factor in their financial success: they can collect their debts when necessary.

[15] One of my poor neighbors in Galpitiya said to me that the reason he would not send his children to the local school was that he was "ashamed" (ladjai) not to be able to dress them in clean clothes. He would rather keep them away.

The schoolteachers, however, had certain problems of their own. Since they might be transferred by the government to another school, it was not always easy to buy land. Usually they managed to overcome this difficulty by deciding to concentrate on one village and having kinsmen buy land for them. They could cultivate it on *ande* and act as absentee landlords.

Associated as they were with learning, schoolteachers were accorded great prestige, and they were often extremely influential in swaying the opinions of the villagers on national issues, particularly at election time. Somewhat similar prestige was accorded to anyone with a secure salary, however; villagers who could afford to were willing to

TABLE 10

The Schoolteachers of Terutenne *

Name	Origin	Hamlet	Land † (in *pale*)
K. (retired)	Low Country	Wekumbura	24
Punchibanda Seneviratne (retired)	Terutenne	Helagama	12.5
Ukkubanda Seneviratne‡	Terutenne	Helagama	7
Kalubanda Nissanka (headmaster)	Terutenne	Wekumbura	2.5
Jayasekera Seneviratne‡	Terutenne	Helagama	2
Wegolle Kalubanda§	Terutenne	Helagama	5.5

* Table shows all schoolteachers resident in Terutenne owning land in the village. Land owned elsewhere is not shown. Two others who teach in Terutenne do not own land yet and are not shown.

† Apart from the lands of the Seneviratnes, all the lands noted have been bought and not inherited.

‡ Teaches in another village.

§ Father is a shopkeeper.

pay substantial dowries to young men who held some kind of governmental posts in order to induce them to become their sons-in-law.

Besides these few who had salaries, the professional practitioners like the native physicians and astrologers also received cash for services. These sums were extremely modest, however, and hardly affected the way of life of the person concerned. Much the same can be said about the ritual healing and tom-tom beating services of the caste of Tom-Tom Beaters. The Washermen and the Blacksmiths, on the other hand, did much better business and were, relatively speaking, quite well-to-do. The Blacksmith family of Terutenne was one of the largest landholding groups, and the Washermen were not far behind. In fact, one of the Washermen, Kiriunga, had done so well that he had paid for part of the reconstruction of the Maluvegoda temple near the washermen's hamlet.

Summary

So far, I have discussed the distribution as well as the sources of wealth in a traditional Kandyan community. I have pointed out that the social hierarchy is related to the limited supply of rice lands and that the economy, mainly of the subsistence type, favors those with some access to sources of cash income independent from land. On this point I suggested that two classes of people were important: the shopkeepers, whose entrepreneurial activities were risky but could lead to considerable accumulation of riches, and the salaried persons, whose steady incomes gave them an advantage over the shopkeepers.

It will be worth considering, finally, the extent to which a money economy had entered the village and the significance of the money economy for social change. On a superficial level this is not difficult to assess. It is possible to calculate the investment in terms of fixed and operating capital into land and compare it with the investment in trading ventures.[16] The results of such calculations, though hardly accurate—since many nonmonetary services cannot be assessed—could be interesting since the ratio of investment in subsistence land, trade, and industry is likely to be different in various parts of Ceylon.

There is, however, a complication in considering the extent of the money economy in Sinhalese villages. In a strict sense, we cannot claim that they are in a subsistence economy at all. It is well known that the government of Ceylon has been providing a high subsidy for rice.[17] The rice of the villages is bought at a fixed price. At the same time, every Ceylonese has a rice-ration book which allows him to buy rice at a price somewhat lower than that at which he sells his produce. Since the island is not self-sufficient, some rice is also imported, at government expense. The net effect of this operation is to bring money into Ceylonese rice-growing villages.

If the villagers are selling their crop to buy rice at a lower price from the state, then they are really outside a traditional subsistence economy. But not everyone sells the rice he produces to the government stores. Many simply sell their rice-ration books to middlemen, who buy from the government stores and then sell the rice on the

---

[16] (a) If we assume that 30 percent of the total acreage is cultivated by casual labor at Rs. 111 per *amunam* (see table 7)—that is, Rs. 55 per acre—we arrive at Rs. 4,950 for casual labor per year. (b) The number of buffaloes in Terutenne may be generously estimated at 100. At Rs. 70 a head, the total investment is Rs. 7,000. (c) The investment in implements may be generously assessed as Rs. 5,000. (d) The seed paddy at Rs. 10 a *pale* may be assessed for the entire 300 acres as Rs. 6,000. (e) Land prices at the 1955 Terutenne levels would total Rs. 800 an acre × 300 acres = Rs. 240,000. (f) Total investment (with operating funds) in rice cultivation = Rs. 261,000. Total investment in village shops and trade = Rs. 10,000.

[17] See I.B.R.D. (1953), pp. 184–186 for a discussion of food subsidies.

black market to make a tidy profit. In this case, since the villagers eat what they produce, they are technically in a subsistence economy. It is probably best to regard them as being on the borderline. Some are aware of the economic possibilities of the market and grow vegetables when prices are favorable. There are others more traditional in their outlook who do not even consider the possibility of growing any other crop than the one they are used to. But a true entrepreneurial spirit is exhibited by the ambitious shopkeepers whose economic sense is so keen that they are referred to as *ganan kariyo* ("calculators") in a pejorative way.

So far as agriculture is concerned, there is a lack of experimentation with new methods or alternative crops not only because knowledge of modern techniques is limited but because at the critical level at which most cultivators have to subsist, mistakes will result in hunger. It is foolhardy to rely on the advice of experts who will themselves not have to starve if their advice is wrong. Hence, even though the economic consequences of conservatism are well recognized, the margin for error is too narrow to permit the luxury of dangerous experiments with the basic food supply.

5

Caste

"Respecting the effect of castes in general on society, it is extremely difficult to form a correct estimate, and to determine
whether the evil or the advantages that result from them, in a
hot climate, preponderate."—J. Davy, *An Account of the Interior of Ceylon* (1821), p. 133

CASTE AMONG BUDDHISTS

Given the somewhat dismaying proliferation of theoretical writings
on the intricate subject of caste, it is refreshing to find that in traditional communities like Terutenne the institution is simple and un-
complicated. Caste is based on the belief that certain groups of people
are inherently different from one another in biological as well as
moral terms. Familial contacts between these separate groups are forbidden, there is no intermarriage or interdining between them, and
the groups are hierarchically ranked. In former times, the organization of the Kandyan kingdom was intimately associated with these
caste divisions, and the hierarchy of castes was upheld by the king or
his officers. It seems clear that one of the functions of the ritual
processions (*perahera*) of which the Sinhalese are so fond was—and
to a certain extent still is—to manifest caste precedence in a public
ceremony. Today, however, the modern states of Ceylon and India
do not officially recognize caste and therefore the hierarchy is a matter of dispute. The top, middle, and bottom ranges of the hierarchy
are generally agreed upon, but there can be considerable difference of
opinion regarding the exact ranking of particular castes.

It is clear that the institution of caste bears a close resemblance to
Negro–white relations in South Africa, in parts of the United States,
and elsewhere. Groups are hierarchically ranked and their interrela-
tions are restricted and formalized; intermarriage is not permitted and
hence access to the women of the superior group in particular is

forbidden (Yalman, 1963). The real difference between the Indian–
Ceylonese situation and the color-bar complex is that, first, the concept
of caste has not been so intertwined with religion and is not an integral part of the religious ritual in the latter case, and, second, the
index of color which fixes a person's social position almost unmistak-
ably is absent in the Indian and Ceylonese context. This latter difference, which permits simple differentiation in the Negro–white context,
compels the Indians and the Ceylonese, who cannot tell caste difference by physiological indices, to utilize all manner of traditional indices (names, occupations, localities, sumptuary rules, strict codes of
etiquette) in order to identify and place individuals on the caste
ladder. The high caste in Ceylon often claimed that they could "spot"
a low caste person by his color and features, but the accuracy of this
claim is dubious.

The legitimacy of the caste hierarchy is most directly questioned in
the towns and cities of Ceylon where the hierarchy of wealth is out of
focus with the caste system. Hence the large and prosperous Karava
caste (Fishers) often claims at least equal, if not higher, rank than the
Goyigama (Cultivators), who are generally accepted as heading the
hierarchy in the interior of the island. On the other hand, the principle of endogamy, which permits the clear separation of one community from another and allows them to be precisely identified, appears to have great resilience and persists at the level of the family in
all castes.

In the small, traditional villages of Ceylon, however, the picture is
so clear as to make caste one of the least interesting aspects of field
work. The larger low castes tend to live in separate parts of the village, often in named and hence caste-associated hamlets. Their personal names distinguish them from the high-caste Cultivators caste.
They are all involved in agriculture, though some members continue
their traditional callings. The code of caste etiquette is still generally
observed, even though certain particular rules are now disregarded.
No kinship can be established across caste boundaries in the village,
and the few individuals who set up house with persons of another
caste are excommunicated by their families. All the castes I came
across in the villages of the Kandyan highlands willingly performed
their traditional duties at temples and other annual rituals. Caste is
so much a part of the villagers' existence that the ethnographer comes
to accept it as a permanent feature of the landscape, like rice fields.

The problem here, therefore, is not one of describing the formal
relations between castes in the villages, but of analyzing the way in
which the institution has become an essential part of every aspect of
thought and behavior. Caste concepts such as purity and pollution

are an integral part of the religious life of the Kandyan village. And,
as we shall see in later chapters, an itinerary in the sphere of kinship
takes us rapidly back to the fundamental aspects of caste.

The caste composition of the Kandyan highlands has been com-
petently described by Ryan (1953). In the highlands there is one large
caste, the Goyigama, at the top of the hierarchy, with all the other
castes in the position of small service castes around them. Of these,
the most numerous are the Beravaya (Tom-Tom Beaters); the Henea
(Washermen), the Valan Karayo (Potters), and the Vahumpura (Jaggery Makers). In the small bazaars, one frequently meets members of
the large and important Low Country castes, such as the Karava
(Fishers) or the **Durava (Toddy Tappers)**. It is not unusual also to
come across hamlets of the very low castes, the Kinnarayo (Mat Weavers) and the Rodiya (Beggars), although these are not numerous. The
third low caste, the Ahikuntakiyo (Snake Charmers) are itinerant, and
I only met them once as a small band deep in the distant division of
Wellassa.

Thus the castes of the Kandyan highlands can be divided into three
layers:

1. The high caste, that is, the Goyigama and its subdivisions (*honda
   minissu*).
2. The service castes, that is, Washermen, Tom-Tom Beaters, Potters, and others (*veda karani minissu*).
3. The lowest castes, Rodiya and the others (*naraka minissu*).

The Low Country castes which do not form caste-communities in the
villages of the highlands do not fit into this simple hierarchy. When
directly questioned, however, the Kandyans tend to place them between the first two groups.

In the largest villages two or three castes may be represented. Terutenne, with a population of about 1,200, had five castes. (I am dis-
counting a few men of uncertain caste origin who had settled with
local women.) This number was considered somewhat unusual, since
a village commonly has only one or two castes. Indeed, in the smaller
tank villages of the northern plain there is ordinarily but a single
caste (Leach, 1961*b*).

In this simple caste structure, Ceylon is different from South India.
Gough (1960), for instance, writing of the Tanjore district of South
India, lists not less than twenty-six castes in a single village with a
population of about 900. The picture drawn by Srinivas (1952) is not
dissimilar. It may well be that in the South Indian context the local
segment of caste and the extension of the family—which I have referred to as the "kindred"—are coterminus. The observation leads into
the further theoretical question as to why, in South India, the kin

group has clearly demarcated "boundaries"—distinct names, traditions, and often a formal structure—whereas among the Sinhalese, as we shall see, all these boundaries are flexible, and a local caste segment can be very large. In the present state of field investigations, this question of relative caste fragmentation has hardly been posed, much less answered.

In Ceylon, at least, there is a significant identification between the caste categories of the Buddhist Sinhalese and the Hindu Tamils. For each, the categories appear to be easily translatable into appropriate terms in the other language. The real difference seems to lie in the nature of the highest category in the scheme: the Buddhist *Bhikku* and the Hindu Brahman.

SINHALESE	TAMIL
Buddhist monks (*Bhikku*)	*Brahman Kurukkal Sannyasi*
Goyigama Cultivators	*Vellalar*
Service castes	
Highly-polluting low castes	

The *Bhikku*, who occupy the highest position on the Sinhalese scale, are recruited from other castes and are so sacred and otherworldly that they are not permitted to raise families. Their position is close to that of the Hindu Sannyasi. The Brahman (who are rare in Ceylon) are also associated with otherworldiness and the gods, but they are permitted to engage in restricted sexual intercourse for the purpose of perpetuating their line. The Kurukkals are discussed further in chapter 15.[1]

The ordinary term for caste in the village is *jati*. The term is associated with "birth" (*jataka*) and carries the connotation of kind or category. Hence it is also used in the sense of "nation." But even single families can be referred to as *jati* when contrasting them with others. *Kulaya* (color) is sometimes heard in the villages, but the scholarly term *varna* is never used. *Wamsa*, which is often heard, and *variga* (variety, kind), used along with *jati*, indicate status gradations between families within the caste.

---

[1] The customs regarding the hair (as symbolic statements) confirm this impression. The Buddhist priests have their hair completely shaved. The Brahman and the Kurukkal (who are half in and half out of the realm of the gods) have half of their hair shaved. The ascetic monks in Ceylon (*Tapasa Bhikku*) are shaved; the Sannyasis disregard it altogether. (Yalman, 1962a; Leach, 1958).

THE LOW CASTES

The castes of the Meda Palata Korale, the administrative division in which Terutenne is situated, are few in number. Most of the larger villages have a number of Tom-Tom Beaters, or Washermen nearby. The largest Potter community is in Terutenne, and I believe that it was the only village with Blacksmiths. On the other hand, in the neighboring village of Udamadura there was a large community of Vahumpura (Jaggery Makers), whose ritual duty is to provide sweet cakes (*kavum*) at weddings and annual offerings to the deities. The lowest castes were not represented in this area.

In Terutenne the high caste, Goyigama, outnumbered the low castes four to one (see table 2). The division between the high caste and the others was very clearly drawn. The Goyigama were referred to as the "good" caste and the others would be the "bad" people. The low castes would also be referred to as simply "low" or "polluted," whereas the Goyigama would be "clean" and "big." These are the terms utilized mainly by the high castes themselves. The low castes could still make the same differentiation, but they would use more neutral terms to refer to themselves: they would call themselves the "working people," and the Goyigama the "big" people. I recall asking a Washerman whether he agreed that the Goyigama were "better" than themselves. He simply answered, "People say so!" and indicated that this was the traditional order. It should be recalled, however, that value-laden terms such as polluted, or bad, cannot be used directly in the presence of the low castes by members of the high caste. The low-caste persons would be offended. Such abusive terms are used only in brawls or disputes, and even then they are considered to be a lapse of good manners.

The high castes in Terutenne were careful to observe caste etiquette in these respects. Hence Tom-Tom Beaters, who are known everywhere on the island as *Beravaya,* were almost never referred to by that term in the village. It was said that the term was demeaning, and that polite persons referred to Tom-Tom Beaters as *Badde minissu.* Almost as soon as I entered the village, I was advised by high-caste people to adopt the use of *Badde* instead of *Beravaya.* This distinction was not made in the case of the other castes.

The Tom-Tom Beaters

The largest low caste in Terutenne was the Tom-Tom Beaters. They lived in a separate hamlet called appropriately Baddegama, which was separated from the rest of Terutenne by a stream. There were only two small *Badde* families in Terutenne who did not reside in the caste hamlet. One lived just below the Galpitiya hamlet, and performed the services at the Maluvegoda temple. The other household lived alone near Helagama and, though very poor, did not perform in temples.

Baddegama itself was a hamlet of about twenty-two dwellings spreading on two sides of a paddy field. The hamlet had a ritual focus in a large Bo tree located in the very middle of the paddy fields and the hamlet. The tree had been made into a shrine and on *poya* days (special days on four quarters of the moon) the inhabitants of the hamlet would offer flowers to the sacred tree.

The total *Badde* community was very highly intermarried within itself. Cross-cousin marriage was the rule, as among the high castes. When directly asked, most persons would say that all the Tom-Tom Beaters were "one people" (*eka minissu*). On the other hand, certain subtle status differences could be noted in this allegedly undifferentiated group. To elaborate, four ancestral names were used by the inhabitants of Baddegama: Udawewa Gedara (up Reservoir House), five dwelling groups; Medawewa Gedara (middle Reservoir House), seven dwelling groups; Meda Gedara (Middle House), five dwelling groups; and Gunnagahawatte Gedara (Gunna Tree Garden House), four dwelling groups. The first three sets of families were considered native to the hamlet, but the last set of four dwelling groups were immigrants from some other locality. It was said that the Gunnagahawatte were "funeral drummers" (and therefore associated with death pollution), whereas the others in the caste drummed only in the temples and never attended funerals. Hence the Gunnagahawatte were lower than the older residents of the hamlet.

Although these differences were spoken of in confidential tones, in fact the Gunnagahawatte were just as closely intermarried as the other groups with the rest of the inhabitants in the hamlet. These claims and counterclaims to status within the caste are one of the most notable features of Kandyan villages, and are further investigated in connection with the kindred (see chap. 9).

The names were not inherited in the male line. They were said to be ancestral names (*parampara nama*) and were used by both sons and daughters. Since a person could use the names of his mother or his father, marriages between persons with the same ancestral name were quite common. There were some young men and women, however, who did not know their names and would have been somewhat surprised if I had insisted on finding out what they were. When directly asked, they would simply use the name by which others referred to the garden or house in which they lived. These local names were sometimes referred to as *padenchi nama* (settlement name) to dis-

tinguish them from the "old names" which carried prestige. The
latter, were by no means coterminous with definable kin groups;
they were more like valued heirlooms which are passed along from
one generation to the next and symbolize a connection with distinguished ancestors.

As in every Kandyan community, there were certain transgressions
of the rules of caste endogamy in Baddegama. Certain liaisons between Tom-Tom Beater women and high-caste men were public
knowledge, and there was a single case of a "marriage" between members of two different low castes. The liaisons between men of high
caste and women of low caste were considered improper but not in-
tolerable. Indeed, young men of the high caste looked upon the
women of the low castes as fair game, and as long as nothing permanent developed, the families of the men would wink at the matter.
There is little doubt that the parents of the girl disapproved of these
affairs and would sometimes make their objections felt, but in most
instances the affair would not come to the notice of the girl's parents;
and even if they suspected that the girl was not so pure as she might
be, neither the low castes nor the poorer members of the high caste
seriously objected.

The Village Headman, who was married to the daughter of the
former Village Headman and had extremely important kinship ties
through this connection, had kept a mistress in Baddegama for many
years. He did not, of course, reside in her house, and he would visit
her very pointedly after mealtimes, in order to indicate that he did
not "eat" with her.

He had had two children by her (who had received low-caste names)
but he always denied in public that the affair had any permanence.
Through the years, he had made gifts of considerable lands to this
woman, so that she was in 1954 the owner of 5.5 *pale* of rice land,
much above the average landholding in the hamlet (see table 11).

No permanent households had been established across the castes

TABLE 11

Ownership of Rice Land among Low Castes in Terutenne

Caste	Adult Pop. (over 20)	Actual Land- holders	Total Land Held (in *pale*)	Average *pale* per Adult
Blacksmiths............	9	2	21	2+
Potters.................	14	—	—	—
Washermen.............	13	4	18.5	1+
Tom-Tom Beaters........	62	14	31.5	0.5
Total..............	98	20	71	—1

in Baddegama. However, in one household on the opposite side of the valley, just below the large hamlet of Galpitiya, there lived a Tom-Tom Beater who had moved there from Baddegama. He was legally married to a girl from the Washermen caste, whose parents

TABLE 12

Household Composition among Tom-Tom Beaters of Terutenne
(Baddegama Hamlet)

	Number
Simple nuclear families*..	15
Compound households: Ego, eldest female.............................	3
Ego + nuclear family of daughter's son (1)	
Ego + nuclear families of 2 sons (2)	
Compound households: Ego, eldest male..............................	4
Ego's nuclear family + mother (1)	
Ego + nuclear families of 2 sons (1)	
Ego's nuclear family + nf of sons + nf of	
sister + nf of daughter's son (1)	
Ego + daughter's nf (1)	
Total..	22

* Nuclear family (nf), *ge* in Sinhalese, is always a unit consisting of parents and unmarried children, cooking as one. The + sign indicates a separate cooking unit.

were members of the Washermen community of Terutenne. In my entire period of field work, this was the only case in which two residents of the community who had been born there and had kinsmen in the locality but were members of different castes had set up house together. The case merits some attention:

Kiri Henea, the father of the girl in question, owned a small shop near Galpitiya. The Tom-Tom Beater worked in this shop and was attracted by the shopkeeper's daughter, who visited the place frequently. Eventually he succeeded in sleeping with the girl without the knowledge of her parents or brothers. When the Washermen at last discovered what had happened they were furious and tried to kill the young Tom-Tom Beater. Babanis, one of the brothers of the girl, and some of his friends from the bazaar town of Nildandahinna, where hooligans are always to be found, laid a trap for the young Tom-Tom Beater, but he was lucky and escaped. The incident aroused his obstinacy and although his own family was opposed and although the Washermen were out for his blood, he told the girl that he loved her, and convinced her to elope with him. As soon as she escaped from her parents, he took her directly to the marriage registrar, and they were married in *binna* (matrilocally—see below). He claimed that the marriage was in *binna* so

that neither of them could leave the other (!), and he promised the girl that
he would always take care of her and love her.

After the registration he took the girl to his hut. In 1955 he was intending
to go to court to claim her legitimate lands, which the Washermen had
naturally withheld from them. (It should be observed here that the father of
the girl is now dead, so there is no one who can legitimately alter the will
and take the lands away from the girl.)

The situation at the time of field work was that Babanis, who had tried
to kill the Tom-Tom Beater, never visited his place. The wife's other brother,
Sinyo, was friendly toward the couple, and they had helped each other during
the chena cultivation cycle. The Tom-Tom Beater claimed that his *nenda*
(mother-in-law) was so friendly that he always called her *amma* (mother)
to show his affection. She apparently visited the hut frequently, but the
Tom-Tom Beater's own parents, who live in Baddegama, seldom came. The
young man claimed that his bride had been accepted by them; he said that
he had been away when she was about to give birth to a child, and that all
his relations, including his father and brothers, got together and helped her.
Nonetheless, his brothers were not happy about the union and refused to
address the Washerman in kinship terms. His children, of course, did use
kinship terms to the Washerman and addressed Sinyo and Babanis as *mama*
(MB, FZH, F-in-L).

At this point I asked the Tom-Tom Beater whether his children,
who were using terms which implied conjugality, could in fact intermarry with other Washermen and/or Tom-Tom Beaters. His reply,
more in the nature of a pious hope, underlined the emphasis placed
on cross-cousin marriage: "They will be *avassa massina–nana* ("own
cross-cousin") and nobody can stop their intermarriage." But he
added significantly that the reason people did not like this marriage
was that it consisted "only of two people," the girl and himself, and
did not bring in relatives on either side.

The Tom-Tom Beater went on to say that he had ceased to care
about intercaste marriage any more: a good Buddhist, who knows
karma, will also not care about caste! When two people like each
other, and if they admit this to each other, then they will marry in
life after life. Finally, he said, "My children are *Badde,* of course,
and will get *Badde* names!" Which is, in fact, an open question.

There are two points of particular interest in this case: first, the
hasty registration. Marriages between close kin are usually begun
very casually: the couple merely start living together, often with no
ceremony whatever and certainly without formal registration. In
marriages between distant or unrelated kin, the occasion is more
ritualized, but even then there may be no registration. In this particular case, where the disruptive elements were particularly intense,
the Tom-Tom Beater clearly sought to counteract them by the legal
union.

Second, the institution of marriage among the Sinhalese always creates or reaffirms the ties of kinship. In this union, which fell into a structural abyss between two castes, there were serious contradictions. Although kinsmen on the two sides had no intention of extending kinship to members of another caste, they had nonetheless acquired nephews and nieces (or "brothers and sisters," "sons and daughters," etc., depending on the vagaries of the Sinhalese terminology)—in the offspring of the couple, who could in the future claim "blood kinship" (le urumaya) with both castes. There is little doubt that these contradictions would be finally resolved with the various marriages of the next generation, when the children of the mixed union would be drawn in one direction or the other. The alternative solution of a new endogamous subgroup emerging is not inconceivable, but it is unlikely under the circumstances of Terutenne.

A schematic representation of the public and private services of the Tom-Tom Beaters in the village is given in table 13. The fact that

TABLE 13

Badde Services (Tom-Tom Beaters)

	Public	Private
Occasion:	Annual festivals of the *devale:* *An-keliya* and *Gam Maduva* *Vihara* ceremonies: Annual: *Katina Pinkama* (offering of new saffron robe to the priest); birthday of the Buddha. Others: *Bana* (preaching), *Pirit* (chanting).	Illnesses—ritual healing and exorcism
Duty:	A few members of the community provide the ceremonial drumming during rituals. Also all public announcements are made by drummers.	Act as dancers, exorcists, astrologers
Reward:	Payment by the Temple Society for Vihara service.	Payment (depending on status and wealth of patron), from Rs. 5 up per night per Tom-Tom Beater

their services, their personal names, and the segregation of their community were convenient indices of separation and ranking needs no further emphasis. It should simply be recorded that, given the segregation of the total community as an identifiable group, the practice of the traditional calling by a few persons is sufficient to reinforce the low-status image of the Tom-Tom Beaters. For this reason, although there were not more than three or four families who actually practiced the beating of tom-toms, the name *Beravaya,* or *Bera Karaya* (drum people) was applied to the entire group. Also, even though most members of the community were engaged in cultivation, the children of Tom-Tom Beaters were taught to play the traditional tunes on the drums. There was no hint that the community was ashamed of its traditional calling; it was simply that, with changing times, there was little demand for their services and therefore only a few families could engage profitably in tom-tom beating.

The Washermen (Henea or Radaw)

Along with the Tom-Tom Beaters, the Washermen are the most important of low-caste communities whose services are considered essential. The function of the Washermen caste is to turn pollution into purity. For this reason they are needed at all ritual occasions in the Kandyan village (see table 14). They participate in births, puberty rituals, and funerals, all occasions on which in Sinhalese belief there is intense pollution emanating from the body which affects the entire household, in which case the house is said to be in a condition of

TABLE 14

Henea Services (Washermen)

	Public	Private
Occasion:	Annual festivals of the *devale:* *An-keliya* and *Gam Maduva* *Vihara* ceremonies: Annual: *Katina Pinkama* (offering of new saffron robe to the priest); birthday of the Buddha. Others: *Bana* (preaching), *Pirit* (chanting).	All *rites de passage:* birth, female puberty, marriage, death General laundry
Duty:	On all these occasions, Henea provide "clean" (ritually pure) cloths to decorate the temples, to protect the Buddhist priests from the public gaze while eating. They make effigies of goddesses from starched white sheets for *Gam Maduva.*	The nature of the service is to change "polluted" clothes into "pure" ones. They wash polluted persons as well.
Reward:	Payments by the Temple Society	Payments from Rs. 2 up, depending on the status and wealth of the patron

kiligedara. The Washermen's function is to purify the house and the subject (the mother and the baby after the birth or the corpse in a funeral), and to wash the soiled clothes. They are also invited to furnish pure white cloths or to purify a special enclosure on auspicious occasions. Thus they will decorate wedding houses with white cloths or will surround the Buddhist priests with pure cloths when food offerings are given to them. They may decorate temples, and may be called in to furnish pure locations for those rituals directed to the gods and goddesses. Payment is made either in cash or in rice at the time of harvest.

These elaborate ritual duties should not divert attention from the fact that the mundane activity of laundering also goes on. Clothes are beaten on rocks and then starched and ironed with heavy hand irons; the efficiency of the operation, at least so far as purity is concerned, is unquestioned, although the condition of the clothes is another matter.

The Washermen of Terutenne formed a very closely interrelated community of but seven dwellings, situated just below the large, poor hamlet of Galpitiya. Compared with the other low castes, they were relatively well off, since they had a fairly steady income from their caste services; a few of them also owned a little land or worked as sharecroppers. One of the Washermen in particular, Kiriunga, was fairly affluent by Terutenne standards; he owned five *pale* of rice land. Still another, a young and intelligent man known as James, owned six *pale*. Both these men had had much to do with the reconstruction of one of the temples in Terutenne. There had been an old temple called Maluvegoda near Galpitiya which had fallen into disrepair. Kiriunga as a good Buddhist had undertaken to rebuild the temple and provide a living for a priest. There is a certain rivalry between the Galpitiya section of Terutenne and the main Wekumbura section where most of the richer high-caste persons live and where they have another temple. The Wekumbura temple belongs to the Amarapura Nikaya; thus the Maluvegoda temple was given to the Siam Nikaya. It is noteworthy that although the Benefactors' Society of the temple included mostly Goyigama, James the Washerman had been elected as its president.

Most of the cross-caste unions occurring among the low castes involved Washermen—as witness the case of the young Washergirl who married the Tom-Tom Beater, described above. Kiriunga's son and daughter had both done the same. The daughter, who had attended a good school outside the village where she had learned English, had fallen in love with a Goyigama man. Though both sets of parents objected, the couple had married, but had settled down away from Terutenne. The same had happened to the son, who had also gone to school outside the village and was clearly emancipated from the traditional influences of the closed community. He, too, had married a Goyigama girl and had not returned to the village.

The Blacksmiths (Achari or Kammal Kariyo)

The Blacksmiths were the smallest, but also the richest, low caste in Terutenne. Like the Washermen and, as we shall see, the Potters, they consisted of members of a single family. Their most important and influential member, Hingappu, was originally from another

TABLE 15

Achari Services (Blacksmiths)

	Public	Private
Occasion:	Same occasions as other castes	Manufacture of utilitarian objects—plows, knives, axes
Duty:	Cleaning the weapons of the saints; making new metal bowls for priests	
Reward:	No payment; free offerings by the Blacksmiths	Individually ordered and paid for

village but had settled with a woman from Terutenne some thirty years before. The woman had had some lands, but Hingappu had bought a great deal of land himself, and had become one of the largest landlords in the village. He owned twenty *pale* of rice land, and there were only two or three other persons in the entire village who could boast as much. It is a reflection of the strength of affinal ties that when his wife died, his mother-in-law (who lived in the same house with the couple) found another woman for him. Hingappu was content with his new woman, and the mother of his first wife continued to share the household with them.

The lands of Hingappu were given out to other members of the village on the traditional sharecropping basis (*ande*). Some of these sharecroppers were high-caste men. Many high-caste men disdained working for him, but for others, who could not afford the luxury of such sentiments, Hingappu was a good landlord. The contradictions inherent in such situations always gave rise to subtle problems of etiquette. The high-caste laborers naturally found it difficult to treat the Blacksmiths as they would other low castes. In Sinhalese villages, it is customary for the low castes to crouch or stand while the high castes are seated. If the high-caste person is on a chair, then the low-caste person may sit on a mat. Hingappu would often come to visit me. Sometimes a few of his workers would also be in my hut, sitting on chairs and gossiping as usual. The arrival of Hingappu would give rise to some embarrassment. The workers had to get out of their chairs, to show some sign of deference to their landlord, yet they had to pretend to me and to each other that they were not getting up for a low-caste man, but only wanted to stretch their legs. It was always possible to create further confusion by my insisting on getting a camp chair and offering it to Hingappu. The camp chair was considered of higher status than an ordinary chair, and this time Hingappu would be embarrassed to show his superiority.

Unlike the Washerman Kiriunga, Hingappu had not given much attention to the education of his children. They had not gone any further than the village school and would clearly remain in the traditional setting. There were no cross-caste unions among Blacksmiths.

The Potters (Valan Karayo, Pandita, or Kumbalu)

The caste of Potters in Terutenne also consisted of a single family who were closely intermarried among themselves. They had apparently arrived in the village about forty years earlier, and had chosen Terutenne because there were no Potters in the near vicinity. The first group to arrive consisted of the old woman, Punchihami, and her four daughters and sons-in-law (see fig. 2). Apart from the branch marked II, which lived in an adjacent garden, the entire group lived in a single fenced compound. An examination of the kinship chart will show that the younger generation had also continued the pattern of frequent cross-cousin marriages between close kinsmen. However, the community in Terutenne was too small to be self-sufficient in marriage partners, and at times the Potters had to go quite far afield to contact kinsmen for suitable partners.

The Potters of Terutenne owned no rice land, but their own compound did belong to them. They eked out an existence based partly on the manufacture of pottery and partly on sharecropping on the lands of other members of the village. Their wares varied in price from 75 cents for a small cooking pot to Rs. 2.50 for one of the large, round water vessels which Sinhalese women usually carry on their hips. In 1955, the Potters were complaining that their community in the village had grown too populous for the demand, and some of them were considering a split in the community so that part could settle in another neighboring village.

The Potters did not have very clear ritual functions in the village (see table 16). However, since all the rituals directed to the Buddha or the deities call for some form of cooking, it had not been difficult

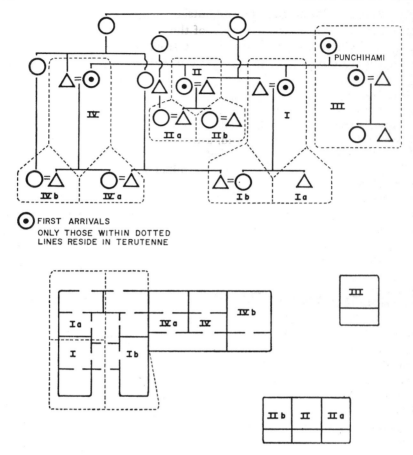

Figure 2. The Potters of Terutenne.

to integrate the Potters into the caste-service system: and so the ritual obligation of the Potters was described as the furnishing of new pots for all *vihara* or *devale* rituals.

There were no cross-caste marriages between the Potters and the other low castes, but there has been one cross-caste union between a

TABLE 16

Valan Karayo Services (Potters)

	Public	Private
Occasion:	Same occasions as other castes	Sale of pots
Duty:	Making new pots for priests and for the rituals in *devale*	
Reward:	No payment; free offerings	Prices: 50¢ to Rs. 3

very attractive Potter girl and an outsider who claimed to be of the highest *Radala* aristocratic subcaste of the Goyigama. The case, which shows a slightly different arrangement from the Tom-Tom Beater–Washer girl example, merits closer examination.

One evening Hinbanda, the husband of the Potter girl, came to visit me. I asked him his name, and he replied with the sonorous EkaNayaka Abeycoon Rajakaruna Wasala Mudianse Ralahami Ketakumbure Walavva Abeysinha Banda. This was, he said, a title of the Radala subcaste, and he described how the Radala had levels of good and bad (i.e., high and low, or polluted and pure) families. The high families would not give women to low families in marriage, but would, with suitable dowry, take women from them. Moreover, he claimed that the name and property of the mother always went to her daughters and the name and the property of the father went to his sons.

At this point in the conversation we were joined by my neighbor, Wannaku, who kept a mistress in Galpitiya but whose wife lived in the next village of Kalanganwatte. Wannaku was a rich landlord of the Goyigama caste and very closely related to the Village Headman.

Wannaku first pretended not to recognize Hinbanda, and remained standing while Hinbanda writhed in an agonized fashion in a camp chair. He questioned Hinbanda's description of the traditional arrangements. In a little while he pretended to recognize Hinbanda, and said that he could not recognize him because of all the elaborate titles, and that he had thought that, since Hinbanda was always with the Potters, he was a Potter himself. This was a terrible insult to which Hinbanda did not respond. By this time Hinbanda had moved to an ordinary chair, and Wannaku had installed himself in the camp chair. After the hierarchy was thus established and Hinbanda put in his proper place, Wannaku lost interest and did not stay much longer.

Hinbanda had apparently come to Terutenne as a friend of the son of the Village Headman. They had started a small shop together, but the venture was bankrupt.

He had first been attracted to the Potter girl by her beauty. He had started to visit her, and in the end had settled with her. He had had some sons from her, and people said that it was not good to leave her, and, he said, this was why he would remain with her. The people in the village say that he has done something bad, and he feels it. His children had been given names that were neither Potter names or distinctively high caste; but there was little doubt that the children would be members of the Potter community.

The case illustrates how Hinbanda became identified with the low caste by setting up a household with a Potter woman. This did not happen to other men who simply "visited" low-caste women, because their relationships were not permanent and did not bring them into close familial contact with the lower community. It should be re-

called that in the cross-caste union of the Tom-Tom Beater and
Washer girl, the children had been given names of the father's
caste, but there was no assurance that they would be able to intermarry with the kin groups of either the mother or the father. In the
present case, the wide status gulf between Hinbanda and his wife
had made even the pretense of high-caste names for the children
quite fruitless. Unless the couple moved into surroundings where
their backgrounds were entirely unknown, it seemed clear that the
children would end up as members of the mother's caste.

THE HIGH-CASTE GOYIGAMA (CULTIVATORS)

The Cultivators, the largest caste in Terutenne, were split into
smaller endogamous segments among themselves. They inhabited all
the hamlets of the village, though there was a strong tendency to
identify the lower sections of the caste with particular "low" hamlets.
The ranking was referred back to the "traditional" institutions of
the Kandyan kingdom. The villagers would say that the Cultivators
of Terutenne were ranked as follows:

(1) The Aristocrats: families descended from the famous houses of
the Kandyan period
(2) Ordinary Goyigama: good people untainted by low castes or
demeaning occupations
(3) Low Goyigama: the descendants of people who had been the
serfs of the aristocratic families of the Kandyan past

Such ranks among Cultivators have been reported from elsewhere
(Ryan, 1953) but the ranks in Terutenne do not correspond with the
widely known categories such as the Radala or the Mudali and are
not distinguished by such subcaste names. The "low" might be referred to as *vahalu* (slaves) in certain contexts, though this is not
usual, and the aristocrats may claim to be of the Radala, though
this would be considered somewhat presumptuous.

The description of the "ideal blueprint" of the village which was
claimed to be the traditional pattern of the "time of the Sinhalese
Kings" did correspond in its broad outlines to the historical details
given by D'Oyly and other early writers on the period. The villagers
said that the division of Walapane was governed by a feudal lord with
the title of *Mohottala,* who owned a great deal of land in Terutenne
and who also enjoyed certain lands (*gam nila*) as perquisites of his
office. The serfs (*veda karayo*) lived in separate hamlets (Galpitiya and
Galkotumulle) and were obliged to provide labor on the fields of the
aristocrats. Between these two classes were people who were neither of
superior birth nor directly obliged to the great families of the village.

The villagers claimed that this traditional pattern existed until about the time of their grandfathers, and that it had later degenerated and become confused. Their notions of history were vague, however; the Kandyan kingdom in fact ceased to exist about 1815, but the villagers often seemed to think of a date perhaps sixty to seventy years ago as the beginning of the confused "modern" period. Thus, although the time when all the institutions were orderly and people lived in the "correct" fashion was always referred to as "the time of the Sinhalese kings," this period was conceptualized to be in the preceding generation.

It is a curious feature of ethnographic accounts that many peoples speak of such a "traditional" period which is presumed to have existed about seventy to a hundred years ago. Ethnographers are sometimes taken in by this, and write neat accounts of the "traditional structure." During my field work I was fortunate enough to be able to examine the accuracy of such claims by recourse to Grain Tithe Registers. These were tax records kept by the colonial government for each village, containing precise details of family name, extent of land, hamlet, and amount of tax. Those for the Walapane district, which in 1955 were in the Nuwara Eliya government offices, provided an important land record for the period from about 1840 to 1895.

In this case, the traditional picture was borne out in its general outlines. There had actually been a *Mohottala* in the village and he had owned much land.[2] The Registers also provided a record in terms of land tenure of the changes that took place in Terutenne in the last half of the nineteenth century. Eight aristocratic houses (*gedara*) are mentioned in the 1856–1861 Registers. These houses owned between them 196 *pale* of rice land. Twenty-one houses of middle rank owned 188.5 *pale,* but eighteen families of low rank owned only 35 *pale* of land. The hamlet of Galpitiya, the same hamlet of serf origin that still exists in Terutenne, is mentioned in the Registers as populated by persons without honorific family names and simply referred to as Galpitiya *ge* . . . (. . . of Galpitiya).

Two changes appear to have taken place in the nineteenth century. First, some of the aristocratic households lost their lands (and some names disappeared); second, more land was dedicated to the Buddhist temples. Comparing the Registers with the pattern of land tenure in

---

[2] The villagers had the story that the local *Mohottala* of Walapane (who resided in Terutenne) had given much of his land as dowry to his daughter when she was married off to the new powerful man in the village, a tax collector (*vi badu lekam*) appointed by the British. The Registers were eloquent: the lands held by Amunumulle Mohottala in an earlier register are passed on to Amunumulle Kirimenika, the daughter, and are signed for on her behalf by the Anderewewe Rate Mahatmaya, also referred to as *vi badu lekam.*

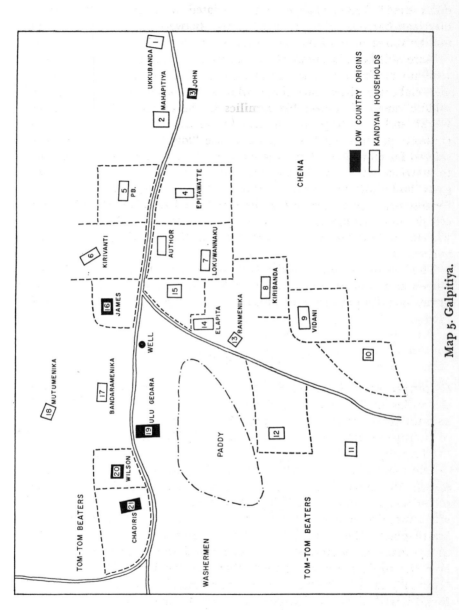

Map 5. Galpitiya.

Terutenne in 1955, one sees that of the eight aristocratic families, four have lost all their lands and the lands of the other four are much diminished.[3] These changes are associated with the fact that such marriage barriers as may have existed between aristocrats and the middle range of families are no longer respected.

More will be said about the aristocrats in chapter 7. In 1955 there were no hindrances to marriage between persons who claimed long and elaborate titles and those who were considered to be of the middle range of respectable families in Terutenne. The criteria of wealth and of caste purity (understood as the absence of any kinship connections with the low castes and the "low Goyigama") were considered far more important: the most frequently discussed impediment to marriage was this informal separation between the ordinary Goyigama and those who were considered "low." There was more cause for discussion on this issue because marriages had taken place between certain low Goyigama and the others under special circumstances, whereas unions would have been out of the question between the various castes.

The "low" category of the Cultivators caste was not specifically named as a unique subcaste, but a detailed description of their case brings out the principles of ranking within the high caste with some clarity.

The Hamlet of Galpitiya

Galpitiya, where I resided for four months, was a hamlet set above the valley of Terutenne in the midst of tall bread-fruit, jack, and coconut trees (see map 5 and table 17). The hamlet proper consisted of twenty-one related households, not counting some low castes who lived nearby.

The place was known all over the Walapane as being of very low status. The explanation was that during the time of the kings, Galpitiya was a hamlet of people who worked for others. Indeed, there was something odd about the name of the hamlet: Galpitiya means "cattle-place." The inhabitants of the hamlet were well aware of the unfortunate connotations of this name and would point out, whenever the subject was mentioned, that the "ancient" (and therefore "correct") name of the hamlet was Karandamaditta, a name which was found inscribed on a talipot-leaf document in one of the local temples.

---

[3] In the Kandyan area land belongs to individuals and not to "joint families." When I mention lands of aristocratic houses, I am simply thinking of the lands of individuals with the same house *name* in aggregate. The nature of these house names is discussed below.

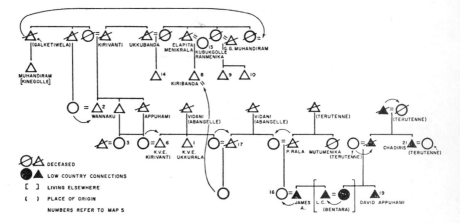

Figure 3A. Kinship connections in Galpitiya.

But these were vain protestations. I never heard the word Karanda-maditta used except in this apologetic sense, and the rest of the village of Terutenne was uninterested in this quaint bit of information. Those who professed themselves to be conversant with ancient lore used to point out that all place names ending with *pitiya* were places where laborers lived: it is true that there were in the vicinity of Terutenne other such villages, also considered to be of low rank, called, for example, Arampitiya, Dodangahapitiya, Hapugahapitiya. The low status of the people of Galpitiya was also considered to be evident in their lack of accepted titles. Kandyans of good breeding

TABLE 17

Galpitiya: Population and Land Ownership

	Population			Paddy Land Ownership	
Ages	Males	Females	Totals	Households*	Extent of Land Owned (in *pale*)
0–20	43	42	85	No. 15	28.5†
20–70	31	25	56	19	5.5
				1	4.5
Total	74	67	141	All others	7

* Numerals refer to map 5.
† The 28.5 *pale* belong to an outsider who keeps a woman of the hamlet. He is not normally considered a member of Galpitiya and has another household in a nearby village (Abangelle); see text p. 113.

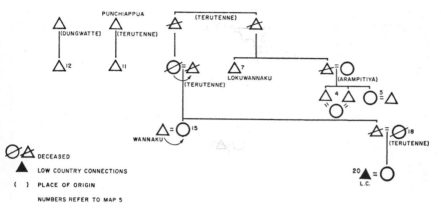

Figure 3B. Kinship connections in Galpitiya.

always use some titles called *pelapata, vasagama, parampara nama,* or simply *mudianse nama* (which we may translate as "pedigree" name) in which the terms *Mudianse la ge* (of . . . Lord), occur. The Galpitiya people did sport such titles, but the rest of the village thought that they were liars anyway and that these names had just been made up.[4]

Galpitiya is very closely interrelated (something of the intricacies of kinship connections may be inferred from figs. 3a and 3b). The population of the village in 1955 was descended from about <u>ten sibling groups.</u> A number of the descendants lived in another hamlet which could be reached by an extremely steep climb from Galpitiya. After forty minutes of tropical mountaineering one arrived at the new hamlet, called Kinegolle. It had been colonized from Galpitiya and was in the process of severing its kinship links with the older hamlet. Another neighboring hamlet above Galpitiya was Dunkalawatte (lit. Tobacco Garden), colonized about 1940; this, too, was very closely related to Galpitiya (see map 6, fig. 4, and table 18).

I had assumed that the people of Galpitiya would be descendants of the original inhabitants, the laborers of the aristocrats referred to in the 1856–1861 Registers. To my surprise, however, I discovered in the course of my investigation that all the present-day villagers are

---

[4] The same idea is prevalent in the Wellassa area. There the villages of laborers are more categorically described as *vahalu* (slave): it was said that the inhabitants had but recently acquired some of these "pedigree" names to which they were not entitled. The Bibile Walawwa (a noble house in the region) still had some hereditary servants of low status, and I was told that in the days of the late Rate Mahatya (the local overlord) such ridiculous insults as the assumption of "pedigree" names would have resulted in the old gentleman himself supervising the whipping of the culprits.

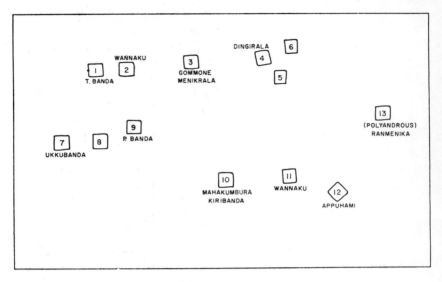

Map 6. Dunkalawatte.

descended from settlers.[5] There had been a complete change of population in the hamlet in the last fifty years; the old Galpitiya people were given land and resettled by the government in another

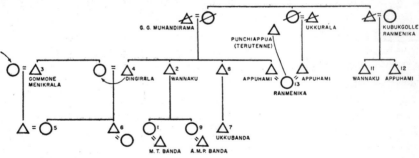

Figure 4. Kinship connections in Dunkalawatte.

region and the hamlet was eventually reoccupied by persons who were obviously not descendants of the people who used to labor for the

---

[5] Not only were the family histories which I collected consistent, but these were confirmed by the Registers in which throughout the last century reference is only made to certain people called *Galpitiya ge*. Only a single member of this family still survives in a neighboring village; he still owns one *pale* of land in a field in which Galpitiya used to own land. The rest of the family have dispersed. In the Registers of 1878–1888 and 1889–1895, 15 *pale* of land are shown as belonging to the Galpitiya family; today, nothing remains of this holding but the tiny portion still owned by the last survivor.

past overlords of Terutenne. Yet the inhabitants of Galpitiya were unable to score even debating points on the question of rank. The prohibition for the ordinary people of Terutenne against marriage from Galpitiya remained as strict as ever.

TABLE 18

Dunkalawatte: Population and Land Ownership

Population				Paddy Land Ownership	
Ages	Males	Females	Totals	Households*	Extent of Land Owned (in *pale*)
0–20	11	13	24	10	1.5
20–70	15	11	26	2	2
				All others	—
Total	26	24	50		

* Numerals refer to map 6.

After I had lived in Galpitiya for some months, the people of Terutenne began to joke about me, in a friendly manner, suggesting that since I lived in the "low" hamlet, I was polluted. The conclusion was that they would not be able to eat and drink with me at the same table and would have to treat me as of the same rank as the rest of the people of Galpitiya. They did not carry out their threats, but even the joking was an expression of the general ideas on the subject of residence. Those who live together in the same place tend to acquire the rank of their neighbors.

The people of Galpitiya had many contacts with the central hamlet of Terutenne—Wekumbura—and were dependent on land-lords who lived in the better areas of the village for the lands on which they sharecropped. Furthermore, Wekumbura contained a number of shops which, as the center of social life, quite naturally attracted the people of Galpitiya. Galpitiya always knew of the happenings in the rest of Terutenne, but Terutenne neither knew nor cared to know what went on in Galpitiya. Terutenne people rarely visited Galpitiya, and, except for youths who had occasional affairs with Galpitiya girls, they had no reason to do so.

Ordinarily, in the fields and in the village a certain distance was kept between the rest of the village and Galpitiya people, but unless one was watching for signs of superiority by the people of Terutenne, their relations with the "low" people would have appeared not unlike their behavior toward the poor in general. In this sense there was nothing that set off Galpitiya from the rest of the landless persons in the village.

During the period of slash-and-burn cultivation, a more definite separation was quite evident, however. Chena cultivation always requires a residence of about four months in the highlands, from the sowing of the crop to harvesttime. The cultivators build little huts in the middle of their plots and the entire community, working together, fences itself in with a single fence running along the outside border of the fields. These groups of chena cultivators are often either close relatives or good friends, but the membership of these highland communities may differ from year to year, and there is occasion for the people who live in different parts of Terutenne to mix with one another on this annual exodus from the village. Even so, the people of Galpitiya never went to the same hillsides as the rest of Terutenne. More often than not, they kept to their own side of the valley, where lands were limited and where the people of other hamlets had no interests. When Galpitiya did cultivate the highlands on the other side of the valley—the area in which the rest of Terutenne usually set up their small grass huts—they invariably remained segregated from the rest.

Why was Galpitiya relegated to a low status among the Cultivators of Terutenne? Why had the change of population in the hamlet not affected their ranking in general? It is immediately tempting to suggest that Galpitiya is, by Kandyan standards, a slum hamlet, a sort of cheap labor pool for the rest of the village, and that its low economic status is responsible for the low caste status. This economic explanation is easily dismissed. There were other poor families in the village against whom the caste sanctions of intermarriage and interdining prohibitions were not applied. A better explanation is that the locality and the name of the hamlet are "tainted" with "low" rank. I have already indicated the connotations of the name. If there had been a clear change in the economic position of the hamlet, some reassessment of ranking might have been expected, but as matters stood in 1955 the poverty of the hamlet still corresponded to the traditional status, and the slow turnover in the population of the community had seemingly no effect whatever.

There are many instances in which Sinhalese, wanting to move in the hierarchy, change their family names, occupations, localities, and thus, by cutting themselves loose from the symbolic anchorages of the ranking system, are able to pass as members of a different group. Some examples are discussed in chapter 7. Here, it is enough to emphasize that the ranking pattern rests entirely on a system of agreed "symbols" or "identification marks." In the case of Galpitiya, there is an association between the name and the locality: both "indicate"

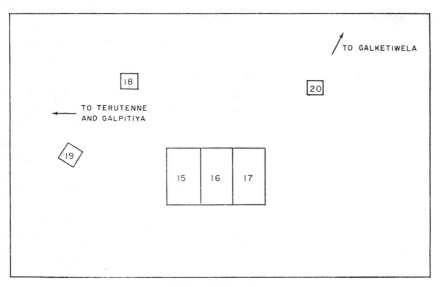

Map 7. Kinegolle.

lowness. In a similar fashion, a caste occupation has the function of identifying an individual and his community with a position in the conceptual model of caste hierarchy which exists in the minds of the members of the society.

The fact that residential areas of the village were ranked, thus having the same symbolic function as caste occupations, is best shown by what happens when a residential area is altered.

Kinegolle, high above the valley of Terutenne in the hills beyond Galpitiya, is a small but flourishing new hamlet close to paddy fields recently brought under cultivation (see map 7 and table 19). The great isolation, the misty and uncomfortable climate only relieved by the truly spectacular scenery beyond, are endured because at this

TABLE 19

Kinegolle: Population and Land Ownership

Population				Paddy Land Ownership	
Ages	Males	Females	Totals	Households*	Extent of Land Owned (in *pale*)
0–20	6	13	19	15 and 16	6.5
20–70	8	5	13	17 and 18	2.5
				All others	—
Total	14	18	32		

* Numerals refer to map 7.

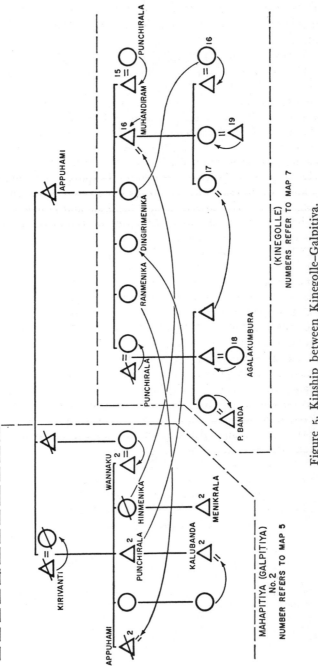

Figure 5. Kinship between Kinegolle–Galpitiya.

altitude the cultivation of certain vegetables as cash crops becomes possible. It is interesting to trace the repercussions of the slightly augmented income and the move on the kinship relations of Kinegolle with Galpitiya.

The ties between Kinegolle and Galpitiya, the parent village, are extremely close, especially through the Mahapitiya family (see fig 5).

Old Appuhami, a resident of Galpitiya, seems to have been the first person to move up to Kinegolle. His sister had married into the Mahapitiya family, one of the largest in Galpitiya, and this connection was reinforced with no less than four marriages of cross-cousins. Ranmenika, Appuhami's eldest daughter, married young Appuhami (the son of Appuhami's sister) and they settled in the large Mahapitiya household in Galpitiya. The marriage of Wannaku, young Appuhami's brother, to his cross-cousin is similar and had many offspring. But the later marriages of Punchirala and Hinmenika (young Appuhami's brother and sister) took them out of Galpitiya to Kinegolle, and in both cases rumors were rife that the unions were not approved of by the people of Kinegolle and that all sorts of attempts were made to break the connections. I was told that Old Appuhami was so opposed to the union between Hinmenika and his son Muhandiram that he threatened to kill Muhandiram unless he left the woman; finally, after the birth of their son Menikrala, a separation was affected. (It should be recorded that when one asks the name of the father of Menikrala in the Mahapitiya household, Muhandiram is never mentioned, and the name of one of the subsequent husbands of the woman is given. I could detect no personal relationship between Menikrala—a young man in 1955—who lived in his mother's hut in Mahapitiya, and Muhandiram—his father—who now and again did come into Galpitiya.) Punchirala's marriage to Dingirimenika was similarly broken, and Punchirala, who had gone up to reside in Kinegolle in Dingirimenika's room, returned to the Mahapitiya compound with one of his sons. Dingiri-menika herself was then given off to a wealthy person in another village.

This painful process of breaking kinship connections between Kinegolle and the Mahapitiya family is only part of the picture. For, as well as obviously denying kinship with Galpitiya, every "outside" marriage link created new connections. Thus (fig. 6) Muhandiram and his brother Punchirala

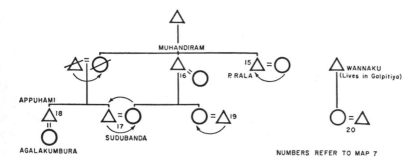

Figure 6. Kinship in Kinegolle.

had acquired respectable wives, and had given their sister to a person of "good" family. In the next generation, too, this process had been pursued, and Appuhami (fig. 6, No. 18) had finally married a girl from one of the respected families in Terutenne. It is true that the girl's family was poor; but they used the title Agalakumbura (the same as the Village Headman), lived in Wekumbura, and would certainly have declined to allow the girl to go to Galpitiya in marriage. Kinegolle was, however, quite acceptable. This particular connection allowed the group at Kinegolle to claim that they were relatives of the best families in Wekumbura hamlet. Their other connections, and ancestry, were conveniently overlooked.

I have discussed two examples to indicate the nature of status among members of the high caste. In the case of Galpitiya, the traditions of serf origin, the poverty of the hamlet, and the connotations of the name of the locality combined to fix the inhabitants of the hamlet at the bottom rung of the hierarchy. In the case of Kinegolle, the move away from the tainted locality combined with a relative rise in the economic scale had allowed the Kinegolle people to alter their status in the village.

It should be emphasized that the status hierarchy in the Cultivators' caste is not simply a matter of where one lives. Ancestral names and family traditions are even more potent indicators of status. And just as there are attempts to change the place of residence for purposes of status, name-changing is also a most convenient gambit for social climbers. A discussion of names and their functions will be found in chapter 7. It should be noted, however, that personal and family names, together with caste occupations and residential areas, are among the important emotion-laden indices used to differentiate the status of the members of the village.

caste status

LOW COUNTRY SETTLERS

In contrast to the undesirability of "marriages" between resident members of different castes in Terutenne, unions with persons of Low Country origin were not thought to be so demeaning and were, in fact, rather frequent. Most of these were between native women of the Goyigama caste and men of the Karava (Fishers) and Durava (Toddy Tappers), who had come to Terutenne and settled. The influx of these Low Country men was not resented by the Goyigama as a whole. There was gossip about families with such connections, but those concerned never denied their Low Country origins and often used such names and David Appuhami and Wilson Baas, which clearly indicated that they were not Kandyans. These names were maintained even in the second and third generations.

While Low Country origin was not denied, inquiries into specific

Low Country caste affiliation had to proceed very delicately. In certain instances, the village was sure that the individual in question was of the Karava or Durava caste, and usually the individual would not deny this ancestry. When a man's origin was vague, he usually resented any suggestion that he was not of the Goyigama.

Some of the Low Countrymen in the Kandyan highlands have been extremely successful. I have already indicated their important role in trading enterprises. One of the most influential persons in Terutenne was a schoolteacher of Roman Catholic Karava origin who had married a high-caste Kandyan woman in Terutenne and had become a Buddhist convert. His case was unusual, however, and the way from stranger to acceptance in the highest circles of the Goyigama had not been easy. His position as a schoolteacher and astrologer had made it possible first for him to marry his sister to a member of the aristocratic Amunumulle family, then to negotiate for the hand of a poor woman from a good family for himself; these marriages had given him kinsmen of the high caste, who would support the claims of his offspring for further marriages into the Goyigama caste.

Unlike the schoolteacher, most of the Low Countrymen who came to settle in the highlands were extremely poor and made their living as carpenters or shopkeepers. These men simply found some Cultivator woman who was also poor and whose parents would not object to her marrying a stranger personally acceptable but of dubious caste origin. In Galpitiya, at least five of the twenty-one households had direct connections with Low Country immigrants. These persons were further connected by many kinship links with the rest of the community, and although their names gave away their origin, they were accepted as members of the Cultivator caste (see fig. 3 and map 5).

The acceptability of Low Country persons was not simply a result of the low status of Galpitiya. Such unions had taken place among Terutenne families generally considered very respectable, and one of the close kinswomen of the Village Headman and the Village Committee Chairman was called Eva Francea Perera. Her mother, Mutumenika, had married a Roman Catholic shopkeeper named Perera and she still recalled with delight the pomp of her elaborate church wedding. After the death of her husband, she had relapsed, probably without any feeling of contradiction, into the Buddhist ways of the rest of her kinsmen. Her attractive daughter with the tell-tale name was unmarried but had had two children from former paramours, and was considered perfectly acceptable by the rest of the Cultivators in Terutenne who noted her relationship to the Village Headman.

In general, then, although the Cultivators always claimed that the Karava were a low caste of fishermen, they actually treated them as near-equals. Again, even when marriages did take place between a person of Karava origin and a Cultivator, there was no public recognition either on the part of the families concerned or their kinsmen that a cross-caste marriage had occurred. The conscious structure of caste rules was so powerful that some story that the two were really of the same caste would have to be invented.

Many of the Karava who had been successful in business and trade in the Kandyan highlands, and who had come to dominate financially and politically such bazaars as Nildandahinna or Harasbedda (in the same area), found themselves in a quandary. There might be certain advantages to marrying into the Cultivator caste, but doing so would undoubtedly mean connecting oneself with a relatively unimportant family, and would imply, in addition, a recognition of a lower caste rank for the Karava. Alternatively, a Karava trader could intermarry among his own caste and thereby could not only acquire kinsmen comparable in influence to himself but could also claim superior status for his own caste.

The villagers in places like Terutenne recognized the power and influence of these Low Country traders who were intimately concerned with the credit and trading system of the villages in their vicinity (see chap. 4). They noted that the District Revenue Officer himself would put on his best white suit to attend the marriages and funerals that took place in the houses of these big traders. They observed that these men knew the ways of the towns and brought in new changes in fashion from the outside. Although the Cultivators claimed the highest rank among the castes, in fact they were compelled to recognize the prestige of the Low Country traders and were pushed into an attitude of mingled dislike and grudging admiration.

Ryan (1953) gives an exhaustive list of Sinhalese castes. In Terutenne most of the castes listed in his survey were completely unknown and quite outside the social universe of the villagers. A clear distinction appeared to be made between castes of the Kandyan highlands and those of the Low Country. When the villagers were asked to enumerate the castes, they usually omitted the Low Country ones. A typical reaction to such a query is given by Wannaku (Irrigation Headman of Galpitiya), who supplied the following list of castes, in the order recorded:

(a)	Goyigama	Cultivators	Terutenne
(b)	Valan	Potters	Terutenne
(c)	Beravaya	Tom-Tom Beaters	Terutenne
(d)	Radaw	Washermen	Terutenne
(e)	Vahumpurra	Jaggery Makers	Udamadura (neighboring village)

(f)	Kammal Karayo (i.e., Achari)	Blacksmiths	Terutenne
[b]	Pandi-Valan Karayo-Kumballu	Potters	Terutenne
(g)	Paddu	very low	not in near vicinity
(h)	Rodiya	very low	not in near vicinity
[f]	Badahallu (i.e., Achari)	Blacksmiths	Terutenne
(i)	Nayyandi (i.e., Ahikuntakiyo)	Snake Charmers very low	not in near vicinity
(j)	Kinnarayo	Mat Weavers very low	not in near vicinity
[e]	Hakuru	Jaggery Makers	Udamadura

It should be observed that apart from four castes, the informant has listed the names of castes with which he comes into frequent contact in normal circumstances. The exceptions, *g, h, i,* and *j,* are the castes that form the lowest end of the Kandyan caste hierarchy, and though they are not often encountered, they are constantly mentioned in conversation as the opposites of the clean and good castes. Second, the repetitions (*b, f,* and *e*) should also be noted. It is clear that the informant is running through all the caste categories in his mind, and, in response to my request to give an exhaustive list, produces all the categories he uses, even though some of them are different terms applied to the same caste.

When the local informant meets someone whom he can place in one of these categories, then he is sure of his position vis-à-vis this person. When, however, he meets someone from another district whose caste name he only faintly recognizes, he immediately classifies him as a stranger and is uncertain about his attitude toward him. It is this uncertainty that gives strangers the opportunity to alter their affiliations, cover up their background, and move up in the caste hierarchy.

THE SYMBOLS OF CASTE

In Terutenne, as elsewhere in the Kandyan hills, the myth of caste divisions *(kula bedimak)* was always referred back to the mythological ancestor, Maha Sammata. It was Maha Sammata who, needing various kinds of service done for him, first divided people into castes and gave them names. So, for instance, the Cultivators, who never use kinship terms in a formal fashion toward the low castes, make an exception for the Washermen, whom they affectionately call *Henea Mama* (*mama,* strictly MB or F-in-L) and *Henea Nenda* (*nenda,* strictly FZ or M-in-L). The usage is curious, and the Cultivators may joke about it by saying that the Washermen are their "kinsmen." (They would not, however, allow me to record this joke in my notebook.) The explanation is that when Maha Sammata was busy dividing the castes, he asked his *mama* (MB) who was actually washing his clothes to take this on as his caste occupation. I have no explanation for this usage except that the Washermen are more frequently and intimately involved in personal and family rituals of the Cultivators.

In the same way, the lower castes of Terutenne had stories about each other. The Tom-Tom Beaters mentioned the Blacksmiths especially, saying that there had been strained relations between the two castes ever since the times of Maha Sammata when the Tom-Tom Beaters took some of the Blacksmiths' women. They said that they referred to Blacksmith women as Hak gedi Amma (conch shell matron) which relates to the ritual task of Blacksmiths to blow the conch at certain rituals (table 20).

TABLE 20

*Some Terutenne Usages Between Speaker and Addressee of Different Castes**

Speaker	Addressee					
	Goyigama	Henea	Badde	Valan Karayo	Achari	Vahumpura
Goyigama		Henea Mama (M) H. Nenda (F)	Personal names; no formal address			
Henea	Hamuduruva (M)		Ayya (M) Malli (M)	Vidani (M) Dingiri Amma (F)	Gurunnaanse (M)	Gurunnaanse (M)
Badde	Hamuduruva (M)	Malli (M) Ayya (M)		Ayya (M) Malli (M)	Vidani Mahatamaya (M) Hak Gedi Amma (F)	Ayya (M) Malli (M)
Valan Karayo	Hamuduruva (M)	Mama (M) Nenda (F)	Ayya (M) Malli (M)		Vidani (M) Gurunnaanse (M)	?
Achari	Hamuduruva (M)	Personal names	Panikkiya (M) Nendiyo (F)	Personal names		?
Vahumpura	Hamuduruva (M)	Mama (M) Nenda (F)	Ayya (M) Malli (M)	?	?	

* Information uncertain regarding women.

There was complete agreement among all persons interviewed as to what were the lowest-ranking castes in the hierarchy. The Kinnarayo (Mat Weavers) are lower than the Rodiya (itinerant Beggars), and the Ahikuntakiyo (Snake Charmers) are regarded as so polluted that if they stop longer than three nights at any one locality, the ground on which they are encamped will begin to rot and smell.

Stories like this were not the only way of manifesting reciprocal relations of superiority and inferiority between the castes. Apart from certain informal signs, there were several traditional and abstract rules which expressed high and low status. These stereotyped signals were as follows:

(a) Each low caste had distinct personal names which often differentiated it from other low castes, and always differentiated it from the high caste. In the Kandyan country, the Cultivators usually utilize Banda (male) and Menika (female), names with various affixes like Black (Kalu Banda) or White (Sudu Menika) or Elder (Loku) or Younger (Hin). These are exclusively Cultivator names, and none of the low castes would appropriate them. Appuhami is also a favorite Cultivator name, though Appu alone is a low-caste usage. Similarly, names like Nila, Kiriappu, and Kirihenea are specific to the Washermen caste. It is likely that most castes do have names specific to themselves on this pattern, but many of the recent personal names used by younger people for their children appear to be taken from Indian mythology and have no specific caste meaning.

The penetration of caste categories into so intimate and almost unconscious a subject as personal names shows the deep roots of these forms. It is noteworthy that if one excludes the qualifying prefixes such as Kalu (Black), Sudu (White), Loku (Big), Podi (Small), and others, the immense majority of the high-caste names in the village would be reduced to the male-female dichotomy: *Banda* and *Menika*. Banda means "Lord" and Menika means "Jewel," and their use as the principal names in the Cultivator caste is appropriate. Similarly, in the case of the Washermen, the principal name is *Henea,* and prefixes are added to this to distinguish individuals such as Sudu-Henea (White-Henea), Kiri-Henea (Milk-Henea), and so on. This example is particularly striking since the term *Henea* itself, which is being used as the root on which to build the personal names, is indeed the category name used for the entire Washermen caste. In other words, it appears that a large number of traditional personal names can be seen as made of a root, i.e. the caste category, and a prefix referring to color, size, or quality to distinguish the particular individual within that category. The villagers do recognize that names contain clues for caste, but the principles of the classification are not, I think, clear to them.

These outlines appear to be getting increasingly blurred even in the villages. The nineteenth century may have been much more orderly in this respect. Davy (1821), who first observed this matter in the Low Country, sums it up as follows (p. 288):

"The name given varies according to the rank of the family; and, excepting the low-castes, is composed of a general name applicable to all of that rank, and of a trivial name to distinguish the individual. Thus all boys of respectable caste and family are either called *rale* or *appo* and are distinguished each by some trivial addition."

(*b*) <u>The low castes may not wear shirts</u>, and their sarongs should be worn short, above the ankles. These rules are only insisted on for special public ceremonies; ordinarily, the low castes in the Kandyan country do wear shirts. The rule about the length of the sarong was somewhat more closely observed, and a polite low-caste person would usually not presume to equate himself with the Cultivators by this index.

(*c*) There is a traditional expectation that <u>the types of houses used by the various castes should be different.</u> This was expressed not only linguistically by referring to the mansions of the Radala aristocrats as *Valawa* (so that the owners could also be spoken of as *Valaw karaya*), and the humbler houses as *gedara,* or *geyak,* but also by the proscription against the low castes' using tiles on their roofs. This rule, though still expressed in ideal terms, is disregarded in practice. In Terutenne there were many high-caste dwellings with simple thatched roofs, and some of the richer low-caste persons had tiles.

(*d*) <u>In seating arrangements, the low-status person must always sit lower than his superior; and if the superior person is sitting on a mat, then the inferior must crouch or stand.</u> This was one of the most direct forms of caste etiquette used in Kandyan villages, and it was never disregarded either in the caste context or between inferiors and superiors in ordinary social intercourse. The low castes, in general, are not permitted to sit on chairs, so one of the first pieces of property an anthropologist must acquire if he wants to be polite to his low-caste friends is a low stool (*kolomba*). If a high-caste man is on a stool, then the low-caste person must sit on a mat. Kandyans will almost never sit on the ground, or on the floor of their huts, because the ground and the earth are felt to be polluted.

(*e*) <u>There are elaborate linguistic patterns</u> which express status. The pronouns are status ranked: the second person singular is as follows:

to	you (very demeaning)
umba	you (familiar or slightly demeaning: can be used between friends)
tamuse	you (equal but somewhat formal)
tamunnanse	you (elevated)
Hamuduruva	"his highness" (used by low castes for the Cultivators; by the Cultivators for Buddhist priests; by the laity for the Buddha and the gods and goddesses.)

Most of the common verbs also have two or three status forms, thus:

palayang	go (demeaning, familiar)
yanta	go (polite)

(f) Low-caste persons must remove their headgear and drop the ends of their sarongs (which are often lifted up, or held in the hand for freedom of movement) in the presence of their superiors. This rule is again a general form of etiquette and is not confined to caste contexts.

The last of the rules of status, but most expressive of ranking, concerns the exchange of women and food.

Ideally, there should be no give and take of food or women between castes (maximum separation and distance). When there is give-and-take, it must be asymmetrical as follows: (a) Low-caste persons may take and eat cooked food offered by the high caste, but not vice versa, and (b) Low-caste women may have sexual intercourse with high-caste men, but high-caste women are prohibited to low-caste men.

Even this rule has certain exceptions. First, these rules are often formulated in such a manner as to imply a complete separation between castes, so it is often said there there is no sharing of food or of women between the castes. This sort of complete separation would, however, fail to indicate just how the castes were mutually ranked; hierarchical position can only be clearly manifested when the groups do come into some asymmetrical relationship with one another. It is noteworthy for this reason that the further formulations of the rule in a and b suggest the existence of asymmetrical relationships in terms of food and women.

Second, with particular castes, there are some formal occasions when members of the high caste will eat food cooked by the low caste. For instance, the Vahumpura (Jaggery Makers) produce small fried sweet cakes called kavum which are of importance in rites de passage, particularly in weddings; even though the cakes are prepared by low caste, they may be eaten by the Cultivators. Similar observations may be made about Toddy Tappers and Lime Burners. But these exceptions to commensal rules are part of formal caste services and the general rule about domestic cooked food holds true.

Third, the offering of food and the disposal of the containers or remains has potent asymmetrical connotations. Thus, food is always offered by the inferior to the superior, hence by the impure to the pure. The inferior must therefore be as pure as possible. In the case of food offerings to the deities (adukka), women (impure) are excluded and the cooking and offering are done by men. When food is offered to an honored guest, it is always offered with the right hand (pure). The left hand (impure) touches the elbow. The disposal of the remains is even more significant. The remains of food are polluted in the saliva of the superior, and can only be handled by an inferior: the offer to dispose of the plate of a guest is an honor. If no inferior is present, the polite guest will not permit his host to place himself in an extremely inferior position and will dispose of the plate himself.

Fourth, although low-caste women do have intercourse with high-caste men, without any objections raised on the grounds of caste, low-caste men of standing try to keep their women from becoming available to men in a promiscuous fashion.

Having made these reservations, I should emphasize that the asymmetrical rules regarding food and women are certainly the most potent symbols of rank in Ceylon. The following conversation clearly indicates these concepts.

Sometime in April, 1955, I moved from the hamlet of Galpitiya where I had been staying to the "good" hamlet of Helagama (Up Village). I had an assistant who was the son of one of the wealthy schoolteachers in Terutenne. He did not get on very well with my new landlord, and one day when I asked him how the relationship was, he suddenly burst out: "We do not eat or drink (*kanni bonni ne*) from these people."

"Why?"

"That's the way; they were working our lands at Pussalketiya [a field] for ten years or so, and they have only stopped now."

"And?"

"We will not eat from them, but they will eat from us; only today he had gone to our house for food!"

"But you ate food from Galpitiya."

"If there is something specially prepared then we can eat. Not otherwise. If they give tea specially then we can have it. But we won't go to their homes and just take tea." (He means that if, in offering food or tea, the other side manifests its inferiority quite clearly, then he will deign to accept the offer.)

"Whom will you eat with?"

"Only Gooneratne (his FZS)."

"What about the other schoolmasters?"

"We have nothing to do with them and do not visit them! [*yanni enni ne:* go come no]."

Ideas regarding food and women are directly related. There is a verbal association between "eating" and "sexual intercourse." The Sinhalese verb "to eat" (*kanava*) is one of the most obscene words in the language. Rogues will come up to women and simply whisper, "Do you eat?" (*kanava da?*) Various compound verbs like "vagina eating" (*hu [tta] kanava*) or "penis eating" (*pa [yya] kanava*) express the same intention, and the same idea is carried on to the eating of bananas, mangoes, jack-fruit seeds, and other objects with sexual connotations for the Sinhalese.

There appears to be a deep psychological identity between eating and sexual intercourse (an identity which is overtly made in diverse cultures), and <u>rules of caste rank utilize both food and sexual intercourse as equally powerful emotionally charged symbols</u>. So, when a Tom-Tom Beater says, "Our women will not 'eat' from anyone but the Goyigama," he means that they will accept neither food nor sexual advances from men of other low castes, but Cultivators will be privileged. The relations between castes are always expressed in this complex idiom of food and sex. It may either be claimed that caste X does accept food from caste Y, and that caste Y does not accept it from caste Z, or, alternatively, that although men of caste Y have intercourse with women of caste X, the same privilege is not recognized in the opposite direction.

We shall also see in the next chapter that the provision of cooked food is the most direct indication of wifely status, and those who cook and eat together are presumed to have sexual relations as well.

<u>We must conclude that the most universal prohibitions of caste, those of interdining and intermarriage, are really different ways of saying the same thing. Those groups whose women "eat" from others are lower than those groups whose women are protected, and who refuse to "eat."</u> Not only the ranking of castes but all status superiority is expressed through this idiom in the Sinhalese and related cultures. This matter-of-fact way of stating the symbolic identity of food and sex should not mislead us to underestimate the power of these notions: families are broken, murders are committed over the refusal of one side to give a girl to the other side. It should also be underlined that this differentiation between eaters and refusers, women-givers and women-takers lies at the root of Sinhalese ideas of hypergamy and dowry. As we shall see in the following pages, in many villages there are no payments upon marriage between equals. But it is noteworthy that when there are differences, then women move up the hierarchy with the aid of dowry. Giving a women to someone down the hierarchy (which could be associated with bride-wealth) would run against the grain of the symbolic system of status definitions described above.

6

The Constitution of the Nuclear Family

"The natives of Ceylon are more continent with respect to women, than the other Asiatic nations; and their women are treated with much more attention. A Ceylonese woman almost never experiences the treatment of a slave, but is looked upon by her husband, more after the European manner, as a wife and a companion."—Robert Percival, *An Account of the Island of Ceylon* (1803), p. 176

"The Batwadenè nilami, using knives and forks and spoons helped the king, who ate with his fingers off a fresh plantain-leaf that was laid on a gold plate . . . He always dined alone; occasionally he permitted, as a great favour, (and it was considered a strong mark of affection,) a favourite queen to perform the office of the Batwadenè nilami, who was excluded, and no one was allowed to be present.—J. Davy, *An Account of the Interior of Ceylon* (1821), p. 154

In this discussion of the Kandyan Sinhalese village community, I have drawn attention to the larger context: the ecology and history, the administration, the economy of the Dry Zone, and the concepts of caste. I now turn to a subject of central interest for the people— kinship and marriage. The general rules have been concisely stated by D'Oyly:

Polygamy as well as polyandry is allowed without limitation as to the number of wives or husbands but the wife cannot take a second associated husband without the consent of the first—though the husband can take a second wife into the same house with his first wife, without her consent. The wife has the power of refusing to admit a second associated husband, at the request of her first husband, even should he be a brother of the first. And should the proposed second associated husband not be a brother of the first, the consent of the wife's family to the double connexion is required. (D'Oyly, 1929, p. 129)

The picture is intriguing. How is this degree of latitude possible in a kinship system? In discussing this subject, I intend to move from the relatively simple smaller units, the nuclear families, to the larger and much more complicated conglomerations of kin which I have referred to as kindreds. This may not be the most logical procedure, but it is the most convenient one. It is difficult to know from the outset just what may be meant by a family in this larger Sinhalese sense. Many persons who may or may not be direct blood relations are considered to be kinsmen (*nädäya*) by Kandyan Sinhalese, and deciding just where the "boundary" of a kinship unit lies is not a simple matter.

On the other hand, the nuclear families not only are very neatly structured in their internal and external relations but they also enjoy considerable autonomy within the larger kinship groups. Out of a total number of 173 high-caste dwellings in Terutenne, 135 were occupied by nuclear families, and we may consider them to be the minimal units from which the other more complex structures are built.

In this chapter, I shall first discuss the economic background of the nuclear family and then proceed to a description of its internal organization and setting; I shall then analyze the more complex nuclear units, such as polyandrous and polygamous families, and I shall conclude with a description of the kinship clusters as they appear in dwelling groups in Terutenne.

THE GE

The Question of Incomes

A notable feature of Kandyan family arrangements is that each married individual has a private income. This private income, usually in the form of grain, is stored in private granaries to which only the spouse has access. I have already recorded the differences between paddy and chena cultivation. On paddy lands an individual can always pledge his labor (or his seed or buffaloes) to a landlord by an *ande* contract. He may at the same time have the assistance of all kinds of other persons in the cultivation, but he pays them off on his own account and a portion of the grain belongs to him alone. He may do anything he likes with this. His parents or siblings cannot claim it.

When there is but one landowner, either man or woman, the crop (or a definite share of the crop in *ande*) is a private income; but difficulty arises when lands are held not by a single individual but by a group of individuals. In such cases there are essentially four procedures possible: (a) the landlords' share of the crop may be divided among the several landlords in the correct proportions to their claims (*gam kariyoge kotas bedenava*); (b) the land may be divided and worked in sections by the different landlords (*idam venas karanava*); (c) the land may remain undivided but each landlord may enjoy the crop for a year (*tattu* or *avurudde maruvata*); or (d) a combination of c and b may be made, with the land being divided into sections and each section enjoyed, in rotation, by a different landlord every year. An example will make this clear (see fig. 7). A,B,C (full brothers), and

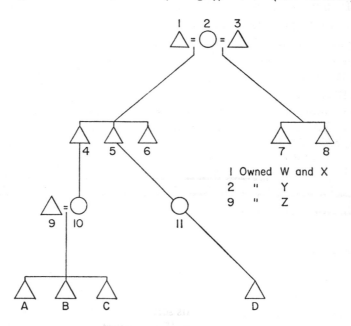

Figure 7. Multiple land ownership.

D (a second cousin), hold some land among them in four different places or sections. Let us refer to these as W, X, Y, Z. The proportions of their holdings are as follows:

(1) In the field sections of W and X the claims arise through 1: his three sons (4, 5, 6) have one-third share each. But 9, the father of A, B, and C, had brought the share of 6. Therefore, A, B, and C have two-thirds as opposed to D who has only one-third share. These sections are each cultivated for two years by A, B, and C, and one year by D. This satisfies all claims.

(2) In section Z the land was owned by 9 alone and is now worked by A, B, and C all the time.

(3) In section Y the shares are slightly different. It was owned by 2, and all her children (4, 5, 6, 7, 8) had shares, i.e., one-fifth each.

Here again 9 had bought the shares of 6, 7, 8, and therefore A, B, and C have four-fifths as opposed to one-fifth for D. The cultivation of this section is not straightforward. D does not wish to wait his turn for five years. Therefore a special arrangement is made. Section Y is subdivided and an area equivalent to its two-fifths is separated. This is worked by A, B, and C. There remain three-fifths in which D has one share and A, B, and C, two shares. This, then, is not difficult. D works it every third year just as he does his other shares. In this fashion—since he has claims in three sections—he has some land to cultivate every year.

The three brothers (A, B, and C) have been treated as a single group. It is important to emphasize that each one draws a separate income from his share in the land. The arrangements they make among themselves illustrate the division of the harvest among close kinsmen. A does not undertake any labor; he has other lands and is too old in any case. Therefore all the land is worked by B and C.

Figure 8 shows the labor arrangements. B and his two sons (who

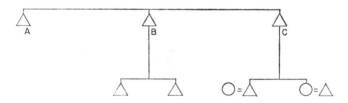

Figure 8. Labor arrangements in multiple land ownership.

are still unmarried) and C with his son and son-in-law make two teams. They work the fields all together. The harvest is then divided as follows:

(1) The landlord's share (one-half) is divided into three for A, B, and C. It goes into their separate granaries.

(2) The laborers' share (one-half) is first divided into two for the two teams of B and C. The share of B goes into his granary, since his sons live with him. The share of C is further divided into three and goes into the separate granaries of each married couple; those of the father, the son, and the son-in-law.

(3) The buffaloes and the seed are provided in proportion by the three landlords (A, B, C) and the laborers (B, C). The obligations of B's sons and C's son and son-in-law are not reckoned (kinship is said to be too close), and A's share is not calculated as strictly as it would have been in the case of a distant or non-kinsman. For, though the persons in the above example happen

to be kinsmen, they are utilizing (with only slight modifications in the case of the rent on buffaloes and seed) the general principles of *ande* contracts which also regulate the relations of non-kinsmen.

It will be observed in the case just described that each of the four factors of production on paddy lands (irrigable land, labor, seed, and buffaloes) is normally rewarded separately. If any of these factors is shared (as in the case of undivided lands, or labor that has been pooled) then each "share" is reckoned separately. In the last resort, the "shares" in all these "factors of production" belong to individuals.

What do the individuals do with their gains? Unmarried persons who live with their parents will put their incomes into the same granary as their parents. As soon as a man is married, his income is put into a separate granary to which only he and his wife may have access. Women may be landlords and have incomes, but, when married, their income and their husband's are pooled in the same granary. Sometimes when the wife is much richer than the husband then only the wife may have access to the granary.

At any rate, a clear distinction between the diverse groups of persons who cooperate on food production, and the smaller discrete units of food consumption must be drawn. The former consist of people who may be said to have "contractual" relations between them (like *ande*), and their membership changes from year to year. There are certainly important and significant questions as to just how close to the core of the family these "contractual" relations penetrate (for instance, full brothers or fathers and sons and sons-in-law do not always use *ande* between themselves), but it is clear that the constitution of the groups that cooperate on food production is predominantly based on contractual principles.

These relations among persons who must cooperate as landlords, *ande* laborers, or providers of seed or buffaloes are among the most important personal bonds in the villages. There is considerable fluidity in kinship behavior in general, but the fact of common land ownership in an undivided estate and the complicated claims on land, as well as the intricate arrangements such as those described above, are among the most important structural factors which constrain the activities of individuals.

In contrast to the "units of food production" for paddy cultivation the "units of food consumption" always consist of the basic nuclear family: the wife and unmarried children and the husband, or, sometimes, husbands. In chena cultivation the situation is slightly different, since in Terutenne there is no scarcity of chena land as yet (though the yields are not so high as in districts with longer cultivation cycles) and any able-bodied man can cultivate one or one and a half acres by himself without assistance. Only when the time for watching, weeding, and harvesting arrives does some assistance become necessary. Weeding and harvesting are women's task and are done by mothers or sisters for unmarried men, or by wives for married men. Thus on chena the "unit of food production" is coterminus with the "unit of food consumption." Those individuals who do work together on chena put the harvest into their own separate granaries.

The Joint Family

I have noted that the Kandyan pattern of land tenure and cultivation is exceedingly individualized. Yet such authorities as H. W. Codrington have referred to the Kandyan pattern as a "survival of the Hindu joint family estate." Codrington writes as follows:

The cultivated land in the village was divided into pangu, or shares, each panguva usually consisting of paddy land, of gardens, and . . . [with reservations] chena. For purposes of service [in the Kandyan Kingdom] the panguva, whatever the number of coheirs may be, is indivisible and the coheirs jointly and severally are liable for service. It seems to be a survival of the Hindu joint family. Of the joint family all the male members own and have right to the family property; no coparcener is entitled to any special interest in the property nor to exclusive possession of any part of it. (Codrington, 1938, p. 3)

These remarks appear to contradict my description of the tenure of undivided lands. It is true that Codrington is referring to the traditional system. The service obligations he mentions (rajakariya), on which the entire feudal organization of the Kandyan kingdom was based, have been abolished everywhere except in the case of temple lands.[1] Even so, there is here an element of confusion that should be clarified.

In legal terms there appear to be two distinct types of Hindu joint family: joint families governed by Mitakshara law, and joint families regulated by Dayabhaga law; the latter prevail chiefly in Bengal. The differences between the two types are crucial. In the Mitakshara case, all the living members of a joint family have coparcenary interests in the common estate. It is notable that "no individual member of that family, whilst it remains undivided, can predicate, that he . . . has a definite share, one third or one fourth" (Mulla, 1919, p. 189). On the contrary, while the estate is joint, he has a fluctuating interest. There are several reasons for this. According to the Mitakshara system, one becomes a coparcener by birth—in other words, if A has a son, B, the son acquires a claim on the property from the moment of his birth. If A has yet another son, and then the estate is partitioned,

---

[1] See Hocart (1931) and Ryan (1953, pp. 211ff.).

it would have to be divided into three equal shares. If B also had two sons, then it would have to be divided into five equal shares. These regulations bear upon incomes as well. The estate being joint, and no shares being specified, the income is also "joint" and must be "brought to the common chest or purse" (Mulla, 1919, p. 214). In this system, partition simply consists of the specification of the shares of each coparcener. The joint family is then considered to be dissolved even though the individuals concerned may not share out the lands but enjoy them as "tenants-in-common."

The differences between Mitakshara and Dayabhaga arise, in the main, from the fact that under Dayabhaga law children become coparceners not by their birth, but upon the *deaths of their fathers*. Thus, if A has two sons, B and C, and C has two sons, D and E, and if A dies, then only B and C become coparceners, and each gets half the estate; D and E have no claims until the death of C, their father. Hence, "[every] coparcener takes a defined share in the property, and he is the owner of that share. That share is defined immediately the inheritance falls in. It does not fluctuate" (Mulla, 1919, p. 248). Moreover, each coparcener may have a separate income which is not pooled (*ibid.*, p. 250). When a partition is to be made under Dayabhaga law, the property is actually divided in specific portions between the coparceners.

The Kandyan pattern of undivided tenure, then, may be said to resemble, in its general features, the Dayabhaga type of joint estate. But the particulars are quite different. The Hindu joint family is normally joint in worship as well. The Kandyan case is merely a matter of undivided property: there are no family idols, and those who have undivided property do not worship in common. Furthermore, the Kandyans allow their daughters much more extensive claims to inheritance than is the case in Dayabhaga law.

GE: THE COMMENSAL UNIT

The "unit of food consumption" in the Kandyan village consists of a wife, unmarried children, and a husband. It always has separate granaries, and it has a separate cooking place. Every married woman has her own pots and stones in a particular part of the house where she cooks. The cooking area is private and other women may use it only with express permission. All else may be shared, but granaries and cooking places may never be shared. Thus the nuclear family, the basic commensal group, is the most clearly drawn cell in the village. It is referred to as a *ge* in Sinhalese.

A dwelling may have a number of such *ge* in it. They may live under the same roof but they are distinct units. Their separateness is brought out by the fact that when one asks the number of "families" (*pavula*) in a village, the answer will refer not to the number of "houses" or to the number of "kindreds," but to the number of *ge* in the community. The word *ge* may also refer to a "house," but the usual term for "house" is *gedara* and the implication of *ge* becomes clear when the question is phrased as "How many *ge* are there in this *gedara?*" (*me gedara geyak kidenek innavada?*). The answer will always indicate the number of commensal units in the dwelling. In practice, it is distinctly rare to find more than a single *ge* in a dwelling. It is true that there are some dwellings with two *ge*, and that in Wekumbura there was a freak household with six *ge*, but as table 21

TABLE 21

Commensal Units (Ge) per Dwelling in Terutenne

	Number of *Ge* and Percent of Total *Ge*									
	1 (58.4)			2 (23.3)	3 (7.7)	4 (3.4)	5 (4.3)	6 (2.5)	Total Dwellings	Total *Ge*
Hamlet	Simple*	Complex†	Total							
Galpitiya and other small hamlets............	45	10	55	10	1	—	2	—	68	88
Wekumbura hamlet.....	36	10	46	10	3	1	—	1	61	85
Helagama hamlet.......	25	3	28	6	2	1	—	—	37	50
Hegasulla..............	6	—	6	1	—	—	—	—	7	8
Total.............	112	23	135	27	6	2	2	1	173	231

* Simple: man, woman, children, or less.
† Complex: man, woman, children, and one or two other relatives who eat together; cf. table 22 for their relationships.

shows, 135 out of 173 Goyigama dwellings in Terutenne consisted of one *ge* only. This picture applied to the low castes as well.

Let us now turn our attention to a closer examination of this primary cell in Kandyan villages.

The Formation of the Ge

It is not always a simple matter to detect the formation of a *ge*.[2] There is much scope for flirtation between persons of the correct standing and a casual affair may turn into a more permanent relationship almost imperceptibly. The turning point is always the establishment of the cooking place: the relationship between a man and woman will hardly be worth mentioning unless a separate hearth has been set up—even if it is only a few rocks placed side by side with a few pots about in one

[2] The term *ge* has been used by other writers and can be ambiguous. Kandyan usage is distinct from that of the Low Country where the *ge nama* (e.g., *Hetti Arachi ge*) is used as a patronymic clan name. Ryan (1953, pp. 25–32, 204ff.) uses it in a Kandyan (Northwestern Province) village. In that case it appears to be similar to the *gedara* name used in Terutenne.

corner of a room. (There is never a chimney, even in well-to-do houses.) For reasons that we shall see, there need not be a marriage ceremony to mark the commencement of such a union.

The traditional time for marriage, as well as for most flirtation, is about the middle of chena season (*kurakkan kapana kali:* finger millet reaping time), not merely because the crops are high and lovers may be hidden in the fields, but also because a man needs a mate to take care of the woman's tasks in chena (weeding and reaping). As soon as the finger millet is in, both a separate granary and an independent cooking place can be established. Indeed, "taking a girl to the chena" (*geniyek henata geniyanava*) is so closely associated with the establishment of permanent relations between them that the phrase is a synonym for marriage. Among the poorer sections in Terutenne this is how most nuclear families are started. With the finger millet harvest safely in the granary, the couple can wait for the ripening of the paddy harvest so that, if the man has worked paddy fields or if either of them owns landlord's shares, their supplies from chena may be augmented. Soon enough there will be two granaries, one for the finger millet (*kurukkan attuva*) and another for paddy (*vi attuva*). In the chena, the couple lives in a small temporary hut made of branches lashed together with a haphazardly placed thatched roof on top. Such a dwelling can be constructed in a day. In the village, more substantial buildings are called for and they are intended to be permanent, but even these present no great obstacles. I knew a man who had built a huge hut in his garden single-handedly in six weeks, working only a few hours a day. Such houses are usually built of wattle and daub. They may be made as annexes to the house of some close relative in the village, or, as the large number of dwellings with a single *ge* show, they may be built in a separate part of a garden in which the man or the woman has a share. If they do not mind living away from the center of the village, an allotment of Crown land may be had for a nominal rent of one rupee a year. If for prestige purposes they want to live in the center of a hamlet, a small garden may cost 200 rupees or more.

The Architecture of a Ge Dwelling

Among ordinary people in the village, the nuclear family seldom needs more than a single room (fig. 9). Those who are slightly better off may have dwellings with two rooms, and the rich have dwellings that look like mansions. Ordinary huts are usually set in solitary compounds. Whether or not the compound is fenced off from surrounding compounds depends somewhat upon the state of relations between the neighbors. If they are on good terms no fence is necessary; if not, it is usual that the trees and the land should be marked by posts. How-

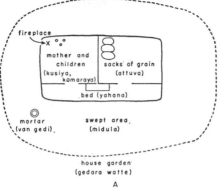

house garden
(gedara watte)

A

AN ORDINARY DWELLING (GEYAK OR GEDARA)

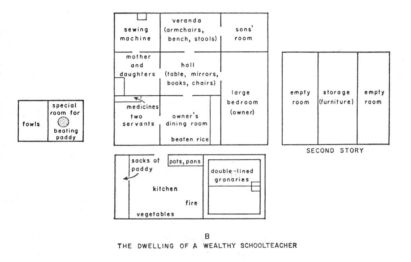

B

THE DWELLING OF A WEALTHY SCHOOLTEACHER

Figure 9. Types of Kandyan dwellings.

ever, there are cattle roaming about, and since Kandyans keep the surroundings of their houses scrupulously clean, it is often more convenient to have a fence in any case.

The layout of the house reflects the fundamental structural division within the *ge:* the differentiation of sex. The wife, young children, and nubile daughters all sleep together inside the dwelling (*ge atulaya*). The father may have a separate room (*kamaraya*) to himself, or, if the dwelling consists of a single room, he may have a bed on the veranda. If he has no bed, he will usually take his mat and spread it on the veranda and sleep there. Husband and wife do not normally sleep in the same place. The wife is visited by her husband, and if he has a separate room they may retire there, but her place is in her particular part of the dwelling. Young sons sleep on the veranda with the father. They may stay—as they often do—on the verandas of their friends, if, indeed, they are not busy pursuing amorous adventures.

The place of the wife is beside her cooking place *(kusiya)*. As was mentioned in connection with caste concepts, cooking as well as eating are among the most highly ritualized activities of Kandyans. Both must take place away from the gaze of strangers. It is exceedingly impolite to watch a person eating, and cooking cannot be done in the open. Husband and wife do not eat at the same time; the woman and young children eat together before or after the father, who is offered the food by his wife. Since the interior of the dwelling contains these private eating and cooking places, most huts do not have any window openings. People say that devils *(yaksha)* may come in through windows, but they also obviously do not like others watching what goes on inside. This emphasis on the privacy of the *ge* is another indication of the structural autonomy of this unit in the community.

The granary is normally inside the house in Terutenne, and if the man has a separate room he may store the grain in one corner. In most other villages, the grain goes into circular-shaped granaries which are raised from the ground by about a foot. But the wealthy in Terutenne were said to be worried about thefts and their granaries were rather like vaults.

With great differentiation in wealth in Terutenne, the furnishings of the houses become important prestige symbols. In the huts of the poor there may be no furniture at all, merely straw mats for sleeping and sitting (Kandyans will not sit on the ground) and perhaps clothes (sarongs, and women's clothes and blouses) hanging on the walls. The average hut, however, would have different varieties of such things as cooking pots; a mortar and pestle for husking paddy *(vangedi* and *molgaha)*; plows, hoes, and knives used in cultivation; water pots (very valuable if made of brass); and almost certainly utensils connected with betel chewing—brass spittoons, betel plates, lime boxes, and areca-nut scissors. Many of these objects have special ritual associations—some are male and female sex symbols, and others are used in special ways in ritual healing ceremonies.

In the houses of the wealthy in Terutenne the furniture may be impressive. There will be tables, chairs, and reclining chairs—evidently one of the most commendable bequests of British rule to Ceylon—not to speak of lockers *(almayra)* and sideboards and radios. Also, in anticipation of low-caste persons who may come on business, every well to do establishment has to have one or more low stools *(kolamba)* as well as mats. There is a specific type of relatively luxurious house that is quickly recognizable. It usually has an elegant veranda with pillars, covered all around with trelliswork looking not unlike some example of the Dutch Colonial style. It may have a separate shed for pounding paddy. Even those houses, however, have the smallest possible openings for windows.

The size and kinds of furnishings of the house are among the most deeply rooted symbols of prestige in the highlands. During the Kandyan kingdom there were regulations as to which category of persons were allowed to whitewash and tile their houses. The dwellings of the feudal lords were referred to by special names (*valawa* as opposed to *gedara*). This preoccupation with the type of house remains, and one sometimes comes across houses with two stories and even balconies in Kandyan villages. In Terutenne there were several houses of this sort which proclaimed the high position of their owners.

The Division of Labor: Rights and Obligations of Husband and Wife

The main division of labor inside the *ge* is based on the separation of the sexes. The man and his woman have reciprocal obligations. Women in Ceylon do not ordinarily labor in the fields, but are kept busy in the house with the cooking and the many children. They are responsible for collecting the firewood, (often merely the charred remains of the burnt jungle) and for fetching water. The collecting of firewood, in particular, is not an easy task, but it is not nearly so arduous as the work on the paddy fields which engages the men every sowing season. Women do assist in the harvest, and they are felt to be indispensable on chena, but the rest of the time they remain at home or visit relatives, and have more children. The basic obligations of man and wife may be listed as follows:

Wife's Obligations

(a) Preparation of food: including fetching water and firewood, and pounding the grain
(b) Sex
(c) Weeding and harvesting on chena
(d) Carrying reaped paddy to the edge of the threshing floor,[3] transporting the grain to the granary
(e) Looking after the children
(f) Cleaning and keeping the house (e.g. spreading cow dung—*goma gahanta*—on floors)

Husband's Obligations

(a) Provision of food; including all forms of cultivation or labor
(b) Sex
(c) Management of property and household
(d) Construction of threshing floor, threshing, winnowing, handling bullocks, etc. See *a* above.
(e) Provision of clothing
(f) Repairs to the house (e.g., taking care of the roof and fences)

---

[3] Women are considered to be slightly "impure" because they menstruate; they may only handle paddy, which is very "pure," with great care. They may not reap nor are they allowed into the threshing floor, which is treated "as a *devale*," lest they cause a drop in the harvest.

These various obligations aside, husband and wife have little to do with each other. They sleep separately; they eat separately, they work separately; and when they have time to spare, they associate with persons of their own sex. It is unbecoming for a man to be seen in the company of women too frequently. Their lives are separate and tend to converge in formalized channels.

The relative wealth of husband and wife naturally makes all the difference to the assiduity and interest with which even the minimum obligations are carried out. It is said that a rich man will treat a poor wife as a mere servant who happens to bear obnoxious children, but, conversely, it is well known that rich heiresses who have poor husbands may treat them none too kindly. Rich women, one is told over and over again, make awful wives, especially if the man stands to lose a great deal by deserting the wife; such unions in which poorer men settle down with rich women matrilocally, are a particular form of Kandyan marriage known as *binna*. In *binna,* the husband is under obligation to work for the rich wife and her parents.

I have placed the provision and cooking of food at the top of the list of reciprocal obligations. As far as the Kandyans are concerned, food is the most fundamental element in the relations between husbands and wives. Indeed, cooking for a man and eating the food he has provided in the same household signifies the marital relationship. A woman will speak of her husband as "the one I cook for" *mama uyanaekkenek*) and a man will refer to his marriage by saying that he needed someone to cook for him. But there is also the aspect of commensality mentioned in connection with caste—the association of ideas between eating together and sexual intercourse.[4] The woman with whom one eats—with the exception of mother, sisters, daughters, and a few other such close relatives—is *ipso facto* a sexual companion as well.

Polyandry and the Ge

The provision of food by the man and the cooking services of the woman form the backbone of the *ge*. The situation is, of course, altered when there are *two* men providing the food that is cooked by *one* woman. The Kandyans have a word for such unions which, indeed, indicates the very essence of the relationship. What we call polyandry is known as "eating in the same *ge*" (*eka ge kanava,* literally "one *ge* eating"). Another phrase to refer to polyandry is "living in

---

[4] This has nothing to do with the fact that even a husband and wife always eat separately, in accordance with the customary etiquette between men and women. They may still be considered to "eat together" (*ekata kanava*) if they form a commensal unit and if the woman merely "offers" the food—cooked by herself—to the man, even though she eats after he has finished.

one peace" (*eka sahaya inni*). The arrangements are simple and straightforward. Two men (whether they are brothers or not is immaterial) come to an agreement to live and work together. They may work on paddy fields as a team and they will put all their grain into the same granary. They agree to share the services of a woman and live with her in the same house. The arrangement is satisfactory; the main obligations of a wife are in the nature of housekeeping, and these are easily shared if the men can get on in the first place. Second, with the deep cleavage between the sexes there is no particular emphasis on the special and private emotional attachments between individual men and women to which Westerners are accustomed. Third, it is of no small importance that two men together can better support a wife than one man alone, with fewer children into the bargain and rather more prosperity and well-being for all. In Terutenne, the poor are sufficiently poor to take this economic issue into consideration.

The three-part alliance depends most of all on cooperation between the co-husbands. If there is cooperation, the household is harmonious; if there is not, one or the other husband is likely to leave. For that reason, the few polyandrous households that did exist in Terutenne were all reasonably happy ones. Polyandry was, however, very uncommon in the Kandyan villages where I worked. Terutenne had four cases, Makulle Watta, in the Wellassa area, three, and Vilawa four. The opportunities I had of observing their arrangements were excellent, for in Terutenne three of them were my close neighbors in the Galpitiya hamlet, and I actually lived in a house in Vilawa where my landlords consisted of two polyandrous brothers.

It should be observed, however, that Prince Peter of Greece has found polyandry to be rather frequent in the Ratnapura area in Sabaragamuva. My own evidence gathered during a brief visit to Ratnapura in 1955 contradicts this view, but it is a question that should be examined further. It would be important if Prince Peter's evidence were to be borne out, for this is indeed what educated people in Kandy and Colombo claim for the Ratnapura area, in rather marked contrast to the evidence from elsewhere in Ceylon (see Peter, Prince of Greece, 1955*b*).

Since the arrangement of polyandry is traditional and not simply a sexual aberration, the rarity in the regions I am familiar with needs to be explained. I think there are two reasons: one moral, one more practical. Throughout the British period in the Kandyan country, no opportunity was lost to point out that polyandry was an "immoral" practice. This view is now generally accepted by the urban upper classes, the District Revenue Officers, schoolteachers, and so on. In my experience, the villagers are certainly aware of it and undoubtedly have the feeling that polyandry is rather frowned on by educated

people. The fact that it is generally confined to the poorest people
certainly does nothing to raise the prestige of such unions. The other
reason for the rarity of the phenomenon is that it is evidently not
easy for two men to cooperate closely and intimately in this fashion.
Those who can do so, however, appear to make a success of the venture.

Fraternal and Nonfraternal Polyandry

That Kandyan polyandry depends principally on cooperation between men rather than on kinship is perhaps demonstrated by the
fact that only one out of the four cases in Terutenne was actual
"fraternal" polyandry. The arrangements in that case were as follows:
two brothers who lived with their mother and had half a *pale* of paddy
land between them brought a wife from another village. She had no
property. There was no marriage ceremony for either of them. The
two brothers work together on paddy, but separately on chena. In the
house in Galpitiya, the two men live on the veranda, their mother
lives in one room, and their wife and four children live in the other.
There is no order about sexual relations and both brothers visit the
wife whenever they like. I know that the men got on very well because my own hut was next to theirs and I could watch their everyday activities. During the chena season, each brother constructed a
separate hut in his highland plot and the woman visited each brother
for a week at a time. The mother cooked for the one who happened
to be alone. The harvesting was done by both women and all the
grain was put into the common granary. The separate chena arrangement was only circumstantial, however; I was told that in years when
they are able to get a single plot of three acres in the highlands, they
build only a single hut and all live together.

The cases in which the men were not brothers were similar. In
each case the men pooled their efforts and, putting their grain into
the same granary, assumed the right to demand both the cooking and
the sexual services of the woman. In all three cases, the men were
natives of Galpitiya hamlet who had known each other from child-
hood. Only two of these men had paddy land, a small amount; the
women had nothing. Nonetheless, the arrangements described were
considered to be very convenient for all concerned.

A variant of the same phenomenon should also be noted. A particular bachelor, said to be a "benefactor of the temple" (*dayakaya*), who
lived in the Maluvegoda *vihara* with the priests but also had a room
in a hut in Galpitiya, used to make special arrangements. Being
friendly with the priests, he could get temple land on *ande*. He cul-

tivated the land by himself, but after the harvest he would approach some of the men in the hamlet and suggest that he put his grain into the same granary with one of them, and enjoy the services of the man's wife throughout that year. He seemed usually to find someone who would accept his offer. This sort of arrangement is only a temporary one, however, and though it may follow along principles identical to those in regular polyandrous unions, it was not considered to be quite the same thing.

Is Kandyan Polyandry "True" Polyandry?
Who Is the Father?

Two further questions need answers. In the first place, is this "true" polyandry?—and, second, who is the "father" of the children?

The inquiry as to whether these are truly polyandrous families arises from the suspicion, noted by Radcliffe-Brown, that only one of the men may be "married" to the woman and the other may merely be allowed sexual access to her. The distinction drawn is between a "husband," whose position has been fixed by a "marriage ceremony" and who has defined rights and obligations, and a second man, who does not share these rights and obligations and is merely a kind of cicisbeo (cf. Berreman, 1962). But it should be immediately obvious that this distinction has no relevance in the Kandyan context. I observed that domestic unions among the poorer people are usually started with no ceremony at all merely by "taking a woman to the chena." Moreover, and more importantly, the rights and obligations of the two men are invariably equal: both must put their grain into the same granary, and it is by virtue of this act that they can demand the right to the wifely services of the woman.

The question as to who is the father of the children is closely related. In Sinhalese terminology, all the brothers, parallel cousins, and many other relatives of the "father" may be referred to in the same manner. The terms loku appa, appa, bappa (bala appa?) signify "elder father," "father," "younger father." In the case of polyandrous men (whether brothers or not) the terms usually applied are loku appa for the elder and bappa for the younger. It is true that the term piya is more specifically applied to a particular "father," but this usage was not unalterable, as I discovered when piya was applied to the younger "father" after the elder "father"—the original piya—died. I have frequently heard informants refer to a polyandrous arrangement of their parents by saying that they had "two fathers" (appochila dennai) —which ought to settle the academic questions. It is of course said that the woman always knows exactly which man is the genitor of which child, but the matter has little significance for the people concerned. No distinctions are made in behavior: for instance, both men appear to have the same rights to discipline the children.

I have been emphasizing in this account that the question of whether polyandry is fraternal or not is irrelevant from the point of view of the rights and obligations of the spouses. Inheritance is also handled smoothly. Shares in the property—if any—of both the men descend to all their children *per capita:* that is, if a man A had three children in a polyandrous union with his brother B, and also had three children from another women he acknowledged, then the shares of A would be divided into six equal portions and those of B into three.

Traditionally the Kandyans used to give two answers to the query as to why they practised polyandry. The wealthy would say that it kept property together and ensured cooperation between brothers,[5] and the poor would say that it was cheaper to keep one woman.[6] Both explanations would still be given, although in my experience the wealthy do not enter into such unions these days. I did not come across a single instance of polyandry among rich people. It is certainly possible —in theory—to preserve the unity of brothers by recourse to polyandry. But the rarity of the phenomenon today suggests either that the method is not particularly effective or that the Kandyans care less about the unity of brothers than they profess to.

"Polygyny" and the Ge

Apart from the four polyandrous *ge* in Terutenne, there were two men in the village who had permanent relations with two women. "Polygyny" is again a rare phenomenon, but it, too, is recognized and accepted. There were no cases of it in Vilawa and only three in Makulle Watta. In contrast to polyandry, no special phrase is used to describe the arrangements; the women are merely referred to as first and second "wives" (*palaveni* and *deveni pavula*).

The arrangements are much the same as those in an ordinary *ge*. A woman, her children, and her husband form a commensal unit, the only difference being that the man has at the same time a similar relationship with another woman and her children. In most of the cases which came to my notice, the women lived in dwellings far sep-

---

[5] Cf. Leach's comments on the influence of female property in such cases (1955).

[6] "The apology of the poor is that they cannot afford each to have a particular wife, while the rich say that such a union connects families and concentrates property" (Marshall, 1846, p. 162). Davy (1821, pp. 286–287) also mentions these sentiments.

arated from each other. In Terutenne one of the men concerned had one wife in the village and another in a neighboring village where he owned extensive lands. The economics and social lives of the two *ge* were completely separate.

One of these women, whose husband, Wanni Wannaku, was one of my best informants, lived next to my hut in Galpitiya. Wanni, nearly seventy but still bursting with energy, had had ten children by her and ten by his other wife. He used to stay in the *ge* in Galpitiya for a few days at a time, depending on the pressure of work, but when necessary would return to the other village. What was expected of him was to keep the *ge* supplied with food, and since this was more than adequately done, the woman had no right to complain about his other connection. Indeed, over the years an excellent *modus operandi* had been reached. The two women almost never visited each other, but they knew about their different family affairs and when they met were polite, but distant, in their behavior.

One could really describe my neighbor in Galpitiya as a "peripatetic husband." Some similar tendency is observable in the ordinary *ge* as well. Given the division of the sexes, the man is often separated from his woman and her offspring. It is suggestive that he usually has a separate sleeping place on the veranda or in another room. It is as if he were on the fringes of the *ge:* he is in it, to be sure, because he is the provider, but he can also be half out of it, and if he decides to share his attentions between two *ge,* there is no serious difficulty. Why, then, if double unions are so easy, are they so rare?

There are two aspects to the question: wealth and kinship. Let me return to Wanni Wannaku for an illustration: Wanni is a very rich man. He is a native of Terutenne but his first marriage was to a woman from Galketiwela, a village nearer the bazaar Nildandahinna. Since he owns land there and since he also has business interests in shops in Nildandahinna, he had a house built for his first wife and their children in her own village. He cooperates very closely with her kin, who are all very rich. On the other hand, he owns lands in Terutenne. These also require his attention, and perhaps as a matter of convenience he has been living with the woman in Galpitiya. He often stays in her hut, but since Galpitiya is a "low" hamlet, he also has another house in the village of Terutenne, opposite the Maluvegoda temple, so as not to be counted a Galpitiya person. All these arrangements are possible only because of Wanni's riches. He is expected to be able to provide for both *ge,* for otherwise he will not be allowed in by the women. Indeed, all the men who had plural wives were very rich by Kandyan village standards. There was one exception in Makulle Watta—a poor young man—but one could not help wondering how long he could continue to keep both the women. At any rate, most people claimed that they could ill afford one wife, let alone two.

The other reason why men rarely have two women concerns kinship obligations. Kandyans cooperate very closely with their in-laws. This cooperation is of such an intimate and all-embracing nature that it would be difficult to share one's attention between two sets of in-laws. Their demands would soon come to conflict.

Here, indeed, lies the kernel of the problem. Neither Wanni Wannaku nor the other wealthy men with two women in Terutenne cared in the least about what happened to the women described as their "second wives" (*deveni pavula*) or their relatives. The woman kept by Wanni Wannaku in Galpitiya was desperately poor and so were all her relatives. And besides, they were "low" people. Wanni lavished all his attention on his first family. His children from his first wife had been superbly married. Each match on that side had been a masterwork of intrigue and politics. On the other hand, he had taken no interest whatsoever in his Galpitiya family. The marriages of the daughters had not been arranged and they all had married very poor men. His "second wife" constantly used to ask me to use my influence and induce Wanni to give some of his extensive property to them, but he preferred to concentrate his efforts on gaining prestige and social position for one of his *ge* only. For these reasons, it is more appropriate to consider these "second wives" as concubines. They are treated as such, but since the basic rights and obligations of both women are similar, no verbal distinction is made by the Kandyans.

Other Relatives in the Ge

So far, I have been concerned with the description of the rights and obligations between the principal members of the *ge*. In some of the *ge*, in Terutenne, however—23 cases out of the 135 in which there was a single commensal unit in a dwelling—other relatives were also present, living and eating with the nuclear family. Who were they? Their relationships to the nuclear family can be seen in table 22. Attention should be drawn to certain interesting features. The husband's mother is present in the *ge* in four instances and the wife's mother in seven instances; in all cases, of course, the mother is a widow, since she and her husband would form a separate *ge* if he were still alive (see table 23). There is no case in which the father eats with his son's or daughter's family. The latter case does occur at times, and daughters do cook for their fathers, but it is very rare to see a daughter-in-law cook for her father-in-law. The reason again has to do with the sexual associations of interdining. There had been an instance in Terutenne of a father being provided with cooked food by the wife of his son. Soon the word spread that he was sleep-

TABLE 22

Dwellings in Terutenne with Single Cooking Units

	Galpitiya	Wekumbura	Helagama	Hegasulla	Totals
SIMPLE NUCLEAR FAMILIES					
Nuclear families (nf)......	40	27	20	5	92
2 polyandrous men.......	1	—	—	—	1
Partial nuclear family (spouse dead or separated)...........	1	—	3	1	5
Single men.............	1	2	—	—	3
Single women..........	2	7	2	—	11
Total nf. (simple)....	45	36	25	6	112
COMPLEX NUCLEAR FAMILIES					
Man's nf + son by another woman........	2	1	—	—	3
Man's nf + wife's children by another man...	—	2	—	—	2
Man's nf + daughter's son..................	—	1	—	—	1
nf + husband's mother...	1	2	1	—	4
2 polyandrous brothers' nf + their mother.....	1	—	—	—	1
nf + husband's father's mother..............	1	—	—	—	1
nf + wife's mother.......	3	2	2	—	7
Mother and grown daughter alone........	—	1	—	—	1
nf + wife's sister's children.............	1	—	—	—	1
nf + husband's brother's children.............	1	1	—	—	2
Total nf + other relatives who eat together...	10	10	3	—	23
Grand Total........	55	46	28	6	135

ing with his daughter-in-law and—whether the allegations were correct or not—the arrangement was quickly discontinued. Although father and son continued to live in the same dwelling, the father laboriously cooked his own meals.

The suspicion suggests first that it would not have been entirely out of the question for father and son to keep one woman. Second, it underlines again the importance of the symbolic association of food and sex for the Kandyans. A father and son keeping the same woman would be considered wrong: wrong because it would confuse relations and make the two men, one of whom ought to respect the other, into co-husbands. But the very fact that it could be considered feasible enough to suspect suggests that the parental relationship is not so powerfully delineated in Terutenne as in parts of India.

TABLE 23

Dwellings in Terutenne with Two Cooking Units

Type of Dwelling	Galpitiya	Wekumbura	Helagama	Hegasulla	Total
PARENTS AND CHILDREN					
Man's nf + son's nf.......	3	—	1	1	5
Man's nf + daughter's nf..	1	—	1	—	2
MOTHER AND CHILDREN					
2 sons' nf + mother.......	2	1	—	—	3
1 son's nf + mother and daughter's children.....	1	—	—	—	1
Mother + daughter's nf + son's son's nf..........	—	1	—	—	1
Mother and children + son's nf..............	—	1	—	—	1
Woman and children and 2nd husband + 1st husband's daughter's nf.	—	1	—	—	1
SIBLINGS					
Man's nf + brother's nf...	1	1	—	—	2
Man's nf + sister's nf.....	1	1	1	—	3
Man's nf + sister's son's nf..............	1	—	—	—	1
Man's nf + brother's son's nf..............	—	1	—	—	1
Man's nf + brother's daughter's nf..........	—	—	1	—	1
Man's nf + sister.........	—	1	1	—	2
Man's nf + brother.......	—	—	1	—	1
Son's nf + mother and sister.................	—	1	—	—	1
AFFINES					
Man + sister's husband...	—	1	—	—	1
Total.................	10	10	6	1	27

+ signs separate *Ge* or cooking units

Although food is provided by the *ge* to various relatives, none but the nuclear family can claim the right to eat in the *ge*. The relatives are looked after as a kindness. Often when a mother lives alone but has several married children in the village, they will take turns feeding her. Frequently, however, the old women are left completely to their own devices (11 cases). In other words, the *ge* is a distinct and compact social unit with clear "boundaries."

Dwellings with Plural Ge

Dwellings with more than two *ge* are rare in Terutenne (see table 21). It is, however, illuminating to consider how the *ge* are associated with each other in the same dwelling. The connections between plural *ge* that inhabit the same dwelling are depicted in tables 23, 24, and 25,

TABLE 24

Dwellings in Terutenne with Three Cooking Units

	Galpitiya	Wekumbura	Helagama	Hegasulla	Total
Man's nf + 2 sons' nf........	—	1	—	—	1
Woman + 2 sons' nf + daughter's nf...........	—	1	—	—	1
Man's nf + son's nf + brother.................	—	—	1	—	1
2 polyandrous men + brother of one + 2nd brother's daughter's nf....	1	—	—	—	1
Man's nf + daughter's nf + daughter-in-law's nf......	—	—	1	—	1
Man and son's nf + brother's nf + brother's wife's sister's nf..........	—	1	—	—	1
Total................	1	3	2	1	6

which sum up a complete survey of the Goyigama households in Terutenne. The figures speak for themselves, showing what kind of social groups make up a plural household. They also throw light on the relative strength of Sinhalese kinship ties.

A dwelling, whatever the number of *ge* in it, is referred to as *geḍara* (house). The people who inhabit the same house may be referred to as *eka gedara kattiya* (one house people) and it is assumed that they are close kinsmen. For greater precision they are sometimes referred to as the people who live "under one roof" (*eka yataliya*).

The main reason for remaining together is that it is convenient for married children to settle in an already existing house and live in a garden with valuable trees which they will, in due course, inherit. (Whether or not the garden is valuable certainly makes all the difference.) Siblings will often divide the garden equitably among themselves and arrange to live in the same dwelling. Sections of the garden may be actually fenced off or only agreed upon. They may even share out the fruit trees. When the property is extensive and the siblings

TABLE 25

Dwellings in Terutenne with Four or More Cooking Units

Four Cooking Units (2 cases)
    Man's nf + son's nf + 2 daughters' nf (Helagama)
    Man's nf + 2 brothers' nf + sister's nf (Wekumbura)

Five Cooking Units (2 cases, both Galpitiya)
    Man's nf + brother + brother's son's nf + dead brother's wife and
    children + sister's son's nf
    Man's nf + son's nf + daughter's nf + brother's nf + sister's nf

Six Cooking Units (1 case, Wekumbura)
    Man's nf + mother's brother's son's nf
            + mother's brother's wife and 2nd husband's nf
            + mother's brother's daughter's nf
            + mother's 2nd brother's wife and children
            + mother's 3rd brother's children and wife's sister

+ signs separate *Ge* or cooking units

are on good terms, then no actual division may take place until the next generation.

I have defined "dwelling" as a single separate building, but let me note that people could build two houses in two corners of a single garden. This will appear as two "separate" dwellings in the tables, but the mere fact of physical separation would not necessarily make their inhabitants more distant in social terms, and the villagers may refer to them as "one house people" by extending the meaning of the phrase. Indeed, siblings who may live in another part of the village certainly continue to keep their shares in the garden as well as in the parental house. They may own trees or even shares in some trees in the garden. Walking in the village I would frequently see men clamber up trees in gardens where they did not reside. When asked, they would usually explain (unless they were thieves) what proportion of a share they held, and exactly how they came to inherit it. As I have noted elsewhere, although claims of this sort may appear insignificant, they are prepetuated for future purposes, and they give the inheritor a toehold, so to speak, on the estate of the people who actually live in the garden.

The value of the property has a good deal to do with whether or not siblings who have built houses elsewhere decide to press their claims. Sisters who have left the village in marriage generally forgo their claims, but those who remain in the village may well live in the same dwelling and hang on to their claims tenaciously.

The various constituent *ge* in a *gedara* are separate economic and social units. Their incomes may be quite different. Unless sons and daughters have remained with their father, and unless the father happens to be a wealthy person—so that his children work his lands— there is no locus of authority in the *gedara*. There is no necessary permanency about these arrangements: the different *ge* may separate out during the chena season, or if they find they cannot get along together, they will simply construct another dwelling for themselves elsewhere. This being so, the fact that some have remained together is a good index of the relative strength of the various kinship ties.

Kinsmen Who Live Together

Let us first consider parents and children. Undoubtedly, most young men and women prefer to live alone in a separate hut if their children are not too young. With young children it could be preferable to reside with parents except that it is not easy for daughters-in-law to live in close quarters with their mothers-in-law, and, for the son-in-law, a definite effort is necessary if he is to reside under the same roof with his parents-in-law at all. In the situation of the daughter-in-law, the difficulties are implicit in the proverb which says that she and her mother-in-law are "like the cobra and the Russell's viper" (*naya polanga vagei*), which are considered to be deadly enemies in Sinhalese folklore. I deal with the position of the matrilocal son-in-law in the next chapter. However, it is a reflection of the relative ease with which young couples may move out that I never came across any formal avoidance patterns between these key relatives.

The number of married men and women who do live in the same dwelling with one or both their parents is about 21 percent of all *ge* in Terutenne. Of the total number of 231 *ge*, 48 contained a married child living with the parents in the same dwelling. Of these, a third (17) were daughters and two-thirds (31) were sons. In other words, in only about 7 percent of the *ge* in Terutenne was the man actually in the same dwelling with his parents-in-law. The daughter-in-law lived with her husband's parents about twice as often (about 14 percent of all *ge*).

These tendencies are reflected also in the case of siblings. Married brothers were found living together in the same dwellings twice as frequently as married sisters living with a married brother, but the incidence (6 brothers, 5 sisters) was very infrequent.

We have been concerned in this chapter with the organization of the nuclear family; the internal and external relations of the *ge* as a social unit. We may summarize the points as follows:

1. In principle, each individual has a separate income.
2. Each nuclear family is a distinct economic unit (*ge*).
3. A "marriage" may be established without ceremony.
4. The rights and the obligations of the man and wife are clear and definite.
5. The duties of the "husband" may be shared between two men (polyandry); or one may discharge them toward two women (polygyny). Both forms are rare.
6. *Ge* rarely remain together in the same dwelling. When they do, married sons are more likely to remain with their parents than are married daughters.

We may now turn to the arrangements of continuity in the *ge* and examine the question of inheritance and descent.

7

Patterns of Inheritance and Descent

"The Singalese being without family names, grown-up people are called either by the names of the places of their abode, or of the offices which they fill."—J. Davy, *An Account of the Interior of Ceylon* (1821), p. 289

Anthropologists when dealing with small, closed, homogeneous communities tend to assume that there is one coherent pattern which can be described and analyzed as a single boundary-maintaining system. This procedure may be justified in the small, truly isolated communities cut off from the world like those in the interior of New Guinea or in the forests of Brazil. When working on peasant communities in parts of Asia and Africa, the assumption of isolation or of invariant structure cannot be justified. Terutenne is no exception. Although there are aspects of this village that I daresay will not change over many decades, it was also obvious during field work that the patterns of behavior in many important respects were not rigid and unvarying. Not only was there considerable difference of opinion as to how, for instance, inheritance and marriage should work, but the individuals concerned felt that there were relatively wide ranges of choice open to them within their varying conceptions of the patterns.

In this chapter I shall be concerned with a description of certain variant behavior patterns in the context of marriage; I shall also describe similar variations in the expectations regarding inheritance; and finally I shall attempt to show how these patterns relate to the theories of descent and status in the social hierarchy of Terutenne.

The problem of "variation" at either the behavioral level or the level of ideal rules is directly related to the questions of change in social systems. In other words, the presence of variant patterns of behavior, or of differing opinions of what is correct, can be interpreted as the intermediate stage between two ideally conceived systems. The variant patterns may crystallize into a new "structure" or both statistical dispersion and the divergence of opinion may continue without crystallizing formally into a definite "structure." Similarly, the complexities of marriage and inheritance behavior of the Kandyan Sinhalese may be seen as variations between two ideal patterns: the poor and the lower castes at the bottom of the social scale and the wealthy and higher castes at the top. On this basis, at least two types of change can be assumed to be going on at any given point in time.

First, the shape of the gradient itself may be changing according to the specific economic conditions, and, second, individual families may be moving up and down the gradient and altering their modes of behavior and expectations in response to new conditions. As we shall see, the various choices open to people in Terutenne have much to do with the question of control over women, who occupy a critical position in the social systems of Ceylon and India.

THE LOCALITY OF MARRIAGE

The Significance of Residence at Marriage

Kandyans classify all marriages as either *binna* or *deega*. In *binna*, the man gives up the place where he lives and goes to live in the house of the woman; in *deega*, the woman comes to live with the man. The term *binna* is applicable not only to the cases in which men have come to live matrilocally with their in-laws but also to those in which the couple have settled on land that belongs to the wife. Hence, even when the household consists only of man and wife the union may be either *binna* or *deega*. It is to be remembered, however, that few married persons actually live with their parents or their siblings.

Binna and *deega* are important for two additional reasons. They influence the inheritance of property in wealthy families, and they define the position and obligations of the son-in-law toward his in-laws. Furthermore, their incidence and nature changes as one moves down the social hierarchy. The *binna-deega* distinction is therefore related to variations in patterns of inheritance.

Deega and Binna

In a *deega* marriage, the groom falls under no formal and specific obligations toward his in-laws. It is true that he has taken a girl from them, but she is by no means lost to her family. If she remains in the same village, she sees them daily and her children remain in close contact with their maternal kin. If she goes to the neighboring village, then much formal visiting takes place between the households.

The connection gains importance if—as often happens—the woman has been given a dowry or if lands have been set aside for her and her children to be used after the decrease of her parents.

If, among families of equal standing, goods have been given by the groom to the family of the bride, these are rarely more than small payments to assist the bride-givers in the preparation of the wedding feast and ceremony. Among equals, the *deega* marriage starts reciprocal obligations which are not immediately discharged, but which are diffuse and maintained throughout the connection. Thus it will be said that a *deega* husband will not press too hard to acquire the control of the property of his wife, for "if he gets it all at once, then he could not turn to them later in an emergency." In other words, the immediate satisfaction of all claims runs counter to long-term interests of reciprocity. Affinity is a long-term alliance and not a transaction which needs to be concluded; hence there is no "bride wealth" and among equals such gifts or favors as the bride may get from her own parents are drawn out over time to secure her husband's connections with her own natal family.

Binna is meaningful only in contrast to *deega*. There are two reasons why the parents of a girl will allow her to bring her husband home: either they have no sons and wish one of their daughters to stay on with them and bear children to continue the family, or the sons are still young and someone is needed to help in the management and labor of the lands. In either case, the groom (who is invariably a poorer man) settles in *binna*, lives with the daughter, and is given lands to work on his own account.

He is distinguished from the *deega* husband, then, in that he works for his father-in-law and uses the land that is allowed him. What is significant, however, is that on the death of the father- and mother-in-law, his wife, the *binna* daughter, will *inherit* an equal share with her brothers in the estate, while her *deega* married sisters and their husbands get nothing of the intestate inheritances. This last is an important point, for it means that whereas in cases of *deega* the children will inherit from the father and be primarily affiliated with the paternal group, in *binna* the main inheritance will come from the mother and the primary affiliations of children will be with the mother's side.

The distinction that is important here is not so much matrilocal residence with the in-laws, but the obligation of the *binna* husband to work for his in-laws and his wife's eventual inheritance. The fact that *binna* men live often under the same roof with their parents-in-law is not a necessary condition, but merely an index of their position and obligations.

The Matrilocal Son-in-Law

The formal differences in the rights and obligations of *deega* and *binna* husbands imply a very real difference of status between the men. The *deega* husband is an equal of his wife's family, and must be treated accordingly. A *binna* husband is considered an inferior by his wife and her family. A man who owns land will not normally contract a *binna* marriage. Moreover, such unions do not set up the balanced kinship relationships between the kinsmen of the husband and the wife which are expected in a *deega* union. It is rather as if the husband has been taken over and adopted by the family of the wife. If he is poor, so, probably, are his relations and there is little reason to encourage them to come on visits too frequently.[1] In all the cases of *binna* that came to my notice in Terutenne there was some element of avoidance with the kinsmen of the *binna* husband. Often, indeed, such men would be outsiders to the village and would allow their connections with their natal village to lapse.

The difficulty of the position of a *binna* man is not merely that he is expected to work for his in-laws, but also that the land will eventually belong, not to him, but to the wife. As a result, the difficulties do not end with the death of the father-in-law; they merely change their character. In many cases, the grain goes into a granary which is under the strict control of the woman. She sells the rice and keeps the money. She gives her husband the cash for his little luxuries: the drinks in the nearby shops, the new shirt and sarong. Needless to add, in the village the position of a man who has to depend on his wife for pocket money is thought to be ludicrous.

The degradation of the *binna* man is reflected in the jocular folklore that has grown about him. He must have a talipot leaf, an oil lamp, and a walking stick with him, it is said, for he may have to leave in the rain, or the middle of the night, or in the heat of the sun when his wife tires of him. Heiresses are notoriously hard to please. It is sometimes directly said, "If you settle on *binna,* you are under the woman" (*Binnata bessot, genige yatata inta one*), or "In *binna* it is the woman indeed who is the husband" (*Binnata giyot geni tamai purussaya*).

There is nothing shameful in such a connection from the point of view of the woman's family. A *deega* marriage alliance with a rich and high-ranking groom undoubtedly brings more prestige, but *binna,*

---

[1] There is an element of adoption in *binna* marriages, and the husband tends to lose his connections with his natal family. Indeed, customarily he may be "fed" by his parents-in-law for six months if he does not have enough capital to begin.

although without such prestige, is useful for the family. It does not depreciate the family's rank.

There are practical drawbacks to *binna*, however. One is that the *binna* husband who can get on with his wife also has to contend with her brothers. Sometimes all goes well, but frequently the *binna* husband cannot cooperate with his brothers-in-law, who treat him as an inferior. I came across numerous cases when such men complained of being sorcerized (*huniyam*) and accused their in-laws. They were anxious and worried over the tense atmosphere in the house. Some who felt they could not continue would break the connection and leave.

These difficulties sometimes persist into the next generation. One day as I was returning from a visit to Kinegolle, in the hills above Galpitiya, I was joined on my walk by Sudubanda, an intelligent young man from Kinegolle. He seemed dejected and preoccupied, and after walking along silently for a while, I asked him whether all was well in Kinegolle with him. He lived in the main house with his two *mama* (MBs), Muhandiram (also F-in-L) and Punchirala, with whom he was on very bad terms. The community being small, it must have been a singularly difficult situation, and Sudubanda said that everyone was all right except himself. "If a person works for them, and slaves for them, then they like him. If he minds his own business, then they are angry with him," he said. He complained that they treated him like a *binna* husband.

As he was describing his difficulties, I recalled that he had consulted my cook Appuhami—a renowned *Kapurala* in the vicinity—about the possibility that he was being sorcerized (see Yalman, 1964). I had also wondered when speaking to him on another occasion why he and his sister's husband had been so ready to criticize the "lowness" of Galpitiya and Kinegolle. When I had pointed out that he, too, lived in Kinegolle, he had said that his connection was on the side of women (*ganu pakse*) alone. It was clear that his connections with his affines had become irksome to him.

About future plans, he said that he had had enough of being treated as an inferior and was going to leave the main house in Kinegolle and go to Morangahatenne to live with his sister's husband. Sudubanda apparently got on very well with him and was proud of his achievements. He added that he would not have stayed so many years in Kinegolle in the company of Muhandiram had it not been for the fact that he lived in his mother's room in the house, and had he not owned considerable land in the Kinegolle field.

The kinship background of Sudubanda is revealing (see fig. 6, chap. 5). His father had settled on *binna* in Kinegolle with his wife's two

brothers, Muhandiram and Punchirala. He was not a Terutenne native and had few connections in the vicinity. He had had three children: the eldest, Sudubanda, had married his MBD and had remained
in the same room that his parents occupied in the main house. He was
not strictly speaking a *binna* husband at all. The second child had
been married to a respectable man from Morangahatenne, where
Sudubanda was considering moving. The youngest son had married
into a poor branch of the aristocratic Agalakumbura group who lived
in the hamlet of Wekumbura, and he lived in a separate hut near the
main house. Sudubanda's troubles therefore were not only with his
in-laws but also with his own MBs, whom he suspected of sorcery.

Wealth and Binna

The distinctions between *binna* and *deega* are only meaningful in the
context of the social hierarchy. The distinctions turn around the
obligations of the son-in-law, and this in turn depends on the availability of sufficient land in the bride's family to call for an extra hand.
But very rich families, whose members do not labor in the fields, will
usually not be interested in *binna* husbands, unless there are no sons
in the family, for the assistance of a *binna* husband in the fields would
not be really necessary. Even so, they would recognize the *binna* and
deega categories.

At the lowest end of the hierarchy, among the ordinary inhabitants
of the village, the distinction loses all significance. In fact, it was amusing to come across many households who did not know and did not
understand the differences between *binna* and *deega*. So far as they
were concerned, there was one kind of union. If the families agreed,
and if the couple were in the correct category of kinsmen, then the boy
would simply take the girl to his highland plot. Whether they then
lived in the same household with one set of parents or the other, or
whether the couple simply built a small hut for themselves, was more
or less immaterial.

Thus, *binna* was mainly relevant for those people who had sufficient
land to welcome the extra labor of a *binna* son-in-law but who were
not wealthy enough to give out the land on *ande* or to wage laborers.

The Incidence of the Types of Marriage

These remarks are directly supported by the detailed evidence from
Terutenne. I collected much material on the locality of marriage and
the obligations of kinsmen, and it did appear that *binna* was mainly
used in the middle category of families in the village. There were some
binna marriages in rich families, but these were almost always confined

to families who had no sons at all to carry on the household and considered it useful to get one of the sons-in-law to live in with the rest of the family, or to families whose sons were very young when the daughters became marriageable.

Among the poorest sections with no property to provide the basis for structured obligations between the in-laws it was largely a matter of indifference exactly where the young couple chose to live. Of course the availability of some garden land for the husband or wife would sway the choice regarding the building of a separate hut or the construction of an additional room to an already existing structure, but there was no clear sentiment favoring one pattern over another. There were a large number of "matrilocal" unions among these people, but properly speaking they should not be referred to as *binna* at all.

I made a survey of the marriages of 316 men and women in Terutenne to determine the patterns with some precision: this covers 77 percent of the total high-caste adult population (410 persons) of Terutenne (see table 26). In tables 27 and 28 I distinguish between natives

TABLE 26

*Adult High-Caste Population of Terutenne, by Origin**
(*Sample Used in Tables 27–29*)

	Men	Women	Totals
Natives.....	130	87	217
Settlers.....	28	71	99
Total...	158	158	316

* Based on a survey of 77 percent of the total high-caste population of 419 persons.

of the village and those settling by marriage. Among the latter, the men invariably settle in *binna* and the women invariably in *deega*. A second division has been made into three categories of wealth. For these purposes, I have used the figures indicated in table 3 in chapter 4: *A* includes those persons who have more than seven *pale* of land; *B* those who have more than two *pale* but less than seven; and *C* those who have less than two *pale,* or no land at all. These figures may be misleading to some extent. Certain shopkeepers who are exceedingly wealthy do not have much land. There are also difficulties in placing sons who will be rich but who actually have no property and daughters who may not have received their dowries. However, since in these cases the final decision of marriage is made by their parents, I have placed the offspring in their parents' categories.

The figures demonstrate what has already been said. There is clearly a greater incidence of matrilocality as one descends the wealth hierarchy. It is useful for group *B* because of the extra labor, but in group *C,* as previously noted, matrilocality is frequent not because it is particularly desirable but because it is largely a matter of indifference where married couples decide to settle. Hence the following remarks may be made:

TABLE 27

Natives of Terutenne: Locality of Marriage and Origin of Spouses*

A. *Locality of Marriage*

Groups, According to Land Owned	Native Men			Native Women		
	No. of Persons	No. of Unions† *b*	*d*	No. of Persons	No. of Unions† *b*	*d*
A (own 7 *pale* or more)..	15	—	19	4	2	4
B (own 2–7 *pale*)........	20	—	27	16	12	6
C (own 2 *pale* or less)....	95	31	83	67	41	36

B. *Origin of Spouses*

Groups, According to Land Owned	Origin of Spouses of Native Men		Origin of Spouses of Native Women	
	Terutenne	Elsewhere	Terutenne	Elsewhere
A (own 7 *pale* or more)....	6	13	5	1
B (own 2–7 *pale*)..........	10	17	10	8
C (own 2 *pale* or less)......	73	41	57	19
				(1 unknown)

* For a comparison of these figures with Udamulla and Vilawa, see table 34, chap. 10.

† *b* and *d* stand for *binna* and *deega*. Neolocal unions classed as *deega* unless explicitly on wife's land.

(a) Wealthy men who are natives of Terutenne do not go on *binna*: this is true for both categories *A* and *B* (table 27). Poor men, category *C,* do settle in *binna*. It is not a high rate, but they are the only men who are natives of the village to do so. Of course, most of these are not formal *binna* marriages but simply matrilocal unions. Out of the 114 unions of 95 men in category *C,* 31 (i.e., 26.3 percent) were matrilocal unions. Note, however, that if the figures were corrected for neolocal unions which are classed with the 83 cases of *deegas*, the preferences would appear more evenly balanced.

(b) The situation is different for women. Those who are natives of the village do contract frequent *binna* marriages. Again, it is less common among the *A* group than among the *B* group. It is the latter group that is most interested in getting extra free labor and hence there are 12 cases of *binna* as opposed to 6 *deega* among them (table 27). Among native women of category *C,* the relative figures for *deega* are again higher and there is a more even balance.

TABLE 28

*Settlers in Terutenne: Locality of Marriage and Origin of Spouses**

A. Locality of Marriage

	Men Settlers			Women Settlers		
Groups, According to Land Owned	No. of Persons	No. of Unions† b	d	No. of Persons	No. of Unions† b	d
A (own 7 *pale* or less)....	I	I	—	13	—	13
B (own 2–7 *pale*)........	8	8	—	17	—	17
C (own 2 *pale* or less)....	19	19	—	41	—	41

B. Origin of Spouses

	Origin of Spouses of Men Settlers		Origin of Spouses of Women Settlers	
Groups, According to Land Owned	Terutenne	Elsewhere	Terutenne	Elsewhere
A (own 7 *pale* or less)......	I	—	13	—
B (own 2–7 *pale*)..........	8	—	17	—
C (own 2 *pale* or less)......	19	—	41	—

* For a comparison of these figures with Udamulla and Vilawa, see table 34, chap. 10.
† b and d stand for *binna* and *deega.*

(c) The incongruity between the figures for men and women is to be noted. It arises from the fact that whereas most native men of Terutenne remain in the village upon marriage, about half of all married women are given out to other villages (see chap. 4). Therefore, *binna* figures are high only among women who have remained in their own villages: those who have left, it may be assumed, almost always go in *deega* (see, e.g., table 28).

(d) The state of affairs among men and women who have come into Terutenne is shown in table 28. Note that there are many more women than men and that all the women have settled in *deega* with their husbands and all the men in *binna* with their wives. Moreover, all the new arrivals have married persons of the village. It is important for them to establish local kinship relations as soon as possible.

(*e*) One further point should be made. There is a marked difference in the places of origin of the wives of Terutenne men. Among the wealthy, *A*, most men marry women from outside villages. Men of *B* do the same. Among group *C*, however, most of the men appear to take women from the village. The reason is simple. Rich families have to look further afield to find suitable spouses for the men. Among *C* families, although there is undoubtedly great prestige attached to unions with women who are not of the village, it is well realized that in-laws are most useful and helpful only when they are close at hand.

We may thus generalize to say that whereas the marriage pattern for wealthy families is mainly patrilocal, among the poorest sections of the village it is frequently matrilocal. Such differences in behavior among persons of the same caste, in the same relatively homogeneous small community, are of considerable theoretical interest. It will be seen that although these variations are not clearly formulated into two distinct formal structures, the differences affect inheritance practices and Kandyan concepts of descent. Indeed, they appear to be closely related to the concepts regarding position of women in the family. The fundamental conceptions are similar for all Kandyans, but the steep gradation of wealth permits contrasting patterns of behavior and divergent concepts of right and wrong to emerge at the two ends of the hierarchy.

INHERITANCE

Testaments and the Rules of Inheritance

A disconcerting fact about field work in the Dry Zone was that there were no categorical rules of inheritance. People gave contradictory accounts of how property descended from generation to generation. One feature was certain, however; testation was permitted. A person who owned property could sell it or grant it as he pleased. This is not a recent development, but was so even in the early part of the nineteenth century. D'Oyly, our main authority on the Kandyan kingdom, writes as follows: "It is stated unanimously by the Chiefs who have been consulted that a person having the absolute possession of real or personal property, has the power to dispose of that property unlimitedly—that is to say—he or she may dispose it, either by Gift, or Bequest, away from the Heirs at law" (D'Oyly, 1929, p. 109; but cf. comments on p. 107 by Tolfrey).

Among anthropologists there is a tendency to assume that rules of inheritance are always clear, imperative, and immutable. The rules tend to be thought of as the backbone of the kinship system—and, of course, in societies that have property-holding corporate kinship groups, free testation would soon break down corporate unity. As Sir Henry Maine observes (1950, p. 42), "the power of free testamentary disposition implies the greatest latitude ever given in the history of the world to the volition or caprice of the individual." Whereas in most societies studies by anthropologists inheritance rules may be treated as constant factors to which the other features of the kinship system may be related, among the Kandyans, who have great latitude in testation, this is not feasible. The rules are changeable and such patterns of inheritance as do emerge demand explanations themselves. In this section these patterns are described and related to what has already been said in connection with marriage.

The most important fact about inheritance, which applied also to our discussion of *binna* and *deega*, is that rich and poor families do not act in the same way. This was particularly evident in Terutenne, where very rich families lived in close contiguity with the large sections of poor laborers. The most important difference between them concerned the position of women, with regard both to their inheritances and to the freedom of choice they were allowed. Both rich and poor allowed sons to inherit. The rich, however, actively controlled the property rights of the daughters and used this as a tool in the arrangement of marriages. In contrast, laborers did not control the property rights of the daughters and all siblings shared alike. There was no emphasis on unilineal descent among them.

The Inheritances of the Sons

Unless sons have been specifically excluded by testament—a rare occurrence—they inherit the property of their parents; this is true among all sections of Kandyans. The normal procedure is to share the estate *per capita* and not *per stirpes*: that is, all the sons recognized by the father and accepted by his close kinsmen—whoever their mothers may be—share and share alike. The same is true in succession to the property of the mother, the number of "fathers" being disregarded.

The Inheritances of Binna and Deega Daughters

The differences between the wealthy and the poor turn on the attitudes toward women, and this is expressed in the daughters' rights in the inheritance.

In principle, all daughters share alike with their brothers in the estates of the father and the mother. In this sense the basic pattern for both rich and poor is bilateral. But for wealthy families this statement is true only of unmarried daughters, for the marriages modify their claims: the *deega*-married daughter loses her rights, whereas the *binna*-married daughter does inherit. This pattern appears to have a long history behind it (D'Oyly, 1929, *passim*). It is also, in general, the present legal position.[2]

The Kandyan Law Commission writes as follows: "according to Kandyan ideas, it was the conducting of the daughter away from the father's family which, with the dowry, was the origin of her exclusion from the paternal estate" (1935, p. 23, para. 168). Much depends here on the meaning of the term "dowry." If these dowries are of sufficient size, it may mean not merely that the daughter is compensated for the loss of her inheritance, but that *most* property is given to *deega* daughters as dowries. If on the other hand, the dowry is a small amount, and if *binna* is rare, then we may assume that the property descends predominantly in the male line.

I deal with dowry in the next chapter. Here we only need mention that there can be no simple generalization about the size of the dowry. It depends entirely on the status of the son-in-law. For our purposes the important point is that in wealthy families the size of the dowry is controlled by the father, or the brothers, and that, in terms of succession, the sons are thought to be the principal heirs of the intestate property.

In these circles, accordingly, a distinct preference for patrilineal ideals is strongly expressed. It will be said that sons remain *in* the family but that daughters go "out," to "other people"; the family seat, the house (*mul gedara*), must always be given to the sons; names descend only in the male line. These preferences among families which are aristocratic as well as wealthy go so far as to exclude the daughters from the property of the father altogether. It is sometimes said that ideally all the property of the father would go only to his sons and that the daughters would take as dowries only the property that their mother brought in as her own dowry. This sex-differentiated double unilineal pattern is claimed to have been the traditional form among the highest section of the Goyigama—the Radala feudal lords—during the Kandyan kingdom. It is reported to be practiced among Tamils today. However, I came across only two or three instances in Terutenne where this tradition had actually been put into practice.

Such emphasis on patrilineal inheritance, in a situation where much property is given to daughters in the form of dowry, is something of a paradox. It is only partly the result of the fact that the unmarried women are, as it were, "owned" by the groups of men, that it is men

---

[2] A distinction is now made in succession to maternal property.

who control the fate of daughters or sisters for their own purposes, and men who decide the size of the dowry. As we shall see, it is also inextricably related to the ideas of caste and family prestige and purity.

The Position of the Daughter among Laborers

The lower orders in Terutenne treat their daughters with much less care and attention than do the higher orders. The rich try to arrange suitable marriages for their daughters, but the poor, lacking property, are unable to engage extensively in such social maneuvers. Often, the marriages of their daughters are left to the girls themselves and make no difference to their inheritance claims. Moreover, since the distinctions between *binna-deega* are lost, all daughters share the same position in inheritance. Briefly, the system of inheritance is that, upon the death of a person, all his children inherit his property and (whether sons or daughters) share and share alike. There is no pretense about property descending in the male or female line. The claims upon inheritance are known as *urumaya;* and there is full agreement that all the children of a person have *urumaya* upon his property.[3]

Perhaps the most important feature of this system is that generally inheritance is *per capita,* not *per stirpes:*[4] all the children of a man, irrespective of their maternity, share the inheritance among them, and all the children of a woman share her property irrespective of their paternity.

The Concept of Marriage and Inheritance

Such a system of inheritance bears upon the very concept of "marriage." Given the fact that the property of man and wife are distinct from each other and not merged, and that they have separate sets of heirs, and granted that inheritance is *per capita* and not *per stirpes,*

---

[3] *Urumaya* is an interesting word. I translate it here as "inheritance claims." It is also used to describe the right of the male cross-cousin to demand the hand of his female cross-cousin. These two can "joke" (*sellam karanava*), owing to his *urumaya.* The clothing of the mother's brother belongs to his sister's son: the latter has *urumaya.* In an extended sense, the word is also used to imply "real," "rightful": *ure massina* (real cross-cousin), *ure mama* (real MB, F-in-L), etc.

[4] But Kandyans themselves are not very clear on the matter. There is general agreement that it should be *per capita* especially when the mother and her children are concerned. In the case of the father, I have come across disputes. Not only were there differences of opinion among the chiefs D'Oyly consulted (D'Oyly, 1929, p. 112), but the Kandyan Law Commission was also faced with the difficulty of making a decision on the issue (*R.K.L.C.*, 1935, p. 25, ¶s 189–196). The commission recommended, however, that it should be *per capita* (p. 25, ¶ 192, for paternal property, and for maternal property, ¶ 294).

certain conclusions follow logically. Most importantly, it means that
the conception of marriage as a powerful, almost indissoluble bond
between man and wife, in which their separate properties are united
and which clearly defines the heirs to the property as the joint heirs
of the couple (to the exclusion of "illegitimate" children, for example),
has no place in the Kandyan way of thinking. The property of the
parents is not earmarked solely for the offspring of the "common
bed"; it may go in other directions. Thus the exact relationship between the man and the woman is also of no importance; it matters
not at all whether she was concubine or "wife," whether he was only
her lover or really a "husband." The property remains distinct and
the inheritance goes to all the children equally. As we shall see in the
next chapter, this is one of the reasons why it is possible for the ordinary people to dispense with the marriage ceremony altogether.

Of course, though succession to the mother's goods is relatively un-
complicated, succession to the father's—particularly in cases where
there has been no marriage ceremony—can present obvious complications. The problem was certainly recognized in Terutenne. There can
hardly be any mistake about the mother, but a child may not be so
certain who his father is and can only hope that he will make himself
known. Furthermore, the man always has a right to use his powers of
testation. If he denies liability, there is nothing further to be done.
Such matters are often raised only after the death of the "father" concerned. It is only then that shadowy claims will be advanced. In that
case the dispute, if not amicably settled, may be taken to the Rural
Courts and may give rise to lasting bitterness.

Inheritance Disputes

The patterns of inheritance described above are certainly complex.
In cases where there is no clear evidence of the exercise of testation in
writing, with witnesses, there can be much disagreement and litigation.

One of the most usual sources of contention rises from the fact that
although the "shares" of each child are separate in principle, the
property may actually remain formally undivided among the siblings
for many years after the death of the parent. Indeed, if the siblings
are on good terms, the property may remain undivided until after
their death. During all this time both men and women with *urumaya*
move in and out of the village on marriage. The land—especially
paddy land—is generally cultivated by those shareholders who are on
the spot, though they may, at times, send the shares of the others in
kind or in cash to their villages. Still, the temptation for those actually

enjoying the fruits of the land to hang on to the portions they have been cultivating and to deny, if possible, the claims of those living far away is very considerable. This is particularly the case with the claims of women who have been given out of the village.

When women have lived away for a long while, their *urumaya* (in principle) will not be denied, but it may be said that they can only "eat" (*kanava*) from the land if they returned to reside in their natal homes (the statistics on women sent out of the village therefore gain an entirely new dimension).[5] The women, too, will frequently say that the brothers are "living off" (*butti vindinava*) the land, but that they have their *urumaya* which they are not pressing. The might say that they are satisfied with what they have and would not wish to disturb their other siblings in what little they may hold. In the case of women, of course, it must be kept in mind that while unmarried they are under the authority of their parents or their brothers and do not often rise against them later. It is proper for a woman to accept the arrangements made for her by her brothers. Moreover, the question of her lands intimately involves the relations between her husband and brother as in-laws, as well as the relations of her children with her brothers. If the women do not always aggressively pursue their claims against their brothers, especially when the property is small, this must be seen in the total context of family relationships and especially in the formal claims (*urumaya*) between MB-ZS.

In many cases, it is the brothers (especially stepbrothers) who start the disputes. If the children are young at the death of their father and if their mother takes them along when she goes to her next husband, it often happens that the brothers of the deceased take over all the lands. They may then attempt to resist the claims of the children when they grow old enough to realize the circumstances for themselves. Frequently they find the lands sold (a clever precaution since otherwise the brothers might have to restore the portions they have usurped), the money gone, and the only chance for justice a long and fierce, and perhaps unsuccessful, battle in the courts with all its consequent bribery and expense. These difficulties, of course, are not merely those of the laborers, but are a marked feature of family relations among all classes in all Kandyan villages I have known.[6]

---

[5] Cf. table 5, chap. 4.

[6] The high fragmentation of land that bilateral *inheritance* implies must undoubtedly have been noted. But when the fragmentation reaches a certain stage it is no longer worthwhile for men and women away from the village to go to the trouble of pressing their claims and antagonizing their kin. The portions involved are too small. At that stage fragmentation slows down very noticeably. Cf. Tambiah and Sarkar (1957, pp. 61–62), who first noted the discrepancy between actual and theoretical fragmentation.

Changes Up and Down the Social Scale

With two such patterns of inheritance operating at the same time in the same village, one inevitably asks where, then, does the dividing line fall between those who follow different patterns? The question is a difficult one, for there is, in fact, no clear dividing line. The two patterns are not systematically formulated ideologies, but rather *ex post facto* explanations by the people to justify and clarify their decisions and behavior.

It is clear that the main differences in the patterns rest in the position and the rights of the daughters. The reasons for these differences have been directly related to differences in wealth. The poor have too little to make dowry settlements possible (they can get the girl married without it) and they do not need *binna* labor. Hence the inheritance pattern is bilateral. Among the rich, this pattern, though basically the same, is modified; and because the hierarchy of wealth is blurred and continuous, the inheritance practices are also indistinct and overlapping. In the middle range, for example, girls may be given in *deega* without any dowry and with no definite agreements about their inheritances, but *binna* husbands may be encouraged. In other words, we are dealing with a continuum and not with two separate communities having special customs. Finally, I should emphasize that the question of the rights of the daughter—whether dowry will be paid, when and to whom, whether her rights in the paternal estate will be defined by legal means, and when she may actually press her claims—form precisely the central problem to be clarified during the negotiations in an arranged marriage. We will return to this in the next chapter.

As a summary, the following points may be made:

(1) Sons and unmarried daughters inherit among all classes.
(2) Among the wealthy, the marriages of daughters modify their claims. They do not inherit, but may receive dowries. Fathers and brothers control the property that is given to women and the concept of descent is patrilineal.
(3) Among the poor, marriages have no effect on inheritance, or on the claims of daughters. Whether they actually do receive their inheritances or not depends on whether they press their claims. Such conception of descent as there is, is bilateral.

THEORIES OF DESCENT AND CASTE STATUS

The Dogmas of Conception

I have been writing of "concepts of descent" in a general, simplified way. And yet we are aware that the Kandyan Sinhalese conception of descent, far from being a simple matter, involves numerous intricate distinctions. Kandyan parents convey to their children not merely property but also certain definite social attributes like "membership" in a kinship group, caste, and status (*wamsa*) within the caste. Some of these, at least, are regarded by the Kandyans to be firmly connected to such matters as "blood." It is therefore of particular interest to consider Kandyan dogmas concerning "biological descent." It will be noted again that these reflect the hierarchical scale described earlier.

The following concepts are relevant and intimately associated: (*a*) blood (*le*); (*b*) milk (*kiri*); and (*c*) semen (*kere*). Blood is considered to be extremely polluting[7] and in the same class as other bodily excretions such as spittle (*kele*), feces (*gu*), and urine (*mu*). Semen is very dirty but very "powerful" (*sarai*), for reasons that will be seen, and milk is held to be at the opposite extreme: it is very pure and auspicious and must be respected.

Some of these ritual elements appear to emanate from a common source. Thus, semen is only a distilled form of blood. During sexual intercourse, the blood at the testicles becomes heated and turns into semen. According to Kandyan theory, semen is very concentrated, eighty drops of blood producing only one drop of semen; it is therefore the very essence of the body, of energy and life, and must on no account be wasted.[8] Among the Sinhalese, as on the subcontinent of India, there is a widespread notion that sexual abstinence brings about supernatural power and strength.

The semen of the man goes into the stomach (*bada*) of the woman. The woman also has semen; but the man's semen is much faster and contains eggs (*bittara*) or seeds (*atta*). They mix and form a small ball which begins to grow. Some of the food it needs it gets from the mother, and some from the father, whose semen in subsequent intercourse becomes food (*ahara*) for the fetus. It will be noted that here is a good justification for polyandry; and multiplicity of fathers

---

[7] Menstrual blood is only much more so.

[8] Another term for semen is *dhatu*. It is significant that *dhatu* also refers to seed in general, and to the relics of Buddha, i.e., the remains that were left behind after his cremation. These relics are the most sacred objects recognized in Buddhism and are held to be very powerful. They are often claimed to be entombed in the famous *dagobas* in Ceylon and India. Some of the well-known *dhatu* are associated with bodily dirt—a "tooth" (*dalada*) in the Temple of the Tooth in Kandy, the "hair" (*khesa dhatu*) in Mayengene, and the "nails" (*nyepata dhatu*), the "frontal bone" (*lalata dhatu*), the "jawbone" (*hakku dhatu*), all in other temples or *dagobas* on the island. The word *dagoba* is a shortened form of *dhatu garbhaya*, which means "*dhatu* in the womb"; thus *dagoba*, or sacred tomb, also carries a distinct association with fertility.

It should also be noted that "caste-blood" and "purity" (or "pollution") are transferred through semen. It is therefore very important that, as in India, the repudiation of sexual intercourse, the celibate existence, is thought to enhance a person's ritual condition. Cf. Stevenson (1954); also see Carstairs (1956) for a psychological analysis of this attitude regarding the loss of semen.

is not merely a fiction, but could in their conception be considered a biological fact. There is, however, no agreement on this point.

A pregnant woman (*gabini*) is in a special position. She is said to be in great danger and as the time for delivery approaches elaborate food taboos multiply rapidly. Her movements into *devale* and polluted houses (*kili gedara*) are restricted.[9] At the same time she is held to be extremely auspicious and is looked upon almost as the very embodiment of fertility (*sampata*; fecund, *sarui*), a concept with which there is great preoccupation.[10]

If the parents of the woman are alive, she is expected by custom to bear the first few children in their home. Accordingly, a few weeks before the child is due, the young couple—or at least the wife—moves to the home of her parents. This return to the home of the woman is, of course, highly significant in terms of the formal claims of the maternal side on the offspring.

Blood does not turn only into semen; it also turns into milk. The principle is the same: the blood arrives at the breast, where it is heated and becomes milk. Again, it is a reflection of these associations with blood—and other bodily excretions—that milk plays a primary role in much of the ritual symbolism of the Kandyans.[11]

Contradictions in Ideas of Descent

So far, milk and semen appear to be two forms of "blood" and there is no undue insistence on the unilateral descent of the child from either parent. But in fact the inhabitants of Terutenne do make certain claims to this effect. In the upper groups, wealthy persons with aristocratic pretentions always emphasize patrilineal descent. This emphasis tends to agree with their *deega* marriage and inheritance practices. But while the attempt is undoubtedly made, there are still unresolved contradictions in their own ideas. The aristocrats will say that children receive their "blood" mainly from their fathers. Moreover, they will claim that all patrilineally related persons form a special category of "blood relatives" (*le nedeyo*). Some argue that all sexual restrictions on the paternal side (cf. chap. 8) are to be traced to

[9] *Kili gedara* is a house in which a birth, menstruation, or death has occurred. *Kili* (*kilutu, killa*) is the common denominator of Sinhalese pollution ideas. It is directly connected to bodily dirt. Low castes may be referred to as being *kilutu*. The opposite of *kilutu* is *pirisithu*: all sacred objects, Buddhist priests, and *devale* would fall into this category. See Yalman (1964) for a discussion of healing rituals.

[10] Much of the village ritual is directed toward the elimination of *leda* (illness) and *duka* (pain, sorrow), both of which are seen as the negation of fertility and auspiciousness. In many festivals, the sexual implications are almost overt.

[11] The sacred bo tree is one of a category of *kiri gaha* (milk-exuding trees); coconut milk (*pol kiri*) is often used in the preparation of special food offerings to deities and the Buddha. The boiling of milk for a deity is an auspicious act. Polluted persons may be bathed with milk to attain purity.

this fact. Sexual intercourse must not take place between patrilineally related persons because "blood would get mixed" (*le kavalam venava*). There are, however, identical sexual taboos between matrilineally related persons, and on one occasion, when I was discussing the question in public, an ordinary villager pointed out that what the aristocrats had said was nonsense; if blood could get mixed and if it only descended in the male line, then there would be no need to obey the taboos on the maternal side. The aristocrats who were present were obviously confused. One of them tried to associate the matrilineal taboo with "milk." Blood goes from the father to his children, but children also get "blood" from the mother—"does she not suckle them? And is not milk the same as her blood?" Hence the restrictions on the maternal side.[12]

I was interested to discover whether there was any agreement on this point—if the blood of the mother goes to her children, is her milk the "same" as that of her daughters? Is a "matriline" of this kind distinguished on the same pattern as the traditional preferences for inheritance? There was no agreement. Finally someone said that it did not matter if "blood got mixed"; the blood of all the Goyigama was the same anyway, and so was milk. It was all the same—the milk of women, of cows, of coconuts, of rice, of milk sap trees!

Indeed, although the people who think of their ancestry as aristocratic go out of their way to maintain patrilineal "dogmas," and although these dogmas support their inheritance practices as well as their opinions regarding names, titles, and other honorifics, they themselves have antithetical theories to justify the dogmas. Even these theories are far from general: it is possible to talk to people of similar high standing who consider the notions of *le nedeyo* and "mixing of blood" to be laughable and advance the theory that "it is only by mixing the blood that kinship is created." Moreover, all kinsmen will also be regarded as *eka le* (one blood), and far from implying incest, those of "one blood" will be said to have "marriage claims" on each other. A male cross-cousin has *le urumaya* (blood claim) on his female cross-cousins. Therefore he has *ahanta balaya* (the "strength to demand") this woman in marriage.

Why are there such contradictions in the ideology of the wealthy? Why do they seem to want descent to be patrilineal among them? To answer these questions we must first discuss the connection between descent and status.

---

[12] The Todas appear to have such an ideology. Emeneau writes in "Toda Marriage" (1937, p. 106), " 'poljol' (matriline) means 'man . . . of the polj.' The most usual meaning of polj is 'sacred dairy,' a meaning which will not explain our word"! It is notable also that the usual term for *lineage* in ·India is *gotraya*, which apparently carries the etymological meaning of "cattle pen." It would appear that the superiority of ancestry is associated with the purity of the cow and the milk.

Blood, Status, and Ancestry

Among the Sinhalese the ideology of descent can never be discussed in isolation from the concept of ritual rank or some kind of birth-status. It is this question alone that gives Kandyans any interest in the subject of descent. The concept of rank is essentially a caste idea, and, much as in Western countries, rank is something that is conveyed to the individual at birth, by virtue of his blood. Indeed, there is such a close association between the concepts of birth and caste that one term means both. *Jati*, the ordinary word for caste in Sinhalese, actually has the three associated meanings of (1) birth, (2) descent, race, rank genealogy, and (3) "a sort of, a kind of." [13]

Blood can be "good" (*honda*) or "bad" (*naraka*). The Goyigama caste has *honda le* (good blood) and the low castes have bad blood. (Westerners speak of qualities of birth and blood in exactly the same way: e.g., high and low birth, "blue" blood.) And since, in Ceylon, castes actually exist side by side as separate communities in the villages, the notions of what determines caste and rank are clearly formulated and tenaciously upheld.

In the context of caste, all Kandyan Sinhalese would not hesitate to say that a child receives "caste-blood" from *both* parents. If one parent is of a lower caste, then, in principle, the child's blood is "polluted" and he cannot become a member of the higher caste. In this sense, the descent of ritual caste status is bilateral. This point has interesting implications regarding caste endogamy. However, though the blood of each caste is distinct, there can be *wamsa* or gradations of blood within the castes: the Goyigama and the Tom-Tom Beaters, for example, believe that in some persons within the caste blood is "purer" (*pirisithu*) or more "polluted" (*apirisithu*) than in others. It is in this secondary respect that the aristocrats can claim the "patrilineal" inheritance of blood. I would therefore make a distinction between caste-descent that is bilateral (at least in Ceylon), and descent in terms of grades within the caste, which may be unilineal.

It is clear that bilateral groups in which marriage is not restricted cannot have clearly defined "boundaries." Alternatively, if status-bearing groups with clear "boundaries" are to be produced in the context of bilateral descent, then such groups must be endogamous. Therefore those groups in which ritual status is conveyed equally by the mother and the father must be structurally identical to castes. To put it in a different way, "castes" are one solution to the problem of ensuring the perpetuation of rank gradations in a social system.

---

[13] Rhys-Davids and Stede, *Pali-English Dictionary* (1925), p. 114.

Another way of perpetuating the recognition of rank gradations in a clear fashion is by unilineal descent of some kind. In this case the groups need not be endogamous, for unilineal descent provides sufficient differentiation between groups. Going back to the Terutenne context, it is clear, first, that the descent of caste status is bilateral, and the castes are endogamous. In the larger castes, however, it becomes necessary to differentiate the various ranks *within* the caste, and here unilineal pedigrees become obviously useful as a way of determining further rank gradations. In mixed communities there is always great interest in pedigrees. Wherever there are suggestions of rank gradation, whether in Colombo (where the Dutch burgers especially keep up very elaborate pedigrees connecting themselves with Holland) or in New England, unilineal pedigrees are one universal method of laying claim to some distinction in a mixed environment.

Let us also observe that the question of social rank is intimately associated with the role of women—the valued commodity—in the system. The symmetrical exchange of women which is implied by the endogamous caste system is an index of the equality of the two parties. At the same time, all rank distinctions in social systems appear to involve an assymmetrical exchange of women. Hence such unions *across* caste boundaries are always hypergamous and some unilineal systems utilize hypogamy for the perpetuation of status distinctions.

In either case, according to Sinhalese dogma, one carries the essence of ritual status, purity, or pollution in one's blood, and since "consanguinity" is necessarily a matter of "blood," these concepts of ritual status become a part of every aspect of kinship. Most statements of family solidarity ("we are *one* family") are expressed in terms of *eka le* ("one blood"), which carries the unmistakable implication that this blood is in some fundamental respect quite different from the "blood" of those from whom one wishes to disassociate oneself and one's kinsmen. All social distance between bodies of kinsmen is expressed in terms of ritual status ("We are good, they are bad people"), and kinship solidarity always implies an "identity" of ritual status.

We may now understand the inevitable confusions among people who claim high aristocratic rank. By arguing that blood descends in the male line, and by demonstrating their own unique descent from an illustrious ancestor (usually a feudal lord of the Kandyan kingdom), their distinction and superiority with regard to ordinary people can be maintained. Moreover, their practices agree with their opinions; women are given "out," the inheritance goes predominantly in the male line, and those who pride themselves on their superiority remain essentially a group of closely related males. Caste status, on the other hand, is obviously acquired through both parents, and kinship links

through females are still of primary importance. In-laws, on both
sides, are still close kinsmen—hence the statement that all the "kindred" is "really" of one blood.

Names

As one might expect, the concern with the "purity" and "goodness"
of blood takes the form of an exaggerated interest in pedigrees, hereditary names, and titles whereby one line may be distinguished from
another.[14] In Terutenne there are certain names that are generally
regarded as highly aristocratic, all derived from the names and titles
of the feudal aristocracy of the village in Kandyan times. Anyone who
has become wealthy attempts to appropriate one of these names.
Aristocratic names, following the upper-class belief in blood descending predominantly in the male line, are patrilineal. Within the lower
groups such patronymies do not exist, and it is felt justifiable to assume any name to which a connection may be traced by paternal or
maternal links. Apart from personal names there are two categories
of names in use in Terutenne. There are *vasagama* names and *gedara*
names. A good name would run thus: *Navaratna Mudianselage/Amu-
numulle Gedara/Gunaratne*. The first part is the *vasagama* (or *mudianse*, "noble," name), the second the *gedara* name, and the last the
personal name.

The *vasagama* (lit. "dwelling village"), which only members of the
Goyigama caste have, has no kinship significance. The same names are
to be found among unrelated people, either within the same village
or in different villages. In the past, when names could not be changed,
they marked the superiority of some sections of the Goyigama, certain
landless Goyigama not being entitled to bear *vasagama*[15] (see chap. 5).
Today, however, old and distinguished names are taken over by those
who can conveniently do so, and the issue has become very complex.

Gedara ("house") names are slightly more significant than *vasagama*
names. *Gedara*, the ordinary term for "house," suggests a kinship
group. It is true that in Terutenne kinship relations can often be
recalled between persons with the same *gedara* name, but in some cases

[14] The many words in the Sinhalese vocabulary that mean "ancestry" themselves
suggest the preocccupation with this subject. *Parampara, pelapata, pelentiya, jamme,
gotraya, wamsa* are all used, and all have the meaning of descent and rank. *Jati* is
also used, but it usually means just caste. *Vasagama* (lit. "dwelling village"—a
reference to feudal origin) also means descent and rank but usually refers specifically to titles and honorifics bestowed by the Kandyan kings (see Raghavan, 1961,
p. 103).

[15] For the usual explanation see von Eickstedt (1927), p. 372. The author dis-
cusses the Bibile family, which I came to know very well while I was in Wellassa.
The Bibiles were once the feudal lords of Wellassa, and the organization of the
Bibile *Valawa* (manor) still follows the traditional pattern.

such relationships cannot be recalled, and in others they do not exist. It is these names which indicate rank most directly inside Terutenne, and again some people have merely usurped them. In those cases where the names have actually been transmitted patrilineally, and where connections are recalled, the relationship chart may look like a patrilineal genealogy, but it certainly does not indicate corporate solidarity or a common estate. The people with the same name do not necessarily have anything else in common and may not even realize that they are related in some way.

The lower groups have a kind of *gedara* name, but their names are *not* hereditary, merely names of the locality where they happen to live. These names are usually referred to as "settlement house" (*padinchi gedara*) names, a designation which appears identical to the original meaning of *vasagama* as "dwelling village."

An example will show what I mean. While living in Galpitiya I had as neighbors two complex households, Mahapitiya and Elapita Gedara, which were closely related (fig. 10). All persons living in

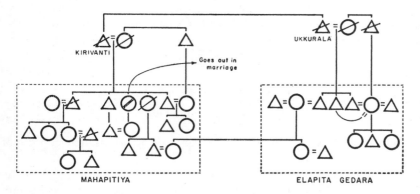

Figure 10. Mahapitiya and Elapita Gedara households, Galpitiya.

Mahapitiya compound were known as Mahapitiya somebody or other; whether they had come to reside there through maternal or paternal connections was wholly immaterial. The same was true of Elapita Gedara. But the ancestors of the two houses, Kirivanti and Ukkurala, had also been known, it seems, as Wela Gedara, and at times all the numerous inhabitants of both these dwellings were referred to by that name.

Whereas among the lower orders the *gedara* name refers to an actual household or to the children of that household, it becomes immediately obvious that the aristocratic names refer to much larger numbers of people. Furthermore, with most of them there is also the claim that they are hereditary (*parampara*) in the male line. Consider, for instance, the widest extension of the Amunumulle mentioned above.

They claimed to be the most ancient lordly house in the village, the descendants of the *Mohottala* (Lords) of Walapane. There had, indeed, been *Mohottala* in Walapane,[16] and working through the earliest Grain Tithe Registers, I came across frequent mentions of Amunumulle Mohottala. Their lands certainly appear to have been of great extent in the nineteenth century. The registers of 1857–1861 give the total extent of the lands of persons with the Amunumulle name as 32 *pale* and 4 *kuruni* in the various fields of the village, and the house appears to have been among the three or four richest in the village, most befitting a family bearing the name of the powerful *Mohottalas* of the Kandyan kingdom. In 1955 only the branches I and II had any common property among them (fig. 11). These did not cooperate,

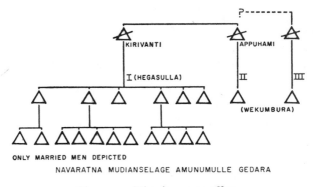

ONLY MARRIED MEN DEPICTED
NAVARATNA MUDIANSELAGE AMUNUMULLE GEDARA

Figure 11. The Amunumulles.

though their links could still be traced; the third branch could not even trace relationships to the other two.

Here, then, is a typical aristocratic *gedara*. All persons related in the male line could use the superb title, Navaratna Mudianselage Amunumulle Gedara. The "rules" were at times rather clearly formulated: Amunumulle women, it was said, kept their *gedara* name, but their children had to take their names from their fathers. Of course, the fact that none of the offspring or the spouses of the Amunumulle women had usurped the title was simply a matter of chance, since the Amunumulle would have been powerless to take common action against the culprit, and in any event would probably not have been particularly indignant.

There were other similar *gedara* in Terutenne. The Field Corner House (fig. 12) was of even larger span. Their title (Senanayika Seneviratne Herat Mudianselage Welakonawatte Gedara) had also been kept in the male line. This house, which had almost as many landholdings as the Amunumulle in the nineteenth-century Grain Tithe

---

[16] D'Oyly (1929, p. 71) refers to them as "Dessavony Mohottale."

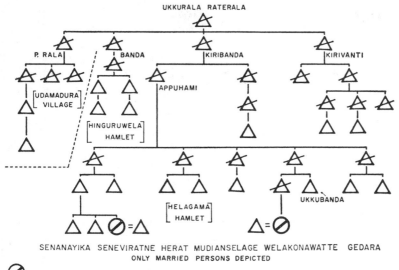

Figure 12. Field Corner House.

Registers,[17] had no common property whatever in 1955, all property having long since been divided among the various branches.

Changing of Gedara Names

Although these pedigrees appear strictly agnatic, there is no necessary unity among the people who call themselves by the same *gedara* name. Of course, actual siblings will tend to cooperate, but by the time one reaches first cousins, let alone second, most people are hardly aware that they have common ancestry at all. Indeed, if one were to ask for a genealogical chart of the people whom an individual considers his closest and most important kinsmen, agnatic, cognatic, and affinal lines would be hopelessly mixed. It is only by consulting old men and by eliminating collateral relations who are always mentioned that neat-looking "lineal" relationship charts can be designed by the anthropologist. The patronymics, then, are kept up mainly for purposes of social distinction even in an isolated village like Terutenne. And it was for this very reason that there was a considerable amount of name changing in the community: anyone who became wealthy tried to acquire a "good name" in order to pretend to aristocratic status.

There were elaborate myths attached to names. Some related to the *vasagama* and others to the *gedara* names. While working in Wekumbura I came across the notebook of a bright girl in the Terutenne

---

[17] The Welakonawatte appear to have 31 *pale* in 1857–1861.

school. In it was an essay on the ancestry of some of the groups in the village; it is worth reproducing here in full:

MYTHS FROM THE NOTEBOOK OF A STUDENT IN TERUTENNE
(translated by P.J.C.)

Parampara's (i.e. Honorable Families) of Terutenne

From this village the people who are belonged to Nissanka parapura, to Weeravairodi parapura, to Ramanayaka Jayasekara pelapata, to Disanayaka pelapata, and to Konara pelapata are the only people who have good paramparas from the time of Sinhalese kings. Out of this paramparas Nissanka parapara is the only one which had not being mixed with the others.

As it can be taken as the first paramparawa, it will be described at first.

In ancient times the chief of the Nissanka's who lived in Anuwradhapura went away from the town to a cave called Nissainkalena near Sripada [Adam's Peak]. He had twelve kinds of servants. In these days King Senanath was living at Maligathuna. He heard about Nissanka and went to see him. Near the Nissanka's house there was a temple and as this man [Nissanka] was not a good Buddhist he played musical instruments in the afternoon and in the mornings. So the King asked him to not to do it and they became very good friends. This king gave Nissanka a golden sword, sannasa [copper title deed], with lots of lands and a ribbon for the forehead. This had a jewel in olden days. But afterwards they loose everything and one Nissanka has given away the golden sword to the God Keerthibanadara at Ekkassa Devalaya. During the riots in 1818, one has hidden the sannasa in the forest and was lost.

When Senanath was returning from Maligatena [sic.] as there was a riot, he has asked Nissanka to protect his queen who was about to give a birth to a child. So Nissanka built a house and a wattarama and protected the queen. So the King sent messenger to Nissanka to bring his wife to Mayyangana [famous ritual center], so Nissanka went to Maiyangana with astrologers and the Queen. And there was a stone plate at Wendarawa which was on the way that they walked. In that time there was a rule to not to use that plate for sitting except for the people who are belong to royal Families. When Nissanka and the Queen sat on this plate people not knowing this [i.e., their royal status] came to kill, but when they showed the letter sent by the King, they respected them and gave food and lodging. On their way to Maiyangana the Queen gave a birth to a child under a great cave. From that day the village was named Willogampitiya, and that prince was the Great Rajasingha II. Nissanka was a very honorable man but at the same time he was swollen headed. Even when the king was coming he don't want to worship him as it was a custom to worship the King. The descendants of Nissanka were also very honorable though they loose everything they had, and even the sannasa they got from the King. Because of their high caste they were so proud as a result they became very poor. And servants of Nissankas also has taken their name Nissanka.

Weeravairodi pelapata

The people who are belonging to Weeravairodi are known as Agalakumbura [Gedara]. First man who lived in this paramparawa, was a very high casted one "known as Radala." And it is said he helped the princes giving food and lodging, who were hiding in the caves in Rajanwella, during Sinhalese wars and it is difficult to say in which King time. And it can be proved as there are footprints on the bank of Rajawella which was the playground of these princes. And this Weeravairodi pelapata got many lands and fields from these princes which were written in copper plates (tamba Sannas) but as they loose these sannas they lost their lands and fields. And now the servants of this paramparawa also has taken the name Weeravairodi.

Dissanayaka pelapata

This paramparawa also a unmixed one which is descending from ancient times. They are known as Kubukgolle [Gedara] too. But it is very difficult to say the old works done by these pelapata.

Konara pelapata

Those who are descending from Weeravairodi pelapata too use this name accidently. But it is their mother's side parampara name. A man who was known a Kosgama Bandara, who was belong to Nawaratna Mudiyanse's, who was a Radala once, he loose his sannasa in which this name was written. Therefore they started to use Konara mudiyanselage. And it is said that the people of Amunumulle has found this sannasa and they started to use that.

Note that the practice of changing names is a well-known procedure. Servants take over the names of their masters, and others "accidentally" take over the names of their mother's lineage.

A splendid example of the acquisition of a name for prestige purposes is that of the Orange Tree people. Their largest extensions are depicted in figure 13. It was Muhandiram who first became rich and influential on a grand scale. Before him the family had been called Dodangaha or Orange Tree Gedara, Dodangaha being the name of a hamlet in Walapane in which the serfs of the ancient and aristocratic families once lived. Its lowly origins were well known. After Muhandiram became the Village Headman of Terutenne, he made vigorous attempts to change his ancestral name. He took two wives (to make the process doubly secure), *both* of whom had real claims to the elegant Nissanka Mudianselage Tunpale Gedara names and titles. Even though he was not married matrilocally, he began to use the names of his wives as his own. After Muhandiram not only his sons but all his brothers began to make use of this title: even the children of Muhandiram's father's brothers gave up Orange Tree for the name with superior prestige.

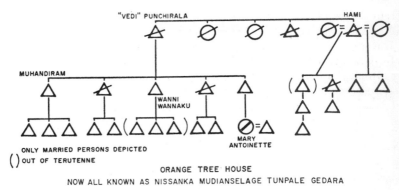

Figure 13. Orange Tree House.

In 1955, there were a great many people in Terutenne who referred to themselves as Nissanka Mudianselage Tunpale Gedara. It was beyond question that many had simply got rid of their real names and had adopted a finer one—they were certainly not descended from the same ancestors. In the profusion of lies and farfetched explanations it was difficult to disentangle the original holders of the title and their estate, but it was evident that they were very impoverished and scarcely in a position to protest the flagrant usurpation of their ancestral titles by persons much richer and more powerful than themselves. Nor were the usurpers generally thought to have done anything wrong. During the Kandyan kingdom, any attempt to change names and titles would have been punishable offenses, for they, like personal names (see chap. 5), safeguarded status distinctions and thereby the political structure of the society. Today, however, the practice of name changing is a familiar and well-established one.

Conclusion

This chapter has been concerned with disagreements in social theory and practice in Terutenne. We have observed, first, the statistical divergence in marriage behavior between the rich and the poor; second, the contrast of the basically bilateral inheritance pattern of the lower levels with the strict control over women and negotiated marriages associated with the father-to-son inheritance of wealthy or would-be aristocrats; third, the way in which the same pattern is repeated for theories of descent as expressed by high and low orders. These patterns mutually understandable to rich and poor alike, are part of the language of status. All members of the community understand this language, though the various sections of the population use it differently: the poor, for example, do know that there is more prestige attached to marrying from afar, with a tremendous public ceremony, with elaborate negotiations and insistence upon virginity; but at the same time they have little reason to engage in the practice. Similarly, a person who has acquired wealth would be foolish if he made no effort to select his sons-in-law judiciously and if he neglected to enhance the values of his daughters with dowries and other lures.

It seems likely—as one is frequently told in the villages—that the so-called "dowry system" is a recent entry to the status gymnastics of Kandyan villages. It is undoubtedly true that the system is not used in the more isolated villages, and Leach (1961b) observes that it is rare in the North Central Province. The lack of a dowry system is associated with egalitarian and immobile villages. Alternatively, dowry—with all that it implies in control over women and solidarity among men as a mark of status—appears to be a function of diversified communities with at least some mobility. It seems likely that the development of social hierarchies is associated with the emerging variations in marriage and inheritance behavior. The high-class patterns appear themselves to be imitations of Low Country practices (where dowry is the rule), but we may also observe that they are developed along the lines of potential behavior such as hypergamy which is to be expected in a caste context. The new institutions are harmonious with the others, and the Kandyans do not turn suddenly to bride-wealth and marriage by capture to express social superiority.

8

The Marriage Alliance

"They are especially careful in their Marriages, not to match
with any inferior Cast, but always each within their own rank:
Riches cannot prevail with them in the least to marry with those
by whom they must eclipse and stain the Honour of their Family:
on which they set an higher price than their lives. And if any of
the Females should be so deluded, as to commit folly with one
beneath her self, if ever she should appear to the sight of her
Friends, they would certainly kill her, there being no other way
to wipe off the dishonour she hath done the Family, but by her
own blood.

Yet for Men it is something different; it is not accounted any
shame or fault for a Man of the highest sort to lay with a Woman
far inferior to himself, nay of the very lowest degree: provided
he neither eats nor drinks with her, nor takes her home to his
House, as a Wife."—Robert Knox, *An Historical Relation of
Ceylon* (1681; repr. 1911), p. 105

"Neither do they reckon their Wives to be Whores for lying
with them that are as good or better than themselves."—*ibid.*,
p. 148

ALLIANCE

I have already noted the lack of unity among persons with the same
patronymic. The lack of cohesion among such lineal descendants must
be directly attributed to the emphasis that is placed on "affinity." To
an ordinary man, the relatives whom he acquires through his wife
(the father-in-law, the brothers-in-law, etc.) are more important relations than, for instance, his patrilineal first cousins. Or, similarly, it
will be said that the mother's brother (*mama*) is important before
marriage, but after marriage the other *mama* (father-in-law) takes his
place. With affinity thus emphasized, one might say that, following first
principles, affinal bonds will counteract bonds by descent, unless—and
this is the Kandyan ideal—relations between descendants are rein-

forced by affinity. The "alliance" aspect of marriage, the formal relations between affines, and the cooperation engendered between them are examined in this chapter.

First, what is an alliance? The term has been used in different senses and a clear definition of the concept has not yet emerged from anthropological writings.

It is possible to identify at least two different senses in which the *definition* concept can be useful. First, alliance can mean the formal relationship between certain categories of persons as proper marriage partners in societies that utilize positive marriage rules. In that case we can speak of a relationship of "perpetual affinity" between these categories, and may observe that any particular marriage between individuals standing in the right categories is an expression of this previous formal relationship between them.[1]

Second, we can speak of "alliance" as a less formal relationship in which persons connected by marriage bonds (not only the husband and wife but also the in-laws) are expected to cooperate very closely. A marriage thus may set up a new relationship of "alliance." It is clear that there is great variety in societies in this respect and in some cases, like the Pathans, a woman is simply transferred from one group to another without there being any establishment, in the process, of special cooperation between the groups (Barth, 1959). In other societies, the Sinhalese among them, it is precisely the brothers-in-law who cooperate most closely. The main difference between the first and the second senses of "alliance" is thus the more or less formal specification of the rights and obligations of in-laws toward one another. In the Sinhalese system, the rights and obligations of kinsmen by "marriage" are channeled into the formal and customary idiom of kinship by "descent." Indeed, it is the intermingling of the two categories that gives the Sinhalese system its special characteristics.

In the following chapter we shall discuss these kinship categories and kinship terminologies in detail; here, briefly, some explanation should be given as background to the subject of marriage alliances.

The Sinhalese together with most other people in Ceylon and South India practice formal cross-cousin marriage. They do not always marry actual cross-cousins, but all marriages are treated *as if* they had taken place between cross-cousins. The key relations beyond the nuclear family are the MB, the FZ, and their respective children. These persons have latent claims upon one another (*urumaya*), and their relations suddenly rise to the surface when a marriage of someone on whom they have claims is felt to be imminent.

---

[1] The literature on alliance is already extensive. See, e.g., Dumont's writings (1953, 1957b, 1961a); the controversy between Fortes (1959) and Leach (1961a, chap. 1), as well as Leach's earlier contribution (1961a, chap. 3), have direct bearing on this subject.

Brothers and sisters.—It is possible to think of these claims as emanating from the relations between brothers and sisters. The brothers have claims on their sisters, and have a definite right to control their marriages. Conversely, sisters frequently retain latent claims on the land and property utilized by their brothers. Even though sisters are said to share equally with their brothers in the property of their parents, it frequently happens that sisters are given out in marriage before the property is divided; in such instances, they may decide to press their claims and divide the lands, or they may withhold any specific claims in the general air of cooperation within the family, and instead demand cross-cousin marriages between their children and their brothers' children. Some writers, like Dumont, have written of these claims— which we also meet in South India—as emanating from the rights and obligations of the in-laws who stand in "perpetual affinity" to one another. It should be clear that they can be looked at from the inside and seen simply as the customary aspect of the relations between brothers and sisters. Let me now turn to these claims on the children of the brother and sister, as expressed between generations.

The mother's brother–sister's son.—There is an implied contrast here with the relationship of father and son. Both are intensely asymmetrical relations. The father and sons will not eat together; the sons are expected to show "respect" and will normally eat after the father is finished. In wealthy families, the father's full rights of testation appear to influence his authority over his sons. The sons will not sit or smoke in the presence of the father, and they always use the language of respectful distance up to an advanced age.

The father is given ceremonial recognition at the birth of a child, which properly occurs at the natal house of the mother. The child is formally handed to the father, who then hands it back again. The father also has a role to play in the naming, first-food-eating, and hair-cutting ceremonies, but it should be noted that this role is always shared with one of the MBs of the child.

The mother's brother–sister's son relationship is again intensely asymmetrical, though Kandyans do suggest that it is not quite so formal as that between fathers and sons. I should note that the term for MB (*mama*) is also used for the father-in-law and FZ's husband as well as for the classificatory collateral extensions of these terms (see chap. 9). There are in practice obvious differences in behavior between these various relatives. I do not make these distinctions here, for the customary idiom of *mama-bena* (ZS) is always expressed in general terms.

Indeed the most notable aspect of this MB-ZS pair seems to be the claims and counterclaims expressed by these persons upon each other, rather than the formal asymmetry in the connection. It is said that the

MB can claim his ZS for marriage for his D; he can also claim his ZD for his own S. Even when he does not press his own claims on them, he is definitely an active partner in the discussions regarding their marriages. Custom expresses these claims by giving a special place to the MB in all the *rites de passage* of an individual, from birth to marriage. The full MB, or at least a person standing in the category of MB, must be present at all these occasions.

Conversely, the *bena* has claims on the MB. He can usually expect to be treated like a son at the MB's house, and there are frequent cases of the MB taking over the education of the ZS and almost adopting him. It is significant that at the death of the MB, the ZS has the exclusive right to all the personal belongings of the deceased. The funeral procession is not complete unless there are persons in the categories of "son" and "sister's son" who walk at the head and foot of the deceased as he is carried to his grave.

The relations between the MB and his ZS acquire a special significance when property remains undivided between the mother and the MB. Under such circumstances there is the latent possibility for unresolved conflict between them. Besides these, there are special relationships between MB and ZD, FZ and BD, and FZ and BS, parallel to MB-ZS but not so carefully specified as the formal connections between the men. They are all, however, colored by the claims on the younger generation for the purposes of cross-cousin marriage.

Within the generation two kinds of relations are distinguished: siblings and cross-cousins. All kinsmen of the same generation fall into one or the other of these categories. The relations between siblings, like the relations between parents and children, are markedly asymmetrical. The younger children are expected to show deference and avoidance to their parents. I found that this avoidance characterized the relations between brothers and sisters as well, even though informants were inclined to say that they were close and friendly. They seem to be close but not familiar. There is also a very strong feeling of unity in the sibling group, expressed most eloquently in the customary usage of the term *ape* (our) toward the parents, or in any context concerning the siblings in the family. The young villager will rarely speak of "my mother" or "my father": he will say "our mother" or "our father." In many other contexts when one would expect the singular personal pronoun, the plural will be used. The adjectives most used to express avoidance are *garu* (respect) and *nambu* (honor).

Cross-cousins.—This is a joking relationship of the most typical variety. Male cross-cousins (*machang*) are frequently to be seen arm in arm, or with their arms over each other's shoulders, in the lanes of the village. Even a mere mention of *machang* will bring smiles to serious faces. Male and female cross-cousins have claims on each other which are restatements of the claims of the parents upon one another. They are sexual companions as well as the proper mates in marriage.

This sketch of kinship categories and their customary content is sufficient to allow us to examine the institution of marriage in detail. These formal customary claims are one of the basic features of Kandyan Sinalese kinship (fig. 14).

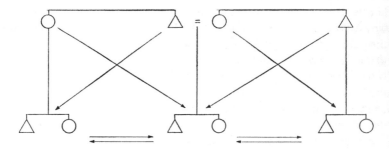

Figure 14. The interconnection and lateral extension of claims for cross-cousin marriage.

The Nature of the Alliance

To what end is all this control over women, this special concern with marriage? The purpose is not mysterious. Men need allies and helpers in the village for all kinds of purposes: helping in the construction of houses, in the annual rethatching of the dwellings, in looking for buffaloes. They are essential in paddy cultivation and are necessary in the hostile world of village factionalism and politics. Perhaps most important of all is that they can act as "witnesses" in all dealings the villagers have with the authorities.

It is true that these allies and helpers need not necessarily be kinsmen. We have observed how the organization of paddy cultivation is essentially "contractual" and how even close kinsmen make use of traditional credit arrangements for sharecropping. But it is also true that contractual relations are highly specific. Each contract has some definite purpose. The reciprocal rights and obligations are narrowly defined short-term arrangements.

On the other hand, the allies and helpers who are needed in everyday affairs, in village factions, as supporters in all dealings with authority cannot be recruited by specific contracts. The reciprocity must be diffuse, and it must be on a secure, long-term basis. In a Kandyan village such a relationship can only be based on "kinship." Indeed, the characteristics that we described—the diffuse reciprocity, the long-term mutual assistance with the pretense that *nothing* is expected in return, the impression of dependability—these mark the morality of Kandyan kinship. It is always said that the duty of kinsmen is simply to help (*udav*).

It is true that good and friendly relations are often established between persons who are not necessarily kinsmen. Such relations spring up between neighbors, for instance, who assist each other in many small ways. It is interesting therefore to observe that if caste, rank, or wealth do not stand in the way, such local acquaintances begin calling each other by kinship terms. Soon enough a marriage between the groups involved puts the affair on a definite footing. When one walks in the hamlets of Terutenne it is quite obvious that each neighborhood is thus closely interrelated.

Hence the association between kinship and cooperation works in both directions. Given cooperation, kinship often follows. When there is kinship, cooperation (*udav*) is expected. And if assistance is not forthcoming between kinsmen, then kinship will go to the winds. People will be bitter. They will say that kinship is "broken" (*nekam kedila*). Among all Kandyans, therefore, a marriage imbues the alliance with the morality of kinship.

The Need for New Allies

Despite the strength of kinship alliances, it sometimes happens that new kinship links need to be forged. This may come about for two reasons. First, given the inherent instability of economic and political conditions, families may become rich or poor, and this will affect tactics. A man who has recently grown rich will prefer to see his poorer first cousins, for instance, less often than before and to create new bonds with others of his own position. The differentiation of wealth is one of the things that can most easily sever bonds between kinsmen. Second, once property is finally apportioned there is no pressing, day-to-day necessity for solidarity between kinsmen by common descent. Even when the property is not yet divided, blood relatives may be neglected. A man's brother-in-law is usually of greater importance than his father's brother.

Thus the importance attached to affinity is both the cause and effect of the relative weakness of descent relationships. The account of a major feud in Terutenne will illustrate some of these remarks.

The Feud in Terutenne

I had been warned by the District Revenue Officer before I set out over the hills for Terutenne that conditions there were very tense. There was a series rift between two influential cliques in the village, and it was causing a great deal of trouble; tempers were frayed, and the

D.R.O. said he would not be surprised if the simmering feud led to open hostilities.

From the very first night in Terutenne I found that people naturally spoke of "they" and "us." They referred to the groups as "sides" —"The village is divided, side, side [*pettak, pettak*]"—or as "groups" (*kattiya*) and sometimes as "kindreds" (*pavula*). I shall refer to them as factions or cliques.

Within a short time of my arrival it became clear to me that—apart from the long recitals of past grievances on both sides—there was a focus to the feud. The main bone of contention appeared to be the office of Village Headman.

It was known that the present Village Headman was going to retire. He was the son-in-law of the Village Headman before him, and Terutenne had in fact been ruled by one faction almost since the turn of the century. The other faction, composed of wealthy and influential persons, was mainly interested in putting a stop to this hegemony— above all, to see that the new Headman was not a member of that faction.

In the last resort, it is the Government Agent who appoints the headman, but both factions thought that if they could blacken the other faction in the eyes of the authorities, they would be rewarded by the appointment. Accusations and counteraccusations of all descriptions flooded the authorities. The situation was made more acute by a murder, an infanticide, an alleged poisoning, and innumerable instances of fornication with under age girls, opium smuggling, and other crimes.

The murder case concerned the eldest son of the Village Headman: had he killed the husband of his mistress? The other faction was also involved because the woman had also been the mistress of one of their best candidates for the Headmanship. The infanticide concerned the rich brother-in-law of the Headman. Almost any incident in the village was enough to arouse the anger of both factions and send them off to hastily called secret meetings, where the other faction's downfall was planned and replanned.

The nature of these factions was of great interest. The core of the "establishment" clique consisted of old Muhandiram, a former Village Headman, his son-in-law, the present and soon-to-retire Headman, and the latter's son, who was at the moment Acting Headman and hoped to secure the job permanently. These three were closely assisted by one of Muhandiram's sons who was the Irrigation Headman and also chairman of the Village Committee, and by two other sons of Muhandiram, who were influential in the village (and, of course, brothers-in-law of the retiring Village Headman). Muhandiram's other son-in-law, the Village Headman of a neighboring village, also supported the faction by doing his best to influence the District Revenue Officer and the Korale.

The relationships between these people were considered so vital

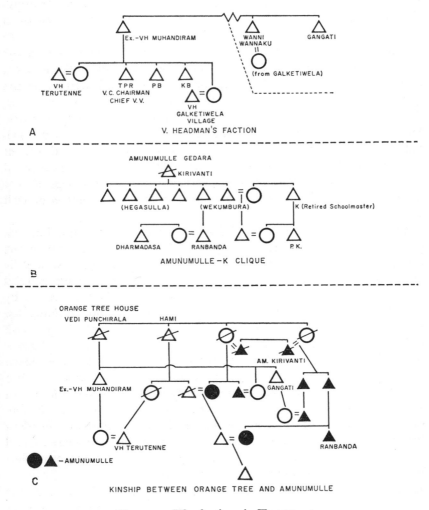

Figure 15. The factions in Terutenne.

that Muhandiram and his faction were all spoken of as "one people" (*eka minissu*) or "one kindred" (*eka pavul kattiya*), even though the ancestral *gedara* names of the sons-in-law were quite different from that of Muhandiram (fig. 15A). Indeed, perhaps the best example of marriage as an alliance is shown by the connection between the present Village Headman and his brother-in-law, T. P. R. The two actually

lived in the same dwelling. Another example was Muhandiram's recommendation of his son-in-law to the Headmanship when he himself
had retired.

In contrast to this close marriage alliance should be set the fact that
Muhandiram's own two brothers (both wealthy men) tended to support the opposition. Indeed, one of them, Wanni Wannaku (see
chap. 6) had a wife in the neighboring village where Muhandiram's
son-in-law was Headman. It was very apparent that the Headman
was making Wanni Wannaku's life extremely difficult because of his
lukewarm attitude toward Muhandiram.

The opposing faction was formed on a similar pattern (fig. 15B).
The central member was old K., a retired schoolteacher of Terutenne.
He was related by marriage to the Amunumulle family (see fig. 11).
(After I left the village, I learned that his daughter had also been
married to the same family to rejuvenate the connection.) The richest person of the Amunumulle was Ranbanda (a shopkeeper, see
table 8) and through him K. was related to Dharmadasa—also a rich
shopkeeper in Terutenne.

The Amunumulle, who thought of themselves as aristocrats, felt
particularly strongly about the Village Headman's supporters. They
accused them of being "low" people of serf descent, and said that their
ancestors had been indentured laborers. Although they now sported
the name of Nissanka Mudianselage Tunpale Gedara, they were really
only "Orange Tree" people and it was Mukandiram who had changed
their titles. They were still "dirty." They were immoral. They drank
toddy and gambled day and night. They had acquired poor villagers'
lands by threat. Relationships? None had ever existed between them
and the pure Amunumulle.

The element of pretense which went with such accusations was
amazing. It is true, I did come to the conclusion that the Muhandirams had changed their name. But little did I know at the time
that the Amunumulle and the Orange Tree people had intermarried
closely and that K. was descended from the Low Country Fisher caste.
There is no doubt about the latter fact since K.'s son himself told me
about it under very tense circumstances.

The Disruptive Effect of Wealth

In the case of the Amunumulle and the Orange Tree people, it turned
out that a change of fortune had estranged them. Apparently the
family connections had started when two women of the Orange Tree
family were married to two Amunumulle brothers. At the time the
Orange Tree people were doing well and the Amunumulle had

lost much of their ancestral lands. Cordial relations appear to have continued until some of the Amunumulle moved out from Wekumbura hamlet to Hegasulla for chena cultivation. About this time, however, Muhandiram became the Village Headman through very obscure machinations (involving cases of kidnaping, murder, and an elephant hunt during which the life of the Government Agent was saved).

From this point onward Muhandiram and his children were very successful. They became rich and powerful and they intermarried with important people. In contrast, the Amunumulle remained impoverished aristocrats. The best sign of strained kinship relations is that the Muhandiram group ceased to address the Hegasulla people by kinship terms. This act was taken as the final breaking of kinship between them (fig. 15C).

Later, however it seems that K., the schoolteacher who had been teaching elsewhere, returned to Terutenne and settled down. He had given his sister to an Amunumulle man, and in the meantime had himself become very rich by buying lands with his salary. Some of the younger-generation Amunumulles also returned to Wekumbura and opened shops. The shops thrived, and they grew rich by the sale possibly of intoxicants. In time, they drove some shops of the Muhandirams' faction out of business.

When this happened the hostility between the Amunumulles and the Muhandirams—who had defaulted on kinship—became open. Since then the Amunumulles, with K. and other malcontents, had been challenging every move of those in power. The prize of the game had become the Village Headmanship.

There is, of course, no end to the story. After the Village Headmanship is decided, there will be the Village Committee elections, and after those, the cliques will undoubtedly form for some other purpose. My intention in relating this affair is to show the purpose of these marriage alliances and to indicate that, though they are not altogether stable, the solidarity they engender is impressive. I also wish to draw attention to the great strains placed on the alliance, as well as on other kinship bonds, by the divergence of wealth and fortune.

THE CONCEPT OF MARRIAGE AND THE CELEBRATION OF WEDDINGS

I turn now to Sinhalese ideas of marriage and wedding ceremonies. Again there is no uniformity: although much importance is attached to affinity, Kandyan arrangements may be completely informal and the wedding entirely eliminated. It is this casual attitude that has prompted the Kandyan Law Commission to note that it often becomes impossible to distinguish between "wives" and "mistresses" or between "legitimate" and "illegitimate" children.

Sinhalese peasants hardly have a term for "marriage" as such. The respectable usage is *kassada bandinava* (tying the household), which derives from the wedding ceremony where the thumbs of the bride and groom are tied together. For the villagers this is an extremely formal phrase. Ordinarily they will merely say *gäniyek tiyegannava* (taking a woman) or *pavul venava* (becoming family), or at times *pavul ganu denu* (exchange of wives). Sometimes the word *sambandha* is used: it would seem to be (I quote from an informant) "a respectable word for sexual intercourse," and endogamy thus expressed is *api e gollanta sambandha ne*. (It will be recalled that the Nayar unions are called *sambandham*.) Sometimes ordinary villagers will say, "Oh no, we had no *kassada bandinava* [i.e., no ceremony]; we are simply *nikang innava* [nothing being, i.e., living together without formality]."

The Kandyan Law Commission, appointed in 1927, certainly got into deep waters in attempting to codify a legal definition of Kandyan marriage. They write: "In early times the conducting of a daughter by by a man of equal caste with the consent of her relations *constituted* a marriage, particularly in the case of persons of low rank who could not afford costly ceremonies," and they go on to examine illegitimacy. Referring to institutional writers, they say, "It must be remembered that when these writers speak of illegitimate children they refer rather to the issue of a marriage which was considered improper or irregular, in the sense, for instance, that the parties to it were of different castes, than to the issue of a casual connection, the word illegitimate not necessarily implying the non-existence of marriage" (*R.K.L.C.*, 1935, pp. 23, 26). The Commissioners eventually ruled that all this was too complicated ("the time has come when an end must be made of the nice questions which arise and the interminable argument and litigation that they give occasion to") and decided that the only definition of marriage to be upheld in a court of law was their definition of marriage—that is, "registration."

It is notable that although there are government-appointed marriage registrars (*lekam mahatmaya*) in or near every village, very few people actually register their marriages. They do register the birth of their children, however, but even then they may sometimes give the names of unlikely men as father of the child.

This informality about what we consider to be the most important point of the kinship and social structure of the Sinhalese may appear surprising and contradictory. Why do the Sinhalese have this lack of concern about the "establishment of marriage"? The matter seems even more extraordinary when one notes that, on the other hand, some marriages are preceded by long and arduous negotiations and comparisons of horoscopes and are celebrated by elaborate wedding rites.

Arrangement of a Match

When a marriage is being arranged between families that are strangers to each other the arrangements are very formal. The initiative is usually taken by the party of the prospective groom. However, a family with a nubile daughter need not remain inactive. The puberty ceremony (which is celebrated in such a fashion as to leave no interested person unaware of the fact that a girl has reached marriageable status) is the first round of propaganda. At times the marriage may be decided upon right then.

If the family is to go much further afield than its immediate circle of kin, then a marriage broker (*magul kapurala*) may be employed. Anyone may act as a *magul kapurala* and there are some who tend to specialize in the occupation. They may receive some remuneration from either party. The *kapurala* is the advance guard.[2] Once the likelihood of a match begins to emerge from his inquiries, more serious investigations take place. It is said that the parties will visit each other's villages in disguise and make discreet conversation in the shops in order to find out whether there are any blemishes in the *wamsa* (rank) of the other party, whether they would be suitable affines who would enhance the family's prestige. If all seems favorable, the boy's side will inform the others through the broker that they are interested in the girl and would like to come to "eat rice and betel" (*bat-bulat kanava*). This request carries the connotation of commensality, and compliance with it implies the provisional acceptance of the other family as sufficiently close in rank as to be marriageable. On an arranged day, the most superior and respected members of both parties meet at the home of the girl. It is usual for both the father's and the mother's brothers to be present. The house is decorated for the occasion and there is much display on both sides, since this initial show of wealth puts each in a better bargaining position.

At the opening meeting the discussion will be concerned with the relations, wealth, lands, and influence of the parties—all of which will no doubt be verified later on in nearby villages or even with the

---

[2] There is always a great deal of joking and amusement when the role of the *magul kapurala* is mentioned, as well as when one is present. The joking is clearly related to his position as intermediary. He belongs to neither group, yet is on the side of both. If all goes well, he is likely to be given credit for the excellent match, but if—as it is feared—the families cannot get on, he is considered the one to blame. This anomalous situation gives rise to much good-natured but rather pointed joking.

Village Headman. This first visit may or may not be returned by the girl's party. Full agreement may be reached quickly, making another visit unnecessary, or serious disagreements may result in the negotiations being discontinued altogether.

The first point of interest at the meeting is "caste"; it is usually referred to as *jati,* but what is meant is the status of the family inside the caste, for it is assumed that the parties will belong to the same caste. We have spoken of such intracaste status as *wamsa. Wamsa* is theoretically related to birth, but in fact depends entirely on the status of the other members of the kindred. Since the marriage of any one member to a "lower" family would prejudice the rank of all, the relatives of both parties must be throughly examined.

If it is agreed that the status of the parties, with their kin, is compatible, there arises the question of land and wealth. These, too, should be roughly equal—or, at least, the groom and the bride should receive equal shares. It can happen that the family of the bride, in order to achieve a connection with a superior family, may settle much of its property on her, depriving her siblings of their fair share.

Last but not least, there is the matter of the personalities of the bride and groom. Their character (*gati guni*) and their physical attractiveness are of considerable importance, and shortcomings in either respect will be taken into account when it comes to payments.

Horoscope

If, after careful discussion, the two parties reach full agreement on all these issues, the next matter to be looked into is that of horoscopes. One of the important observances of the Sinhalese on the birth of a child is to record the precise time of the moment of its appearance; this is then taken to the astrologer, who produces a horoscope which foretells the whole story of the infant's life. Even its name is chosen with regard to the ruling planet in the horoscope. The horoscope is taken to an astrologer at every important occasion in an individual's life. The astrologer may then give advice—knowing what is in store for the person—as to what should be done. He also can provide astral charms (*yantram*) to allay an illness, and may even predict the illness— which may often grip the unfortunate individual shortly thereafter.[3]

---

[3] It may well be that some expert astrologers still make astral observations, but those I met relied on a book of astrology printed in Colombo and said to be a copy of one printed in London. Illness and the arts of healing are part of a complete and consistent system of belief. Thus, some illnesses are brought about by *karma*—a particular configuration of the *grahayo* at birth—and certain ceremonies may be concerned with attempts to tamper with the constitution of the horoscope. The individual may be made to go through a complete rebirth and avoid the period of difficulty (*apele*) foreseen in his old horoscope. See Wirz (1941) for descriptions of these ceremonies.

Marriage with new kinsmen is a venture that arouses great anxieties. For the perfect match, the nine *grahayo*—that is, planets and supernatural beings—that influence men's lives must foretell the same future for both the bride and the groom. They must also show that their characters are compatible, that they are fairly similar in miserliness, or in nonchalance, in temper, or in their bodies. Indeed, quite apart from general character, the horoscopes even allow the comparison of the astral nature of the sexual organs. One may be characterized by the elephant, and the other by the mouse, and if so, the astrologer quickly predicts that it is useless to go on with the venture.

Here one touches upon the effects of "social distance." All these trimmings are likely to be dispensed with when the couple are already very closely related. But when one is getting related to distant persons who are only vaguely known, one is sure of little. It is the time to turn to the *grahayo* and the deities for their special intervention.

After the agreement of the astrologer has also been secured (one may be obliged to apply to a different astrologer), and after he has given a date as well as a full timetable, showing the "auspicious times" (*honda velava*) when each particular step of the ceremony should take place, the new alliance is considered complete and it is time for the wedding ceremony.

The Ceremony and Conspicuous Gift Exchange

A wedding is known simply as a *magul gedara* (ceremony house). The term associates the occasion with other *rites de passage*. Thus, a birth, the reaching of puberty, various minor occasions—when a boy first works in the fields, when the children read for the first time, when the earlobes of girls are pierced—all call for celebrations. The houses in which these celebrations take place are also known as *magul gedara*. A death occasions ceremonies as well, but these being inauspicious the house is then known as *ava magul gedara*, literally anti-*magul* house.

There is much conspicuous show of wealth at *magul gedara*. The guests arrive in their best clothes (the men, very uncomfortably, in shoes and starched jackets); the women display all their gold jewelry. Huge amounts of food are prepared and set out on long tables, and there is a great deal of drinking and some gambling. The poor, of course, can hardly rival the spending sprees of the rich, but they do what they can. The burden of the expense is mainly upon the groom, though he may receive help from his brothers, his father, his sisters' husbands, and his mother's brothers (in which case he is obligated to return the favor later on).

The urge to display becomes particularly evident when the guests

first arrive. They are immediately given a glass of water to wash out
their mouths and are then seated, in silence, along the walls. (The
position of the guests depends entirely on their status; lower castes
are never mingled with the others.) When a fair number are assembled a special bronze betel-plate is passed around the company. This is
a tense moment and each guest produces a certain amount of money
from within the folds of his cloth and places it ostentatiously on the
plate. Considering the economy of the villages, the sums that appear
are quite extraordinary. The richer guests try to outdo one another
and in a well-to-do household very large amounts may be collected.
At the wedding of the Terutenne Headman's daughter which I attended one of the guests put a 500-rupee bank note on the plate.

These sums do not go in only one direction. The payment (always
in public) is a gift that must be returned. At the next *magul gedara*
in the house of the donor, the gift will be reciprocated. Only people
of the same wealth can keep up this kind of gift exchange and the
sheep are quickly separated from the goats.

Some Basic Ceremonial Patterns

A formal wedding often includes the following traditional elements.

   (a) The feasts (*astom*).—The word is derived from the English
phrase "at home." When the families are unrelated or socially distant,
there are two "at homes." The most important point is that each
"kindred" has a communal meal *before* they unite. When they are
closely related, one "at home" is sufficient.

   (b) "Auspicious times" (*honda velava*).—As on all ceremonial occasions, every important step of the ceremony is carried out according
to an auspicious timetable provided by the astrologer. This enhances
the formality of the occasion.

   (c) The arrival of the groom.—The groom, together with some
kinsmen including at least one woman who is *nenda* (FZ, MB's wife,
or M-in-L) to the bride, go in procession to the bride's house. The
bride is given to the charge of the *nenda*. Henceforth she may not
speak to anyone directly but the *nenda* must act as an interpreter. The
two must not be separated. The whole group eats a communal meal.

   (d) The changing of the dress.—At an auspicious time, the bride
takes off her own dress in public and puts on one brought by the
groom. She must not wear the old one again.

   (e) The tying of the thumbs.—In very formal weddings the couple
goes into a big cagelike structure (*magul poruva*) and stands on grain.
Their thumbs are then tied.

   (f) The pardon of the cross-cousin (*avassa massinagen samava illima*).—As the bride leaves the house with the groom and his party,

she hands one hundred betel leaves (*kadulu bulat:* gate betel) to a *massina* (cross-cousin). His acceptance indicates that the cross-cousins have forgiven her for marrying someone else and are allowing her to go.

For less formal weddings, some of these elements may be omitted— or all of them may be dispensed with. Occasionally, for a very sumptuous wedding, other castes may be invited to perform their caste duties (for which they are paid): Washermen may come to decorate the house with "pure" cloths, and Jaggery Makers may bring highly symbolic sweet cakes (*kavum*) in procession.

The Details of a Wedding in Terutenne

While I was in the village of Terutenne a marriage took place between the daughter of the Village Headman and Ukwatte Gedara Tikiribanda, an aristocrat of the village, who had been working in an important shop in a bazaar (*Harasbedda*) which serves the village. It was a good marriage for both parties, and Tikiribanda being rich (his father was dead, but his mother and brothers were living), the bride was to receive a dowry of Rs. 2,000 in land and cash. There were two "at homes," which lasted a week, with much ostentation, gambling, and gift exchange. Courtesy visits to the house were made by those who worked in the fields of the Headman and his relatives, the Orange Tree people. The actual ceremony took place at the end of the week on an "auspicious day" and at the "auspicious" hour of three-thirty in the morning. The kinsmen of the bride and groom had eaten a communal meal the evening before. What follows is an eyewitness account of the ritual from start to finish.

3:00 A.M.: The *magul poruva,* decorated with white paper and special flowers (areca-nut, and coconut flowers, various leaves), has been prepared and the Washermen are putting on the finishing touches. Standing at the entrance outside are earthen pots full of unhusked rice (*vi*). The floor within is covered with husked, washed, but uncooked rice (*haal*). (Note, incidentally, that the husking of rice takes place in a mortar [*vangedi*] with a pestle [*molgaha*], both of which are often spoken of in sexual terms, and the husking itself likened to the sexual act.) Fresh papaws are being cut into two and placed on the pots—these will be used as lamps. There are two uncut coconuts on the floor.

3:27 A.M.: The changing of the dress at the auspicious time takes place indoors but it is a public ceremony. The bride is sitting with a *nenda* (FZ in this case) but the mother of the groom has not come. The brothers of the groom are much in evidence.

The couple stands on a white cloth provided by the Washerman. The *mama* (MB) of the bride gives the groom another white cloth. He puts it around her diffidently just over her dress. Some jewellery held in a box by the *mama* of the groom is put around her neck. *Nenda* (FZs) are standing beside the bride. The groom is overcome with shyness and leaves off halfway. The bride goes into a separate room and changes into a white sari provided by the groom. This ends the dress-changing ceremony: the white cloth symbolizes the dress. In less magnificent weddings, the bride actually changes in public.

The next "auspicious time" is 4:15 A.M. The guests are sitting about in the outer room. There is a crowd of about fifty. They consist of all kinds of relations but are mainly members of the kindred. There are some Jaggery Makers (Vahumpura) from the next village (Udamadura) who have brought *kavum* for the occasion. They are given food and will later be paid. The women are not to be seen much among the men.

There is some more work to be done. The *mama* (MBs) of the girl are rushing about while her *appa* (father) looks on by one side. The papaw lamps are lighted. Pennies are put into the earthen pots. As the time approaches, guests start changing into formal dress. Some who have been wearing only sarongs put on stiffly starched and obviously uncomfortable jackets. Some are putting on shoes and sandals. Still others have taken off their sarongs and are wrapping *dhoties* (Tamil dress, which is considered more elegant) made of gabardine. There are two layers put on for formality and display, as well as a jacket of the same material. The wearers are obviously acutely uncomfortable.

4:15 A.M.: The auspicious time arrives. There is a great crowd. Some dressed-up girls come into the room: they are in white and must be virgins—one cannot be sure of the latter fact if they are past puberty so they are between six and twelve years old. The bride enters from one side and the groom from the other. She is surrounded by *nenda* (FZ, mothers-in-law) and *nena* (MBD, sisters-in-law). The groom also has a *mama* (MB) beside him. They enter the *magul poruva* at what is hoped to be the precise time (the watches and clocks do not appear to agree) and stand on the rice-covered floor. As they enter, the *mama* of the bride (therefore, formally *appa* [F] to the groom) breaks a coconut in two on the threshold. This is a very common ritual act. It is usually done on a threshold and marks a special change of status in all ceremonies. The future can be foretold from the fall of the two neatly divided halves. The breaking of the coconut—and the flow of its water—is considered to draw the blessings of the deities upon the couple.

The virgins start singing the *Jayamangala Sutra* in Pali. This is auspicious, though not many understand what it means. As the singing goes on, the thumbs of the couple are tied together by a gold chain. The *mama* of the bride then pours water over the thumbs. They are then untied and the couple remains standing side by side. The singing stops. As the bride and groom come out, the *mama* breaks another coconut. They want a picture to be taken by me. I suggest going out of the house into the feeble morning light, but no, the bride cannot go out of the house before another "auspicious time."

The fact that most of the ceremony is directed by *mama* and *nenda,* and not by the parents of the couple, gives the impression that the rites are in the charge of intermediaries. The families of the couple are shy and avoid one another. There is much sitting and waiting, for the "auspicious time" to leave the house is 9:00 A.M. Men and women separate again to different rooms.

A hut had been constructed outside the wedding house and decorated by Washermen. Gambling had been going on in it until a little before, but now the party is to move into it for speeches. The couple moves out at the exact moment they are supposed to, and gunshots sound. All the important members of both kindreds take their places. The bride is on the left with *nenda* and *nena* (FZ and MBD) sitting next to her. The groom has "brothers" and *massina* (cross-cousins) on his side.

It is notable that again neither the father of the bride, nor her mother, nor, indeed, the mother of the groom is taking part in the celebrations. The house of the groom's family is only about two hundred yards away from that of the bride and yet the groom's mother is nowhere to be seen.

The procedure in the hut consists only of speeches—the first by the elder brother of the bride, the second by the groom's employer from the shop in Harasbedda—both of which are highly rhetorical. The main sentiment is that the two "people" are now as "one": "one family" (*eka pavula*), "one people" (*eka minissu*), and everyone hopes that the union will be auspicious and fertile.

The time has come for the bride to be taken to her new home. She rises and starts handing around betel leaves to her close relations. One of the Jaggery Maker women who is standing beside her passes out a few at a time. The bride, accompanied by the groom, eventually moves out of the hut and goes toward the ceremonial gate which has been constructed for the occasion. A young *avassa massina* (real cross-cousin) is brought forward at random, and she gives him one hundred betel leaves, "worships" him with the traditional gesture, the palms of the hands pressed together, and moves on. As she leaves the compound she is met by two women carrying pots of water on their hips—auspicious signs even if prearranged—and an open umbrella is held over the heads of the couple. The "brothers" and "mother's brothers" of the bride as well as the relations of the groom are all in the procession. Again, although the distance the procession must traverse is but a short way, the formality is remarkable. Both the bride (probably for the first time in her life) and the groom are wearing shoes. The "social distance" between the families is well marked. This is a new marriage between them, and it is hoped, the first of a series.

The Elimination of the Ceremony

The wedding I have described—with all the changing of clothes, the leave-taking, the formality—very clearly symbolizes the giving of a woman by one "group" to another. Yet in other contexts the whole elaborate affair may be omitted. In that case, why is it necessary to have weddings at all?

The people themselves cannot give consistent answers. When Terutenne people were directly questioned, they would reply that the marriage ceremonies were all newfangled inventions. In the "times of the

Kandyan kings" there was no arrangement or ceremony at all. One merely went to the mother of the girl who took one's fancy and asked for her daughter as a companion during the chena season.[4] If one found that she did no work, she would be sent promptly back. There being no formal marriage, there was also no divorce.

We need not, of course, accept these details as historical facts. It is true that we do have the words of Robert Knox: "Here are no Public whores allowed by Authority. . . . Indeed the public trade would be bad, and hardly maintain them that exercised it, the private one being so great." But if one considers the elaborate ritual of an aristocratic wedding provided by D'Oyly (1929, p. 82), little doubt remains that some, at least, had different ideas. Clearly, the idealization of the past as a time with no marriage follows, as usual, the contours of the present. But this does not bring us any nearer to the reasons why the present is as it is. Why is it that Kandyans will sometimes not bother about any arrangements, discussion of dowry, wedding, but will allow a couple to start cohabiting quite informally, whereas at another time the whole affair is fraught with tension and takes weeks to arrange and to celebrate?

The Ceremony as an Expression of Wealth and Social Distance

The answer to these questions is that the ceremonies and arrangements may vary in two respects. In the first place, wealthy families prefer elaborate weddings. Second, the elaboration of the ceremony and the necessity for careful preliminary arrangements depend entirely on "social distance" between the two groups concerned. If the bride and groom are already very closely related—they may even have been brought up in the same house—then no ceremony is called for. They will say, "We are merely among ourselves [*api apata:* literally we to we]; why should we feed a lot of strangers?" [5] If the families are com-

---

[4] Sometimes a *hetti* (blouse) and *redi* (lower cloth) were taken by the man as gifts to the girl. Gifts of cloth appear to be widespread symbols of cohabitation in South India as well. The Nayar *sambandham* is also commenced in this fashion.

[5] Even though all formal acts can be dispensed with, there is nonetheless a certain ritual that is frequently observed by close kinsmen who set up a household. Following what is described as an "old custom," the *massina* may take a *redi* and *hetti* to the girl, and if she accepts them she changes her clothes and goes with him to his hut. Her own clothes then become the property of her unmarried sisters. I interpret this act as part of the reciprocity of the household. The custom is widespread in South India (even the Nayar *Tali kettu kalyanam* contains it), and it is reflected in the dress-changing ceremony of the elaborate Sinhalese wedding. An unmarried girl works in the parents' household: she gets food and clothing in return. After her union the responsibility for her food and clothing falls to her husband. These are the return, as it were, for her services as a wife. My informants commented jocularly on these offerings of cloth and the changing of the dress by saying that her family "gives her naked to the man" (*helueng denava vagei*).

plete strangers to each other or only distantly related, then they must, of course, tread with care. There will have to be preliminary discussions, and the wedding when it comes will be a relatively grand affair.

The Permanent Categories of Affinity: The "Cross-Cousins"

That there should be elaborate preparations and weddings when new kinsmen "unite" is not very surprising. It is surprising and important that a marriage can be established between close relations without any formality. It is here that some of the fundamental features of Kandyan kinship appear with the greatest clarity.

"The Tallensi," writes Fortes, "draw a sharp distinction between . . . kinship, and . . . in-lawship. They are irreconcilably contradictory. They must not be 'mixed' . . . Marriage implies the absence of kinship ties between the parties; kinship, the impossibility of marriage. Kinship ties exist in their own right; [in-lawship] is an artificial alliance of a contractual nature" (1949b, pp. 16–17).

A clearer statement of the exact reverse of Kandyan concepts would be difficult to find. The Kandyans make no verbal distinction between kin and in-laws; *näkam* covers all of them. And as to marriage, it is the *nädäyo* who may and are expected to marry; those with whom one may not marry are persons of another caste, or families of bad standing within the caste. It is the notion of "endogamy" that permeates all thoughts of kinship and marriage and gives rise to the inevitable feeling that those with whom one has intermarried, and whom one must marry, are nearer than others who are set apart from one by barriers of endogamy. Community contains the implications of conjugality. Therefore, affinal relations and relations arising through common descent are expected to be intermingled, and marriage is the cement that holds "kinsmen" together.

It is undoubtedly because those persons we refer to as "affines" are an especially important category of kinsmen for the Sinhalese that there are customary elaborations which, first, formalize the relations between marriageable kin, and, second, indicate the permanent bonds between such persons. The most important and noteworthy of these customary features are the formal statements regarding cross-cousins.

We shall see below that the Sinhalese, as well as many other peoples in South India and Ceylon, utilize a Dravidian kinship terminology. Accordingly, they practice prescriptive cross-cousin marriage. In other words, so far as the ordinary Sinhalese is concerned, there is only one category that is marriageable in his or her kinship universe. This category (*nana* for the male, and *massina* for the female) is usually translated as "cross-cousin," although it should be noted that it would include a wide range of relations: *nana*, for example, can be MBD,

FZD, MBMBDD, S's M-in-L, ZHZ, BWZ, etc. (see chap. 9). The customary bonds between these categories of *massina* and *nana* contain the key to Kandyan kinship. It is the expressed principle that *massina* and *nana* have "blood claims" (*le urumaya*) upon each other. This means that they "belong" to each other from their birth, since they find themselves in categories of kinship established by the kinship positions of their parents. They may therefore "play" (*sellam kara-nava*) with each other, and they may have sexual relations. They are, as it were, in a permanent relationship of "marriage" by virtue of their formal positions in the kinship framework.

Hence not only are they allowed to set up house together without ceremony, but a woman who has not married her close *massina* must formally ask for permission from an *avassa massina*. This particularly expressive customary obligation takes place as the last ritual act before the bride leaves her parental home—as described above. The act is explained as the *nana* asking for permission from her *massina* to leave with the other man and ceremonially receiving it. Needless to say, this ceremony is omitted when the couple are themselves *avassa massina–nana*.

Let me describe two cases to indicate the practical effects of these customs:

My cook Appuhami, the renowned *Kapurala,* had six sisters, all of whom had marriageable daughters. Until recently his relations with them had been cordial. In 1955 his son decided to get married and started looking around for a suitable girl. His actions brought family relations to a simmering point. The son did not want to take a *nana* from his FZ. He argued, though without much conviction, that "the *nenda* [FZ] relationship is always with us and will not change, but we must get new relations!" Apparently the real reason was that the families of the father's sisters were not well off, and the boy did not want to get involved with them. In the end a suitable girl was found among some distant relations, and the negotiations proceeded to an advanced stage. All Appuhami's six sisters became extremely angry with him, however, for having disdained the immediate cross-cousins, and though the wedding went on as scheduled, they refused to attend. Appuhami said that he had not visited his sisters for the last four years, and dreaded to do so now.

This first case, showing the tensions that arise in the family when formal claims are disregarded, also indicates how serious the formal relationship is considered to be. The second case indicates the connections between these formal bonds and small group endogamy.

I was speaking to a Tom-Tom Beater who lived above Helagama hamlet. Tom-Tom Beaters have the same kinship system as the Goyigama, although since they are usually poor, the low-class pattern

—no dowry, no formal marriage—predominates. I asked the Tom-
Tom Beater whether he had many relations in the Baddegama hamlet,
which is the main Tom-Tom Beater community in Terutenne. He
said, "No. We do not have *näkam* (kinship) with them and therefore
do not intermarry." I was surprised and wanted to know whether he
attributed this to some status distinctions. He said there were simply
no relationships between his *pavula* (family) and the *pavula* in
Baddegama; and since there was no *näkam* (kinship), they could not
intermarry with them (*Nädäkamak neti nisa bandinni ne:* literally,
kinship absence [because of] do not intermarry). I pursued the subject
further. With whom did they marry? He said, "Our father's sisters
[*api nendala*] live near Galpitiya; our mother's brothers [*api mamandi*] live below the hills; our father's brothers [*bappala*] and our
cross-cousins and brothers [*massinala avyala*] live on the way to Nildandahinna; so those are our kinsmen and we intermarry with them."
"Well, don't those people have some connections with Baddegama?"
"No. There is no proper kinship relationship [i.e., the correct *nana* or
massina category] outside, and we intermarry among ourselves.

Actually after some investigation I did uncover certain connections
between the kinsmen of this informant and the people of Baddegama,
but the Tom-Tom Beater disregarded these, and his conception of
marriage as a relationship that can occur only between strictly defined
and previously interconnected categories of kinsmen illustrates my
argument with some precision.

The structural implications of these formal customs—all the more
striking since Sinhalese kinship has often been described as "loosely
structured"—are clear. These formal bonds between categories of "affines," who are kinsmen at the same time, are an expression of the attempt to treat "marriage" in the same categorical framework as "consanguinity." Or to put it differently, an attempt is made to turn
the inherently contractual relations which emanate from marriage
into noncontractual permanent kinship relations by confining marriage
to certain isolated and formalized categories.

It may indeed be suggested that this problem of differentiating
and at the same time reconciling consanguineous ties and ties of marriage appears in all endogamous castes where concepts of lineage
exogamy are not strongly developed. This in turn may be the reason
why these formal bonds between the cross-cousins among the Sinhalese are a well-known feature of many South Indian kinship systems.

We may further observe that these preoccupations appear with
particular force in those communities where the marriage relationship is relatively informal and flexible. Thus, among the Nayars we
are told of the *enangar* relationship, which, though originally de-

scribed as "ties of clanship," is obviously a relationship of perpetual affinity between matrilineages (taravad). The function of the enangar institution, that is, the provision of ritual husbands for the women of the linked lineage, is structurally similar to that of the nana-massina bonds among the Sinhalese. In both cases, "marriage" is turned into a noncontractual bond which precedes any particular union. I have provided much evidence elsewhere to show that the Brahman rule of prepuberty marriage, very widespread in India, is also directly related to the concern to fix the partners of the women permanently in a hierarchy of castes.[6]

In kinship terms, therefore, the reason why a marriage ceremony may be omitted among close kin is that structurally nothing happens. The particular relationship is already in existence since it is implied by the kinship categories of the rest of the relatives and the cross-cousin rights and obligations. Since the cross-cousins are permitted sexual intercourse, even their own personal relationship need not change. The children fall into place in an orderly kinship universe. All this world, of course have been true for any other "correct" partner. There is no danger about "caste" nor difficulties about membership in other social groups: the parents being in the "correct" categorical position, the children are assured of places. Nothing changes in the kinship terminology, and the behavior of all persons in the kinship constellation remains the same.

Claims on property do not come into the question in any case. As we have already seen (chap. 7), the offspring of the union will inherit separately from the mother and the father. Whether the parents were "married" or not will normally be immaterial for inheritance claims.

These are the reasons behind the problems encountered by the experts of the Kandyan Law Commission. And these remain the reasons why registered marriage is considered something of a luxury by Kandyan villagers, who continue to take their women up to their chena when the season is ripe.

HYPERGAMY AND DOWRY

Status and Marriage Portions

Marriage payments among the Sinhalese usually take the form of a dowry. In rare cases there are payments which go in the opposite direction, from the bride-receivers to the bride-givers. What are the purposes of marriage payments and what factors decide their size and direction?

We must return yet again to the concept of status. When describing Terutenne, we spoke of two hierarchies: those of "wealth" and

---

[6] See Yalman (1963); also Gough (1952a).

"rank inside the caste" (*wamsa*). These hierarchies are distinct in principle, but when Kandyans speak of particular families they may refer
to their status in general. The word that is used is "level" (*tatvaya*). It
connotes neither wealth nor rank, but a combination of both. Of
course, distinctions may still be made. They may say of someone that
he is "good" *wamsa* but very poor, or vice versa, but people will not
be of the same level with one another unless there is some kind of
correspondence between their individual wealth and rank.

This correspondence need not be exact. A somewhat impoverished
man of high rank may be said to be of the same *tatvaya* as another
man of lesser rank but greater riches. It is these slight discrepancies
in wealth and rank that are utilized to advantage in the arrangement
of marriages. The intention is recognized to be social climbing on one
scale or another.

Unions between Equals.—Ideally, a Kandyan marriage should take
place between two groups of kin of "equal" wealth and rank.[7] It is
said that only then can the association really prosper. There is give
and take between the groups; they may visit each other without
being "ashamed or afraid" (*lajjai-bayai*); they can really become "one
people." In marriages of this kind, there may be a ceremony if the
parties are strangers or only very distantly related, but there will be
no cash payments. There may, however, be a slight inequality in the
gifts of food which are taken by one family to the other. In the discussion that precedes the wedding, the bride-givers may point out to
the bride-receivers (in a *deega* marriage) that they will invite a certain
number of people to their "at home." They may ask for a certain
number of *kat*.

A *kat* is a food parcel. Its contents are traditional and include plantains, rice pudding (milk-rice: *kiribat*), *kavum* cakes, and dried fish
of various kinds. In 1955 the value of a *kat* was reckoned to be twelve
rupees. At a normal "at home" among ordinary people, the bride-
givers may request six to seven *kat* from the groom. This is quite apart
from the food they will provide on their own account. The groom's
party, who also have their own "at home" if the families are strangers
to each other, do not get *kat* from the bride-givers. On the other
hand, the *kat* are not all provided by the groom himself. All his close
kinsmen—his mother's brothers, his own siblings, his sisters' husbands,
his father's sisters' husbands—will make arrangements among themselves to provide the *kat*. Two or three households may get together
to make up one *kat*. In this fashion not merely the food that is taken
in formal procession to the bride-givers but also the food that is con-
sumed in each "at home" is provided by the kinsmen of the bride

---

[7] This is suggested even by the term for marriage and sexual intercourse: *sambandha* means "marriage," "intercourse," and "equal."

and the groom. These gifts are later reciprocated on similar occasions. For these reasons a *magul gedara* (ceremony house) plays an important part in becoming the focus of "kindred" solidarity.

When the groom's procession comes to collect the bride and have a meal with their new kinsmen, it will be said that they have brought their own food with them and that they will not be a burden on the bride-givers. In this sense, there is a rather scrupulous balance in the exchanges. I have been told that at times the groom's party may offer cash in lieu of *kat*. But this was always rejected by the bride-givers with the proud exclamation, "We are not selling the girl; this is a wedding!" In other words, her family does not intend to lose any of their claims on the girl. On the other hand the groom becomes entirely responsible for her food and clothing.

The Compensation of Status Differences: Dowry.—There is thus a balance in marriage gifts among ordinary people when both parties are similar in wealth and status. Yet it is also well known that the so-called "dowry system" prevails among the Sinhalese. As soon as one arrives on the island one begins to hear tales of astronomical dowries which are given to daughters. There is no mystery about the fact that these are directly related to status. The greater the status difference, the larger the dowry.

It may be recalled that among wealthy families daughters leaving the house in *deega* marriage lose their inheritance but are given a dowry. There is even some suggestion that the dowry compensates this loss. But the differences between "inheritance" and "dowry" are extremely important, even though they may sometimes shade into each other. There is the question of timing and the size of the endowment.

An inheritance, by definition, becomes the property of the children only on the death of the parent. Until then the property belongs to the parent, and he may sell it or give it to someone else if he wishes to do so. A dowry, on the other hand, is a payment that is definitely agreed upon—and quite frequently even actually paid—at the time of marriage. It may be cash only, or a combination of land, houses, and trees as well as cash. After the agreement, the dowry is conveyed by a signed deed to the person of the daughter. It is noteworthy that the payment is not made to the groom or his family. The groom becomes the manager of the land, though the parents of the girl continue to have a finger in the pie through their influence on the daughter.

Unlike an inheritance, which is usually a portion of an estate divided among a number of heirs, a dowry is adjustable in size. Two daughters will not receive the same dowry. The size depends upon the status of the groom and is decided upon after heavy bargaining.

These differences arise because female inheritance and dowry have two different purposes. The former is merely a reflection of the general descent ideology of the Kandyans that sons and daughters both inherit in the same fashion. Dowry, on the other hand, is the result of a bargain and has a specific intention: that of linking the daughter—hence her family—with a particularly desirable son-in-law.

It is the position of the son-in-law that dictates both the timing and size of the dowry. If he is an equal, and a member of the family, the girl will get nothing. If he is equal but of another village or a distant family, he may insist that the rightful "inheritance" of the girl be signed over to her name, even though she will get control of this property only when her parents die.

If the son-in-law is superior and demands a dowry, then some action will be taken: if he is a stranger or a very distant relation, then both he and his family will insist that a dowry deed be actually signed and given to the girl. If the young man is a close relation (though superior), there may merely be an agreement without a signature—quite in keeping with Kandyan kinship morality.

The timing of the dowry is also adjustable. We have said that the dowry is owned by the daughter and managed by the son-in-law. If he is a very rich man, he may decide not to take the produce of the land but to allow the parents or brothers of the wife to cultivate the land for the time being. This gesture will be a good sign of the closeness of relations between the affines.

It is clear, then, that "dowry" is paid when the groom is somehow "superior." But this superiority is not merely one of rank. He may be superior because of his position and influence. He may be a Village Headman, or a Village Committee Chairman, or he may be one of those petty government servants—a clerk in a District Revenue Officer's office, a food production overseer, a health officer. There are many such people, employed by the Ceylon government and receiving reliable salaries, who are in contact with the villages. The combination of prestige, influence, and some stable income make such men the most desirable sons-in-law that wealthy people in Terutenne can imagine. And conversely, of course, it is the hope of every country youth with some initiative to get some such employment.

Dowry may be paid, however, even when the son-in-law has no such position but is only richer than the father-in-law. In this case one wonders how it is possible for the dowry to be paid at all. What often happens it that one daughter receives all the cash and even much of the lands owned by her parents in order to become acceptable to the wealthy man.

People say that it is the couple themselves who must be "equal" in wealth. The dowry brings the woman "up to the same level [tatvaya] as the groom." They "must be equal, for otherwise she will be treated as a servant and not respected." And if she is treated as a servant, her natal family will also not be respected as kinsmen. Hence, as long as a girl of a poor family gets enough of a dowry to raise her up to the level of the groom, the union will be considered successful even though her natal family may be impoverished as a result.

Of course, there are good reasons why a father may be tempted to such a course of action. For if the son-in-law is reliable, and if he also happens to be rich, the family of the daughter may receive great benefits from the connection. The parents may be allowed to cultivate their daughter's lands during their lifetime, and they have the privilege of turning to the son-in-law for general assistance. Thus the very size of the dowry is a reflection not merely of the status of the son-in-law but also of the closeness and the permanence of the affinal relationship.

The Compensation of Status Differences: "Bridewealth."—Such is the connection between dowry and status. However, since dowry is given to women, our arguments carry the implication that dowry is always connected with hypergamy. But what of those marriages in which the wife is superior to the husband? In Terutenne as in the rest of Ceylon and India there was a strong feeling that women of high *wamsa* must never associate with men of low *wamsa*. In this respect the preference for hypergamy (and the ritual purity of women) is very strongly expressed. If a rich woman were to marry a poor man of the same *wamsa* it would be foolish and ridiculous, for she could just as well marry an equal; but there would be nothing morally reprehensible.

Indeed, most *binna* marriages would fall into this category. It is true that the man would be treated as an inferior, but only because he would be a "poor" laborer under the control of a wealthy "wife." There are always enough poor men of the same *wamsa* who would like *binna* connections and there is no need for a wealthy man to have a *binna* son-in-law who is of low *wamsa* as well as being poor. Of course, reciprocity is maintained in *binna* marriages. The husband compensates for his poverty by his extra labor to his father-in-law.

Do these arguments mean that women of high *wamsa* never marry men of low *wamsa*? In fact, though rare, such instances could always be found both in Terutenne and in other villages. In every case, the women concerned were of high birth (*wamsa*) with "good" names, but of very poor families. They were espoused to men of low *wamsa* but great wealth. These were clear cases of the exchange of rank for money. This exchange, furthermore, was often in terms of cash.

The cases were almost identical. An aristocrat who had encountered difficulties would mortgage his property. Later, being unable to redeem the mortgage, he would give his daughter in marriage to a man of low *wamsa* who would undertake the payment of his debts. Almost invariably, the husband would then change his name and titles to those of the woman. If he failed to do it, his children would certainly do so. In these cases what is particularly interesting is that such "payments" are always secret. They are some kind of "hidden bride-price" of which both sides are ashamed, standing in contrast to dowry, which is always open and aboveboard and even a matter for pride. All parties are embarrassed by "hidden bridewealth" because, in the case of the groom, the payment is a concrete example of his own admittance of "low" *wamsa*; it is even worse for the family of the bride: the acceptance of payment for the girl makes her into a prostitute.

The Principle of Hypergamy

Here we touch upon some of the most deep-seated ideas of Kandyans. Women may have sexual relations with equals and superiors. They may marry men of higher ritual status. But they must not fall below. Men, however, may do what they like; even if they have sexual intercourse with women of lower castes, this does not matter much. They may deny or repudiate all connections, and in any case they can keep low women as "concubines."

It is of great interest that there should be such preoccupation with the ritual purity of women and not of men. Of course, this is true not merely of the Sinhalese but of all Indian and Ceylonese castes (see chap. 5). In all cases, there is a categorical assertion that the consorts of women should not fall below their own ritual rank, though in general they may be higher.

The Kandyans would say that "the honor and respectability of men is guarded through the women." "Women's lineage [fecundity] must be protected." There have been various suggestions as to why there is this concern about the ritual positions of women, when it is said that men may do what they like. H. N. C. Stevenson (1954), in his analysis of Hindu pollution, makes the singular suggestion that men are only "externally polluted" by sexual intercourse with women, whereas women are "internally polluted" when they sleep with men of low caste. External pollution can be dealt with by lustrations, but internal pollution is difficult to cleanse.

There is undoubtedly some evidence to support this view. In Terutenne men thought nothing of sleeping with low-caste women— some, like the Village Headman, kept regular "mistresses"—but they always insisted that they never *ate* any food cooked by the women. That would have polluted them internally through their stomachs.

But there is more to this question of hypergamy. I believe that hypergamy is related to the concept of caste and the descent of ritual status. In South India and Ceylon, it seems clear that caste membership is always a matter of bilateral descent. In other words, the individual receives ritual rank (caste-blood) always through both parents. The matrilineal Nayar, the patrilineal Nambudiri Brahmins, the patrilineal Tanjore Brahmins, and the Coorgs are not negative instances. We must make an analytical distinction in the concept of descent as signifying, on the one hand, ritual status and membership in a caste and, on the other hand, membership in corporate descent groups within the caste. All the groups mentioned above are bilateral in the former sense, though they may have a variety of unilineal descent groups, within the castes or subcastes.

The Nayar are the most obvious test case. Those of South Malabar and Cochin are always described as having exhibited extreme forms of matrilineal descent groups until quite recent times. But in fact, in terms of the descent of ritual status, they are, and always have been, bilateral. The ritual status of the "father" is of the first importance, and it is for this reason that the princely Nayar lineages encouraged connections with the Nambudiris; for "chiefs and royalty alike revere their Nambudiri *genitors,* and boast that the blood of these Gods of the earth is running in their veins" (Gough, 1955*a,* p. 54). The Nayar of lower subcastes, in turn, had hypergamous connections with men of slightly higher groups. What was forbidden, on pain of severe punishment, was the association with low-caste men.[8]

The question that now rises is why the bilateral descent of ritual status should be associated with hypergamy. Here seems to be a contradiction in terms. Theoretically, one would say that if ritual status descends bilaterally, and if there is a desire to preserve ritual status, then all marriages should be endogamous. I think that this is indeed the reason why castes in South India and Ceylon are normally endogamous. Moreover, since kin groups carry ritual status, they too

---

[8] If one accepts the view that the Nayar had bilateral descent of ritual status, their rather puzzling prepuberty *tali* rites can be seen to have a definite structural role. We know that marriage as *sambandham* was an uncertain relationship. We know that Nayar women had considerable sexual freedom. The prepuberty "*tali*-tying marriage" ceremony may be interpreted as an attempt to unite the Nayar woman once and for all to a particular, well-known person of "good," "pure" ritual status. He then becomes the *ritual genitor* (the conveyor of ritual status) to the children that the woman may subsequently bear. And, this indeed appears to be what Nayar claim themselves: "The *tali*-tier of a woman was regarded . . . as the ritual father of her children. If they knew him, the children called this man *appan* (the Tamil word for 'father,' used for *genitor* by Tiyyars and Christians) as distinct from *acchan* . . . the Malayalam word used by Nayars for the *genitor* and all lovers of the mother . . . Nevertheless . . . informants stressed that the *appan* was a child's 'real father,' as the *tali*-rite was a woman's 'real marriage.'" Gough (1955*a*), pp. 50–51.

have a strongly endogamous tendency. Still, it is important to recognize that when unions between persons of different ritual status (caste or *wamsa*) do occur, they are expected to take the form of hypergamy. The Laws of Manu state unequivocally that *anuloma* unions (with the hair or grain: natural) between a high-caste man and low-caste woman are acceptable, but that *pratiloma* unions (against the hair or grain: unnatural) between a high-caste woman and a low-caste man must be punished by excommunication, if not more severe measures. In Ceylon, before British rule, the punishment was drowning.

Given bilateral descent of ritual status, hypergamy is, as it were, a second line of defense, and is related to the fundamental difference between men and women, that women can bear children and men cannot. With men there is always at least the possibility of repudiation of the offspring. The tie is tenuous. But when a woman has intercourse with a low-caste man, the connection may result in a child that will remain perpetual witness to her deep pollution, and the mother will be forever associated with another caste. Moreover, unless she and the child are excommunicated, they may together bring "polluted blood" into the rest of the caste and family and in that way threaten the ritual status of their natal group.

For men, the situation is quite different. It is true that they, too, convey ritual status through their semen, but there is never any danger that they may themselves be irrevocably polluted by sexual intercourse with women of low caste or low ritual status. Furthermore, although a man's children may take pleasure in the high ritual status of their genitors and in their own relatively "purer" blood, the father can disregard them in a manner impossible for a mother.[9] Therefore, the sexuality of men may always be allowed much greater freedom. The sexual freedom of men stands in contrast to the stringency of other prohibitions.

"In hypergamous unions [among the Nayar], the higher caste father might not eat in the house of his mistress, and, after taking a bath, might not touch her nor her children" (Gough, 1955*a*, p. 48). As we have already seen, food prohibitions among the Sinhalese follow those of the Nayar.

"Hypergamy" Within and Outside the Caste

There is an ambiguity in the use of the word "hypergamy." It implies, first, the connections across caste boundaries like the Nambudiri–Nayar or, in the case of examples provided from Terutenne, Cultivator–low caste, and, second, hypergamous marriages within the castes. Cross-caste connections, of course, hardly merit the appellation of

---

[9] Consider Wanni Wannaku's treatment of his Galpitiya family, pp. 113–114.

"marriage." On the Malabar coast the Nambudiri certainly do not think of their connections with Nayar women as being the same as their "real" marriages to Nambudiri women who bear legal heirs; similarly, the cross-caste unions in Terutenne, as we have seen, are at best no more than "concubinage." In both cases, caste boundaries remain intact, and the cross-relationships are always those of men of high ritual rank sleeping with low-rank women.

In the context of "marriages" within the caste, with dowry, the situation is different. Obviously the father does not repudiate his children. They inherit from him. But the statement that "the honor of men is guarded through their women" should be recalled. A man's "pollution" is superficial, and it may be overlooked altogether with the help of the dowry; but if a woman is polluted she can never again be cleansed. The ritual purity of each sibling group must, of necessity, by fundamentally safeguarded through the women. Hence the bias for hypergamy remains even inside the caste.

However, if the man is to accept the woman or his children into his home, the status differences must not be too great; hence, in hypergamous unions with dowry the ritual positions of the couple are usually fairly equal. Indeed, it is amusing to recall that although my informants were as one in asserting that "women go up" with dowry, they were all very puzzled when I remarked that, by their own reasoning, the men obviously married "low" women. This piece of logic was not entirely welcome: men married "equals," even though the women "went up."

From an entirely different point of view, I have already indicated that, with this intense preoccupation with the "purity of women," the notion of hypergamy has come to symbolize all kinds of status distinctions (see chap. 5). A family will often say, "They are low; we do not give our women to them." If the other group is considered very low, then they may say, "There is no give and take of women between us" (*hira ganu denu karanni ne*), though, of course, the men would not be averse to sleeping with these "low" women. Even so, it is the refusal to give women that is the most forceful public statement that the other group is considered to be of lower rank. (One could always take a woman and treat her as a concubine.)[10]

THE JOKING BEHAVIOR OF MASSINA

Differences in status influence the behavior of brothers-in-law in significant ways. Both the somewhat standardized behavior and the terminology of address show important variations. Brothers-in-law

---

[10] For a further discussion of the relationship between caste and hypergamy, see Yalman (1963).

are known symmetrically as *massina* to each other. The chief meaning of the term is male cross-cousin (again symmetrical). The fact that brothers-in-law are referred to as cross-cousins is a logical concomitant of the Kandyan marriage rule which stipulates that only a male and female cross-cousin may have sexual relationships or marry. They may, naturally, be cross-cousins only in the classificatory sense.

The most interesting fact about the *massina* category is that it stands in direct contrast to the category of classificatory or real "brothers." Whereas *massina* is a symmetrical term, the sibling terminology is markedly asymmetrical. Elder brothers (*ayya*) and younger brothers (*malli*), and their various grades (big elder brother, small elder brother), are always distinguished.

These terminological distinctions are related to certain kinds of behavior. *Massina* are expected to joke and play with each other. The very utterance of the word *massina* (or its various other forms such as *machang* or *hura*) will bring broad smiles to all faces in the villages. Even those *massina* with great age discrepancies between them will be seen speaking and amusing themselves as if they were peers.

Among siblings, in contrast to this free equality between *massina*, age differences are magnified. Their behavior toward one another is expected to be one of great reserve. They must pay respect to, and honor one another. I have even heard it said that brothers should turn their faces away (and indeed turn their backs to each other) when they meet in village paths lest they give offense.

Why is *massina-massina* a joking relationship? In answering this question it is best to distinguish the relationships between brothers-in-law from those between cross-cousins. In Terutenne both cross-cousins and brothers-in-law (with the important exceptions which will be described) joked with each other.

(a) First cross-cousins are known as *avassa massina* (real or own cross-cousins). It is often said that although they are very closely related, and often on better terms than siblings, they do not usually have property in common as a full-sibling group. The *massina*, however, do have claims on each other's sisters, and their position of being close kinsmen and potential affines as well appears to introduce the contradictions of intimacy and tension which have often been considered as conducive to joking relationships.

(b) Similar observations apply in the case of brothers-in-law as *massina*. The brother-in-law has come as close as possible to his *massina* by his marriage to the sister, but he is still an outsider. Since no marriages are permitted between generations, he is also of the same generation, usually an equal. Thus, with the same contradiction of intimacy and tension, it is not surprising to find joking relationships in this case as well.

Avoidance Between Brothers-in-law

The equality between cross-cousins and between brothers-in-law is an important aspect of their joking relations. How important this factor is may be gauged from the cases in which the brothers-in-law are not equal. When there is great wealth or status differences between them, the normal joking behavior is completely reversed and the brothers-in-law avoid each other scrupulously. The inferior must pay "respect" and "honour" to the superior. Symmetrical *massina* terminology completely disappears; instead, the superior is addressed as *ayya* (elder brother) and reciprocates by *malli* (young brother).[11] These manifestations often accompany dowry payments.

This sort of unequal cousinship existed for my interpreter in Terutenne, whose sister had been given to a very wealthy and influential shopkeeper of another village. The brothers-in-law rarely visited each other, and when they did—always at prearranged times—it was a formal occasion. Had they been equals such formality would have been ridiculous. Among equals, alliances are often made doubly certain by an exchange of women. Two men exchange their sisters and this union is considered to be best of all.

These various remarks on hypergamy, the relations of cross-cousins, joking, and avoidance may be illustrated by the following discussion which took place one day in Terutenne.

Piyasena, the son of a schoolteacher, said, "School starts today!" I asked him whether many boys from Galpitiya went to school in Wekumbura, the main hamlet. He replied, "No, as soon as they can walk, they go to the chena. And young men consider it a waste of time to go to school when they can do something else. But education is really very important; you can get jobs with it and raise your status." I expressed some doubt about the jobs. Piyasena said, "Look, if you have passed your Senior School Certificate exams you can get a job as a schoolteacher; but of course then you would not accept work as a tea-maker [low occupation], or in hotels and shops."

"What about marriage?"

"If you are educated, you can get better girls. The Headman's sons all went to school but none of them graduated and so they are not educated, but Nissanka [a schoolteacher] did give his children an education, so he can marry them off well. We would never give a girl to the T. P. R.'s [Village Committee Chairman and *massina* of the

---

[11] These changes are only in address: they remain in the category of *massina* for reference and kinship. They would say, "We call each other *ayya-malli* but are really *massina* by kinship.

Village Headman]; they may be rich but they are low and unedu-
cated."

"But they married the Amunumulle [an aristocratic family] in the
last generation; they can't be all that low!" (A baited remark since
Piyasena himself is related to the Amunumulle.)

"You can't say that! They have done so in the past but today we do
not recognize that relationship any more! We are not related to
them. Anyhow, we are only related to this village through my *nenda*
[FZ] who was given to the Amunumulle."

"Would you now give a girl to the Amunumulle?"

"No! And they would not ask for my sisters!"

"Would you give a girl to anyone in this village?"

"No, we can marry them to better people."

"Your sister has been married to a very good person [rich Low
Country *Karava* shopkeeper in Abangella]: now what about you asking
for one of his sisters for yourself?"

"Oh no! If they refuse, then our relationship will grow distant and
will also create trouble for the brother-in-law. My father and mother
will never ask it, and they [the in-laws] will not suggest it. If anything,
I would have to fall in love with the girl [i.e., have an affair with her],
then something might be done. But, similarly, we would never give a
girl to the Amunumulle, and they will never ask us for one."

"Well, what will you do?"

"A boy can marry anyway he likes, he can arrange it himself, but a
girl's must be carefully planned. I can marry anyone I like from this
village. They would all want to get related with us, but the dowry
they can give is not much."

"What happens when, as in your case, you give a girl to better people with a lot of dowry, and the brother-in-law's sisters become your
nana? Can you ask for them, and if you can't, what is the use of such
a marriage?"

"We cannot ask for the *nana*, but could get around to them [start-
ing sexual relations]. The point is that the brother-in-law's sister will
be married to a rich man, her children will get education, and will be
rich, and they will be married to even better people."

"Well, how does that help you?"

"Why, they are our relations, we can be proud of them! And having
good relations is a good point in marriage. My brother is a clerk in
the Kachcheri [Government Agent's Office]: that is very good too!"

"But you are slightly below these people in Abangella?"

"Slightly."

"What would be a good match for you?"

"The postmaster in Nildandahinna has children just like us. They are rich. But my father is well known to them and in the vicinity. The best would be to marry one of his daughters; they are also 'Low Country' and they would give her to me. And we could give our sisters to them. That would be very good; exchanging sisters would make us something like one [ekata], very close."

"What about the people of Galpitiya? Why do they not try to arrange better marriages for their girls?"

"They have no land, therefore that idea is gone. The best thing is that the girls have brothers. That is important; they can help in difficult times, and the number of brothers works like dowry! But most of the marriages in this place are between equals, and dowry does not come into it. They have nothing to arrange better marriages with, and therefore they do not care about their women. In our family the girls are well guarded!"

The point of this account is that Piyasena gives full recognition to the implications of a system in which women are supposed to go up, but men may marry beneath them. The avoidance and formality patterns which develop in a significantly hypergamous marriage are also clearly indicated. The rich massina Piyasena was talking about has a house with seventeen rooms in the village of Abangella, and is very well known in the vicinity. He never comes to visit his father-in-law in Terutenne, though Piyasena's family does go formally to visit him with announcements at various times of the year.

EXCOMMUNICATION

Marriage draws those who cooperate, or intend to cooperate, into a kinship pattern, and a certain compatibility of status in both wealth and wamsa is essential. Kinsmen are naturally identified with each other. They are "one people," and the status of one branch inevitably reflects upon the others. For a marriage to be effective (i.e., to set up cooperation and kinship), the agreement of the kinsmen is essential. When such an agreement has not been secured, then the relationship between the couple is hardly to be described as "marriage."

If a man and woman decide to set up house together against the will of either family, they are excommunicated. Such excommunication is always the result of a runaway marriage in which the status of the bride and groom (either in wealth or in wamsa or, indeed, in caste) is felt to be incompatible by either kin group. After the runaway union, the superior group announces as widely as possible that all relationships with the erring man or woman have ceased. In particular, the excommunication is effected as follows: (a) all visiting is forbidden (yanni enni ne), and (b) all interdining is forbidden (kannit bonnit ne! literally, we do not eat and we do not drink [with them]).

The wrongdoer and the mate are treated, in short, like outcasts. If the groom is a member of another caste, the family of the girl preserves its "purity" by not coming into contact with its "polluted" member.

In the case of a man living with a woman of lower caste, the matter is less serious. As long as he does not publicly or obviously "eat" with her, he will not be excommunicated. But the union will be mere concubinage; neither the girl nor her family will have any hope that kinship can be established between themselves and the kinsmen of the man involved. Since the girl will be in the position of a paid prostitute, her family will not look upon this liaison with much favor.

How deeply the idea of "equality" is embedded in kinship is shown by the use of the word *sambandha*. People will say that they have no *sambandha* (lit., joined) with another kin group. This will mean (a) that they do not intermarry, and (b) that they are not equals. Those with whom there is *sambandha* are the people who are considered "equal" and with whom there is intermarriage.

Caste Climbing and Role of Affines

We have said that excommunication takes place when status is threatened. There are instances when a family of superior caste or rank will establish both cooperation and kinship with an individual of doubtful and shadowy ancestry. One may be quite sure that the family will receive some material benefit and that the individual does not have many kinsmen of low rank or wealth in the village.

If these conditions are satisfied and one does succeed in establishing affinal kinship with a superior family, a climb from one caste into another will almost have been effected. One's children will have definite matrilateral connections with the "other caste." True, they will be of low *wamsa* in the caste owing to the "pollution" in their blood. But they are quite likely to make further marriages themselves in the same group. By the third generation the incident will almost have been forgotten and, at the same time, the "boundary" between the castes or (to a lesser extent) between *wamsa* groups inside the caste, will still be considered "impregnable."

STABILITY

The question of stability is best treated when the two aspects of marriage—the alliance and the domestic union—are considered separately. For obvious reasons, kinship cooperation can wax and wane without necessarily disappearing entirely. Certainly, affines may quarrel and cut off relations with each other without the domestic units being affected. On the other hand, the alliance may remain even though the couple which brought it into being break up their domestic unit. I have seen men who, though separated from their wives, still considered their former brothers-in-law among their closest kinsmen and allies even though the marriage had been the only bond between them. The stability of the affinal alliance is independent of the stability of the domestic unit. This does not mean that these two aspects of marriage do not influence each other.

The stability of the domestic unit is one of the remarkable features of marriage in Terutenne. When the in-laws quarrel, if there are no children, there may be pressure brought upon the bride to return home to her parents. But it is rare to see this happen when there are children. The alliance may fall into abeyance, but the domestic unit remains.

The stability of the domestic unit may be seen from the figures of remarriage in Terutenne (table 29). Certain reservations are called

TABLE 29

Marriages and Separations in Terutenne

	Men			Women		
Relative Wealth	No. of Men	No. of Marriages	No. of Separations	No. of Women	No. of Marriages	No. of Separations
A (own 7 *pale* or more)....	15	19	1	4	6	0
B (own 2–7 *pale*).	20	27	4	16	18	1
C (own 2 *pale* or less).....	95	114	12	67	77	6
Total.......	130	160	17	87	101	7

for. First, it is impossible to get reliable figures about domestic units in which the couple were young and separated without having children. In the case of separations between couples who had children, I believe the figures are not unreliable. Field observations that domestic units with children tend to be stable agree also with the figures given regarding the *ge* (chap. 6). Note that children are living with stepparents in very few cases (table 30). The material about full-sibling groups is reliable, and I doubt that I missed many cases of this kind.

Generally speaking, one could say that young people do tend to experiment to some extent with various partners especially among

TABLE 30

Children Living with Stepparents or Other Relatives in Terutenne

	Cases
Man's children by another woman	3
Woman's children by another man	2
Daughter's son	2
Wife's sister's children	1
Husband's brother's children	2
Wife's brother's children	1
Total	11

lower classes. But the appearance of children gives a greater stability to their relationship.

On the other hand, there is no formal difficulty whatsoever about divorce. There are no payments to be returned, no authorities to be consulted. A couple who cannot get along may simply separate; their property is separate in any case, though property acquired during the marriage ought to be divided. Young children normally go with the mother; older children may live with either parent or other relations.

It may seem surprising that in a society with such formal ease of marriage and divorce, with few marriage payments, a system of property rights for women, no unilineal descent groups, and with both polyandry and polygyny, there should be such stability in the domestic unit.[12] Two important reasons explain the seeming inconsistency:

(a) The tasks and domestic roles of men and women are so distinct and so specifically allocated that each partner is quite clear as to what his rights and obligations are. No more can be demanded. In this respect the *ge* is well isolated from purely personal difficulties unless these happen to be great enough to upset the basic rights and obligations.

(b) Great sexual freedom is granted to both partners. The criminal nature of adultery (when it occurs within the same caste) is minimized. This is, I believe, a direct result of the lack of interest in descent especially among the lower orders.

It is well known that married men often sleep with other women. If their wives were asked about it, they would say, "How should I know what he is up to? I do not follow him around!" In the case of women, it is generally felt that their husbands cannot easily prevent their wives from sleeping with other men. They do attempt to catch

---

[12] See Gluckman (1950); but see also "Aspects of Bridewealth and Marriage Stability Among the Kachin and Lakher," in Leach (1961a).

the culprits, but if the man is a friend or a good relation, nothing more will be said. Otherwise, he may escape with a beating. Of course, if low-caste men were to be caught at such adventures they would be very severely handled.

The figures of remarriages cover up an important fact. The certain men and women who seem to change domestic par astounding frequency. These people are in complete contr great majority who tend to remain in the same domestic uni lives.

One woman, for instance, Mary Navaratne, had started by setting up house with two brothers, and after about ten had four children from them. Then one of the brothers d day Mary went to visit a relative of hers in another village, a met a man whom she liked. She set up house with him, a bearing him two children, brought him along to the house first husband. The two men then formed a polyandrous unit. another child. When I was in the village, her second "lover" (husband) had died, but she was again separated from her first h and was living in the house of one of her married daughters.

Such cases, however, are exceptions. They are not confi women. There was one man married in *binna* in Terutenne, brothers-in-law had worked out with great amusement that he had had serious connections with twenty-two women. One does not know, of course, whether to believe such stories. But it is clear that most separations concerned certain eccentric individuals. Terutenne villagers described their antics to each other with obvious amusement. If any disapproval was felt it was not, I believe, particularly strong.

9

The Structure of the Micro-Caste

"And thus by marrying constantly each rank within itself, the Descent and Dignity thereof is preserved for ever."—Robert Knox, *An Historical Relation of Ceylon* (1681; repr. 1911), p. 66

THE BOUNDARIES OF THE KINDRED

In the village of Terutenne the idea of innate purity or pollution was not considered to be entirely or even mainly a matter of caste. The wider family loomed much larger than caste in the discussions of this topic. Indeed, each single individual was felt to possess an innate ritual quality which placed him in a particular position in relation to others. In this respect, the individual was like a unique ritual cell whose balance of purity and pollution would be deeply affected by his personal fate (*karma*). Similarly, the larger kin group to which he belonged was a ritual cell modeled on caste. Such kin groups were ideally endogamous. Their members viewed their distinction from other kin groups around them in terms of purity and pollution.

These significant features—the ideal endogamy, the unique ritual status, the conception of clear boundaries—are indeed the crucial structural factors in the organization of castes. Since we can only properly speak of castes when they are definitely recognized and identified by name and other indices by the people concerned, we ought, perhaps, to refer to these small kin groups, which utilize the same structural features as the named castes and which are in fact the cells from which the larger status groups are built, as micro-castes. To avoid a certain inevitable confusion with castes, however, I shall continue to use the term "kindred." The Sinhalese themselves refer to such groups as *pavula*.

One aspect of the *pavula* is the convergence of the "personal kindreds" of a certain number of individuals.[1] By this is meant not a

---

[1] *Ape pavula*, also *eka minissu* (one people), *avessa pavula* (near or real family), *ape kande* (our mound), etc.

series of overlapping circles that include parts of one village or a district, but an interconnectedness, reinforced again and again, of persons who have many kinship links in common among themselves but few or none with other kindreds. Marriage, of course, is responsible for many of these connections. Women are likely to hold property: it is as if the kindred is formed for the sole purpose of keeping both land and women inside a circumscribed circle.

There are two ways, therefore, by which an individual may become a member of a kindred. He (or she) may be born into it by the fact that both his parents were members of the kindred; or he may make a marriage alliance, which, however, must be treated as an expression of previous kinship ties. Descent and marriage are the two principles on which these groups are formed. The former makes for continuity of ritual status and membership and the latter allows some flexibility and leaves an open door for those who wish to move out of or enter the *pavula*.

Although the *pavula* is not in fact entirely endogamous, its members (as well as outsiders) think of it as a clearly demarcated group. In the first place, there is the dogma that one should intermarry only with people with whom there is previous kinship and previous intermarriages. The lack of earlier ties would indicate that the parties were not of equal status. In the second place, when marriages are arranged with unknown strangers with the full agreement of the kin group, the new relations "become" kinsmen and are assimilated into the group. Indeed, it is rude to suggest in their company that they were not related in the past. Third, when a union is undesirable, those who flout the wishes of the kin group are excommunicated. Although the anthropologist may discover marriage links between members of the *pavula* and outsiders from whom they claim to be separate, these may be denied or they may be referred to as "wrong marriages" (*varada kassada*) which must be disregarded for kinship. In this way, the whole *pavula*, and not merely its individual members, will cut itself off from other *pavula*.

The formal denial of intermarriage is significant. Among people who consider all kinship links to be equally important, kin groups can be clearly demarcated only by the denial of all intermarriage. This is also the reason why castes must be endogamous if caste affiliation is equally traced through both parents.[2]

An example will clarify the nature of these caste-like kin groups.

The Pavula in Helagama Hamlet

I lived in the hamlet of Helagama for many months. Its inhabitants included aristocrats as well as "low Goyigama," and there was one

---

[2] Note, however, the reservation made for the purposes of hypergamy pp. 177ff.).

household of Tom-Tom Beaters (dwelling 8 in map 8). The hamlet was divided into two large *pavula* with some people remaining un-committed. I list the dwellings below as numbered on map 8. Each dwelling is treated as a single unit, for in this village all the members

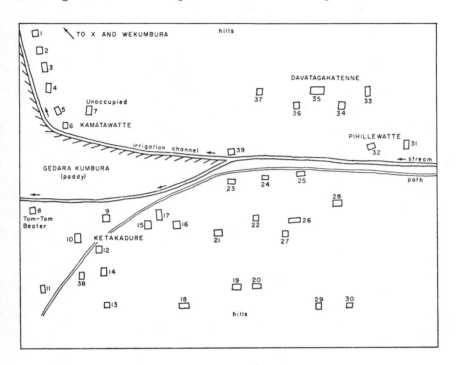

Map 8. Helagama in Terutenne.

of a dwelling were of the same *pavula*. There were two major *pavula,* A and B:

> *Pavula* A (16 dwellings): Nos. 1, 2, 3, 4, 13, 17, 19, 20, 28, 29, 33, 34, 35, 36, 37, and X
> *Pavula* B (13 dwellings): Nos. 10, 11, 12, 15, 16, 21, 22, 24, 25, 26, 27, 32, 38

Those who were not entirely committed were these:

> *Pavula* C (3 dwellings): Nos. 5, 6, 9
> *Pavula* D (1 dwelling): No. 39
> *Pavula* E (four dwellings): Nos. 14, 23, 24, 31
> *Pavula* F (two dwellings): Nos. 18, 30

Household 24 was in a specially difficult position discussed below. For obvious reasons it is impossible to show all the kinship relations which obtained in this hamlet and in so doing demonstrate how the

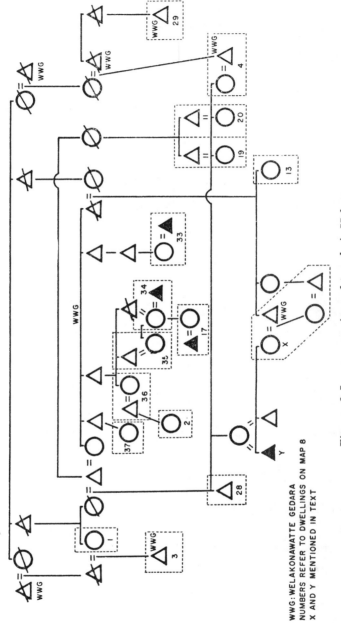

WWG: WELAKONAWATTE GEDARA
NUMBERS REFER TO DWELLINGS ON MAP 8
X AND Y MENTIONED IN TEXT

Figure 16. Interconnections of *pavula* A, Helagama.

pavula were not related. It is possible, however, to show how one of these *pavula* was internally related and how, when I discovered some connections with the others, special explanations were furnished.

Figure 16 shows the internal connections between members of *pavula* A. I have only traced the relationship to one of the senior members in a dwelling and I have disregarded extra-hamlet relatives. Some persons are shown in solid black. It was possible to link *pavula* A through these persons with some of the other *pavula*. The actual connections are depicted in figure 17. Thus, through household 34,

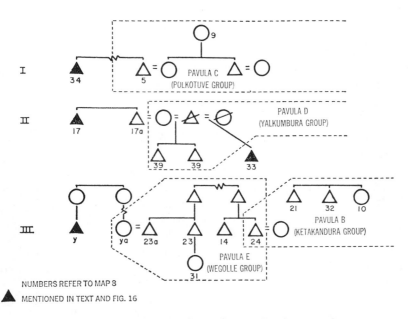

Figure 17. Connections of *pavula* A with other *pavula*.

pavula A was related to *pavula* C known as Polkotuve and considered by all the hamlet to be of very low ritual status. It was said that the Polkotuve people did not have traditional *mudianse* names and were of the same kind of low Goyigama as the people of Galpitiya (chap. 5). They had been workers on the fields of the aristocratic households in "traditional" times.

Moreover, through Y, who was the brother-in-law of one of the leaders of *pavula* A (a schoolteacher who owned much land in the village), the kindred had some connection with *pavula* E. *Pavula* E (known as the Wegolla group) was fairly wealthy in 1955, but it was known that its members had come from a low Galpitiya-type village in the region and that they had intermarried with some people known as Galkotumulle in Wekumbura who were also said to be persons of the lowest category of the Goyigama. Hence the connection with *pavula* E was uncomplimentary and therefore conveniently over-looked. *Pavula* E, in turn, had some connections through its poorer members (notably household 24) with *pavula* B, which, as we shall see, consisted mainly of poor persons of very low ritual and economic status.

These unpleasant connections were isolated cases in the total com-plex proliferation of inter-*pavula* kinship which had to be discovered as a result of lengthy investigations in the hamlet. They would not have been freely mentioned by *pavula* A. In each of them kinship was categorically denied, and it was asserted that "we" do not eat or drink with "them" and do not exchange women with "them." In other words, the polluted members were excommunicated. So, 5, who lived with the low Polkotuve woman, was never invited to the *magul gedara* feasts of the kin group even though the brothers 5 and 34 did see each other now and again. Another man, 17a (who lived in part of dwelling 17) was separated from a poor woman who was also regarded as low, like the Polkotuve. Though the households 17 and 39 were very close neighbors, they carefully avoided each other and there was some hostility between them.

The case of *pavula* E (the Wegolla group) was the most complicated. Here, as we noted above, there had been a double renouncement: Y did not not consider Ya to be his kinswoman any more, and at the same time, status distinctions inside *pavula* E had led to a further split in the group. Two men, 23 and 23a (both of whom had fairly success-ful shops and one of whom had the distinction of having a son who was a schoolteacher), and a woman, 31 (the daughter of 23), had ceased to keep up close kinship with 14 and 24 (both miserably poor and quite hostile to their kinsmen) on the grounds that these people had made "bad marriages."

In this fashion *pavula* A quite frankly thought of itself as uncon-nected with the other *pavula* who lived in Helagama. I do not show the internal connections of B, but it may be assumed that they pro-liferated quite as much as those of *pavula* A.

Cooperation and the Identity of the Pavula

One immediately wonders, of course, why a kindred pretends to this separation and insists on its distinctions. In order to answer this ques-tion, we must investigate the *pavula* from a nonritual aspect, looking at the material basis on which the *pavula* is formed and the specific interests which bring people together.

We noted in the previous chapter that kinship demands cooperation and dependability. When these exist, then closer kinship can be created by a well-arranged marriage, and when they do not exist, such kinship as existed is denied and forgotten. Pursuing this logic, one may say that although all the personages in the *pavula* are assimilated into the kinship idiom, they are not brought together merely because of consanguineous kinship.[3]

What, then, does bring them together? There are, in fact, quite a number of spheres of village life which require men and women to work in unison. These informal groups will overlap but will not coincide. If these groups are regarded as overlapping, there will be an area where the overlap is greatest. This nexus of greatest cooperation is where we would also expect the greatest number of kinship ties— and thus the *pavula*.

The *pavula* is not formed around one common material factor or a single principle; it consists not simply of the people who own land in the same field, or who live in the same neighborhood. Other considerations always enter in, and these may vary from place to place. The interests noted below are the foci around which cooperation develops in Terutenne. Some are obviously more important than others, and there may be many others in the bazaar towns and trade centers of the district.

(1) Property (*pangu karaya*: shareholders).—People who have some undivided property between them or are "holders of undivided land" (*havul idam tieni minissu*) are usually, though not invariably, in the same *pavula*. There is pressure to bring in unrelated members (who may have bought a share) as part of the kinship group.

(2) The paddy field (*idam karaya*).—Those who own land on the same water line or in the same field need to cooperate closely. Their unity is sometimes remarkable. I have seen the landholders of a whole field walk up a hillside to demolish the dams made on the water line by the owners of another field. These people need not necessarily be of the same kindred or even of the same caste.

(3) The dwelling (*gedara kattiya*).—Those who live in the same dwelling (with the exception of servants) are almost always of the same *pavula*.

(4) Neighborhood (*gama*—hamlet, or *hen yaya*—chena community). —Generally speaking, those who inhabit the same neighborhood tend to be close kinsmen. There are two neighborhoods in

---

[3] This duality appears in the nomenclature. Often the terms *pettak* (side) or *kattiya* (group, faction, lot) will be used interchangeably with *pavula*. The former have no kinship implications, whereas the latter (together with *variga*, which is also used) always carries the connotations of consanguinity.

Terutenne. There is the fairly permanent one in the hamlets, and there is the annual chena community which is formed by the slash-and-burn cultivators. In both cases those who live in very close contiguity tend to be members of the same *pavula*. *Pavula* A in Helagama, for instance, tends to inhabit a number of dwellings that are fairly close together.

(5) Agricultural cooperation (*attang veda karani kattiya*—those who cultivate paddy in association).—The nature of these labor exchanges, which are "contractual" and carefully calculated, have been explained in chapter 4. During the harvest in Terutenne in June, 1955, I carried out very detailed investigations into reciprocal labor exchange. Two facts stood out clearly: first, cooperation was almost entirely confined to the individual hamlets, and, second, members of the kindred were always the first to be invited to an *attang* group. Nonkinsmen are also occasionally found in these coöperative groups, however.[4]

Ande (sharecropping), too, may frequently be between kinsmen. But since it is a relationship between landlord and tenant, unless land is given on *ande* by two men to each other, it remains a relationship between a superior and an inferior. Many *ande* tenants are therefore not related in any way to the landlord.

(6) Cooperation in trading ventures (*Kadei karaya*: shops; and *tavalam karaya*: transport).—Certain persons in Terutenne, who had some capital in cash or bulls, were interested in these more sophisticated cooperative enterprises. Indeed, assistance in shopkeeping and trading is expected between wealthy persons, and they frequently finance one another's trading ventures. Again, in Terutenne, the shopkeepers were very closely related. Moreover, as the feud described in chapter 8 may suggest, many of the deepest enmities, as well as the closest associations, were greatly affected by the competition engendered by the shops.[5]

(7) Politics and elections.—I have already mentioned the political role played by the *pavula* in the village. Here groups of kins-

---

[4] There is an interesting problem in *attang* reciprocities. The residential unit makes use of its labor resources without special calculations. *Attang* is not reckoned among members of the same dwelling and between fathers, sons, and sons-in-law. They all have the general obligation to assist and the right to be assisted. Buffalo loans, too, may not be specifically within this circle. Beyond it, all reciprocities are calculated in detail.

[5] Dharmadasa and Ranbanda, members of the younger generation of the old branch of the Amunumulle, opened shops in Terutenne in direct competition with T. P. R., a shopkeeper of the Muhandiram faction. T. P. R. had a hand in arranging a marriage between his niece and Ukwatte Tikiribanda (p. 165), an important shopkeeper.

men coöperate closely for or against factions in positions of authority in the village. They act as pressure groups in all elections in the village. The stakes at these elections are high[6] and it is very important to get one's own candidate into office.

I have been describing specific interests which bring about coöperation in Terutenne. Any single one of these need not be based on kinship. Friendship and good will would be sufficient. But eventually the whole becomes greater than its parts: "One of the great processes of society . . . is that . . . the common is built out of the like, common interests growing out of what were at first merely like interests." [7]

Stresses in the Pavula

On the other hand we must be careful not to define the *pavula* as a sharply focused corporation: its unity is only relative, its solidarity rests upon convenience, and may be broken.

In *pavula* A, for instance, there were deep tensions which would undoubtedly make themselves felt in the future. Consider figure 18, which depicts the core of *pavula* A. Though on the surface this group of people had appeared quite friendly with one another when I first settled in the hamlet, there had been an uproar over some undivided land between A and his sister B. B was born in the neighboring village of Kalaganwatte and had come to Helagama as a wife. Part of the reason for this marriage was that her family owned ten acres of garden land in Helagama through some earlier connections. There had been no other claimants and for many years B's son, Tikiribanda, had made use of this land. But the arrangement did not last and other claimants started to arrive. A, the brother of B, married his daughter, Tikirimenika, to Kalubanda, who was also of Helagama and of the same *pavula* as Tikiribanda. Then the trouble started in earnest.

Kalubanda wanted to use the garden land along with Tikiribanda, but Tikiribanda refused to share the land because it belonged exclusively to his mother. Sometime later Tikiribanda died and the unsettled dispute was inherited by his children. In the meantime, A, who was still alive, confounded the issue even more by asserting that B had no rights whatsoever on the land. He argued that a daughter given in *deega* during the lifetime of her parents had no future claims on the paternal estate unless a portion was granted to her by testa-

---

[6] I have noted above the significance of government grants in this context (see p. 31).

[7] Nadel (1951*a*), p. 17, quoting from MacIver.

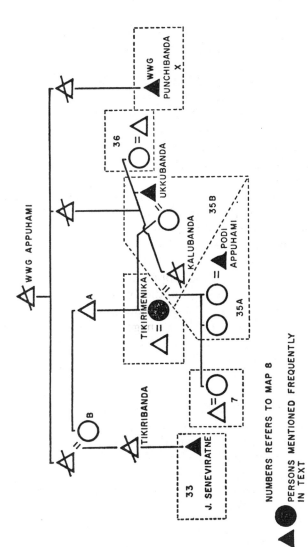

Figure 18. The core of *pavula* A.

ment. He proceeded to write out a deed on a talipot leaf (on which ancient deeds were written), signed by many numbers of witnesses, by which he conveyed the whole of the ten acres to Tikirimenika (his own daughter).

This added more fuel to the fire. J. Seneviratne countered by asserting that his grandmother B had married after the decease of her parents, and therefore did have valid claims to equal shares with her brothers! And so it went. The dispute had not been taken to the Rural Courts, but it had also not been settled for many years. It continued as a source of friction between these very close relatives.

The case illustrates an important aspect of the *pavula*. Claims on land can rarely be substantiated by actual written and witnessed deeds. When difficulties arise, one has to depend on one's kinsmen to validate one's title to property. In general, the system does work—though it also generates a considerable amount of litigation. But it is also true that there may be other occasions, such as the one described, when the *pavula* splits into smaller factions.

A faction seldom forms around a single dispute, however. There are wheels within wheels which determine one's alignments. Let me describe another instance to explain the division in this *pavula*.

Consider the position of Podi Appuhami, the *binna* son-in-law of Kalubanda. He was a man from another village, but he had been in Helagama for fifteen years. After Kalubanda died, Kalubanda's brother, Ukkubanda, had hoped to manage the lands alone. He therefore made an arrangement with Tikirimenika, Kalubanda's widow and his own wife's sister, to get rid of Podi Appuhami. He did not succeed; Podi Appuhami was well liked by other members of the *pavula*. In particular, W. W. G. Punchibanda (a very rich schoolmaster), who had had a dispute with Ukkubanda (also a schoolmaster), made it clear that he would support Podi Appuhami to the hilt.

It thus came about that the potential line of cleavage in the *pavula* assumed greater clarity during the spring of 1955. W. W. G. Punchibanda, Podi Appuhami, and J. Seneviratne supported each other's claims. On the other side were Ukkubanda, Tikirimenika, and A, but many others sat on the fence. In 1955 during the Buddhist New Year feasts, when the *pavula* traditionally dines together, there were two feasts in two houses. Most people could not decide which to attend and went to both.

Somehow, with all these strains the *pavula* had not entirely broken down. It still had a considerable degree of cohesion which could be drawn on in the struggles against other groups. Thus, the *pavula* co-operated against the *pavula* of the Village Headman in all elections and similar issues when a large base of support was essential. They still claimed themselves to be "one people" (*eka minissu*).

THE QUESTION OF ENDOGAMY

Despite internal stresses, it is clear that unity can be maintained in the *pavula*. But the argument regarding common interests does not explain why a kindred formed on such a basis should make an attempt to deny kinship with other kindreds.

Two things explain why there is a strong endogamous tendency in the kindred: land and ritual status. The role of land is obvious. The kindred has a certain amount of landed assets controlled by a group of people who coöperate as best they can. Every marriage carried potential, if not actual, implications about ultimate claims on these lands. The allegiances of the young men and women (who may inherit) must be contained in the *pavula*. Therefore their marriages outside will be disapproved of on principle unless, of course, the marriage is particularly desirable. Women also are potential claimants of land, and here again there is a strong desire to marry them to dependable people. Hence evident material considerations point in the direction of endogamous marriage.

But quite apart from the rights on land that women may inherit, there is the question of ritual status and its protection. Here, leaving the materialist arguments, we return again to a subject of cardinal interest to the people from a different approach.

Social Distance and Pollution

It was certainly true that *pavula* A had bitter disputes within it, often arising out of claims to land, but in contrast to the other people in the hamlet it considered itself to be in a unique position. It was different, separate from the other inhabitants in the hamlet because—as they insisted—its *wamsa* was different. Their superior rank was allegedly apparent in their titles. The people in *pavula* A had such aristocratic names as Senanayika Seneviratne Herat Mudianselage Welakonawatte Gedara, Jayasekera Mudianselage Polgaha arawa Gedara, and Nissanka Mudianselage Tunpale Gedara, whereas the others were all people of serf (*vahalu*) descent with degrading names like Polkotuve Gedara and no *mudianse* titles! Because of their low ancestry they lacked *wasagama* names and in many cases their whole descent was obscure, so it was well known that *pavula* E consisted mainly of people called Wegolle Gedara, who were said to have been the descendants of settlers from a "low" village, like Galpitiya in Terutenne. In this fashion, claims about status were referred to the past. But there is more to these claims.

In general, there was evidence to show that the claims of *pavula* A did contain some grain of truth. I concluded from a study of Grain

Tithe Registers kept in the nineteenth century that the "aristocratic names" were the names of high feudal officers and that the Wegolle group had obviously come in as outsiders.[8] But, on the other hand, it was obvious that some of the closest relations of *pavula* A who were said to be of high aristocratic rank had actually been very "low" persons who had become rich. For instance, the husband in No. 36 was called Tunpale Gedara Gangatirala. It turned out that he was the brother of the retired Village Headman (Muhandiram), whose low origin and flagrant name-changing have already been related.[9] They welcomed this man as a kinsman with open arms, and if they could accept him, they could accept anyone of any *wamsa*.

Let us therefore reconsider the positions of these *pavula*.

TABLE 31

Landholdings of Pavula *in Helagama*

Pavula A (16 households)		Pavula B (13 households)	
No. 1	—	No. 10	2 *pale*
2	—	15	2
3	7.5 *pale*	22	1
4	6.5	24	2
13	2.0	32	1
17	2.0	38	1
19	2.0	Others	—
20	2.0		
28	5.5		9 *pale*
29	—		
33	1.5		
34	2.0 + 4.5*	Pavula E (4 households)	
35	3.0 + 7.0*		
36	3.0		
37	1.0	No. 23	5.5 *pale*
X	12.0 + 7.5 + 2.0*	24	2
	71.5 *pale*		7.5 *pale*

* Separate figures indicate different landlords; siblings' shares are differentiated.

The Reinterpretation of Wamsa

Living in the hamlet, I quickly saw that there was a clear and decisive difference in wealth between *pavula* A and the others (table 31).

The members of *pavula* A held a total of 71.5 *pale* of paddy land. They had fairly valuable gardens and three members were school-

---

[8] They bought a paddy field in 1889 (which they still own) and eventually assumed the name of the field.

[9] See pp. 147ff.

teachers who had regular cash salaries. They thus considered themselves cultured as well as aristocratic and rich.

In contrast, *pavula* B owned only 9 *pale* of land. (Seven of the thirteen households in the *pavula* held no land at all.) Many of the men in this *pavula* worked as both coolie and *ande* laborers on the fields of the landlords of *pavula* A. Hence the alleged *wamsa* superiority of *pavula* A was at least partly a rationalization of their direct superiority in wealth. They looked upon *pavula* B as "their workers" (*veda karaya*). Whereas *pavula* B would accept cash payment for labor from anyone, *pavula* A insisted that they would never allow themselves to be so degraded. I do not wish to imply here that the feeling of *wamsa* superiority rests simply on an economic base. The notions of caste, of ritual rank, of purity and pollution are so clear in their minds that they undoubtedly do think of their claims as being "true" and justified, and quite unrelated to material considerations. *Wamsa* is a quality inherent in the blood. But the ethnographer must take note of how often wealth comes into some alignment with ritual rank within the Goyigama caste.

The example is typical of the rationale whereby the different *pavula* conceptualize their distinctions. "They" (*e golle*) are "separate (*venas*); they are "not of us" (*apata ne*). Hence they are of different *wamsa*. In this fashion, the ideology of ritual status in Terutenne was always called upon to express or justify a sense of distinction, that is, social distance, or of identity.

This phenomenon is a direct result of the cohesion of the kindred. Because members of the kindred feel that they are "one people," they must have "one blood." And if they have "one blood" then they must be of "one *wamsa*." Thus, social distance between kindreds is always expressed in the idiom of "pollution." Indeed one can go further. If other people are of different *wamsa*, by the very logic of this ideology it is necessary either to make certain that they are really "pure" or to protect oneself from them. For if they are of "low" *wamsa* they are *naraka* (polluted). Pollution can affect one as suddenly as the plague, and therefore extreme caution is necessary to avoid being polluted; one must above all avoid intermarriage and interdining with the people of low *wamsa*.

It is thus the *pavula* comes to consider itself a completely distinct, clearly defined group, even though an anthropologist can frequently trace marriages between *pavula*.

Equality and Endogamy

I have observed that an equality of status is intimately related to the sense of identity and community in the *pavula*. It is only a corollary of this notion that all marriages should be confined to members of the *pavula*. Some of the people of Terutenne would claim that those with the same *wasagama* title (who are or should be of the same *wamsa*) should marry only among themselves, though they would agree that this was not always what people actually did.[10] If the *pavula* kept all marriages to itself it would be a perfect model of a small caste. However, there is wealth. There is the desire to marry people who are not merely of the same *wamsa* but who are also fairly equally rich. As we noted in the case of the marriage alliance, for enduring reciprocal kinship relations it is imperative that the families should be more or less comparable in both *wamsa* and wealth. The same observation applies to the *pavula*.

Inside the *pavula*, discrepancies are magnified and lead to recriminations. The ideal of communal equality is lost when one branch rises far above the others in wealth. Reciprocity becomes lopsided; gifts among equals turn into tributes; and soon enough the party that is slighted begins to feel *irishiya* (jealousy). And this, people in Terutenne assured me, often leads into sorcery (*huniyam*) and disputes. All are the result of "climbing" (*naginava*). Therefore, they said, "only kinsmen can really hate each other."

Thus, while *wamsa* expresses the sense of community and demands endogamous unions, the discrepancy of riches breaks the close circle and induces members to look outside for their partners.

Ideally, the *pavula* is drawn on the same lines as a caste. Ideally, one should intermarry only with close relatives. But although there is this centripetal tendency, the circle can never be completely closed. The divergence of wealth introduces an element of instability. Past kinsmen strike bad fortune and fall; then new links need to be forged. The old ones are crossed out as best one can.

Thus every *pavula* is organized on these two dimensions: it is closed on the basis of putative ritual status, but it is open to wealth. We must not underestimate the intense passions that are aroused over the question of the perpetuation and denial of kinship obligations. The residual claims of the members of the *pavula* are given formal expression in the rights and obligations (the "blood claims") of the cross-cousin categories which were described above. Each outside marriage, therefore, has to be negotiated against the background of such claims from kinsmen, and it is precisely such maneuvers that lead to "breaks" in kinship.

---

[10] D'Oyly (1929) mentions the traditional preferences: "the parties must be of the same caste and equal family, respectability and rank, which is chiefly ascertained by the families having previously intermarried" (p. 127).

Feasts and the Act of Eating Together

The cohesion and putative "equality" of the *pavula* are publicly expressed on ceremonial occasions, *magul gedara*. The most significant are weddings, especially when new kinsmen are being introduced into the old circle, but births, deaths, puberty ceremonies, New Year feasts —any occasion when the *pavula* meets to partake of a meal together —also serve the same purpose.

Eating is a highly ritualized act in Ceylon. "Strangers" must not be allowed to watch one eating. To watch others engaged in this intimate act is thought to be an expression of hungry jealousy or hostility. People will be afraid of intentional or supernatural foul play. Therefore, one normally eats in the company of those who are familiar and close. Eating together is an expression of trust and friendship. The fear of being watched by a stranger induces Kandyan villagers to consume their food in the darkness of their huts, away from the public gaze. Equality is expressed in customs of eating in many societies. Although the rules are flexible there appears to be an inherent inconsistency, in master and servant sitting down to a meal together. The same in general appears to be true of sexual relations. Caste ideology has carried these concepts with rather wide currency to their logical extremes and crystallized them in formal categories.

These customary sentiments surrounding food, the feeling that only "familiars," people who are "close," who are "equal," eat together, make the ceremonial feasts of the *pavula* particularly expressive. The elaborate food exchanges which are a marked feature of weddings have been described. The night before the actual ceremony, the members of the *pavula*, the sari'ed women and the heavily powdered men, meet for a special dinner. The special dinners at *magul gedara* (lit., ceremony house) reflect the *pavula* as it is constituted at that moment. These are also the occasions when the defections from the *pavula* are made public. The members of the house in which the ceremony is held issue the invitations, and some, naturally, are pointedly omitted. The internal affairs of the kindred are thus brought to a head. It is when the whole group "unites" for a feast that the absence of old members, or their refusal to participate, is felt most strongly.[11] When two kindreds intermingle at weddings the procedure may be highly electrified. Those who are at the table should be of

---

[11] Consider the following item from *The Times* of London, April 16, 1957: "Fourteen persons were murdered in Ceylon during the weekend, when the Sinhalese new year was celebrated. It is an annual feature that the murder rate, which is usually more than one a day, rises sharply during the new year celebrations, but this year's figure sets a new record. A total of 157 persons have been murdered in Ceylon this year—40 in April alone."

similar status. But this means that no diner should have any kinship relations with others of "low" *wamsa*. Standards of this sort are, naturally, difficult to achieve to everyone's satisfaction. If there is a diner who is not free from suspicion, the new bridegroom (or anyone who feels insulted) may be induced to turn over the dining table or mat and start a dispute. Thus, it is not infrequent for wedding ceremonies, like New Year feasts, to end in violent brawls.

The ostensible reason for these last-minute disputes is said to be *wamsa*. Since those who dine together are looked upon as one *wamsa*, it is said that one must make a break before it is too late if there is any suspicion that someone in the group is "polluted." But it is in the nature of *wamsa* that opinions concerning it may be poles apart, and herein lies the trouble. These claims about *wamsa*, whereby one pushes others out of the *pavula* or cuts the connections oneself, are often no more than pretexts, when the real problem, if one can but discover it, is a quarrel over property, land, or debts. The language used is that of caste, but the complaints are very material ones indeed.

The Kindred and the Castes

It is clear from my description of the kindred that the principles which are at work at the level of the major castes are also operating at the level of the micro-castes. It is proper to speak of the *pavula* as a microcosm of the Sinhalese castes. This is partly expressed by the use of the word *jati*, which is equally applied both to the castes and to the kindreds. Two of the most important features of caste—the concept of endogamy and the complex of ideas regarding purity and pollution—are present in the *pavula*. The further elaboration of these basic features, the sense of separation as expressed in food customs, the practice of excommunication by the refusal to exchange food and women, the preference for hypergamy, all indicate that we are dealing with the smaller cells from which the larger groups are built.

I do not, of course, claim that the micro-caste and caste are identical. It is obvious that the micro-castes lack the cultural paraphernalia by which the castes are identified. The micro-castes do not have the traditional names, the occupations, the sumptuary rules by which castes are distinguished. Though their unique status is expressed in terms of the purity-pollution scale, their sense of endogamy is only an ideal to be lived up to. Micro-caste endogamy is seriously practiced only in the most traditional communities (as in the account of the Tom-Tom Beater in chap. 8). The status differences between the micro-castes are hardly comparable to the immense crevasses between the major castes. Yet important consequences follow from this analysis of the micro-castes.

The castes in Terutenne (with the exception of the Tom-Tom Beaters, who had a society)[12] were not formally organized. There was no formal machinery, as there was in feudal times, for punishing breaches of caste etiquette. In view of this informality we may well ask ourselves why the castes have not entirely intermingled.

The answer lies in the structure of the micro-caste. If the kin group looks after itself, then caste boundaries are also maintained. This was certainly the case among the Blacksmith, Potter, and Washer castes in Terutenne. Each of these groups was a single kindred and was kept separate by its own decisions. In other words, in these cases the boundaries of the caste and micro-caste were the same. But the issue was clearer in the case of the large Goyigama group, which, though it had no formal machinery, not merely maintained its boundaries against the low castes but also perpetuated its own internal status divisions.

It is important to observe that the breaches of the rules are dealt with in the caste idiom. When intercaste or *wamsa* cohabitation does occur, either or both of the culprits are excommunicated. One could, by much questioning, bring "scandalous" unions to light. I discovered, for instance, that the daughter of Pihillewatte Kirivanti of Helagama (household 32 in *pavula* B) had eloped with one of my neighbors in Galpitiya. Her family was also poor and was also considered to be "low" by people in Helagama, but a connection with Galpitiya had evidently been too terrible for her parents. It would have been visible proof of what the superior *pavula* A in Helagama had claimed all along. So the girl had been excommunicated. She had not been home to Helagama for three years. This excommunication, however, had been a purely private decision by her family, which perpetuated the status cleavages among the high caste in Terutenne.

Micro-castes in South India and Ceylon

For the sake of clarity, I have restricted my analysis of the micro-caste to the *pavula* in one hamlet of Terutenne, but it is evident that these arguments may be extended beyond the unique features of the Sinhalese case to illuminate aspects of caste behavior at the kinship level in other communities in India and Ceylon. There is increasing evidence in ethnographic writing to suggest the presence of micro-castes, even though the authors are not always aware of it. Gough (1960), for instance, says of the Tamils of Tanjore: "The endogamous group had

---

[12] Societies like the Tom-Tom Beaters' are rare among Sinhalese low castes, where the smallness of number makes formal machinery unnecessary. The Tom-Tom Beater caste was larger than the other lower castes in Terutenne, and its society was one way of coordinating its activities against the Goyigama. In this sense it is a remarkable index of cohesion in this local caste group.

no formal organization. It was *merely a clearly demarcated group* within which *marriage,* visiting (especially for family ceremonies), and free commensality took place" (p. 45; my italics). She does not examine the structure of these groups. Similar material is also reported from Kerala by D'Souza (1959). In a highly interesting paper, D'Souza discusses the internal structure of the Islamic Moplah community: "While marriages between members of the same patrilineal *taravad* cannot take place, several *taravads* form an endogamous group. Generally, in any locality of father right Moplahs there are several endogamous groups" (p. 493). Specifically, he says of the matrilineal Moplahs (p. 497): "White the interrelated *taravads* form exogamous groups, several such exogamous groups constitute a larger endogamous group. Families of an endogamous group have the same social status in the community, and different endogamous groups have different social statuses. In any particular Moplah locality the various endogamous groups can be arranged according to a hierarchy of status differences."

For Ceylon, Banks (1960) discusses his material on Jaffna Tamils in terms of small endogamous groups: "These fictionally endogamous groups are viewed by the society as mutually stratified. I have termed them 'sondakara caste's; they lack not only proper names, but also a local generic name" (pp. 63, 70). And finally, going farther south in Ceylon, Leach (1961b) has an important discussion of two groups in the small Sinhalese village of Pul Eliya in the North Central Province. He refers to the first group as *variga* (subcaste) and to the second as *pavula;* I should note that his conception of *pavula* is somewhat narrower than mine. He distinguishes between the " 'ideal' *pavula*" and the " 'effective' *pavula*"; the former is restricted in meaning to the "direct biological descendants of one woman" (p. 105) whereas the latter "is a group of kinsmen allied together for some specific political purpose." In this latter sense his conception of the *pavula* is similar in its fundamentals to my discussion of the basis for cooperation in the kindred, except that the ritual status preoccupations of the Terutenne kindreds appear to be lacking in the Pul Eliya case.

This difference seems to be very closely related to the presence of the *variga* (subcaste) in the north central provinces and the absence of any such semiformal structure in the Terutenne region. It is quite clear from Leach's analysis that in Pul Eliya the *variga* is the main status-bearing group, which makes it possible for *pavula* to be little concerned with purity and pollution so long as marriages are confined to the *variga* circle. Leach observes (p. 72) that "the judgements of the *variga* court . . . were always designed to maintain, as a fiction, the caste dogma that only kinsmen standing in the relationship of *massinā-nāna* ('classificatory cross-cousins') may legitimately co-habit." Following this he gives a vivid description of how the neatly structured endogamous *variga,* which has a court mainly intended to try offenses against caste purity, is about to lose its clear boundaries as a result of the breakdown in its court system.

If it is correct to say that the *pavula* in Pul Eliya were little concerned about ritual status and kin group endogamy because the strict rules of the *variga* ensured that all members of that endogamous group were *ipso facto* of equal status, then we are left with an important theoretical problem. On my argument, with the breakdown of the *variga* system, we should find a parallel development of the Pul Eliya *pavula* into a status-bearing micro-caste of the Terutenne type. This is certainly the case in other villages of the Pul Eliya type such as Vilawa (chap. 11) which now retain only some vague conception of the *variga* as a "traditional system" which has been given up, and it may also become the case in Pul Eliya.[13]

Apart from South India and Ceylon, there is also the evidence from other parts of India regarding groups of the micro-caste type. There is evidence from Gujarat and from Mysore[14] that such circles of kin play a significant role as effective social groups beyond family or lineages. Since there is little detailed material on this subject, we are not yet in a position to discuss these groups in general terms, but it is obvious that in those areas where the "micro-castes" exist in a context of corporate lineages, a host of organizational problems not encountered in the Sinhalese context will undoubtedly make their appearances.

At the present moment, it is clear that we have only just begun to understand the relationship between caste and kinship systems. The suggestion that endogamy is in fact a function of centripetal kinship systems may bear further examination.

Some of the problems we have noted regarding the kindred may have relevance outside the "caste" context. Freeman (1961) has recently raised the question of the definition of the "kindred." He excludes affines from his definition of the kindred, but correctly observes (p. 200) that, in a bilateral system, it is impossible to produce clearly defined groups of kin on the principle of descent alone. He also notes (p. 207) that close intermarriage may be a second principle which can produce a "closer cognatic network" than is otherwise possible. I have also argued that "endogamous" marriage can be the second principle which

---

[13] The ideal concept of the *variga* was very clear in Terutenne. Although the villagers had no idea of the *variga* court and used the term interchangeably with *pavula,* they sometimes formulated it in the same way as in Pul Eliya: "One may only marry relations from the same *variga;* of course it is possible to say exactly who is and who is not a member of the *variga.*"

[14] Personal communications from A. Shah and A. Beals (1960).

helps to produce cohesive groups, which in the limiting case of full endogamy are clearly circumscribed "castes." Indeed, Freeman himself observes (p. 209) that marriage with the kindred accounts for 75 percent of the marriages of the Iban, 80 percent of the Sumbawa, and 90 percent of the Bisaya. Moreover, in an example he quotes in detail (p. 211), it is the "affinally related relatives" who unhesitatingly join the "kindred proper in seeking vengeance" for a murder. In view of these facts, as well as of the vital importance of affinity in what Freeman calls "kindred based action groups," there is all the more reason for including the "affines" in the kindred as we have done in this chapter.

There are doubtless different types of kindreds. But if social groups based on the sentiments of kindred loyalty are to be found in a society, I would suggest that the bonds of affinity will be the main mechanism by which the groups attain cohesiveness.

THE CATEGORIES OF KINSHIP AND THE RULES OF MARRIAGE

A good many anthropologists tend to dismiss the whole complicated study of kinship terminologies as a barren puzzle. Yet the Sinhalese terminology does play an important part in its kinship system, and it raises significant problems about the regulation of sexual relations within the family and the nature of the concepts of incest and exogamy.

It is not entirely accurate to describe the system of kinship terms as simply a "terminology." This usage carries the implication that kinship terms are relevant only in speech; if this were true in the Sinhalese case, it would obscure the most interesting features of the system. I prefer to treat kinship terms as "categories" whereby the Sinhalese organize their kinship universe; these categories are definitely associated with certain rules of behavior.

Since there has been considerable confusion on the chicken-and-egg argument of whether the behavior or the categories come first, I must proceed carefully.

In Sinhalese villages one often comes across dwellings in which two brothers and their children are living together, or two sisters with their children, or perhaps several brothers and sisters with their children. In such households, the children of the two brothers are categorized as brother and sister; the children of two sisters are also brother and sister. No sexual intercourse would be permitted between them. But the children of a brother and a sister, even though they live in the same household and hold property in common, are not brother and sister but find themselves in a special category. They belong to each other and would be permitted to have sexual intercourse, and they are regarded as ideal marriage partners.

The basic rules are also extended far beyond the household. When one asks a villager anywhere in Terutenne whether he may intermarry with people in Wekumbura hamlet, he will reply, "If there is a *massina-nana* relationship, then we can intermarry. If not, then not!" As an ideal rule this carries the implication that there must be previous kinship between the parties to a marriage, and that this kinship must fall into the specified categories. All other types of kinsmen are forbidden.

It is in this specific sense of kinship that Needham (1962) has correctly drawn a distinction between preferred and prescribed marriage, and it is in this sense that Dumont (1953) speaks of marriage in South India as an "expression" of kinship. A "preference," which carries the implication of volition, is in no way involved in the Sinhalese case. The permissible kinship category is strictly prescribed.

The ideal rule is unequivocal; it is directly mentioned by other field workers (Leach, 1961*b*, p. 72) and makes sense only in relation to the total system of categories. So much understood, there are a number of questions which legitimately arise: what happens when non-kin are in fact married? Can the categories be changed? How is all this related to cross-cousin marriage? Why do they bother to make such a prescription? And finally, to what extent are the rules followed?

Before proceeding to these questions, we ought first to look at the Sinhalese kinship categories. The following list shows kinship terms and their referents.

The first problem to deal with is, How do the Sinhalese allocate persons to the *massina-nana* categories? In other words, what are the principles of the terminology? In fact, the Sinhalese, together with many other peoples in South India and Ceylon, use a Dravidan terminology, which is basically similar to the Kariera terminology of Australia and has been noted for its association with symmetrical cross-cousin marriage. The categories are so constructed as to presuppose regular and consistent marriage between the categories of *massina* and *nana* usually referred to as "cross-cousins."

A cursory examination of the categories will indicate that only sex distinctions are made in the grandparents' and grandchildrens' generation. The main structure of the categories is contained in three generations—that is, ego's generation, the first ascending, and the first descending generations. In reciprocal terms, we are in fact really dealing with but two levels in the terminology, depending on whether Ego is located in the superior level or in the inferior level.

Sinhalese Kinship Terms

(e = elder, y = younger)

mutta   FFF (or any father of a grandfather)
siyya   FF, MF (or husband of a grandmother)
achchi   FM, MM (or wife of a grandfather)
kiriatta (same as *siyya*), also *atappa*
kiriamma (same as *achchi*), also *atamma*

                     munubura Grandson
                     minibiri Granddaughter

taata   F
appa   F
appochi   F
piya   F
loku taata, loku appa, maha appa, FeB
kuda appa, (kudappa), bala appa (bappa) FyB
amma   M
mavu   M
loku amma MeZ
punchi amma, balamma, kuda amma (kudamma) MyZ

                     puta   S
                     loku puta   eS
                     podi puta   yS
                     duwa   D
                     (*loku, podi* as required)

ayya   eB   *malli*   yB
   loku ayya   ("big" eB)   (adjectives as opposite column for
   madhyama ayya   ("medium" eB)   seniority)
   punchi ayya   ("small" eB)
   pin ayya   ("merit" eB)
   podi ayya   ("small" eB)
   hin ayya   ("youngest" eB)

akka   eZ   *nangi*   yZ
   (adjectives as in *ayya*)   (adjectives as opposite column
                                       above)

massina, machang, hura   "cross-cousin" (male)
                     nana   "cross-cousin" (female)

mama, mamandi   MB,   FZH,   F-in-law
nanda, nandamma   FZ,   MBW,   M-in-law

                     bana   ZS,   S-in-law ⎫
                     leli   ZD,   D-in-law ⎭ male sp.

                     bana   BS,   S-in-law ⎫
                     leli   BD,   D-in-law ⎭ female sp.

sahodari   sibling (female)
sahodara   sibling (male)
pavula   wife
gänu (woman) wife
miniha (man) husband
purussaya   husband

Within the generation of Ego, two distinctions are made—between the sexes, and between "siblings" and "potential affines." That is to say, all parallel cousins are classified as "siblings," in which case seniority and juniority are always specified: e.g., *ayya* (elder brother), *malli* (younger brother), *akka* (elder sister), *nangi* (younger sister), and further, e.g., *loku* (big) *ayya,* and *podi* (small) *nangi,* and so on.

The "potential affines" are symmetrical terms: males call each other *massina-massina;* females, *nana-nana. Massina-nana* have claims on each other; they may have sex relations and are the only categories who are in a marriageable relationship. The sister of a *massina* is a *nana* and vice versa. Hence two classifications, a socio-biological one into male/female, and a cultural one into prescribed/prohibited mating categories, cross-cut each generation into four primary classes.

In the first ascending generation, then, the parents of all those classified as "siblings" in Ego's generation are "mother" and "father." The parents of all those called "potential affines" are *mama* (MB and F-in-L) and *nenda* (FZ and M-in-L).

The same assumption of consistent cross-cousin marriage is also clear in the first descending generation; thus all the children of "siblings" in Ego's generation are classified as "son" and "daughter," and all the offspring of "potential affines" are classified as *bena* (S-in-L) and *leli* (D-in-L). If a male is speaking, then his "sisters son" is *bena* and "sister's daughter" is *leli;* and vice versa in the case of a female speaker. Thus the children of the "potential affines" in Ego's generation are, in fact, located in the prescribed categories of potential spouses to Ego's children.

So much for the description of the interconnections between the categories. I need to emphasize that the categories can be extended in any direction according to the principles inherent in the system. Thus, the wife of any *massina* is "sister"; her brother is "brother"; his wife is *nana;* her father is *mama;* his wife is *nanda;* her brother is "father," and so on. It should also be quite clear that we are dealing with a system of categories which are completely unrelated to such matters as "local descent groups," or "residential compounds," or indeed any other specific grouping of persons on the ground. The interest of the Sinhalese case arises precisely from the fact that the principles inherent in the terminology cannot be attributed to the configurations of people into lineages or any other kind of groups in the villages. What, then, is served by these elaborate categories, and why are the Sinhalese villagers so strong in their support of them?

The answer is, in my view, simple. The Sinhalese, like all other peoples in the world, must somehow restrict and channel sex relations in kin groups. They do not use "exogamy" or any other alternative sets of specific prohibitions. They use a single positive rule: that the only persons who may legitimately have sex and may marry are those standing in the prescribed categories of *massina-nana*.[15]

But note how well the rule fits into the context of caste. Much of the interest of sex regulations in Sinhalese villages lies in the prohibitions of non-caste mates, that is, endogamy. The rule of *massina-nana* unions, on the other hand, must be seen as a corollary to caste endogamy intended to restrict and specify the legitimate sex mates within the castes.

Our observations that Sinhalese sexual regulations are entirely dependent on a single rule, and the fact that this rule in turn depends on the orderly specification of kin categories makes it imperative for the Sinhalese to retain their terminology in a systematic fashion particularly within the confines of the family.

It is not merely "wrong marriages" (*varada kassada*) which would introduce inconsistencies into this most logical structure. If a person merely addresses another by a kinship term which is not "correct"— if, for instance, one calls a classificatory "sister" *nana*—and if the mistake is not corrected, relations would similarly be confused. The villagers are quite aware of these significant connotations of the terms. *Nana* implies a person with whom one may have sexual affairs. If one called a "sister" *nana,* that would be nothing less than a lewd sexual suggestion. The villagers say that the "sins" resulting from wrongful intercourse are the same as those arising from a willful confusion of the categories by addressing kin by the wrong terms. It is *dos* in both cases and may result in serious illness or, worse, the revenge of some deity.

I have described cases of "wrong" marriages elsewhere (1962b). Here I shall describe a further case, showing the informants' reactions to the difficulties that arise in the applications of the roles.

Podi Appuhami from Helagama explained the disadvantages of "wrong marriages." First he described the situation shown graphically in figure 19. I asked him why this was so bad (*naraka*). He replied, "It confuses people's relations inside the family."

"Does it matter what you call people? Why can't you call them what-

---

[15] It must be pointed out immediately that "actual" cross-cousin marriages are not very frequent. In Terutenne, out of 139 men, who had made 169 marriages, only 22 were married with "full" cross-cousins:

	Uxorilocal	Virilocal	Total
MBD	6	7	13
FZD	4	5	9
Total	10	12	22

The rate with other "cross-cousins" would be very high indeed, but is difficult to assess exactly. The low rate of "actual" cross-cousin marriages does not, of course, prejudice the point that all marriages must take place between "categories" of "*massina-nana.*"

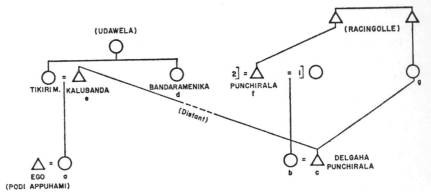

Figure 19. A case of "wrong" marriage. (1) *e* and *c* are *ayya-malli* of the same
kin group; (2) therefore *a* is *duwa* to *c*; (3) *c* marries *b* (i.e., a *nana* [MBD]
on the maternal side); (4) then *f* marries *d,* thus making; (5) *a* and *b* *akka-nangi* (sisters); (6) so *a* has to call *c* *bappa* (FyB) and *b* *akka* (eZ).

ever you want to? Delgaha Punchirala is not all that close; why not
call him *massina*?"

"Oh, no! He is *mama* to me, and I could not call him *massina*. It
would be very bad, very wrong. He is one of the family [*pavula*] and
one has to call him according to his *pevatigenima* [position; generation; birth]."

We were joined by my landlord, Polgaharava Ukkubanda (see fig.
20).

I asked Ukkubanda, "What does Podi Appuhami call Talagaha
Dingiribanda?"

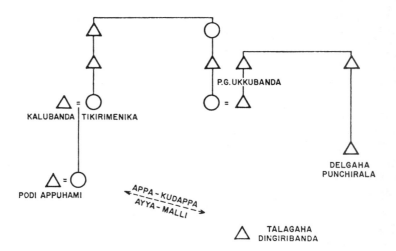

Figure 20. More of a case of "wrong" marriage.

Podi Appuhami chimed in, "I ought to call him *kudappa* [*Kuda appa:* lit., small father]."

"But what do you call him?"

"Well, I can also call him *ayya-malli!*"

"What do you call Ukkubanda?"

"Ukkubanda is *mama* to me and I call him that."

"Can't you call him *massina?*"

Podi Appuhami, indignant, "Oh! that is impossible; Ukkubanda is also a close relation [*api pavula ekkenek:* one of our kindred]."

"So with Dingiribanda, it does not matter what you call him but with Ukkubanda it does. Why is that?"

"Well, it all depends on the family. Ukkubanda is near to us, but Dingiribanda is not so near. But he has now come as a neighbor to Ukkubanda; he has married *binna* and lives in the next house. So I must call him something." He looked around, "Yes, I think these things are really important only with those who are very near [*langa langa*]. When the relation is close, then it is *dos* [sin] to say the wrong thing."

"But how far do you reckon it is important to say exact relations?"

"Oh, now you have got us!"

Podi Appuhami emphasized the relation of nearness. If you live near people especially, then you can call them all to work (*attang*). You have constant dealings with them. And if they are relations, then you simply have to keep to the categories. If the relations grow "distant" (*dura*) then the categories become less important.

This said, it is also true that certain changes in address are accepted. Thus, it is frequently the case that male cross-cousins (*massina-massina*) call each other elder and younger "brother" (*ayya-malli*); this is always so when there are status differences between them (see chap. 8). Such changes in the terminology, highly suggestive though they may be, are confined only to address. For purposes of marriage they are always disregarded; the people would say, "by kinship we are *massina*. it is only out of respect that I call him *ayya*. His sister is still my *nana*."

There are also certain other alterations in the terminology confined to address. I provide below an account of permissible variants.

The informant commenced with the statement again, that it is *dos* (sin) to alter the terms in the family, because "kinship is confused" (*nakam kavalam venava*). Having said this, he went on to describe the conventional alterations.

1st ascending generation: *nenda, appa, amma, mama* ("None of these can be changed, and they must be said as they are").

Ego's generation: (*a*) *ayya-malli* (siblings) cannot turn into *massina*, though vice versa is permissible; (*b*) *akka-nangi* (f. siblings) cannot turn into *nana,* but vice versa is permissible; but (*c*) *massina-nana* can turn into *ayya-nangi* ("That depends on age and respect").

1st descending generation: (*a*) *puta* (son) cannot become *bena* ("son-in-law"); (*b*) *duwa* (daughter) cannot become *leli* ("daughter-in-law"); but (*c*) vice versa is possible and "not harmful."

To my query as to why, in respectable families, brothers-in-law who were *massina* rarely addressed each other by that term but instead used the *ayya-malli* terminology, the informant replied, "The kinship [*näkam*] is well known, so no harm is done!"

It may be observed from this account that all changes for address are in the direction of further formality and avoidance. Thus, terms that carry the implication of joking and sex are turned into the formal "no joking, no sex" terminology of siblings; changes in the opposite direction would always be associated with ulterior intentions regarding marriage or sex.

There are two further questions that arise. First, what is in fact the range within which there is an interest to keep these rules? Second, why are the categories in this form?

The Range of the Rules of Marriage

The answer to the first question can be given definitely: the range in which the rules and the categories are carefully reckoned and where there is preoccupation with consistency in the terms is related to the widest extension of the kindred (*pavula*). Among people who think of themselves as close relatives, it is a sin to have sex relations with persons in the wrong category; and even, as we have noted, to call these people by wrong kinship terms is looked upon as reprehensible. Though villagers were often highly amused when "wrong unions" were pointed out to them, they were not amused when close relations of the *avassa pavula* (own kindred) were involved in such scandals.

On the other hand, the membership of the kindred does change over time, and those who consider themselves kinsmen at the moment may, for unforeseen reasons, become enemies. Or, alternatively, as we suggested, new members can make their way into the kindred. In such cases the kinship categories of the two groups are enmeshed on the basis of a single marriage assumed to be between the categories of *nana* and *massina.* The remaining categories fall into place, but in practice there are always some inconsistencies even in the most systematic kindreds.

The Form of the Terminology

It will be noted that the rule of cross-cousin marriage has certain implications: as a corollary all "parallel" cousins are prohibited from entering into sexual relations or matrimony. This extension of the rules has had a great charm for theorists. It has been frequently assumed that the rules imply the existence of "exogamous patri- or matri-lineal descent groups." [16] The arguments seem to take the following form:

As an extension of the *massina-nana* rule it could be said that all persons related "in the male line" are prohibited. Thus, all the children of the father's brother are "brothers" and "sisters," but the children of the father's sister (who may be said to marry a "stranger") are not related in the male line to Ego and are allowed to have sexual relations and to intermarry. Here, then, is an imaginary "exogamous" line! It is obvious, of course, that the same argument can be turned around to apply to the female side, and theoreticians can discover imaginary "exogamous matri-lines."

These formal aspects of the Dravidian type of terminology have worried many anthropologists. The distinction between parallel cousins and cross-cousins makes no sense on its own. Why should the children of sisters or of brothers be forbidden to marry and those of a brother and a sister encouraged? It is a puzzling question. It is clear enough that the children of "sisters" in a matrilineal society would be of the same exogamous descent group (assuming that there are exogamous groups) and that the offspring of "brothers" in a patrilineal society would be in a similar position. But it is not so clear why there should be prohibitions on both patrilateral and matrilateral parallel cousins at one and the same time.

Two categories of answers to this puzzle have been suggested: first, there are the "general" answers of Rivers (1907), Lévi-Strauss (1949), and Dumont (1953, 1957*b*); second there are the explanations in terms of single societies by Emeneau (1937, 1941), Gough (1956), and Srinivas (1952), to mention only some of the work concerning South Indian kinship systems. The general issues are discussed in chapter 16. To anyone familiar with the area, however, it must be obvious that the "single society" kind of explanation is theoretically unsatisfactory. This type of terminology, embodying a marriage rule as well as incest prohibitions, is in use among groups that exhibit widely different kinship structures.

In Ceylon, the Sinhalese are not the only people who use this type of terminology. It is used also by the Muslims of the east coast, who are matrilineal and matrilocal (see chap. 13), by the Tamils of the east coast, who have a similar pattern (chap. 15), and by the Tamils of Jaffna, who have a different organization altogether. In India, the low castes of Tanjore, the Todas, the Coorgs, the Iravas, the Pramalai Kallar, and many others, all have formally the same terminology.

---

[16] See, e.g., Tambiah (1958).

It is too simple to give local explanations for each single society separately, disregarding all others—especially when, as in South India and Ceylon, the groups are historically and culturally related. Further- more, single society explanations always seem hopelessly forced. Gough, for example, in an excellent article, attempts to explain the prohibitions of the low castes in a Tanjore village on their maternal parallel cousins by saying that "sisters" retain ties in their natal fami- lies and are often identified, so that the restrictions safeguard good relations between them (1956, p. 846). Apparently these low castes have patrilineal exogamous lineages which "explain" the positions of paternal parallel cousins.

The Coorgs are patrilineal and have exogamous *okkas* with joint estates. It is quite clear both from Srinivas (1952) and from Emeneau (1938) that they have the same formal terminology as the Sinhalese. As for the rules, Srinivas remarks that "The only relative a man may marry is his cross-cousin" (1952, p. 145). It is clear enough that the prohibitions on the patrilateral parallel cousins are explained by the rules of exogamy in the *okka,* but the extension of these complex systematic regulations on the matrilateral side is hardly convincing: "Such accordance of importance to maternal relatives is an attempt to balance the enormous importance accorded to paternal relatives" (p. 145).

In the case of the Muslims of the east coast of Ceylon, there are matrilineal *kudi* (lineages) with formulated notions of exogamy, but again this does not explain why paternal parallel cousins should be unacceptable for marriage.

All these short-range arguments which revolve around unilineal groups giving out women—local exogamy—are inadequate in that they fit only certain societies and are clearly ill-suited to others. For the Sinhalese, as an example, it must be pointed out that there are no exogamous patrilineal lineages, and scarcely any recognition of descent. There is no local exogamy. On the contrary, the basic group is one that is formed by in-marriage; it is largely endogamous. Here, in fact, is the advantage of the Sinhalese case over the South Indian. The *massina-nana* rule stands as an abstract principle on its own and can- not be traced to "real" or specific groups on the ground or to any other kind of "exogamy" at all. If we can understand the function of the rule in this case, we may then be able to provide a more general hypothesis to be tested in South India and even Australia.

I should emphasize that it is very misleading to regard the marriage rule as simply or predominantly the result of lineal "exogamy." This confounds the issue. As I indicated above, quite apart from the exclu- sion of parallel cousins, it is obvious that the "correct" category is found only in Ego's own generation. In other words, there is a prohibition on the union of persons in different "generations." This prohibition is no less important than the exclusion of parallel cousins or "exogamy." Moreover, there is an obvious lateral spread in the categories: the affines of affines of affines are brought within the scope of the system. I see no reason, therefore, why the particular rule regarding the association of *massina-nana* categories should necessarily be traced back to "exogamy." Indeed, exogamy is simply another abstract rule which some societies, and not others, employ.

I would suggest, therefore, that the Dravidian kinship categories, and the cross-cousin marriage rule embedded in it, are not related to exogamy but exist in order to regulate sex, marriage, and other kinds of behavior within bilateral kin groups. The bilaterality of the group should be stressed: the system can never be understood in terms of "exogamy" and "lineages" even where they do exist, for it is always mainly concerned with the interconnections between all the categories in the total kinship universe of Ego, which spread far beyond any particular "lineage." (See fig. 21 for a representation of the non-lineal but "bifurcate-merging" aspect of the terminology.)

Again, an important aspect of the categories is that they are a permanent constellation. Since the marriageable categories are also previously defined, the framework remains unaltered in the case of any particular marriage. It is clear that a union in accordance with the rules entails no changes in the kinship positions of the people involved. In a correct Sinhalese marriage, even the relationship between the couple is not expected to alter, aside from their cohabiting, since they already have strong claims, including sexual ones, on each other. It is precisely in this sense that we must emphatically agree with Dumont when he suggests that each new marriage is actually the reiteration of previous bonds. "What we are accustomed to call cross cousin marriage . . . is a perfect formula for perpetuating the alliance relationship from one generation to the next and so making the alliance an enduring institution" (Dumont, 1953, p. 38). In this sense, then, the entire universe of kin is seen as a permanent and ordered constellation. The individual falls into it by virtue of correct parentage and is at once given a place that he and everyone else understands and accepts. But though we may speak of "prohibited" and "prescribed" categories, I doubt that it is useful to speak, as Dumont does, of "kin" versus "allies." The system is one of kinship which entails affinity. And this is why Dumont, in trying to maintain this unnecessary distinction, has had to classify the FZ as an affine, and has turned to such clumsy concepts as "terminological kin."

I have argued that the cross-cousin marriage rule should be recognized as a method of organizing sexual relations and marriage within bilateral kin groups, and that it should be treated as being of the same

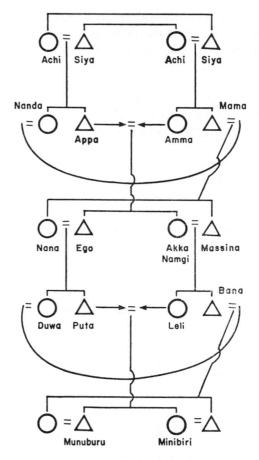

Figure 21. Bifurcate merging.

logical order as the other rules such as "exogamy" which anthropologists have come to accept. It should be recalled after all that "exogamy," too, is by no means universal, even though anthropologists whose field experience is in Africa always seem to feel cheated in some indefinable way when reminded of the non-exogamous lineages of the Middle East. It is obvious that some of the kinship terminologies we meet in Australia are extremely elaborate logical systems of the same nature as linguistic systems. It seems unnecessary to seek one-to-one functional correlations between parts of such terminological categories and specific exogamous local social groups. I would go further. The bias toward explanations based on "exogamy" has prejudiced the analysis of South Indian materials since the nineteenth century. It has prevented us from understanding that we have here a different but coherent system which separates the question of intercourse and the sexuality of women from the problem of defining the social position or paternity of her offspring. And for this reason it becomes possible to release the sexuality of women within the endogamous caste (to the appropriate persons in the correct categorical position) and to allow all the extraordinary combinations and permutations of polyandry, polygyny, "group marriage," etc. which we meet in South India and Ceylon.

Of course, even with these reservations, it is still true that not all kinship terminologies exhibit the neat logical rigor of the Dravidian —or the more elaborate Australian—systems. It is also clear that societies "categorize" certain aspects of their social universe more than others. If endless varieties of pigs are differentiated in New Guinea or if the Nuer do the same with cows, we accept and understand their preoccupations. In the case of the Dravidian terminologies of South India and Ceylon, we may conjecture that they are peculiarly suited to caste conditions. These terminologies systematically categorize and define marriageable partners in the entire kinship universe of any person. Logically, they are closed systems: one has to be a kinsman to enter the system in the first place. In this respect the boundaries of caste or indeed the micro-caste coincide with those of closed and systematic kinship terminologies.

The Situation in the Urban Areas

I should stress that the above observations apply in their particulars to the villagers of the Dry Zone, and that they are used only in the rural sections of the Low Country. Given the elaborate nature of the system, it is striking to see that the terminology and the rules with which it is associated lose their form among the urbanized sections of the Sinhalese. During investigations in parts of Negombo and Colombo, I was impressed by the seeming lack of awareness in my informants as to the "meaning" of *nana* and *leli* categories. The idea that marriage must be prescribed to the categories of *massina* and *nana* was unknown. Some said that "in the past" their ancestors had had such rules, and others referred to them as country ways. In view of these observations, the difficulties experienced by the Commission on Marriage and Divorce in attempting to define "prohibited degrees of relationship" are surely chastening. The Commission appears to think entirely in terms of Anglo-Saxon cultural categories and thus fails to see that for the Sinhalese the defining principle is not a prohibitive marriage rule but a positive one. The Commission writes, for instance, "[We] feel we might accept the following conclusion which Hayley reaches . . . 'he may marry his Leli his Nana and his Loku amma or Kuda amma, except when these terms are applied to his full aunt or full niece.' " It should be quite clear that a statement such as this would have been received with astonishment, if not ridicule, by villagers in the Dry Zone.[17]

The reason for these fundamental differences in conception must be sought in the relatively complex circumstances of the urban areas, where it would be difficult and impracticable to maintain the dogma that those who marry are already closely related as kinsmen, and that the marriage is a reinforcement of an earlier existing kinship link. On the contrary, it is understandable that the city would emphasize the attempt to spread kinship links so as to make life easier under the more complex circumstances. We may see in this the disintegration of the positive marriage rule and an attempt (as exemplified by the Commissioners' efforts) to grope toward the formulation of new rules of prohibition which take care of the sexual taboos in the immediate core of the family and leave the boundaries open for new connections. The precise analysis of this shift from a closed system in the villages to a relatively open system in urban areas must await further work in the towns of Ceylon.

To conclude this detailed examination of the forms of kinship, endogamy, caste, and descent in one highland community, certain general formulations may be made.

(1) We do not often come across systems in which a bilateral kinship group appears as a large and fairly distinct unit with a sense of solidarity. Firth has rightly noted that bilateral kinship groups can be perpetuated only if they exhibit a high degree of endogamy.[18] This observation fits the Kandyan case admirably.

Apart from status, endogamy arises from a context in which women are potential carriers of important property claims, and consequently must be actively controlled.[19]

The fact that the marriages of women carry property implications emphasizes the importance that is attached to affines of all kinds. The affines of one generation are the paternal and maternal kin of the next; hence, the allowance of property rights to women as well as men imparts a distinct lateral spread to kinship.

In structural terms the rich Tikopia material provides excellent comparative data. It will be recalled that women on that island are endowed with property at the time of their marriages, but this property must be returned to the *paito* (patrilineal house) when the woman dies. I think that this interesting marriage portion may be

---

[17] *R.C.M.D.* (1959), p. 46; see also p. 49, "the Marriage of Cousins (very popular)."

[18] "The other type of bilateral kin unit is of a corporate order. . . . Here it is possible that completely bilateral groups may function for two or even three generations. . . . But unless birth and marriage are highly restricted or there is a high degree of endogamy such bilinear continuity is unlikely." Firth (1957), p. 6.

[19] See Peters (1964) for similar issues in a totally different cultural context.

considered as being directly related to the importance attached to affinity in Tikopia. That affinity is very important may be observed from the great indignation aroused by adultery on the one hand, and from the attitude toward the maternal kin and the MB on the other. We may venture the suggestion that the value attached to the bilateral kindred (the *Kano a paito*) for purposes of cooperation, assistance in emergencies, and life crises is also related to the impetus given to affinal relations by the "marriage portion." There is greater lateral spread to kinship in Tikopia than one would expect in a purely patrilineal society.

But here the differences between the Tikopia and Kandyan systems are instructive. In the Kandyan system the property does descend to the children of the women; therefore her marriage, as well as those of her children, is circumscribed. The Tikopia marriage portion returns to the *paito,* and we need not expect, in that case, an endogamous tendency.

(2) These remarks have an important bearing on the nature of descent. The Tikopia kindreds seem much more amorphous than those of Terutenne. This is an aspect of the importance of unilineal descent groups in the society. In Tikopia the property-holding group is a named house. This house has a head; the name carries rank; and we are told that marriages are patrilocal. The convergence of these elements gives an unmistakable identity to the group.

In Terutenne, on the other hand, most marriages among the higher groups are patrilocal, and they do have patronymics which carry rank, but members of the *gedara* have no cohesion and do not act in unison. The essence of the matter is that *gedara* property is not kept within the group but goes out with its women. Moreover, affinity is stressed at the expense of lineal solidarity, and the identity of the *gedara* is diffused within the *pavula*. In Tikopia the house does not lose its identity, and consequently the kindred appears to be less cohesive than the *pavula*.

The suggestion, then, is that the endowment of women with property, unless counteracted by restrictions on their marriages, weakens the solidarity of patrilineal descent groups. The more their endowments resemble those of men, in kind and size, the weaker the cohesion of the descent groups is likely to be.

(3) It is obvious that the concept of descent need not always be associated with "groups." In the Kandyan case, were it not for the concern with ritual status, "descent" would have played an insignificant part beyond the elementary family. It certainly does not provide that basis for the formation of corporate unilineal descent groups, and with the *pavula* we reach a situation in which its use is restricted to the very minimum.

On the other hand, there is caste, which is a matter of bilateral descent, and there is the concern with relative rank inside the caste. Regarding the latter, again, there is more concern with unilineal pedigrees among persons of high rank; as one descends the scale, one finds less and less awareness of such ideas.

The Kandyan evidence suggests that when society is organized into small semi-endogamous groups, descent, and particularly unilineal descent, may be discounted as a means of establishing an individual's position in the community. Instead, there is a bilateral and wide-spreading framework of kinship to which the individual may be attached by an affinal tie. Therefore, if rank gradations are to be perpetuated within such a system, there would seem to be two solutions: either the groups become entirely endogamous, as in the case of the castes, or some form of unilineal descent may be recognized, such as status-bearing pedigrees, as among some sections of the high caste in the Kandyan highlands.

Book two is concerned with the logical transformations in the bilateral kinship structure which give rise to patrilineal and matrilineal structures. Here, again, these are found to be associated with a significant diversification of ritual status in both Ceylon and South India.

BOOK TWO:

Toward South India

PART IV: THE LOGIC OF STRUCTURE IN CEYLON: FROM THE BILATERAL TO THE PATRILINEAL

10

A Visit East: Uva Province

"Of these *Natives* there be two sorts, *Wild* and *Tame*. I will begin with the former. For as in these Woods there are Wild
Beasts, so Wild *Men* also. The Land of *Bintan* is all covered
with mighty Woods, filled with abundance of Deer. In this land
there are many of these wild-men; they call them *Vaddahs,*
dwelling near no other Inhabitants. They speak the *Chingulayes*
Language. They kill Deer, and dry the Flesh over the fire, and
the people of the Countrey come and buy it from them. They
never Till any ground for Corn, their Food being only Flesh
. . . "—Robert Knox, *An Historical Relation of Ceylon* (1681),
p. 61.

In Book one we were concerned with the elucidation of the principles
of Sinhalese kinship as they appear in one highland community. We
shall now set out on a trip through the less familiar parts of the
island. We shall visit small communities in the broad eastern jungles
and shall also see their neighbors, the Tamil Moors, and we shall go
on to the eastern littoral, where conditions similar to those of the
Malabar coast of India appear to exist in miniature.

In Terutenne we detected the attempt to construct patrilineal
models out of an essentially bilateral structure. We shall now observe
the same pattern on a wide geographical dispersion. The attempt is
successful in the Low Country, where a patrilineal ideology is consistently formulated. On the other hand, the opposite path has also
been explored: we shall observe exogamous matrilineages on the east
coast. Indeed, in one village, Panama, we shall see the two models
existing side by side in perfect order.

Part iv has two related purposes. First, we must consider how far
the principles of kinship organization, which we have described for

one village, remain applicable in other villages where the agriculture
is based on a different balance between paddy and chena than in
Terutenne. Second, the general principles of kinship organization in
the Kandyan Dry Zone should be contrasted with the situation in the
Low Country to provide an example of the possibilities inherent in
the system if the model is taken further in the patrilineal direction.
In chapter 10 we consider Makulle Watta in Uva Province, which is
largely dependent upon chena cultivation. Chapter 11 describes the
situation in the tank village of Vilawa in the Northwestern Province.
We shall examine the differences in the organization of these communities and the preferred order for caste, marriage, and kinship.

In chapter 12 these general patterns are contrasted with those
evident in a fishing community in the Low Country, where there is
a full-fledged development of a patrilineal ideology.

These variations on the theme of kinship must not be seen as determined by ecological or economic considerations, or reified into
something "other" than the means of defining and expressing certain
social relations. Indeed, we must make a clear distinction between the
specific contexts (the actual relations of A and B in a particular household) in which the "language" of kinship is embedded, and the
general principles, which, like the structure of language, are the organizing and communicating patterns behind the empirical data. We
shall consider the particular communities in the following pages only
to arrive at a more accurate description of those general principles.
At the end of part iv (chap. 12) and of the two parts that follow,
I hope to show just how the specific modifications in the structure
(often reified into discrete and different "matrilineal" or "patrilineal"
structures) more closely resemble the "dialects" of a system of communication than the skeletons of different species (for instance) which
biological analogies so crudely bring to mind.

MAKULLE WATTA

Terutenne was a hill village. Its economy was centered around the
many streams which gush full during the wet season and irrigate the
elaborately laid-out paddy fields like many waterfalls. Wellassa Division (see map 9), where our next village is situated, is different. Here
one is in lush parkland, with jungle clustering up into thick bushland
in places, or here and there opening up wide vistas in the tropical
haze. Around Monaragala, the small bazaar nucleus which serves the
village, the country is slightly rolling, and one is mostly in the shade
of great trees; it is one of the most attractive areas of the island.
There are two main roads here: one cuts across from Monaragala to
the east coast, with little by way of habitations along the way until

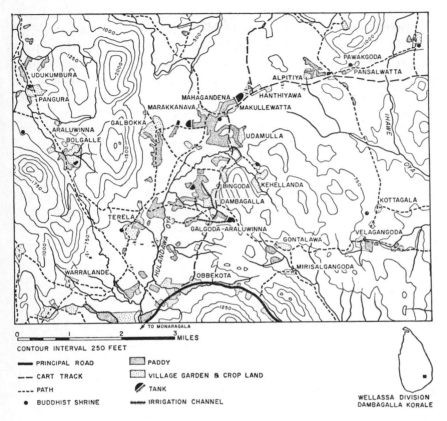

CONTOUR INTERVAL 250 FEET

▬▬ PRINCIPAL ROAD   ▨ PADDY
▬ ▬ CART TRACK   ▨ VILLAGE GARDEN & CROP LAND
▬▬▬ PATH   ▨ TANK
● BUDDHIST SHRINE   ▨ IRRIGATION CHANNEL

WELLASSA DIVISION
DAMBAGALLA KORALE

Map 9. Wellassa Division.

one reaches the populous districts of the Eastern Province; the other runs north from Monaragala, through to Bibile (due east of Teru-tenne), and then on through the Vedda country, described by Selig-man, to the charming Dutch Colonial town of Batticaloa.

If one were to go south, one would reach the Hambantota region, the subject of a perceptive novel by Leonard Woolf (1913), who was a Government Agent in these parts.

Makulle Watta is a few hours' walk from Monaragala, on a jungle path leading into the interior of Wellassa. In the last century this district was one of the wildest parts of the island, and its remoteness from the centers such as Kandy made it possible for a great uprising to be organized a few years after the conquest of the Kandyan king-dom by the British in 1815. Until recently, the area was left much to its own devices, but now with the impressive projects of land colonization in the Eastern Provinces, and in particular with the development of Gal Oya—one of the largest irrigation projects in South Asia—the isolation of Wellassa is coming to an end. The people

still bear the marks of their long isolation, however: they speak in
the Kandyan dialect with special accents of their own, and in fact
refer to themselves as Vedda people. This is partly a reflection that
they are jungle people unfamiliar with the ways of the towns, and also
partly a way of claiming high status, since the Vedda are thought to
be people of high birth and good caste. I should emphasize, however,
that there was no one in these villages who could utter more than a
few grunts of imitation Vedda; they were in truth Kandyan Sinhalese,
although with slight modifications in every aspect of their culture.

I stayed in the hamlet of Udamulla. Like the hamlets of Terutenne,
Udamulla was one of a cluster of hamlets situated on the edge of a
large paddy field; the other hamlets were considered part of the environment of Udamulla, mainly because they were all under the
jurisdiction of one Village Headman who lived in Udamulla. (For
the populations, see table 32.) Of these hamlets, only Makulle Town

TABLE 32

The Population of Makulle Watta*

Hamlet	Population	No. of Houses
Udamulla	300	51
Makulle Town	35	1 (+ 10 shops)
Hanthiyawa	29	6
Makulle Watta	28	5 } all estimates
Maha Gandena	260	40
Marakkanava	91	15
Total	743	

* Also known by villagers as Makulle or Maha Gandena or indeed Udamulla.
These figures are V.H.'s census. My own census of Udamulla hamlet gave a total
population of 225 (114 men, 111 women), and 41 houses; 10 houses were not included,
since 3 were empty and derelict, 2 were shops on the road outside the hamlet, and
5 were temporarily empty because their owners were far away in Chena. The adult
population (over age twenty) was 103 (45.5 percent of total).

and Marakkanava require any special comment. The "town" was in
fact an area of shops much like the central section of Wekumbura
in Terutenne, and it was for that reason distinguished from the rest.
Marakkanava was one of the largest settlements of Tom-Tom Beaters
in the region. I should mention also that the population of the Udamulla area was unusually large for the region, and a short walk in any
direction from these hamlets took one into sparsely settled open parkland, with only an occasional small community of not more than
20–30 people.

The Temples

There were two small and rather poor Buddhist *pansalas* near Uda-mulla. They were called *Pingoda* (heap of merit) and *Bingoda*. They belonged to the same order and had frequent quarrels, mainly over the administration of temple lands dedicated to them by the villagers. There was little resemblance between these temples and the elaborate sacred complexes which are common sight in the more prosperous parts of the island.

The gods and goddesses, too, were not very well provided for. There was no *devale* or village temple in any of the hamlets, though a section of the paddy field was known as *Anpitiya* and seemed to be set aside for the sacred game of breaking of the locked horns of the goddess Pattini and her consort. I was told that it was an annual festival, but it had not been performed for several years. When it was performed, it apparently repeated the ritual at the shrine of Kataragama: a temple for the goddess was constructed in *Anpitiya,* and her consort was brought in great pomp and splendor from the village of Deluve, further north, which does have a *devale.* After the unification of the goddess and her consort "like man and woman" (*pirimi gani vagei*), the game was commenced. In 1955 the only ritual that took place was a *Mangalla Davasa* (Festive Day) at the village of Deluve. Few people from Udamulla bothered to attend (the visit entailed a three-hour walk), apparently satisfied that they could stay on good terms with the supernatural by going to the local Buddhist temples on festive days or perhaps making the pilgrimage to the famous shrine of Kataragama in the jungle to the south of the village.

The Economy

There were important differences between the economies of Udamulla and Terutenne. Perhaps most significant is the fact that, until some years ago, most of the paddy fields of Udamulla had no assured water supply. There are no mountain streams, and paddy cultivation of a limited sort could be done only in hollows in the ground where rain-water could collect in the rainy season. Not surprisingly, these plots, called *malan kumburu,* had a very low yield. A few years before my visit, some new water tanks had been constructed for the village, and the land situation had changed radically.

The traditional system of rice cultivation, though similar to that of Terutenne in general method and in the use of *ande, attang,* and *kayya,* had special characteristics in the details of the contract between the landlord and the worker. Whereas in Terutenne the harvest was divided equally between the landlord and the worker, in Udamulla the landlord received only a portion of the crop, referred to as *bima giya vi,* which was the share equal to the extent sown. In other words, on a piece of land of five *pale,* the landlord would receive only five *pale* baskets of rice; the rest of the crop would belong to the worker. It should be evident that even with low yields the system favored the worker. The division undoubtedly reflects not only the low pressure on the land in this area but also the difficulties of cultivating non-irrigated land and, most importantly, the predominance of chena cultivation. In 1955 in the Wellassa region, the chena cycles were anywhere from seven to twelve or fifteen years—long enough to allow the fields to regain some measure of fertility. Fortunately, the relative flatness of the terrain makes it less subject to erosion than highland terrain.

Chena cultivation was really the mainstay of agriculture in Wellassa, particularly in the very sparsely populated interior. Indeed, in some areas the people were so unaccustomed to paddy cultivation that they vigorously protested attempts by the government to improve their lot by requiring them to take over rice lands in the Gal Oya valley. Some of the resentment was certainly due to the fact that their ancient communities were to be inundated by the Gal Oya reservoir and that they were forcibly evicted from their lands, but at the same time it should be noted that on fertile lands chena is much easier and cheaper than rice cultivation, and it provides a greater variety of crops. Whatever the reason for the fondness for chena, there is no doubt that it was an important aspect of social existence in this province.

With the development of new tank-irrigated rice lands in Udamulla, there was a flurry of buying and selling of lands in the community. In 1955, much of the rice land of the village appeared to have been bought up by the shopkeepers of Makulle Town. This appears clearly in the figures for landholding (table 4, chap. 4): only 7.9 percent of the total adult population of all the hamlets bordering the main paddy field own 78.2 percent of all the available paddy lands. Only 25.3 percent of the adults own any land at all; and if we include persons with more than two *pale,* 93.6 percent of all paddy lands are owned by only 14.1 percent of the adults. This should be compared with the figures from Terutenne (table 3), where 36.4 percent of the adult population hold paddy lands, and those who own more than seven *pale* are 3.2 percent of the total adult population, owning some 40.8 percent of all the available land.

It is noteworthy that the landlords in Udamulla who have these large holdings do not farm according to the traditional system of that area, which so clearly favors the worker. Most of the large landlords employed coolie labor, but they paid them the going daily wage, assumed all the expenses, and kept the harvest for themselves. The only persons who could still get land on a *bima giya vi* basis were close kinsmen and others who had special reasons to be so favored.

To conclude, the specific differences between the Makulle Watta complex and Terutenne in terms of the economy was that slash-and-burn cultivation was much more prevalent in the Wellassa area than in Terutenne, and that the ownership of paddy land was concentrated in the hands of a small group of landlords. This polarization made it appear that much of the population in Udamulla were in the position of landless laborers in Terutenne, but there seemed to be less frustration with the situation than there was in Terutenne, no doubt because of the availability of fertile highlands suitable for chena.

CASTE IN MAKULLE WATTA

The subject of caste in Makulle Watta introduces one element that we did not encounter in Terutenne—Christians. There were only a few Christians in Udamulla, but their marriages bring out the delicate position of Christianity in the Kandyan country. There were also considerable numbers of people who had settled in Udamulla from the Low Country, whose caste origins were somewhat nebulous. Like the Christians, they had become so integrated into Kandyan society as to be caught on both sides of the fence. The positions of both communities were in striking contrast to the Ceylon Moors (Muslims) —also a new element—who appeared to keep their distance and seemed to spurn kinship connections with the Kandyan communities.

The story of the Christians in Udamulla was this: There was a schoolmaster in the village, a Kandyan born in the village of Medagama, who had gone to Badulla in his early youth to a Wesleyan Mission school. There he had become a Christian, and had married a Christian woman. They had had no children themselves but had adopted (*hada gatta*) several, who also became Christians. One of the two adopted sons now lives in Udamulla; he is still a Christian, but he has married a Buddhist woman from the village. Their children are being brought up as Buddhists, but the father does not go to the Buddhist temples.

The other adopted son has also remained a Christian, in the town of Badulla, and though the villagers of Udamulla do not know with certainty, he too is said to have married a Buddhist woman. This second son, in the words of the villagers, goes "to the church there, and to the temple here" (*eha Palliyata yanava, meha Pansalata*).

The schoolmaster's sister and her husband, a marriage registrar who also attended school in Badulla and became a Christian, also live in Udamulla. The marriage registrar has returned to the Buddhist faith and both he and his wife attend the Buddhist temples in Udamulla. The villagers say that they are "ashamed" (*ladjay*) and are therefore feeling the pressure to take up Buddhist practices. Of the three children of the marriage registrar, Charlie, Albert, and Edmund, only one has remained a Christian; he now lives in Buttala and works as a clerk in a government office. But Charlie, still in Udamulla, has become one of the main organizers (*dayakaya*) of the village to provide for a priest during the Buddhist lent (*vas*).

The story of this Christian family in Udamulla illustrates that caste transcends the boundaries of religious affiliation, and that persons of the same caste find it possible to straddle the fence between Buddhism and Christianity and intermarry across religious divisions. It is also true that the ending of the colonial rule in Ceylon has weakened the self-esteem of the Christians and has given added force to Buddhism as the magnet Sinhalese nationalism. We shall see this tendency again in different circumstances in a discussion of the village of Panama later on.

If caste affiliations can override religious differences, the position of the many Low Country persons in Makulle Watta shows that caste differences, too, may be overridden. I shall not go into a detailed discussion of Low Country families in Makulle Watta, except to observe that there were numerous families associated in one way or other with persons of uncertain Low Country origin in this village as well as in Terutenne. It is of some interest, however, to draw attention to the composition of the hamlet of Makulle Town, as a way of illustrating the picture of caste affiliations and also as a way of giving a simple example of the growth of complex bazaar towns around a nucleus of a few shops in one locality. Makulle Town is in many respects typical of the many bazaar towns to be found in every part of Ceylon (see map 10).

It should be emphasized that Makulle Town is a distinctly separate part of the community of Udamulla, a trading post, quite set off from the familial areas of the hamlets. There is a small hamlet called Makulle Watta, but the separation of trade activities is emphasized by the use of the term "town" (*tauma*). The "town" consists of several shops (one a bakery) and a dispensary. Three of the shops are owned and operated entirely by outsiders not related locally. One of these is a Muslim shop, owned by some people from Batticaloa. The bakery is owned by some Low Country people, of uncertain caste, from the town of Ahangama. And one shop is owned by people from Dondra, said to be (though without certainty) of the Durava caste.

Besides these outsiders, there is another set of shopkeepers, also of

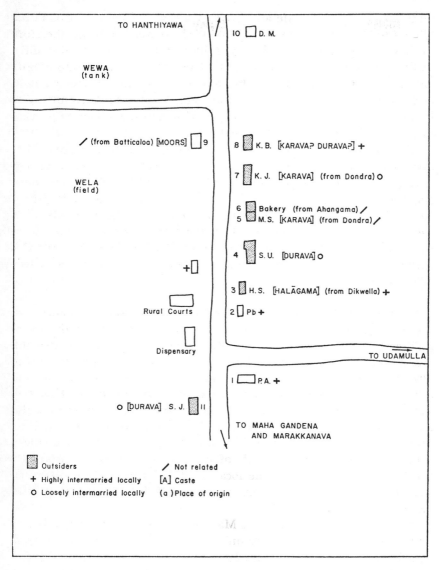

Map 10. Makulle Town in 1955.

Low Country origin, who are loosely intermarried locally. One of these is known to be of the Karava or Fisher caste, and the other two are Durava, but all have relations in Udamulla of the Goyigama caste. The next stage of integration is illustrated by two shops that have been in the locality for a very long time and are closely woven into the kinship structure of Maha Gandena. In their case again the Low Country connection is known and commented upon by their enemies, but their specific caste affiliation is somewhat vague. Bentis, one member of this family, who is one of the largest landholders in the area, is said to be "of the Karava, Durava, or some such caste."

The percentage of Low Country people in the bazaarlike Makulle Town is, of course, much greater than in ordinary residential hamlets like Udamulla. It was generally assumed in the Kandyan country that most of the traders were of Low Country origin. The reasons for their expansion into Kandyan areas must be sought in the economic condition of the Low Country itself. The Low Country is economically the most developed part of the island, and not only is capital for business more readily available there but the connections in the Low Country are themselves a valuable asset for business in the interior of the island. The most common caste of the Low Country found in the highlands is the Karava (Fisher) caste. The reason again is that the Goyigama of the Low Country are relatively less involved in trade and transactions than the fishing community, whose entire activity and subsistence is almost completely dependent on their ability to sell their catch.

The attitude of the inhabitants of Makulle Watta to the Low Country immigrants was uncomfortably ambivalent. In general, they seemed to think the Low Country people were of lower caste than they, though they did not specify their caste connections; and indeed they mainly came across persons of such castes as the Cinnamon Peelers or Fishers, whom highlanders usually relegated to lower rank. Yet it was patently clear to the villagers that the Low Country people were in almost every way more sophisticated than they were. When discussing differences of marriage customs, one villager of Udamulla put the issue directly. "These people," he said, "know how to dress. They put on starched coats, and belts, and the girls just go for them. We cannot keep them from getting married to these people. Our customs are simpler; in our marriages we do not even have receptions. These people will make a big show and impress all the village girls with their new ways!"

KINSHIP AND MARRIAGE

With the background of a jungle village with paddy land concentrated in the hands of a few shopkeepers, and with most of the inhabitants making their living on chena, it is not surprising to find that the patterns of kinship and marriage are similar to those of the landless laborers in Terutenne. The general impression is like that given by the Galpitiya hamlet, except that where the people of Galpitiya felt that they were poor, ignorant people who knew no better, the people of Udamulla were proud of their ancestry and knew that they were keeping up their old customs even though new models were being carried into their society by strangers. In this sense, the wealthy natives of the community were closer to the ordinary people than in Terutenne; and the scale of economic wealth had not yet drawn the social hierarchy along its gradient, and the polarization that was evident in Terutenne was not immediately clear in Udamulla.

Slash-and-burn cultivation was part of the economic foundation of the community. As we have seen, this tends to emphasize the separation and the independence of the nuclear family, and it is essentially only the energy and power of the man in the household that limits the amount of land that can be cultivated. It is a way of life that gives a distinctly egalitarian tone to the entire community. In the general similarity of economic background, such caste differences as are delineated stand out as clear and lasting rents in the social fabric. Accordingly, there was little talk of subtle differences in *wamsa*. Members of the village appeared to take it for granted that they were all much the same kind of people, except in those cases where caste differences had tainted particular families.

So far as names were concerned, Udamulla was much like Terutenne. People seemed to feel that names should be inherited in the male line so as to give honor to the family, but everyone recognized that this never happened. People were referred to by the name of the garden in which they resided, and if the brothers were scattered, they would be referred to by different *gedara* (house) names. Some informants claimed that very few persons in this region had ancestral rights to feudal titles like *wasagama* and that these initials were now being taken up by all and sundry. One of my informants, Sudubanda Vidani, was emphatic about the present customs. "Look here! Here is a man whose mother ran away with another man. Who is his father? Who knows? It is difficult to know that anyway! What name will he take? Any name! I found him the other day simply using my name— saying T. R. M. [*wasagama*] as if he had any rights to it!" Turning to me, he said, "Do not investigate this subject [of names]; it is all lies [*boru*]!" The consensus in Udamulla appeared to be that most people could and did take any name which seemed to them to have the proper sonorous roll.

The terminology of kinship, too, resembles what we recorded for Terutenne. But in their inheritance system—although the aristocratic patterns were known and recognized—the people of Udamulla followed the basic pattern described as that of the landless laborers in Terutenne. In the first place, they were emphatic that sons and daughters all had identical claims on whatever the parents had. But they appeared to contradict this by saying that "in this country we do not give land to women [*me rata gani kattiyata api idam denni ne!*]." What they meant was that the women could always return to the houses of their parents or brothers, and that they did not lose their claims on the property by their marriages; but that, on the other hand, they were not given anything specifically for themselves when they were married. In other words, informants wished to emphasize the fact that marriages in this area were rarely arranged, and that women were not given dowries separate from the common holding.

These statements, ill-defined as they are, could certainly lead to contradictory claims and to bitter disputes, except that there is not very much property to dispute in any case, and that the people who do have much land would probably specify their heirs by testament.

The customs of marriage were in many ways familiar ones. The usual practice of setting up a household in Udamulla was for a young man simply to take a girl to the chena fields. As in Terutenne, he would need her in particular during the *kurakkan* harvesting time, and this season was always spoken of with much amusement by the villagers, as if every field hid a pair of lovers. Usually there was no ceremony of the marriage, but in most cases the young man asked the consent of the girl's parents before taking her to the chena fields. My informants indicated that if the man was a close kinsman and cross-cousin and there were no specific objections to the union, the parents would say "*Ha! Hondai!* [Yes! it is good!]" and the man was then free to take the girl to his hut. The informants were aware that rich people, Kandyans, and Low Country people all had somewhat more elaborate rituals at this time. They knew, for instance, that a respectable ceremony in other parts would involve the setting up of a marriage *poruva* (ceremonial structure) and that even in the simplest of ceremonies the thumbs of the couple would be tied together by some elder in the family. But the villagers in Udamulla would make fun of these pretensions and say, "We do not tie hands and feet like that!" (meaning, as the corpse is tied at the funeral). The most formal recognition they gave—and this was not common—was a special meal to which kinsmen from both sides were invited. This would indicate the support of the girl's parents to the project, and the responsibility for the girl would be tacitly conveyed (*bara denava*) to the man.

There was a government-paid marriage registrar in this village (the Christian referred to above), but it was evident that he lived a life free from pressing duties. In general, a marriage was registered only if some sort of dowry transaction were taking place, a rare occurrence in Makulle Watta. The registrar did have some business recording the birth of children so that they could get rice ration books permitting them to buy rice below the open market price. Until the Second World War, I was told, no one used to register their marriages. "Then," Punchibanda said, "a rumor spread in the village that unmarried bachelors would be drafted and sent to fight. You should just have seen these old men with long beards running to the registrar to get their women legalized. The entire *wasama* [Headman's Division] was married in the space of two weeks!"

The Marriage Ritual

Even though households were set up informally, the villagers of Udamulla Makulle had vivid notions of how an elaborate marriage ritual *ought* to be carried out. Just how many times anyone of my informants had witnessed such a ceremony I cannot say, but their accounts offered an interesting comparison with highland and Low Country customs. The egalitarian tone and the lack of dowry are notable features of the ceremony.

(1) First there is the informal period when the young man visits the house of the girl frequently, helps his *mama* (MB and F-in-L), and gives them presents.

(2) Then the elders of the young man's family visit the girl's house to find out whether the parents of the girl are pleased with the developments.

(3) *Bulat puwak siyak denava* (Hundred Betel Giving): Then a marriage broker (*kapu mahatmaya*) goes to the house of the girl to distribute one hundred betel leaves and one hundred betel nuts among the relations of the girl. One or two are given to each person.

(4) *Maha bulat adukku* (Grand Betel Offering): This is a second visit, when the marriage broker dresses up in a special costume to take bunches of betel leaves and betel nuts to the house of the girl. A man of the Vahumpura (Jaggery Makers' caste) goes with him this time. The marriage broker gives the betel leaves and the nuts to the Vahumpura, who hands them on to the relations. The Vahumpura then presents a handkerchief (*lensuvak*) to the girl; this is a gift from the young man, and the girl expresses her pleasure with the match by accepting the handkerchief.

(5) Finally a day is named and the groom's side prepare for a procession. In this, two elders from the community (*denu mutta:* Knowing elders?), the broker, and a man and woman from the Vahumpura caste again dress up in special costume and go to the house of the girl. The Vahumpura man goes in front carrying a large torch (*pandura*), the phallic significance of which is not lost on the guests. The side of the groom also takes along on this procession food parcels (*kat*) carried at the end of sticks. They may joke about the fact that they have brought their own food with them.

(6) The two kindreds then join together in a feast: The elders (*denu mutta*) may preach *bana* (Buddhist sermon) to the couple, telling them

TABLE 33

Cooking Units in Udamulla and Vilawa

A. Dwellings with One Cooking Unit

	Udamulla (44 dwellings)	Vilawa (49 dwellings)
Nuclear family	26	27
2 polyandrous brothers	—	1
Incomplete (spouse dead or separated)	2	2
Man's nf and children by another woman	1	—
Man's nf and wife's children by another man	3	1
Single man	2	1
Single woman	1	1
Man and daughter's nf	1	—
Man and adopted son's nf	1	—
Woman and daughter's nf	1	1
Woman and daughter	—	1
Woman and daughter's children	—	1
2 brothers	1	—
Total	39	36

B. Dwellings with Two Cooking Units

	Udamulla	Vilawa
Man's nf + son's nf	—	3
Man's nf + daughter's nf	—	1
Woman + son's nf and daughter's nf	—	1
Woman and children from 1st husband and from 2nd husband + son's nf	1	—
Man's nf + wife's brother	1	—
Man with son's nf + son-in-law's nf	—	1
Total	2	6

C. Dwellings with Three Cooking Units

	Udamulla	Vilawa
Man's nf + son's nf + daughter's nf	1	1
Woman and children + son's nf + daughter's nf	1	—
Man's nf + son's nf + sister's daughter's nf	1	—
Woman and children + son's nf + brother's son's nf	—	1
Woman and children + brother + sister	—	1
Man + son's nf + daughter's nf + wife's brother's daughter's nf	—	1
Woman, daughter, daughter's children + son's nf + 2nd son's son's nf	—	1
Total	3	5

TABLE 33 *(Continued)*

D. Dwellings with Four Cooking Units

	Udamulla	Vilawa
Man's nf + son's nf + daughter's nf + brother's son's nf..........................	—	1
Man + brother's wife's 1st husband's son's nf + 2nd brother's 1st daughter's nf + 2nd brother's 2nd daughter's daughter's nf...	—	1
Total......................................	0	2

of village lore *(gama kata)* and instructing them how they should behave as husband and wife. At the end of the feast, one of the *denu mutta* will say, "Have you all eaten and drunk well?" Then he will turn to the Vahumpura man who has also been invited (though of course seated apart), and say, "Have you eaten and drunk well?" Then he will signal the formal end of the feast by saying, "Well, now we can all wash our hands! *[Deng api ata hodanta puluvan!]*" Since it is one of the purposes of the feast to demonstrate the ritual equality between the kin groups, the elder must ask in formal terms whether everyone is satisfied. If there had been difficulties about ritual status, trouble would have arisen between the people concerned long before this stage. The formal washing of hands together is an indication of the assent of the kins groups to the new alliance between them.

Polyandry

In 1955 there were no polyandrous households in Udamulla. There were said to be some in Dambagalle, Maha Gandena, and other hamlets. The usual term for the arrangement was the same as in Terutenne: *eka ge kanava* (one-house eating). The informants generally expressed the sensible aspect of the arrangement. One said, "It is very good for all. The woman gets food from each husband, and they all have more. Sometimes the elder brother will start the woman, and if they are on good terms they will all live together. There was a case in Hanthiyawa where one of the co-husbands wanted to have another woman for himself and left the household. But the polyandrous woman did not want to give him up and eventually got him back again. The children call one man *tatta* (father), and the others *loku appa* (big father), *bappa* (small father), and so on. These people do not need to hide the arrangement, there is nothing to be ashamed of. What they do is very good for them all."

TABLE 34

Locality of Marriage and Origin of Spouses, Udamulla and Vilawa

I. THE LOCALITY OF MARRIAGE: NATIVES

A. Marriages of Native Men (binna-deega)

Relative Wealth†	Terutenne* No. of Persons	No. of Unions‡ b	No. of Unions‡ d	Udamulla No. of Persons	No. of Unions‡ b	No. of Unions‡ d	Vilawa No. of Persons	No. of Unions‡ b	No. of Unions‡ d
A	15	—	19	5	—	5	6	—	9
B	20	—	27	6	—	7	20	6	22
C	95	31	83	26	11	31	9	3	9

B. Marriages of Native Women (binna-deega)

Relative Wealth†	Terutenne* No. of Persons	No. of Unions‡ b	No. of Unions‡ d	Udamulla No. of Persons	No. of Unions‡ b	No. of Unions‡ d	Vilawa No. of Persons	No. of Unions‡ b	No. of Unions‡ d
A	4	2	4	1	—	1	3	2	3
B	16	12	6	4	3	1?	12	12	8
C	67	41	36	18	18	9	12	9	5

II. THE ORIGIN OF SPOUSES OF NATIVE MEN AND WOMEN

A. Origin of Spouses of Native Men

Relative Wealth†	Terutenne* No. of Persons	No. of Unions‡ In	No. of Unions‡ Out	Udamulla No. of Persons	No. of Unions‡ In	No. of Unions‡ Out	Vilawa No. of Persons	No. of Unions‡ In	No. of Unions‡ Out
A	15	6	13	5	1	4	6	1	8
B	20	10	17	6	3	4	20	10	18
C	95	73	41	26	22	17	9	4	5
						(3?)			

TABLE 34 (*Continued*)

B. *Origin of Spouses of Native Women*

	Terutenne*			Udamulla			Vilawa		
		No. of Unions‡			No. of Unions‡			No. of Unions‡	
Relative Wealth†	No. of Persons	In	Out	No. of Persons	In	Out	No. of Persons	In	Out
A	4	5	1	1	1	—	3	2	3
B	16	10	8	4	3	1	12	10	10
C	67	57	19	18	14	12	12	5	9
		(1?)							

III. THE LOCALITY OF MARRIAGE: SETTLERS

A. *Men Settling in the Village*

	Terutenne*			Udamulla			Vilawa		
		No. of Unions‡			No. of Unions‡			No. of Unions‡	
Relative Wealth†	No. of Persons	b	d	No. of Persons	b	d	No. of Persons	b	d
A	1	1	—	—	—	—	—	—	—
B	8	8	—	2	1	3	3	3	—
C	19	19	—	10	9	6	6	4	2

B. *Women Settling in the Village*

	Terutenne*			Udamulla			Vilawa		
		No. of Unions‡			No. of Unions‡			No. of Unions‡	
Relative Wealth†	No. of Persons	b	d	No. of Persons	b	d	No. of Persons	b	d
A	13	—	13	3	—	3	5	—	5
B	17	—	17	1	—	2	12	—	12
C	41	—	41	11	—	12	6	—	6

TABLE 34 (*Continued*)

IV. THE ORIGIN OF SPOUSES OF SETTLERS

A. Spouses of Men Settling in the Village

Relative Wealth†	Terutenne* No. of Persons	No. of Unions‡ In	Out	Udamulla No. of Persons	No. of Unions‡ In	Out	Vilawa No. of Persons	No. of Unions‡ In	Out
A	1	1	—	—	—	—	—	—	—
B	6	8	—	2	2	2	3	3	—
C	19	19	—	10	14	1	6	5	1

B. Spouses of Women Settling in the Village

Relative Wealth†	Terutenne* No. of Persons	In	Out	Udamulla No. of Persons	In	Out	Vilawa No. of Persons	In	Out
A	13	13	—	3	3	—	5	5	—
B	17	17	—	1	1	1	12	12	—
C	41	41	—	11	11	1	6	5	1

V. SIZE OF SAMPLE FOR TABLE 34

	Terutenne*	Udamulla	Vilawa
Native men	130	37	35
Native women	87	23	27
Men settlers	28	12	9
Women settlers	71	14	23
Total in sample	316	86	94
Total adults in village (over age 20)	419	103	185
Percent in sample	77%	83.4%	50.8%

* The Terutenne figures are the same as those in tables 27 and 28 but are here included for ease of comparison.

† The distinctions for A, B, and C are based on the same principles as in earlier tables.

‡ Nos. refer to the marriages of persons interviewed; *b* and *d* stand for *binna* and *deega;* In and Out refer to spouses who are natives of the village or outsiders.

A case for polyandry is often made on the grounds that it prevents
the division of the land between brothers. However that may be, in
this region it derives its rationale from the fact that two men can
work larger areas of chena, and if they have only one household between them, not only do they all have more food (an important issue
when the people live near the subsistence level), but the presence of
two able-bodied men is a good insurance against calamities like sick-
ness which could practically wipe out all hope for the small family.

Whatever the situation in the past may have been, it would appear
that nowadays men are not easily satisfied by polyandrous arrangements. This is shown by the scarcity of such unions even in these areas
where it was distinctly approved. On the other hand, there were any
number of men, both rich and poor, who had more than one woman
for themselves. This was not approved of. The largest shopkeeper in
the region, the Orange Mudalali, had numerous women, some of
whom actually lived together in the same household. Most of these
women were of poor families who appreciated the connection with an
important man. There was, however, one poor man who had no land
except what he could cultivate, without help, on the chena, and yet he
too maintained two households. When asked about it he simply said

TABLE 35

The Stability of Marriage in Udamulla and Vilawa

A. *Udamulla*

Relative Wealth*	Men			Women		
	No. of Men	No. of Marriages	No. of Separations	No. of Women	No. of Marriages	No. of Separations
A.........	5	5	—	4	4	—
B.........	8	11	—	5	6	1
C.........	36	56	11	29	37	4

B. *Vilawa*

Relative Wealth*	Men			Women		
	No. of Men	No. of Marriages	No. of Separations	No. of Women	No. of Marriages	No. of Separations
A.........	6	9	—	8	10	—
B.........	23	31	3	24	32	8
C.........	15	8	2	18	20	3

* A, B, and C are based on the same principles as in earlier tables.

that he did have two families, and had enough strength to satisfy both of them; that, he felt, answered all criticism.

I have underlined the differences between this community and Terutenne. From the point of view of the principles of kinship and marriage the differences are largely confined to the lack of any emphasis on the unilineal descent. Tables 33–35 show that the patterns of kinship resemble those of Terutenne. These tables also include figures for the village of Vilawa, a tank village of a type common to the North Western Province, and the subject of the next chapter.

11

More on Bilaterals:
The Northwestern Province

"The first tank in Ceylon was formed by the successor of Wijayo, B.C. 504, and their subsequent extention to an almost incredible number is ascribable to the influence of the Buddhist religion . . ."—Sir James Emerson Tennent, *Ceylon* (1859), I, 431

"No people in any age or country had so great practice and experience in the construction of works for irrigation . . ."— *ibid.*, I, 468

We observed the prevalence of chena cultivation in Uva Province. We had already noted the relative autonomy given to the nuclear family by slash-and-burn cultivation. In the circumstances of eastern Ceylon this autonomy, together with the lack of heritable land, valuables, or indeed social position, appears associated with the unconcern toward unilineal descent. The framework of kin categories seems sufficient for the internal organization of small communities.

We turn now to the Northwestern Province. The ecological conditions here are quite different both from Terutenne and from Uva Province. We are in a region with highly focused communities. The ordinary village shows a unity much greater than any we have met. How does this affect the nature of the family and the institution of marriage?

THE DESIGN OF A TANK VILLAGE: VILAWA

The district known as *Wanni* was considered wild and inaccessible even in the late nineteenth century, but today, with the dense population, the villages bordering on one another in close contiguity, with good roads frequently traversed by ancient buses, with energetic shop-

keepers well connected in such circles as Kurunegala and Colombo,
Vilawa is a community well in touch with Sinhalese national life.

The Wanni Hat Pattuva region of the Northwestern Province (see
map 11), almost on the line dividing the Dry and the Wet zones of

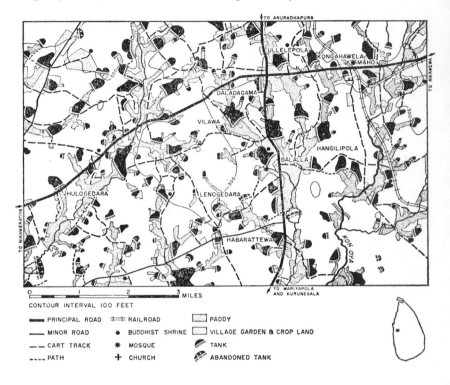

Map 11. Wanni Hat Pattuva Region.

the island, conveys a vivid impression of cultural uniqueness. The villages here seem to be more prosperous than the jungle villages, and
one is struck by certain unusual features in the architecture, women's
dress, and the like. The older houses are often built around a court-
yard—a style which was considered the traditional but long-aban-
doned Kandyan style by the people of Terutenne—and the rice and
kurakkan harvest is kept in raised granaries that look much like the
great stacks of rice one sees at harvesttime. Among the younger
women, the usual present-day Sinhalese female dress of the cloth and
the blouse has recently become popular, but the older women in
particular still wear a sort of a sari, not unlike the Tamils.

The most singular feature of these regions in the northern half of
Ceylon is the village tank, around which the village is clustered. These
carefully constructed reservoirs, usually built in a natural basin with
an earthenwork bund, fill up during the wet season and can be used

for controlled irrigation for the elaborately laid-out paddy fields during the dry season. Sometimes there are three or four tanks utilizing
the contours of one catchment area.

We know that there were in ancient times very clear principles for
the establishment of such tank-based communities (Codrington, 1938).
First, a number of kinsmen got together to cut the jungle, prepare the
ground, and construct a bund for a tank. After the bund was prepared
and the spills and sluices made, the group would cooperate in the
preparation of the paddy field to be watered by the tank. The area
below the tank would be laid out in the form of an elongated rectan-
gle. Each person in the group would be entitled to one share (*pangu*)
not merely in the paddy lands below the tank but also, as it were, in
the community. Ideally, this was an equal share in a corporation. Since
the corporation signified, in this case, the tank, the bund, the paddy
land, the garden lands, and highlands for chena cultivation, the original shareholder was entitled to one equitable share in all these different assets of the corporation. The share carried not only specific
rights to certain sections of land but also important obligations having to do with the upkeep of the main water-supply system (Leach,
1961*b*).

In 1955 Vilawa was a village of seventy households (see table 36).

TABLE 36

The Population of Vilawa
(Census of 38 Households out of 70) *

Age	Men	Women	Total
Above twenty (adult)......	65	54	119 (48.7%)
Below twenty.............	61	64	125
Total................	126	118	244

* Total population (V.H.'s census), 380 (all Goyigama). Estimated adult population, 185.

The population was 380 and as is usual in this area of more unified
communities they were all members of one caste, the Goyigama. The
low castes, such as the Tom-Tom Beaters and the Washermen, each
had their own villages nearby with separate water supplies. The most
immediate neighbors of Vilawa were the villages of Daladagama, only
a few miles across the jungle, and Balalla, to the south, again not more
than twenty minutes' walk from Vilawa. I was assured as soon as I
arrived in the village that Daladagama was really a "low" village, like

Galpitiya. Balalla was considered to be no more than ordinary in rank, even though it was a richer village than Vilawa. This had not apparently always been the case, but it had benefited from the main road that passed through it and had developed a large bazaar to serve the vicinity. It is significant that in the past Balalla had not had a village tank and had been obliged to use the leftover waters which spilled from the Vilawa tank. Vilawa, on the other hand, was an ancient tank village, and could boast among the ancestors of the community an official whose post was referred to as *Wanni Nayaka* and who had had jurisdiction over large parts of the Northwestern Province. I was proudly shown the document which confirmed in English the position of the *Wanni Nayaka* in Vilawa by a Government Agent sometime in the nineteenth century.

THE FOUNDING OF THE VILLAGE

In 1955 the knowledgeable and responsible members of Vilawa had a lively idea of the principles on which their community had been founded. They were not sure about the date when this had taken place, and, significantly for this area, there was even some suggestion that the original inhabitants had come from South India. But they were very clear as to how it had occurred.

The original founders had built the main tank at Vilawa (*wewa bendala:* lit., tied the tank) and had laid out the paddy field below the bund. (The first distinction here was between the tank [*wewa*] and the field [*wela*].) The land around the tank was considered common (*gamata podu*) to the village community, except for lands specifically shared out among the members. Thus (fig. 22), the paddy field was divided into "strips" (*issara*) which were continued on into the highlands on either side of the field (*ismatta*). Each strip therefore carried a distinction between paddy land (*mada idama*) and highland (*goda idama*). The highland strips were considered to be the appurtenance of the strips in the paddy field, and they could be used for house gardens (*gedara watte*).

Such lands which could be brought under paddy cultivation on the *ismatta* on either side of the main field were also considered to belong to the owners of the *issara*. These included the small new tanks (*dalupata*) that could be constructed near the field by the shareholders. The rest of the highlands that could not be brought under paddy cultivation, and were not part of the house sites of the village, were used as a common chena without specific rights accruing to particular persons.

The accepted story in the case of Vilawa was that the original founders of the village were eight brothers. The village had for that reason been divided originally into eight shares (*panguva*), with each share-holder receiving paddy fields, house sites adjacent to the paddy field, reserve lands for future paddies on which small tanks had later been built, and a right to the highlands of the village. Even the fish in the village tank were shared equally by the eight brothers, and I was told that this particular custom was still honored: in the dry season when the village tank is low, the fish caught would still be divided into eight shares.

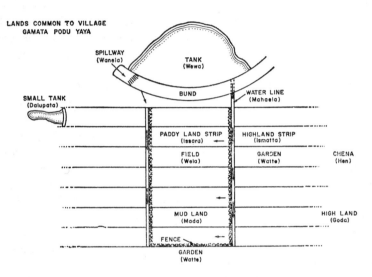

Figure 22. A tank village in the Maho area.

All this was the theory, and it may have been true, except that certain changes had occurred making it difficult to trace the legend. Around 1900 the village tank was extensively repaired by the government and the field was increased from the original size (said to be eight *amunam,* i.e., one *amunam* per share) to the present twenty *amunam.* I was defeated in my attempt to trace the present distribution of land in the main field to the supposed original one of eight shares. Certain features of the original pattern remained. In 1955 there were still lands on the *ismatta* of the strips (*issara*) where the identity of the pattern of ownership with the main field could still be detected. Some small tanks (*dalupata*) had been built on the *ismatta,* and in 1955 the owners of the *dalupata* and the main field *issara* were the same. The position of house lands was already highly complicated by the fact that house sites were being sold quite separately from the paddy field, and only the barest outlines of the original pattern were discernible.

The division of the village into a fixed number of shares is referred to in Ceylon as the *pangu* system. In the past it seems to have been related not merely to the cultivation practices of the village but also to certain feudal rights and obligations, which we noted earlier (see also Codrington, 1938). The Vilawa *pangu* system invites a direct comparison with that described in remarkable detail for the North Central Province by Leach (1961*b*), in the village of Pul Eliya. The differences both in practice and spirit are very considerable. In Pul Eliya the field below the village tank is so designed as to ensure an equitable distribution of the rewards and obligations involved in the cultivation between each specific share (*pangu*). The general idea is that each share is made up of strips of paddy land in different sections of the village field, so as to give each shareholder some of the best, the middling, and the poor portions of the land; furthermore, to anticipate the likely event of a drought, when the entire field cannot be cultivated because of insufficient water in the tank, the dispersal of the holdings of each share is arranged in such a way as to place the cultivable lands of the field near the water supply, again without affecting the rights and obligations of each share. As we have already noted, the entire field has to be fenced against marauding animals: the share system makes it possible to compensate the owners of the strips of land at the head and the foot of the field which require more fencing than the strips in between. We need not go into the details of the system here. It is sufficient to note that the total "design" of a village field which will fulfill all these requirements is so intricate and amazing as to be quite a severe challenge to any modern town planner or engineer, yet it is put into effect as a traditional system in the isolated jungle villages of the North Central Province of the island. The implications of these brilliant feats of plane geometry on the part of simple villagers have not been sufficiently realized. This single instance is enough to dispel any lingering notions of "primitive mentality" that we tend to associate with people who live near a subsistence level.

The *pangu* system of Vilawa was much less remarkable in design than the one in Pul Eliya. Not only was the "ancient" blueprint less complicated, but there was not so much ingeniuity in the procedure followed when there was insufficient water in the tank to cultivate the entire field. In Pul Eliya the field is laid out in such a way that it can be cut in half or quarters without affecting the relative return per share. In Vilawa a significantly different rule was followed.

The reduction of the irrigable field into a half, or a third, or two-thirds as the case may be, is called *bethma*. In Vilawa, when there was not enough water, a formal meeting of all the landlords was held (Cultivators' Meeting) under the general direction of the Irrigation Headman. Once the meeting had come to an agreement on what proportion of the field could be cultivated, the land was reapportioned among all the landowners in precise proportion to their original extent of ownership in the field. A person who held three *pale* of land, for example, was given one *pale*, and all the cultivators moved in closer to the main water supply. There is little doubt that this procedure results in tension, but there are reports of similar land reallotments by other observers and it does not appear to have been a recent development. It is quite possible that the system reflects the far greater reliability of the rainfall in the Wanni region than up in the north where Pul Eliya is situated, where recurring dry seasons long ago forced the villagers to work out a system that was fair and acceptable by all.

In Vilawa, various other obligations besides the one just mentioned were reckoned in terms of the proportions of the total landholding in the fields. Thus the important obligations involved in the upkeep of the bund, the cleaning of the water lines, the fencing of the top and bottom sides of the field were all reckoned on the basis of landholding. To give one instance—it was customary for every person who worked one *pale* of land in the main field to construct three fathoms (*bambu*) of fence at the upper and lower ends of the field. The two sides of the field, however, would be fenced by the workers in each strip as in Pul Eliya. The repairs to the bund, when not undertaken by the Irrigation Department of the government, would also be decided on according to the extent of land held in the field. Again, the measures for the amount of earth needed to keep the bund in good repair had become traditional. A *katti* of earth was about twelve feet long, six feet wide, and one and a half feet deep. In the past about twenty *katti* were needed annually for the upkeep of the bund.

Such obligations on the part of landholders were very specifically reckoned. When the small tank of Alut Wela Dalupata was constructed, all the owners of the main field strip (and only those) got together and provided *katti* for the new bund according to their holdings (*vapa saraya*: sowing extent) in the original strip (*issara*). They thus became entitled to proportionally the same extents of land on the "highland strip" (*ismatta*) as they owned in the "mainland strip" (*issara*).

Quite apart from the original division of the village into eight shares, it was said also that the communal part of the village was originally divided into three sections, called *tulana*—an *ihela* (upper), *meda* (middle), and *pahala* (lower) *tulana*. Here again the village was to some extent still divided in this way in 1955, but the population had spilled on to new lands on all sides, and whatever the former significance of the threefold division, it had ceased to play a part in village organization. My informants did say, however, that when the village was thus divided each *tulana* was "as one." "All you had to do was to go out into the middle of the field and shout Ho! and people from each *tulana* would come in equal numbers to help you with your cultivation!" But that was in the good old days.

THE RETURNS ON LAND

Chena land is not plentiful near Vilawa as around Terutenne or Udamulla. This makes the paddy lands of Vilawa a matter of even greater interest for the inhabitants. Attention should be drawn to an important fact in this connection. The yields on paddy even on the most fertile fields in Terutenne were rarely more than 16 to one and varied between 8–12 to one. In Vilawa, however, during the main harvest, the yields were of the order of 24–32 to one. It is certainly true that Vilawa enjoyed a more reliable rainfall than Terutenne or Udamulla, but the difference in yield cannot be attributed simply to that. Different techniques of cultivation seem to have made the crucial difference. Terutenne may not provide an entirely accurate comparison since its lands were subject to erosion and were probably less fertile than those of Vilawa, but on the good lands around Wellassa one could certainly have expected much higher yields than the 8–12 to one which was reported. But even the superficial observer could see that the cultivators of Vilawa tended their paddy fields with great care—double plowing, careful sowing, elaborate fencing, and so on—whereas the fields in Wellassa got very little attention. They were rarely plowed but only "mudded," and the owners, or workers, seemed little concerned with trying to get as much as they could out of the land. It appeared that most of their energy and care went into the cultivation of the chena lands which abounded in the area.

If these remarks are accurate—and they are based on close observation—it seems that we are facing an even more flexible situation regarding the pressure on land and general economic problems in the Dry Zone of Ceylon than has generally been realized.

It is important to realize, too, that in Vilawa, where most of the agricultural income came from paddy lands, there was a more equal distribution of land ownership than in Terutenne and Makulle Watta (see tables 3 and 4, chap. 4). Nearly twice as many inhabitants in Vilawa own paddy land as in Makulle Watta (44.3 percent as against 25.3 percent). And far fewer of those are big landowners (that is, owners of more than seven *pale*) than in Makulle Watta: 3.3 percent of the adults in Vilawa own 29.9 percent of the paddy land in the village, whereas 7.9 percent of the adults in Makulle Watta own not less than 78.2 percent of the total available paddy land. Note also that although the average amount of land per adult is 1.38 *pale* for Vilawa and 1.77

pale for Makulle Watta, Vilawa farmers can get two harvests a year, whereas attention is directed to the chena in Makulle.

KINSHIP AND MARRIAGE

As in the case of the ideal blueprint which guided the founders of Vilawa, the ideal pattern of kinship, too, was out of focus with the facts. I was impressed when I began to work in the Wanni area by the insistence of the informants that each village had a prescribed circle of villages within which all marriages allegedly took place. Such "circles" were not named and although the term *variga* was applied to them, this was not an exclusive usage and *variga* also meant "line," "family," "ritual status," and the like. More frequently specific distinctions would be made by saying that certain villages were *"sambandha gama"* (marriage villages—also equal, connected) and that others were "not of us" (*apata ne*).

The justification for such an in-marrying circle was expressed in caste terms. The people of Vilawa only married with villages of equal status. They could not intermarry with Daladagama (their closest neighbor) because, in the days of the Kandyan kings, that village had had service obligations to carry oil to the famous Temple of the Tooth in Kandy. Similar reasons were brought up when certain other village names were mentioned. Or the village would simply be dismissed as "not of our status" (*api tatvaya ne*). Again, certain villages were dropped even though they had originally been of acceptable status because they had allowed marriages to take place with "low" villages.

In theory it should have been possible to make a list of the *sambandha gama* of Vilawa, but in fact this was not possible. Even though the informant would say that Vilawa only married into its *sambandha gama*, his list would not necessarily agree with those given by others, or even by himself on an earlier occasion. This was recognized by the informants by saying that these old customs were now getting confused, and that people would now marry for reasons of money and not status (*wamsa*).

Even so, certain important distinctions remained. While certain villages with traditional low connotations were "out," others were said to have excommunicated the families which had intermarried with another particular "low" village and were acceptable as *sambandha gama* as long as one carefully chose the family one wanted to marry into. Thus, whatever the situation in the past with a clearly demarcated endogamous circle, the communal distinctions in Vilawa were in 1955 very similar to those among the *pavula* of Terutenne.

Some of the traditional divisions were of long standing. This suggested that the practice of *variga* endogamy may have been a matter

of serious concern in the not too distant past. At the very beginning
of my stay in Vilawa I was told that one of the original *pangu* shareholders in the community had been excommunicated. There were
three households descended from this particular line, and in 1955
they had no kinsmen in Vilawa, although they were recognized as a
very old family.

There were interesting disagreements in the explanations given for
the excommunication by the villagers and by the family concerned.
The villagers said that one of the ancestors of this family had married
a person in the unacceptable village of Imbulgodayagama. The shareholders of the village had thereupon held a meeting and agreed to
excommunicate these people and segregate their particular *pangu*
(share) from the rest of the village.[1]

I should emphasize that the conception is more important than the
incident. The villagers evidently saw some identity between cutting
off all kinship connections and the "separation" of the share in the
lands. The statement was undoubtedly symbolic, and not merely practical: the severance of kinship relations with the rest of the community
meant, in effect, that the excommunicated family could not gain control of lands in the village fields by inheritance or marriage. At the
same time the formal separation of their lands was intended to thwart
their hopes of reestablishing kinship across the division. However, in
1955, the "excommunicated" family did in fact own land in the main
field in Vilawa, and they cultivated it according to the usual complicated reciprocal arrangements with the rest of the respectable
members of the village. Some of these lands were said to have been
bought by the senior generation just deceased and others to have been
inherited from earlier ancestors. Kinship, however, had not been re-
established and, although the vagaries of Kandyan kinship make it
foolish to predict, the prejudice against them seemed so strong that
future connections within the village are unlikely. They continued to
intermarry with villages which were claimed to be unacceptable by
Vilawa.

This symbolic association between land and status is inherent in the
historical service tenure system of the Kandyan area and is simply an
example of the general principle whereby the various castes were given
lands in separate places. One recalls, for instance, the lands of the
Tom-Tom Beaters in Terutenne who had independent water supplies.
We may note also that in the Wanni area the low castes normally
live in their separate tank villages. The mode of thought, therefore,
by which the villagers expressed the excommunication of the particular family was one which had its roots in the feudal symbolic language

---

[1] Expressed as *idam kadam venas kirima* (separation of land), *nedekam venas
kirima* (separation of kinship).

of the land. The case of Devale Gedara, as these people were called, is unusual only because it has become by the passage of time part of the traditional lore of the community, much as the hamlet of Galpitiya had become in Terutenne. Since the initial flaunting of the rules, many other breaches had taken place which unfolded day by day as I continued to work in the community.

Vilawa, too, was split into kindred groupings, each one of which viewed its distinctions from all the others in terms of its putative purity. Thus it became clear that the Village Headman himself had been responsible for a breach. His connections were solely with the neighboring village of Daladagama. His deed was at least understandable since it was politic. He had married a wealthy woman, the sister of the wife of the Village Headman of Daladagama. My landlords, who told me the story, claimed that the Village Headman and his family had therefore been "separated" (*ayin karala*) from the village. But these claims and counterclaims appeared to be similar in their nature to the divisions between the kindreds in Helagama hamlet. Since we have examined those in detail, it is enough to note here that these divisions bore no relation to the eight *pangu* divisions in Vilawa except for the one instance noted above.

From the point of view of my landlords in Vilawa (two polyandrous brothers), the village was divided into many kindreds (*pavula*). They would sometimes refer to them as "factions" (*kattiya*). Yet when questioned closely about these "barriers" of excommunication, they would smile and draw attention to those past and present marriages which connected otherwise proud kindreds.

KINDRED AND LAND

The reasons for the proliferation of kinship "connections" within the kindred, as well as the excommunications on its boundaries, are sometimes said to be related to the facts of land tenure. As in Terutenne, I went into the question of land tenure carefully in order to understand to what extent the motivations and tactics of individuals were based on their interests in land. Hardly to my surprise, I found that land tenure could be used to "explain" both close kinship and great enmity, and all the shades of social relationship in between. The inheritance of land in the village certainly seemed to give a distinct form to the genealogies which the villagers were prepared to recall. Otherwise, land entered into the picture of *pavula* formation as one of several factors.

The facts of land tenure and cooperation in Vilawa are so complex and yet so clear that it is illuminating to examine the detailed evidence regarding one *pavula* and one small section of the paddy field

where some members of this *pavula* owned land. By doing so, I hope
to indicate the fascinating organization of paddy cultivation in Vilawa
as well as to underline the complexity of the connection between
land and kinship. Consider map 12 and figure 23. There is a neighbor-

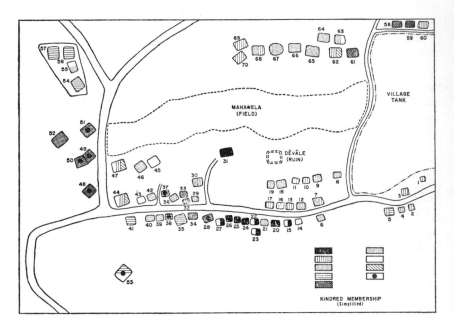

Map 12. Vilawa.

hood near the bund of the village tank (dwellings 1–18) related in
many different ways. In this neighborhood the households shown in
figure 23 considered themselves to be one *pavula*. They justified the
denial of kin relations with others shown as I–V (all coaxed out of
them by the anthropologist) on the grounds that those people were
"polluted" by having intermarried with people from "low" villages.
There was a definite attempt made to confuse the connections and
"forget about" those people.

At the same time there was great precision in the kinship links of
certain persons considered to be at the center of the *pavula*, A and B in
figure 23. In group A, Hora Punchibanda (4) was claimed to be "out"
since a nasty dispute had developed between him and 9 over the division of an inheritance. No. 13 (V. V., the Irrigation Headman) had
sided with No. 9, and 10, 11, and 12 followed. However, the mother
of V. V. had not been given paddy lands, and in 1955 there were no
common landholdings between groups A and B. V. V. had extensive
landholdings, and No. 2 (a person I came to know well) addressed
him ostentatiously as *Mama* (MB)—a correct term since V. V. was

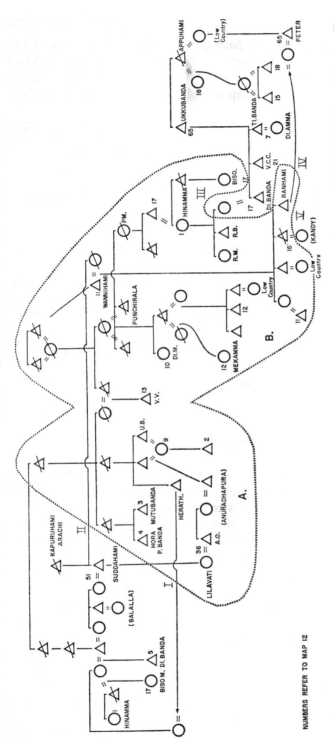

NUMBERS REFER TO MAP 12

Figure 23. Kinship connections in Vilawa. Specific denials of kin links are shown as I, II, III, IV, and V. Household 17 is internally split. Some persons are depicted in different positions: Hinamma (1), Bisomenika (17). Household 14, occupied by a Kandyan woman (outsider) and a Tamil man, and households 6 and 8 are not shown.

cross-cousin (brother-in-law) to No. 2's polyandrous fathers—and 2 also hoped to be able to marry V. V.'s daughter (which I heard he succeeded in doing in 1963).

Turning to group B (10–13), my informants traced the complicated relationships between old Wannihami and the others in detail and again with considerable precision. It should be observed in this connection, of course, that it was important to keep these relations absolutely orderly, because they were the basis of complicated rights on paddy lands outstanding between these various persons (see below).

Even though it can be argued with some effect that undivided lands were one of the major reasons for keeping complex kin connections alive, it did not necessarily follow that those who had undivided lands or had bought shares in an estate (see below) were kinsmen. Sometimes efforts would be made to turn such associations into kinship by a specially arranged marriage, but it could also happen that close neighbors in the paddy fields or in the village were the ones who kept up intense antagonisms against one another.

Let us now examine the situation from the point of view of land-

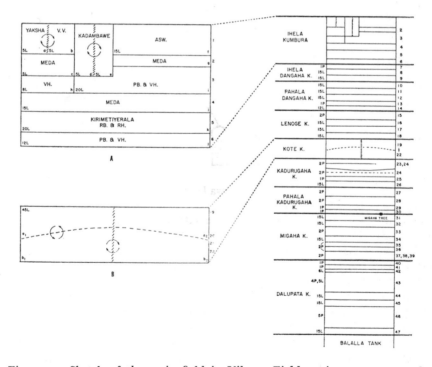

Figure 24. Sketch of the main field in Vilawa. Field sections are separately named; distinct strips (*issara*) are numbered. P and L denote sowing extents of each strip (10 *laha* = 1 *pale*). A (Ihela Kumbura) and B (Kote Kumbura) are discussed in the text.

holdings in adjacent plots, and observe what sort of kinship relations obtain among people who work together. Consider figure 24, which shows the large field, and, in detail, two of the sections (measured in *laha*, i.e., one-tenth of one *pale*).

(1) Plots a and b (fig. 24A) belong jointly to V. V. (No. 13) and to Ausuddahami Vedarala; the sections they own are exchanged every year. (An attempt at the establishment of kinship between the two families was unsuccessful.)

(2) Plot *c*: cf. with (*g*) below.

(3) Plots d and e were bought by V. V.'s father and sister. V. V.'s share is one-half, so he works d one year and e the next. The other half is owned by numerous persons: the half-share is worked one year by Dingirimenika (see fig. 25A) and the next by the children of Appuhami. In 1955 there was a

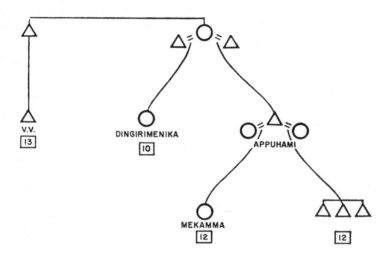

Figure 25A. Vilawa landowners.

dispute as to whether Appuhami's share should be divided one-half between Mekamma and the others or one-quarter for all his children.

(4) Plot f is owned one-half by Punchibanda (No. 4) and one-half by V. H. and his two brothers. It is worked year by year (*avurudda maruvata*): one year by Punchibanda and the next by the others. Punchibanda's MZ (*loku amma*) was MBD (*nena*) to V. H.; she had no children and Punchibanda got her share. (Parties not of the same *pavula* yet.)

(5) Plot h belongs to V. H. and siblings. (Kin links with others denied.)

(6) Plot i belongs one-third to Punchibanda and two-thirds to V. H. and siblings. It is worked one year by Punchibanda, two years by the V. H. group. (Not same kin group.)

(7) Plot j is treated together with plots c and g. For this purpose it is divided into three unequal sections, x, y, and z; x is five *laha*, y plus one-half g is five *laha*, z plus the other half of g is five *laha*, and c alone is five *laha*.

The people involved are Ranhami, Herathami, Punchibanda, and Dingiribanda; they are said to be "brothers" (see fig. 25B), but each one gets five *laha* in a four-year rotation.

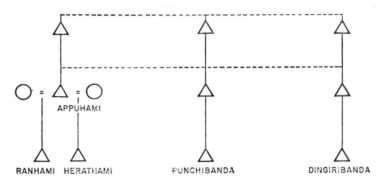

Figure 25B. Vilawa landowners.

(8) Plot *k* is owned by Ranhami and his half-brother Herathami. Twenty years ago one-half was given to Diba's father on a mortgage (*ukas*), and until 1955 one-half of the *gam ande* (landlord's share, i.e., one-fourth of the total, see chap. 4) was given to Diba. In 1955 the mortgage was redeemed.

(9) Plot *l* was owned and worked on the same principle as plot *f*.

Sometimes the complications are remarkable: consider figure 24B. In this case the field is divided into two unequal sections, *a* and *b*. Of section *a*, three-quarters belong to V. V. (No. 13) and one-quarter to Wannihami (No. 11) and Kaluhami equally. It is worked the first year by V. V. alone, the second year half by V. V. and half by Wannihami and Kaluhami, the third year by V. V. alone, and the fourth year half by V. V. and half by Wannihami and Kaluhami. In the second and fourth years V. V. and the others change sides from a_1 to a_2. The other half of the field, *b,* is owned three-quarters by Ranhami and one-quarter by Mudianse and Appuhami. This, too, is worked on a four-year cycle like *a*. In addition, the entire halves (*a* and *b*) are also alternated between the two sets of shareholders, though in these exercises only the landlord's portion is involved. Add to this the possible contracts for seed, labor, and buffaloes, and the number of permutations and combinations of those who could cooperate and enter into contractual relations for the purposes of paddy cultivation become enormous.

In a large community like Vilawa, the common ownership of land is without doubt one of the most powerful incentives to recall kinship links with other co-owners in the most precise fashion. Apart from co-residence in the same household, no other form of association necessitates the precision required for the validation of rights to paddy land. On the other hand, although those who cooperate on paddy cultivation in one form or another tend to channel their association into a kinship idiom, this is a tendency that one observes also between neighbors, or between shopkeepers with common interests. The very complexity of the many factors which seem to influence the creation and perpetuation or the dissolution and severance of kinship links draws our attention to the specific quality which "kinship" imparts to otherwise ordinary associations. And this is indeed the particular kinship "idiom" which we have underlined.

WOMEN AND LAND

The complex problems arising from the rights of women to land, and especially paddy land, were clearly recognized by many informants in Vilawa. Unlike other Kandyan villages, there was here fairly complete unanimity as to what constituted the ideal and traditional arrangements. I was told with many examples that in the past land was not given to women. This question is fundamental to the Sinhalese kinship system and should be briefly reconsidered.

First, property was divided in Vilawa into immovable and movable property (i.e., *niyachala* and *chanchala badu*). Land, houses, gardens, fruit trees were "immovable" property, and gold ornaments, money, clothes were "movable" property. In the ideal system no immovable property was given to a woman upon her marriage, but she could be given gold and valuable ornaments.

Second, all the children of a person, whether male or female, had equal rights to all his or her property upon death. This right was interpreted in effect to mean that women always held ultimate claims upon parental land but did not have the right to sell it—even upon the death of the parent—or to have it worked on some sharecropping system and receive the fruits. Women given away in marriage could, however, always return to the parental home and then enjoy their portion of the estate. In other words, only such persons resident in the parental house, or maintaining close relations with the parents, could claim the right to "eat" the land. As one informant put it, "You can give women gold and money, but how can you give them a piece of earth to take with them? [*Polova denta be ni!*] Nobody can move the earth!"

This would be the case whether the woman remained in the village after her marriage or went to another village: she would go with her husband. Only if her marriage was in *binna,* which would of course mean that she and her husband were residents in her parental home, did she have a direct right to land. Hence a lively distinction was maintained in Vilawa between *binna* and *deega* marriages. The distinctions were the same as in Terutenne; the only note to add here is that Vilawa informants had very clear ideas as to divorce in *binna* marriages. In accordance with the distinction maintained between movables and immovabales, if a divorce occurred in a *binna* family, the sleeping mat would be split into two, all movables would be divided between the couple, and even the children would be treated as "movables" for this purpose and separated. But the land could not be split.

Although women given away in marriage (*deega*) could not "eat" the land of their parents, their claims on the land were not affected. They retained *urumaya* (inheritance claims). In Vilawa this was expressed as "In the past, women given away in marriage had *urumaya* with the rest of the children, but they would not beg for it [*Gani urumaya tibbe, illanni ne*]!"

The concept of *urumaya*, one of those important terms which sum up many of the imponderables of this kinship system, is today not necessarily enforceable. It reflects the rights and obligations among brothers and sisters and among the children of brothers and sisters. The act of giving a woman away in marriage does not affect her ultimate position in her natal family. She does not lose her rights nor does her family renounce claims on her in favor of the family of the son-in-law. The perpetuation of these strong links with the natal family on the part of women is fundamentally different from those other systems where rights over the women are surrendered to the bride-receivers, and it leads us to the essentials of Sinhalese kinship. The informants would express the situation thus: "We do not give immovable goods to women, but they continue to have their *urumaya*. Later, one of the offspring of that woman will return to this house [*gedara*] to claim the *urumaya*."

Such claims between the offspring of brother and sister or between Ego and his MB reflect the unsettled nature of the rights of the woman at her marriage. Custom gives expression to these claims in a variety of contexts. We have already examined cross-cousin marriage at length. The claim of the cross-cousins is only one expression of *urumaya*. In the same way a woman could go to the puberty rite of her BD and say to her brother, "*Me lamayek mata one* [I want this child for me]." Note the way the claim is expressed. She does not simply wish that the girl be married to her son; she claims her as a child for her own purposes!

In the same way the sister's son would inherit the clothes of his MB upon the death of the latter. One of my informants, explaining the customs at funerals, surprised me by his emphatic assertion that he simply marched into the house of his MB and, without asking anyone, just collected all the clothes and brought them back to his hut. This was by no means an expression of impatient greed; it was meant to indicate the closeness and intensity of the formal relationship between these two men.

Again, the custom whereby women in all the villages we have discussed return to their natal house for childbirth is an immediate expression of the intimate relationship kept in good repair between their parents and themselves as well as an indication of their claims on their natal household. It was often said in explanation of this custom that women would need their mothers at such critical times, but in Vilawa I came across a woman who had returned to her parental house for childbirth even though her mother had died long before. As usual, the informants themselves were hazy about the significance of their customs.

In Vilawa, just as the loss of rights on land by *deega*-married women was strongly expressed, their ultimate rights in the next generation were taken as a very serious aspect of kinship. They could not be disregarded without serious trouble in the *pavula*. The expression of my elderly informant Wannihami against a woman who, after the death of her parent, would return to demand the land which her brothers were "eating" was noteworthy: "*Chee, chee, e golle enni ne, enni ne* [Those people (i.e., the married sisters) will not come to press claims]!" Since *chee* is an expression of disgust used against filth or filthy animals, its use here indicates the strength of feeling.

Some tension seems inevitably a part of the system. Take, as an example, the Village Headman of Vilawa who had married a woman from the "low" village of Daladagama. She had wanted her own son to get the daughter of her brother as a wife. Ironically enough, this was refused by her husband's family, who had earlier accepted her. They did not wish to continue the connection with Daladagama. The young man had a good salary, and the family found him a wife from a "good" village. In 1955 the relations between the woman and her "good" daughter-in-law were hardly cordial.

Although the traditional *urumaya* pattern was still regarded by my older informants as the proper state of affairs, it could no longer be followed consistently. The chief difficulty seemed to be that the differential claims of *binna* and *deega* daughters were more and more disregarded in Vilawa. It was now felt—and informants noted this change—that all children should inherit equally. Often elderly men would make out testaments specifying how they wanted to distribute their lands. Sisters and sisters' children felt that "their" lands should be given to them by their brothers. If there was but a small amount of land, the claim would perhaps not be pressed, but if it was extensive it probably would be.

One informant, Banda, who had good relations with his MB, said emphatically that he would get his mother's land after her parents died, and that his MZ and MB would naturally want him to receive his shares. But relations were often not so friendly as in this case.

Some informants would say, "Our MB (and their group) are 'eating' the land. We have *urumaya,* but in order to get it we will have to go to court against them." It appears then that in the traditional system the resolving of the outstanding claims of women was left to the general reciprocity and prestations system of kinship. The outstanding debts in one generation would be repaid in the next, and this intricate web of kin relations would be an element of cohesion within the kindred. Today, with a money economy allowing the sale of land, a social system in which families can grow rich and poor rather quickly—and, in addition, with much wider communications than before—there is an increased tempo in handling social relations. Instead of keeping claims unspecified until the following generation, kinsmen seem to want their claims more clearly expressed, so as to be free to deal with any eventuality. It is as if a cycle that has been operating at two revolutions per year has been speeded up to two per month.

We must place the limited practice of dowry giving in the Kandyan area into the specific context of the rights of women. At the moment the tendency is for ordinary people to declare the property intended for their offspring by testament. Some have gone a step further and specify the lands to be given a daughter at the time of her marriage negotiations. The lands will not be given until the parent dies, but the parent undertakes to specify the portion of the daughter at that moment. This is only a distant acknowledgement of the full-fledged dowry system, but it is there nevertheless. I shall have more to say about dowry a little later, but here I must point out that in Vilawa the general opinion, among those who knew anything at all about dowry, was that it would be unwise for a son-in-law to press his father-in-law too hard for premature possession of those lands that were marked for his wife. Informants would say, "If we get everything now, then we cannot go to them when we need something later. It is best to wait!" In other words, it was thought better to have unspecified claims upon in-laws than to clinch the transaction early. Obviously, Kandyan minds were working as acutely as ever on time-tested principles.

MARRIAGE RITES IN VILAWA

In Vilawa ordinary unions between close kin involve no celebrations. Rites are called for in the case of special marriages and the following account could only be coaxed out of informants by demanding information about "old customs [stuff!]" (*parana deval*). It is worth considering the traditional arrangements from the point of view of gift exchanges between categories of kin.

(1) The initial approach between families is made by the *mama* of the boy or a Tom-Tom Beater. The exchanges must be kept very secret to prevent loss of face in case of refusal on either side.

(2) The boy's father or *mama* and other elders go to visit the girl's family for a formal betel-chewing and meal (*bat bulat kanava*).

(3) There may be further visits to examine the property of the girl's family, and these visits may be returned.

(4) On an auspicious day, determined by an astrologer, the boy gives the girl a necklace and she gives him a ring. The real MB and FZ of the girl may decide the number of food parcels (*kat*) they will need for the celebration. They may want ten *kat* and 1,000 betel leaves.

(5) The *kat* will be prepared by the kindred of the boy, and various members of his kin group will take over the preparation (*kat bara gannava*) of a certain number of *kat*.

(6) Certain traditional gifts are essential: these include "twenty yards of cloth" (*visiriyena*), "areca-nut cutters" (*gireya*), and a "silver betel box" (*killote*). If the girl's MM is alive, the "silver box" goes to her.

The *visiriyena* goes to the mother and father of the girl. It may also be known as *kirikada hale* (as it belongs to the *kiriamma* MM). This cloth may be given to the MM. It is interesting to note here that when a child is born to the girl later on, they will visit the MM (*kiriamma*) and this same cloth will be given by her to the grandchild. If the MM dies before a grandchild is born, then she is dressed up in this cloth and buried with it. I interpret these customs as indicating the claims of the girl's family on her offspring and vice versa. They are parallel to the custom of the girl returning to her natal home for childbirth. The "areca-nut cutter" and the "box" may also be given to the girl's parents, who will later present them to her offspring together with some cattle.

(7) The bride may also receive a set of clothes, necklace, and bangles (*valala*), false bun (*boru konde*), cloth for a blouse, umbrella, handbag, shoes, sari; these may be taken to the girl by the marriage broker.

(8) There may be a visit from the girl's side to the parents of the boy. The visitors may bring a present like a betel spittoon or betel stand to the parents of the boy, who, in turn, may hand the areca-nut cutter and the silver betel box to the girl as a present.

(9) On the wedding day the house of the bride will be decorated with fresh white cloths by a Washerman, who will later be paid about twenty-five rupees by the groom for his services.

(10) At auspicious times the clothes of the girl will be changed and she will wear the cloth brought by the groom. The informants

emphasize that "you get the girl and you have to dress her up." All the jewelry she owns must be left in her house. She is not allowed to take anything with her.

(11) The groom's party in coming with the *kat* will jokingly claim that they are bringing their own food and will not receive food from the bride's house. Observe that food is almost always given from the superior to the inferior whereas women go from the inferior to the superior. It is therefore appropriate that the transaction here is either equal or that food is offered by the side of the groom.

(12) The bride wears the cloth given by the groom for a week. She may be visited by her parents after three days, but this visit is formally returned in two weeks when the bride goes back to her natal home with the kinsmen of the groom. She is allowed to put on her old dresses and jewelry on this occasion and may then take some of this back with her. There is also a feeling that these clothes should be given to her younger sister.

This might be the course of a formal wedding according to tradition. The symbolism is noteworthy since it repeats the theme of the outstanding relations between the bride and her natal family. It also marks an exchange between equals—hence there are no unbalanced payments from one side to the other. The household of the bride loses a helper and is not compensated for it. The attempts to commute the food parcels to money may be refused by saying that "we are not selling the girl!" On the other hand, in the emphasis on the *kat* we may detect the opening toward hypergamy.

Throughout this chapter I have pointed out the differences in customs between Terutenne and Vilawa, but it seems clear that the main differences are those of village layout and agricultural organization, which do not affect the institution of the family except as they emphasize the "bilateral" aspects of the kinship model. There is in Vilawa no concern with patrilineal charters, and in keeping with the desire to confine marriages to small circles, we find also that hypergamy is not at all a well-developed practice. The gradation between the rich and the poor is not so steep in Vilawa as it is in Terutenne and Udamulla.

The similarities are many. All that was said about the *ge* in Terutenne also applies to Vilawa (table 33). In general, Vilawa appears to exhibit the same variation in the locality of the marriages of its rich and poor people (table 34). The comments that were made in connection with affinity and the stability of the marriage bond also apply to Vilawa (table 35).

When we turn to the figures having to do with the movement of people in and out of Vilawa, however (table 5), we find two important differences from the Terutenne figures. First, unlike Terutenne, few men leave the village permanently for outside employment. This appears to be true of Udamulla as well, and I think the difference is explained by the geographical propinquity of Terutenne to towns and tea estates. The second point is also striking. Proportionally many more women are given out of the village in marriage in Vilawa than in Terutenne. I know of no categorical reason for this difference in the figures. It may be related to the lack of chena cultivation in Vilawa—that is, the greater dependence on paddy land may possibly be a reason for sending more of the potential claimants on land out of the village (in which case they may forego their rights).

Finally, a few comments on names in Vilawa. Feudal *mudianse* names were used in this village as in others. But whereas Terutenne had a number of diverse aristocratic patronymics, in Vilawa everyone had the same *mudianse* name (Wanni Nayaka Mudianse). *Gedara* or house names, on the other hand, were localized like their counterparts in the Galpitiya hamlet of Terutenne. Anyone who lived in the same garden or house (whether related or not) could use the same *gedara* name.

The use of names in Vilawa is, in fact, another instance of the cohesion of the community. Since the people considered themselves to be descendants of siblings—which was never suggested in Terutenne—they used the same patronymic, and the *gedara* names were considered to be of equal rank. It should be noted that when marriages took place between villages of unequal rank, it would be said that the name of the father should be perpetuated. These observations agree with our remarks about the function of patrilineal descent in Terutenne. Names and titles that descend in the male line are supposed to preserve the status gradations in the community. Among equals they may be redundant, but in more diversified populations they appear to be more scrupulously used.

There appears to be a continuous gradation from the formally closed circle of a subcaste (*variga*) in Pul Eliya as described by Leach (1961b), to the less formal, only ideally endogamous (*pavula*) met among commoners in Kandyan villages, to the development of patrilineal pedigrees among aristocrats (Terutenne), all the way, as we shall soon see, to a clearly formulated patrilineal ideology in parts of the Low Country.

Even so, my experiences among commoners in Kandyan villages gave me the impression that in this region at least there was a subtle balance between patrilineal and matrilineal concepts—rather as if a push in either direction could take the kin structure further in the matrilineal or the patrilineal direction. We shall observe the patrilineal end of the spectrum in the next chapter. It is true, however, that there is some limited evidence showing that the Sinhalese descent system was matrilineal, at least in the former royal household. There have been some suggestions that matrilineal concepts were brought to the Kandyan Sinhalese by the Tamil consorts of the Sinhalese kings. At the present day there are only subtle tendencies in the matrilineal direction, but they are unmistakable (see Paranavitana, 1933).

On my last day in Vilawa I had the good fortune to be visited by one of the charming and intelligent old men of the village, Dingiribanda Tennekoon, and we talked about some of these matters. It is impossible to give our conversation in full, but these few comments of his (quoted verbatim) are more eloquent than pages of description. On the subject of the role of the father: (a) "In this world one can only believe the mother: Who is the father? Don't know who he is? People say he is nothing. The mother is one; the mother one really knows!" About father and son: (b) "Once my son is married, he is no longer mine—finished—no respect! He belongs to the daughter-in-law. He goes in her direction. Daughter not like that; more love. Who cares if the son-in-law is angry? You have the daughter—she will respect the father." In other words, it is best to keep the daughter in the house; she will look after her parents, but the son belongs to other people. He sums up his thought with a proverb: (c) "In the past people say this: 'Daughter's son goes in the arms [of the grandmother], son's son goes on foot.' The daughter's son is picked up—he belongs to me. But the son's son belongs to other people—to the daughter-in-law." And he recalled the days of the Kandyan kingdom: (d) "Now we give gifts [meaning lands] to the sons; in the past, in the time of the Sinhalese kings, gifts were given to the daughters, not to the sons." [2]

We shall find in part v that these almost Nayar-like principles expressed by Dingiribanda, which are mere hints in the context of Vilawa, have been blown up and made the cornerstone of an elaborate and consistent structure of kinship among the populations of the east coast of Ceylon.

---

[2] For reference, I give the Sinhalese: (a) "Me lokaya ammata tamai visvasa karanta puluvan; piya kauda? kauda dannava ne; nikang kiyanava minissu. amma ekai! amma hariyata dannava!" (b) "Mage puttu kassada bendeng passe mata ne—iveray – salakannit ne! Lelita tamai aiti. lelige paruseyin yanava! Duva ehema ne; adaray vedi. bena taraha mokadda? Duva innava ni – itn piyata salakanava." (c) "Issara minissu kiyanni mehemai: 'duwage puta wadagana yanava, putage puta paying yanava' duvage puta ihelata ganni, eya mata tamai, putage puta vena kattiyata – lelita aiti!" (d) "Deng devedde denava ni, puttunta; issara, Sinhala rajakali, genita dayade deela tienava, piriminta ne."

12

The Patrilineal Hypergamous Variant:
The South Coast

"For there is a great difference between the People inhabiting the high-lands, or the mountains of Cande, and those of the low-lands where we now are placed . . ."—Robert Knox, *An Historical Relation of Ceylon* (1681), p. 121

THE LOW COUNTRY

The thought and behavior of the Kandyans, people of the Up Country, stand out in sharper outline when they are contrasted to the patterns of the Low Country. In Terutenne, the tendency toward hypergamy—in other words, the treatment of the daughter, together with her dowry, as a "gift" to be given to another family of higher status—is only a stated preference expressed mostly among the rich families. But in the Low Country hypergamy reaches an impressive elaboration. We should place the tendencies of the upper sections of Kandyans in a Low Country cultural setting in order to see them properly.

The exercise is worthwhile, because, in practice, Kandyans are in contact and do hear and learn about Low Country practices through visitors, relations, shopkeepers and others. They are affected by what they hear. In theoretical terms the Low Country model of the dowry system may be regarded as a further development of the model described in connection with the wealthy aristocrats in Terutenne.

The dowry system of the Low Country has never been systematically described, and I shall rely on material collected in the Dondra–Tangalla area, just east of Galle (map 1), during brief visits in 1955–1956. The Dondra–Tangalla Area is one of coastal fishing villages well integrated into a money economy and well connected with such historic towns as Galle and Colombo. Between Colombo and Tangalla

—a distance of 120 miles—stretches an almost continuous ribbon of
settlements, where the population density is among the highest on the
island.

The fishing village of Kottegoda, on the farthermost eastern end of
this ribbon, a few miles west of Tangalla, is comparable in size to
others in this area. It has a population in the Village Headman's division of about 4,000. Of these by far the greater number—some 3,500
—are said to be of the Karava or Fishers caste; the remainder are of
the Durava or Toddy Tappers[1] caste. Apart from a few lands owned
by eight or ten individuals, the village has no cultivable rice lands,
and almost the entire population is dependent upon fishing for livelihood. In all, the village possesses about three hundred fishing boats,
all privately owned, ranging in size from the one- or two-man out-
riggers to those that hold seven men. The price of the boats varies
in the same way, from Rs. 200–300 to as much as Rs. 6,000. Because
it is necessary to fish different waters according to the monsoons,
large and small boats are necessary. From the beginning of November
to the beginning of May, during the northeast monsoon, the fishing
is concentrated on the south and west coasts of the island, fairly close
to the village. But when the southwest monsoon hits the south coast
after the month of May, the fishermen leave the women, children, and
old men behind and take the large seven-man boats up the east coast,
to Batticaloa or even as far as Trincomalee, for a fishing season of
about three months. In 1955, I was told that sixty of the seven-man
boats had gone up the east coast that season.

In Kottegoda one immediately senses the fact that this is not a land-
based economy like that of the Kandyan village. People own houses,
jewelry, boats and nets, but not paddy land, and the anthropologist,
even on brief stays, finds here, in this community where possessions
can easily be converted to money, a distinct air of mobility, flexibility,
and heightened tempo of social and economic life. This is also the
area of Ceylon for which the highest figures for crime, murder, and
sucide have been quoted.

The community is divided into various *pelapata* (pedigree) groups
whose names are vividly associated with status. The usual pedigree
names in Kottegoda are Abeydira Vijesuriya, Saonda Hennedige, and
Marakkala[2] Manage, which sound extremely alien to Kandyan ears.
There is much honor attached to such names and the rules of pa-
tronymy are claimed to be very strict.

All conversations in the Low Country return to the subject of status
(*tatvaya*) and honor (*nambu*). Rights between adjacent castes and

---

[1] Toddy is a drink made from the sap of palm trees.

[2] Marakkala is the usual Sinhalese term for the Ceylon Moors, although these
people claim to be Sinhalese Buddhists.

fights between members of the same caste on questions of status are common and often reported. It is for this reason that there is so much concern with patronymics and such matters as which named pedigree groups should walk in front of the others in the annual processions of the Buddhist temples.

These districts have been under European influence since the Portuguese first turned up in the Indian Ocean, and the influence of Roman–Dutch law has had important effects on family life. What concerns us particularly here is the fact that the legal codes of the Low Country provide that a legally registered marriage entails community of property between the spouses, so that when one of the spouses dies the estate is divided between the living spouse and the children with full rights of alienation. In concordance with such a legal system, the kinship system, too, turns around the firm bonds which are established at marriage between affines.

I shall have more to say on the nature of affinity in the Low Country, but it is important to emphasize here that, whatever the differences, the Low Country kinship system is, in general, the same kind of system analyzed in the preceding pages. The differences in the system of the Low Country Sinhalese and the Kandyan Sinhalese are not those of fundamentals but only of specific features, of which the most arresting is the large dowry. The terminology as well as the rules of marriage are the same in Kottegoda as in Terutenne. However, in keeping with patrilineal ideology there are no formal *binna* (matrilocal) marriages. The general emphasis on endogamous marriage is present. Polyandry, though extremely rare, is sometimes heard of, and polygyny, too, is not unacceptable in terms of custom, though both are legally out of the question.

DOWRY

Dowry (*devedde*) or (*dayade*) is a "gift" given by the persons who are responsible for a woman, to her and her husband upon marriage. In the Sinhalese case these persons are primarily the woman's father, her mother's brothers, her brothers, and her sisters' husbands. The "gift" is clearly a prestation which, though made to the girl, places the son-in-law under powerful obligations toward her guardians. The gift may be in the form of lands, cash, jewelry, or other valuables, and it is negotiable before the marriage between the two parties. The future son-in-law will press for a dowry in cash or at least in lands written over to the girl, and the family of the girl will negotiate to hold as much control as possible over various items in the "gift." Cash is, of course, the least controllable, whereas lands and houses allow considerable influence to be exerted on the son-in-law. Again there is a difference between a promise to be fulfilled and a legal document. It is hardly surprising that the intricacies of the "gift" are the most absorbing subject in all Sinhalese—indeed, all Ceylonese— conversations about social practices.

There is no doubt that we are here concerned with a prestation of the classic type as described by Mauss (1923). The dowry is not a simple transaction (this would defeat its purpose), nor is it merely a payment to equalize the status differences between a superior son-in-law and a humbler father-in-law, though this is often claimed by the Ceylonese to be the reason. It is like all prestations, a powerful symbolic device which acts as a flywheel to perpetuate social relations between two person and two groups. The dowry is repaid by allegiance and return gifts over a long period of time. As we shall see, we are here undoubtedly concerned with one of the fundamental features of Indian as well as Ceylonese family structure, for the "dowry gift" must be seen in the context of the Hindu idea of the "gift of a virgin," one of the most sacred obligations in the Hindu family.

In the Low Country the dowry gift is first of all a matter of honor: it is dishonorable (*avanambu*), especially for the father of the girl, to omit it. Hence in this region some negotiation regarding dowry precedes every marriage. There is more money utilized in this region than in Kandyan villages and even humble persons engage in the custom as much as they can.

The negotiations in Kottegoda are usually opened by the marriage broker. He compiles the horoscope for examination and arranges for the elders from the family of the young man to call upon the family of the girl. At this meeting the girl herself appears to pass around the betel tray to the guests. If an agreement is reached, the young man may receive a gift in gold from the father-in-law, handed to him by the girl. Rings are exchanged and a day is set for the wedding.

The single most striking feature about the dowry gift in this community is the complex backlog of obligations and prestations it activates within the family of the girl. For the dowry gift is not simply given by the father of the bride. He is responsible for it, but the gift is a collective effort on the part of the girl's close kinsmen. Old obligations that now come to the surface are binding, public, and serious. A former gift has to be properly repaid on this occasion. Indeed, the obligations are regarded as debts: if they are not repaid, kinship breaks!

The family of the girl immediately responsible are the MB's, FB's, brothers, and brothers-in-law. Before the agreement on dowry the family group meets to decide on the issue. Kinsmen get together and ask the father of the girl, "*Ayya*, etc., how much are you giving?" The sum is then apportioned among the kinsmen concerned. The side of the father of the girl and the side of the mother and mother's brothers are said to engage in a friendly battle expressed as a "tug of war." The amounts to be given are pledged at this time. The sons-in-law fall under special obligations, and it is said that they are supposed to pledge more for their wife's sister than her own brothers. After all, one is told, the husbands of sisters are very close to one another and will have to work together.

To take an example, as in figure 26, if *a* pays 100 rupees for the

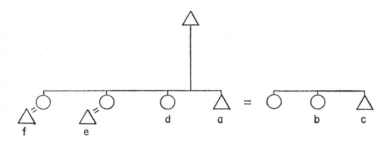

Figure 26. Dowry obligations in the Low Country.

dowry of *d* (his sister), *c* will offer only 25 rupees. But when *a* gives 100, *e* and *f* (*d*'s brothers-in-law) will be under pressure to pay 300 or 500 rupees. Note that while *a* is obligated to *c*, *c* is less obligated to *a*; likewise *e* is more obligated to *a* but *a* not to *e*'s sister.

There is no question of the tense nature of these gifts and obligations. One is told of feuds, even murders, arising from disagreements on these issues. The dowry gifts which are agreed upon are actually paid in public during the marriage ceremony. At that time the gift list (*dayade lestuva*), including the amounts paid by the various kinsmen, is read out over loudspeakers to the onlookers, not only the assembled guests but the whole village. Thus every member of the community knows just what obligations are set up by these gifts.

One Kottegoda informant pointed out, to emphasize the lasting nature of the obligation, that some time earlier he had given a large sum on the wedding of his elder brother's daughter. The elder brother had subsequently died but his wife had repaid the gift recently upon the marriage of the informant's own daughter by selling a section of land. The informant said he had not known about the sale of the land and that if he had he would have tried to halt it, but his observation did not sound very convincing.

Although marriage among the Karava is said to be patrilocal and the names strictly patronymic, it is not considered odd that the son-in-law should often come to live near or with the father-in-law. In the case of the informant above, the son-in-law had bought a house near the wife's father and had moved in soon after the marriage.

The preoccupation with ritual status associated with these patronymics can hardly be overemphasized. In a recent work on the
history and traditions of the Karava, an entire chapter is devoted to
a discussion of the honorable connotation of Karava names.[3] The
concern with ritual status is an important part of tradition in the
community, and it is particularly evident in the formal procedure
laid down for a wedding.

THE MARRIAGE CEREMONY AMONG THE KARAVA

In contrast to the situation in the Kandyan country, even a cursory
examination shows an element of hypergamy to be built into Low
Country marriage ceremonies. Some of the features of the rite are
similar to the standard Sinhalese practices. Thus the house of the
bride is decorated with white cloths—called here *pavada*, rather than
viyana as in the highlands—by the members of the Washermen caste.
The groom pays for this service, and the amount he pays reflects upon
the honor of the bride's household. A *poruva* or marriage cage is
constructed and elaborately decorated—this too as in the highlands.
And the groom's party sends a messenger before they arrive with a
set of betel leaves indicating the number of people on the male side
who will be attending the ceremony.

The most important detail in the ritual, however, is one not present
in highland weddings—the washing of the feet of the *massina* (cross-
cousin–groom). When the groom arrives at the house of the bride,
and before he enters, the brother of the bride (who stands in the relation of cross-cousin to the groom) ceremonially washes the feet of the
groom. This act is a public recognition of the superior status of the
brother-in-law-to-be. The act recalls that of the washing of the feet of
Buddhist priests by a member of the laity when the priests arrive at a
"preaching hall" or other ceremonial location for a ritual purpose.
Just as that act symbolizes humility, so is humility shown in this ceremony toward the groom, who must reciprocate by dropping a gold
ring into the water basin (*koraha*) for his wife's brother. "The washing
of feet" is part of the traditional status idiom. Davy, for instance,
vividly describes how, on his first trip to Kandy, he saw noble Kandyan
lords, in all their colorful raiment, waiting while servants washed
their feet before they entered their palanquins.

After the foot-washing ceremony, there is more exchange of gifts.
When the groom enters the marriage cage he presents the mother of
the girl with a white cloth with a sovereign tied into a corner. The
mama (MB) of the bride has an important role to play. It must be a
person in that "category" who ties the thumbs of the bride and the

---

[3] Raghavan (1961).

groom together and who pours water onto the tied fingers, thus solemnizing the *sambandham* (equal tying; marriage; sexual intercourse). After this he is given a present of a gold ring by the groom. The Washerman holds the water basin, and is paid again. The bride is presented with an entire wardrobe of clothes and jewelry; her mother may also be given many gifts.

Throughout the proceedings the high status of the groom is a dominant theme. All my informants emphasize that he has to be "honored," specially received, respected. The feast which takes place before the solemnity is particularly tense: as usual, all who eat together must be of the same status. But since this permits some interpretation, it is often feared that the groom may take offense, turn the feasting table over, mess up the proceedings and leave. It is of course unlikely that this will happen, if the preliminaries are agreed upon, but the statement shows how anxious the family of the bride is that the son-in-law will be pleased. At the end of the feast a tray of "curd and treacle" (*kiri-päni*)—two items of food which go especially well together, according to Sinhalese gastronomic traditions—is offered around to the guests. This may be intended to symbolize harmony, but the difference in status between the groom and the bride is never lost sight of. A most respectable matron with a well-known noble name expressed the attitude succinctly: "She must be low, otherwise she will control the whole household!"

The difficulties are not over until the morning after the wedding, when a Washerwoman makes a ceremonial inspection of the sheet used by the couple to verify the claim of the bride's virginity: it is said that the proof has to be shown to the members of the groom's family to allay their concern.

The course of the marriage rite in Kottegoda thus clearly fits into the special context of hypergamy in the Low Country. It would be interesting to have further evidence on the stability of marriage in this region. By Roman–Dutch law the properties of the bride and the groom are merged into a single estate, and it is my impression that divorce in this region is far from the simple matter it is in the Kandyan regions, where under customary arrangements the estates of the bride and groom remain separate. Divorce or the decease of one partner in the Low Country gives the other spouse absolute rights over half the joint estate. These, again, are an indication of the strong reciprocal obligations put into effect by the marriage.

An illustration will show how tensions can arise. The informant, a Food Production Overseer, had married with a dowry. He pugnaciously asserted that honorable men would never settle with the *mama* (F-in-L) and would not render him special honors. But for him the annoyance of dowry was the difficulty of controlling the wife!

Now his *nenda* (M-in-L) had decided to live with them to see how he managed the property. This, too, was irritating. He claimed, furthermore, that the mother's property was to go to all the daughters, and the father's property to the sons; and that in his case the *mama* (F-in-L) was living with his sons and the *nenda* had come to live with her daughter.

Apparently the informant's own father had received a large dowry from his *mama*. But the informant's mother and her father were given to drink, so there was a good deal of tension in the family. The informant claimed that after his father received the dowry, his mother and her father tried to control his father's actions, but since he would not give in to their wishes, he was finally murdered! Dowry, then, is no outright gift, but a prestation to which vital reciprocal obligations are attached.

We may now return to the question of patronymics. Why is it that we find the greatest elaboration of patrilineal ideas precisely in the region where the formal hypergamous marriage bond is most emphasized? Anywhere in the Low Country, the anthropologist is impressed by the vehemence with which the patrilineal point of view is offered. In Dondra, for instance, one is immediately told which *pelapata* (pedigrees) are respectable, and the best names are reeled off: Vira varuna Nila vira Ran pata bendige, Loma Badu Varuna kula Suriya pata bendige, Andrea Hennedige, Naratotahevage, Henda vita Ranage, Pata bendi Maddumage, Sellahevage, Vakki Hennedige. It is always said that these names are quite separate from one another, that each pedigree group has its own burial grounds and certain other privileges. Part of the *kula-sirit* (caste custom) means taking only the father's name. The mother's side is unimportant; it gets mixed up and cannot be remembered. The "pedigrees" are also called *janmaya,* a term with "feudal" associations implying land grants to specific groups.

On the other hand, it is also quite clear that we are not faced with patrilineages in the strict sense of the term. People with the same name certainly do not always cooperate, for any one of these names may be used by as many as two hundred households, which would certainly never come together. They would not live in the same neighborhood or even in the same village. Moreover, the pedigree lines are not exogamous: the question as to who has the same name always elicited some answer like *mamala* (MB's), *bapala,* (FB's) *sahodariya* (B's). When asked whether marriage was possible with person of similar name, the reply would be, "Why not, if there is a relationship to marry?"—meaning, a cross-cousin in the group. We are therefore obviously not dealing with one strongly unified group. What, then, is the purpose of these patronymics (*pelapata*)? It seems clear that they are kept up for purposes of tracing ritual status in the complex conditions of the Low Country; and their rank is expressed by hypergamous marriages between them.

CONCLUSION

We are now in a position to conclude our examination of the Sinhalese kinship system and to relate it to general problems. In Sinhalese kinship, we may observe the most general theme of South Indian kinship systems stripped of all structural embellishments: in the ordinary system of the commoners we are dealing mainly with a system of abstract "categories" which order social relations in the most general sense. Descent concepts are not stressed; the choice of locality is theoretically open; inheritance is equally divided among sons and daughters; authority depends on the head of the household and can be exercised by the MB or even the F-in-L; dowry is not emphasized, but bride-wealth is disapproved. What stands out is the insistence on cross-cousin marriage and on a small circle of endogamy —that is, micro-castes in the form of *pavula* or *variga*.

This pattern, which I shall call the general structure, can be contrasted to that of the Low Country, where again we are not in the presence of unilineal property holding kin groups but where there is a definite formulation of patrilineal ideals. There is a lively concept of "family honor" which appears mainly linked to groups whose unity is expressed by their attachment to the patronymic. This is still a far cry from the patrilineal corporations described for South India, as we shall see later on, but we can regard it—for purposes of system building—as a stage between the patrilineal systems and the ordinary Sinhalese system, which we have taken as the general theme on which there may be variations.

The importance of this exercise, the distinction of the general from the unilineal systems, is that it focuses our attention precisely on the particular features of Ceylonese kinship systems which, though similar in fundamentals to certain features of the general structure, differ from them in important respects. By thus focusing our attention we close the door to certain kinds of explanations and are made to look for the concordances between the specific variant features in each particular system. In the Low Country system, for instance, our attention is drawn to the simultaneous appearance of patrilineal ideals, dowry and hypergamy, carefully arranged marriages, women specially protected, and so on, all of which is in contrast to the general Kandyan pattern of no stress on a line of descent, no dowry, endogamous circles, free marriages, and relatively free sexual access to women.

Such a study is in accordance with our general model for the preservation of status gradations in these systems, which we shall come to in chapter 15. The more emphasis is placed on a unilineal principle of descent, the less there is need for strict endogamy, for the patronymic can be made to carry the status distinction. Alternatively, when marriage is strictly confined to a small endogamous circle, then the unilineal principles are rendered redundant for these purposes, and

TABLE 37

Three Sinhalese Patterns of Kinship

	Low Country	Kandyan Noble	Commoner
1. Descent membership....	Patrilineal (stressed)	Patrilineal (weak)	Unspecified
2. Residence at marriage.......	Neo-local and patrilocal	Neo-local and patrilocal	Unspecified
3. Property, inheritance.....	Equal and patrilineal	Equal and localized succession	Equal
4. Authority........	F or MB	F or MB	F or MB
5. Dowry..........	Developed; general	Minimal	None
6. Bride-price.......	Secret; rare	Secret; rare	Secret; rare
7. Categorical cross-cousin marriage.	General	General	General
8. Endogamous kindred........	Recognized	General	Emphasized
9. Hypergamy.......	General	Some	Rare
10. Caste endogamy...	General	General	General

A) *Similarities*

   Categorical cross-cousin marriage (7)
   Disapproval of bride-price (selling girl!) (6)
   Authority may shift from F to MB (4)
   Caste endogamy: general (10)

B) *Differences*

	Low Country	Commoner
Patrilineal ideals stressed (1, 2, 3)	+	−
Dowry (5)	+	−
Kindred endogamy (8)	−	+
Hypergamy (9)	+	−

women are freed from sexual constraints toward appropriate members of their endogamous group.

Table 37 summarizes these similarities and differences. We shall see in the next two chapters that just as the general structure is open on the patrilineal side, it is also open to matrilineal structures. And this intermediate stage from patriliny to matriliny renders the Sinhalese system of fundamental interest in the context of South Indian kinship systems.

13

The Tamil Moorish System:
The Matrilocals

"In the western extremity of the province adjoining Bintenne,
a custom prevails, and has acquired the recognition of law,
whereby nephews by the sister's side succeed to the inheritance
to the exclusion of the possessor's sons."—Sir James Emerson Tennent, *Ceylon* (1859), II, 458

We have now concluded our examination of the Sinhalese ideas concerning marriage. The central features of this system can be studied
in sharper outline when contrasted with a similar but different system.
In this chapter, I describe the kinship system of the Muslim Tamils,
the so-called Moors of eastern Ceylon. They are particularly appropriate for comparative purposes because the community I describe is a
neighbor of Makulle Watta in the same province, and their mode of
life, agriculture, villages, houses are practically identical to those of
the Buddhist Sinhalese around them. Moreover, they have until recently taken part in the annual rituals of the god Kataragama, which
are held in the jungle near Kotabowe Vidiya, the Moorish village from
which most of my material is drawn. A further reason to include the
Muslims in this volume is the general paucity of material or even
reference to matrilineal-matrilocal systems in Ceylon.

The Muslims of Ceylon themselves recognize that they cannot all be
descended from the original Arab traders who came to Serendip in
search of spices: they know that there have been strong infusions of
Indian Muslim blood into their community, and this is realized to
be still going on. The Malays of Hambantota are another group of
Muslims who seem almost completely absorbed; but the most charming tale of origin is told by Muslims of the Batticaloa district, who
rather reluctantly explain that, a long time ago, seven Moors (Muslims)

with seven Hindu Tamils came over from South India to fight against the Jaffna Tamils who were then in control of the east coast of Ceylon. A terrible war was waged and the newcomers vanquished the older settlers. The Hindu Tamils, who had their womenfolk with them, then turned to the Moors and asked them whether they would like land or women. The Moors knew that the Hindu Tamils were matrilineal, so they asked for the women, for in getting the women they also got land which descended in the maternal line.

The tellers of this story, if they are Hindu Tamils, always point out that this explains very well why Muslim women in Ceylon cover up their faces so that they will not be seen: they are obviously Hindu Tamils who are ashamed of their connection with Muslim men. They cover up their faces so that their brothers and fathers will not see them.

We need not be concerned with the veracity of the myth. But it must be observed that Muslim kinship customs bear a striking similarity to those of the matrilineal Mukkavas who are governed by the Marumakkatayam law of South India.[1]

A number of matrilineal, matrilocal Muslim communities have been noted in Southeast Asia, like the Minangkabau and Negri Sembilan of Sumatra and Malaya and the Mapilla of South India. Matrilineality and Islam are indeed an extraordinary combination, and it would be worthwhile to investigate these communities more fully. So far, the only authoritative account of the customary laws of those in Ceylon would seem to be the Mohammedan Code of 1806 which Sir Alexander Johnstone had translated from Dutch when he assumed office as Chief Justice of Ceylon. This is contained in the report which Sir Alexander made to His Majesty's Government in November, 1807, which is not generally available. The customs of the Ceylonese Muslims appear to be similar to those of the Mapilla of South India, who are also Muslims and who have been described recently in Schneider and Gough (1961).

The Muslims of Ceylon who have not kept up myths and stories of recent arrival—like the Indian Muslims, or the Malays, or the Borah community—sometimes speak of themselves as Sonagar, which connects them with the Goldsmith caste of South India. They deny, however, this connotation of the name.[2] The Sinhalese refer to them as Marakkala people (Morocco?).

The Muslim Tamils are frequently to be found as traders in all

---

[1] For a full treatment of this and related subjects, see H. W. Tambiah (1954), chaps. 10–12.

[2] Iyer, in writing about the Jonakan Mapilla in South India, notes that Jonakan "according to a Malayalam song (Payyanur pattu) is a sailor known as Jonavar or Yanavar, i.e. the Greeks." He probably has in mind the Ionians. It is possible to imagine that the word Sonagar, as used in Ceylon, may be derived from Jonavar as used in South India. Iyer (1937), p. 459.

parts of the islands, usually living in very heterogeneous bazaars inhabited by people of all races and descriptions. In their rural environment in the Kandyan country they live in homogeneous villages
identical in outward appearances to other Kandyan villages. Such
villages usually contain one or more mosques, according to their size,
and in them the Koran is read in the native language, Tamil. By
religious affiliation they claim themselves to be orthodox *Shafi*, and
in so far as mosque behavior and general theology are concerned,
they would seem to be right. It is in matters of the family that they
follow quite different rules.

The material presented in this chapter is based on observations in
the village of Kotabowe Vidiya in Wellassa, which is one of numerous
other Muslim villages around the Bakinigahawela—Bibile region. Although Kotabowe Vidiya differs but little from these other Muslim
villages, it is of special interest historically as the site of a fierce battle
between the forces of the Kandyan kings and the English in the 1820's,
and culturally as the place where one of the major Buddhist–Hindu
rituals of the Wellassa region is held (see Yalman, 1964). Until fairly
recently, the Muslims of Kotabowe participated in the annual rituals
of the Kotabowe Devale, though nowadays they do not even attend
the celebrations, which draw very large crowds to this exceedingly isolated spot in the jungle.

The village of Kotabowe Vidiya, in which I settled after attending
the annual rituals, is in most outward details identical to a Kandyan
village. The only immediate sign that one is in a variant culture is
that the women wear saris and cover their heads, and chickens are
to be seen running about in the village. The people speak excellent
Sinhalese, but their normal language is Tamil. Otherwise all that we
have said about the topography, economy, and ecology of Makulle
Watta applies to Kotabowe as well.

The most singular difference in Muslim villages from Kandyan
villages is the existence of a *Palliya Jamaat* (Mosque Council), which
consists of a body of elected representatives (*Marikkars*) of the laity—
their number depending on the size of the village—who choose one
among themselves as a *Matticham* (lit. mediator: chairman) and also
elect a secretary, a treasurer, and various mosque servants like the
Muaddin (who calls the faithful to prayer) and the *Lebbe* (the main
religious functionary).

This body is responsible not only for the affairs of the mosque, the
conducting of services, the safe-keeping and running of the mosque
chest, but also for all the public affairs of the laity.[3] In the latter role,

---

[3] It would seem that on the east coast such an organization exists also with the
Tamil *kovils*, (temples) and that the *Marikkars* (or *Mahamakkaran* among Tamils)
are the heads of named matrilineal descent groups, who represent their descent
group at the mosque or temple council.

they act as marriage registrars, as well as a court of law. The main business is conducted after the Friday prayers, and attendance at this prayer is obligatory—one may stay away only with special permission or on pain of a fine of one rupee—so that the boundaries of a group with a mosque and the limits of the judicial powers of the mosque council are coterminous. Even in highly differentiated urban centers like Puttalam, the Muslims always "belong" to some mosque or another: all disputes are heard first before these councils, and only when the council fails to make a settlement—which is apparently rare—are they taken to regular law courts.

In terms of habitat and environment, Muslim villages are in close contact with other Kandyan villages; many are indeed surrounded by Kandyan villages. The Muslims in Wellassa also work paddy fields of the same kind and practice slash-and-burn cultivation in the same way as the Kandyans. Apart from poultry, which the Muslims keep and the Kandyans do not,[4] the property held by the two groups is exactly the same. Indeed, even customs regarding the division of the crop in cash-cropping are identical.

It would be no exaggeration at all to say that, so far as the villages from which the material is drawn are concerned, there are no ecological or economic differences between the communities of the Muslims and the surrounding Kandyans. When such differences do exist between societies, whatever theoretical opinions one may have concerning their effects on kinship, they are always a complicating issue in comparing kinship systems of different groups. In this case such factors can be entirely disregarded as variables.

Both the Kandyans and the Muslims inhabit villages in which they own low-lying paddy lands, house and garden sites planted with coconuts and areca nuts, and highlands for slash-and-burn cultivation. The village consists essentially of a group of people who are drawn together by a multiplicity of bonds, all related to the owning of paddy lands in the same fields and to kinship. In this the Muslims are no different from the Kandyans, and their villages also contain all sorts of kin who may be related to one another through the father or the mother, through their wives, or through the affinal relations of their own affinal relations. It should be clear from table 38, based on a study of all the thirty-eight households in Kotabowe Vidiya, that most of the marriages take place inside the village.

---

[4] I had thought that the Muslim Tamils would eat poultry, but this did not turn out to be the case; there were restrictions against the taking of life by ordinary human beings and poultry had to be killed specially by the *Muaddin* for feasts. Their eggs were used.

TABLE 38

Marriages in Kotabowe Vidiya

Type of Marriage	Men (33)	Women (33)
Within village...........	37	29
Outside village..........	12*	9
Total...............	49	38

FZD (full) or MBS (full) marriages: 0
MBD (full) marriages: 5
FZS (full) marriages: 6
Patrilocal marriages: 3 (1 man, 2 women)

* Men have left the village in these cases.

MARRIAGE

In turning to arrangements of marital unions of the Muslims, we immediately come up against some fundamental differences from the Kandyans: all marriages are registered and legalized by the *Jamaat,* and the marriage ceremony includes religious observances. The approved form of marriage is matrilocal: the husband takes up residence in the home of his wife and there is no concept of bride removal. The children of these unions belong to the family of the woman and affiliation is said to be *tai vali* (mother way). In all matrilocal unions large dowries are paid, or are agreed to be paid, in cash, lands, cattle, and property. One encounters a few examples of patrilocal marriages, but these, although accepted, are far from customary, and it is to be noted that there are no dowries paid for such patrilocal unions. It is said that these are degrading for the wife, who is always much poorer than the husband, and that only rich men can afford them. These two types of union clearly do not correspond to the *deega* and *binna* of the Kandyans, and they will be examined separately.[5]

The Muslims call the family, in Tamil, *kudampam,* and it is interesting that they tend to think of it as an extension of a sibling group, which perpetuates itself only through the offspring of its sisters and daughters. The normal arrangement is for the brothers to go out to form matrilocal unions with other *kudampam,* leaving most of the property to their sisters, who in turn get husbands and have children.

The Muslims say that the father is really a "stranger," and I was told that especially in moments of tension in the family, people may

---

[5] Muslim matrilocal marriages will not be called *binna,* which is a specifically Kandyan term.

claim that the father is not even of their blood, and that their real
relation is their mother's brother. It is also said that "the father's
blood comes to me through my mother; he is close, but his brothers
and sisters are not our people; they are strangers!" And I heard it said
to my interpreter, "If you marry my sister and come to our house,
then your children are ours!"

It is noteworthy, however, that although the husband is a "stranger"
in a "strange" house, he gradually acquires more and more rights in
the family so that when his children are ready to be married, it is he
who principally arranges their marriages—in consultation with his
wife's brothers—and has the rights of management of lands and other
property which has been transferred to his wife's name on their marriage. As in most other societies where affiliation goes through women,
the roles of men as fathers and as mothers' brothers tend to be contradictory, and when, in the context of the Muslims, the "father" is
mentioned, it must be understood that in normal circumstances he is
a person who has acquired certain rights in the household of his wife,
and that he has to work in close cooperation with her siblings.

If there is undivided property between his wife and her siblings,
then the nature of this cooperation is put on a more definite footing;
however, this is not always the case, and the Muslims, as indeed the
Kandyans, have complete powers over the transfer of property to the
succeeding generation. In this way, a man may leave his, or his wife's,
property unequally to his children.

The nature of the Muslim *kudampam* is particularly to be seen in
this matter of jurisdiction over children: I have noted many instances
when mothers speak of the houses into which their sons have married
as "other people's houses," and their children as belonging to "other"
women; accordingly, when the husband's parents come to the house
of the wife to visit and see the children of their son, it is a formal
occasion and preparation must be made. The husband's parents or
siblings have no rights to punish or admonish his children, whereas the
parents of the wife, and her siblings, may do so. If indeed the parents
or the siblings of the husband do attempt to discipline unruly children, their mother considers this to be an insult to her and her family.

Another index of the *kudampam* are the arrangements of cooking
and eating: again as among the Kandyans, one of the most significant
obligations of a wife is to cook for her husband. When the couple
have married daughters the situation changes slightly: in Kotabowe
Vidiya there were definite and recognized cooking obligations on the
part of the daughter toward her father. Every day the married daughter would set apart a portion of rice called *pava panga* (father's share)
intended for her father, who could have it if he wished. Men used

to go and eat in the houses of their daughters very frequently, particularly after all their children had been married off and most of the landed property was being managed by their sons-in-law.

Apart from the recognized *pava panga* it would seem that almost everywhere among Muslims, the brothers have the right to come back to their natal homes for food, and it is part of the obligations of the sister to provide food—obviously within reasonable limits—to their brothers.

On the other hand, it is unthinkable for a man to go to his brother's house for lunch or dinner, and indeed, as emphasized above, the house into which a man has been married is a stranger's house to all his family; it is, however, a home to the siblings or the parents of the wife. A Muslim man will refer to his wife as *vidi kari* (Sinh. *gedara kariyo:* the owner of the house), whereas a Kandyan will refer to her as *gedara inni ekkenek* (the one in the house).

In the custom of the *pava panga* the increased importance of a man after long years of residence in the household of his wife becomes apparent. It may be interpreted as if in the "father-daughter" type of matrilineal societies of Richards (1950) the man had acquired rights of bride removal, except that among the Muslims his interest in his wife's property ties him to her lands.

It is now possible to examine the arrangements and realignments of marriage. The first question that arises is, "What interest do the parents have in keeping the daughter at home, and allowing the sons to go out?" The answers to this question were always consistent with facts stated above, but seldom really satisfactory. Thus, it was claimed that it would not be respectable to allow daughters to go away with their husbands: they would become servants and be treated badly by their in-laws. But there was no point in keeping sons at home, because after they were married they would be swayed by their wives and would not help their own parents. The daughters would love their fathers—do they not always give them food? If one kept the daughter at home, one could get good sons-in-law to work for one. All these statements are quite true, but ultimately they do not answer the original question.

It is certainly true that with daughters it is possible to acquire good sons-in-law; so it is fully consistent with Islam that among the Muslims daughters are very carefully guarded, and informal unions are not allowed to take place. The marriage, particularly of a first daughter, is an extremely important affair, and its arrangement may take a very long time. It is generally recognized that the first daughter is given the greatest share of the property that her parents have at their command, and, accordingly, the first son-in-law is intended to be of great assistance in arranging the marriages of the other daughters.

This has immediate effects on the marriage age of daughters. The interest of a girl's parents in getting a son-in-law as soon as possible is evident, and girls are frequently married as soon as they reach puberty. The sons, on the other hand, are usually not allowed to marry until their sisters are married. It is realized that once a young man is married, his primary obligations will be directed to the family of his wife; before he can be married himself it is his duty to help his parents secure a good son-in-law (he has to help to augment his sister's dowry) who can take his place.

The first son-in-law is obligated not only to assist the father-in-law generally but also to help secure good husbands for his wife's sisters. Evidence of this is to be found in the inequality of the dowries given to elder and younger daughters: Ismail, the father of six children, had two of his daughters married. To the first he had given a dowry of Rs. 1,000 (a very large sum for a poor village), a house, nine head of cattle, and about two and a half acres of paddy. To his second daughter he had given Rs. 250 and promised to give more (Rs. 250 again) and some highland. The house was supposed to be built later. When I asked why the inequality of this distribution, I was told that the first man was rich and the son of a Marikkar, and would not accept less, whereas the second man was poor and quite happy with what was given.

The Ceremony

It is in keeping with the importance of the daughter that among the Muslims the offer for marriage should come from the family of the prospective bride. Seven female cross-cousins, with seven plates (*madane machi*), go to the house of the intended bridegroom. An acceptance of the food implies an acceptance of the offer. After this the *Jamaat* (Mosque Council) in a body repairs to the house of the prospective groom, where also representatives of both parties meet to argue details of the dowry. If agreement is reached, all is well, and the details of the agreement are registered by the *Jamaat*.

The dowry itself is listed in great detail, including, apart from cash and lands, such items as chairs, trees, pots, even mats. After the agreement, the food brought to the husband is returned. This return gift is supposed to match the initial gifts of the bride's family exactly, and it begins a relationship of *kantankudatan* (give and take) between the two families. It is interesting to note that, after the agreement on the dowry, which is to be paid by the girl's family, a further sum is agreed upon to be paid by the son-in-law in case he divorces the bride; this is called *mahar*.[6] *Mahar*, it was said, was a fixed sum, but larger sums were often agreed upon.

On an auspicious day chosen by an astrologer, members of the two families gather at the home of the prospective groom; a feast may or may not be provided, but the relatives of the bride are supposed to give sums of money to the household of the groom—apparently not less than five or ten rupees apiece. On this occasion the female members of the bride's household, though not the bride herself, also visit the female members of the household of the groom and give presents. The husband is then taken to the mosque, thence to the house of his prospective wife. Here a feast is prepared for him and two cross-cousins referred to by a special name (*mapilla tolergar*),[7] but before the feast the marriage is finally legalized.

The officials of the *Jamaat* are present and the list of dowry is read again; then the cash agreed on is handed by the father of the bride to the father of the groom, who in turn hands it on to his son. The husband is given here, it is said, "in charge of the *mama*" (the father-in-law). The father-in-law and the son-in-law shake hands with arms crossed, and the same action is repeated between the son and his father. The brothers of the wife then take the groom into the house and give him and his cross-cousins (but not his father) the feast that has been prepared.

After the feast—or sometimes before—comes the ceremony of the tying of the *thali*. The bride is veiled; the father-in-law takes hold of a lock of his daughter's hair and passes it on to his son-in-law, who holds it and recites some verses from the Koran. At this point a bowl of milk containing bits of plantain is brought to the son-in-law by the parents-in-law. The son-in-law is supposed to drink the milk and say—and feel—"this is just like the milk given to me by my mother." [8] Here the main part of the ceremony ends. Later the new couple visit the husband's parents, and return, and are in turn visited by the sisters of the husband; but henceforth the son-in-law is said to "belong" to the father-in-law (who may of course be his mother's brother).

There are other formal elements concerning the "feeding" of the

---

[6] *Mahar* is the bride-wealth payment according to Islam, which has to be paid by the husband to his bride's father upon the marriage: it is interesting that among the Muslim Tamils it takes the form of a payment to be made if there is a divorce.

[7] I could not discover whether this pointed to any connection with the Mapilla of South India (see chap. 16).

[8] This is important: those who have sucked milk from the same mother count as siblings and cannot intermarry. Milk is said to be one of the closest physical bonds between a mother and her children: because of the milk the child's body is like its mother's body. Muslim women take particular care to hide their breasts from strangers, including sons-in-law. Milk kinship may have a Koranic derivation. See Bell (1953), p. 169.

son-in-law by the family of his wife. For a period of six months it is
obligatory for the couple to reside actually with the wife's parents:
during this period cooking is done by the mother-in-law, and the
daughter does not cook for her husband. (In some cases this function
is delegated to a sister of the mother-in-law.) There are other obligations besides dowry that fall on the father of the wife: for one season
he works a paddy field for his new son-in-law, and puts the grain into
the son-in-law's granary. It is said that this is done to allow some time
for the young man to settle into the household, but clearly, as with
the milk, there are some aspects of adoption in these customs.

Dowry

It is through the payment of dowry that most property and wealth
are transferred from generation to generation among the Muslims.
In view of its importance, we ought to analyze this payment in more
detail, to see just what is transferred and to whom, what reciprocal
obligations arise from this payment, and to what end it is directed.
Unfortunately, there are no customary formulations on the subject.

As with the Kandyans, the superior generation has power to transfer
the property of its offspring quite unequally if necessary. There is
some evidence cited by H. W. Tambiah (1954) for Muslims of the east
coast that, in the past, maternal *muthusom*[9] was allowed to pass only
by matrilineal succession, but that paternal *muthusom* and acquired
property could be dealt with freely. From my limited field work it
would appear that such distinctions no longer continue, and that all
categories of property are freely transferred when necessary by those
having rights to them.

A Muslim may acquire wealth and property in four ways: by inheritance from the mother, by inheritance from the father, by acquisition, and by the cash dowry of the wife. For the ordinary male villager, the first and second ways are rare. The same ways apply in the
case of a woman, except that there is usually no cash dowry but rights
over immovables. Let us consider, first, the timing and delivery of
dowry, and, second, the significance of undivided property among
siblings. The first of these two matters takes us immediately into the
question of dowry debts.

All Muslims are quite aware of the great distinction between the
transfer of cash dowry to the son-in-law and the transfer of rights of
management over landed property to the daughter. They realize full
well that once cash has been given, little further control can be exercised over it. With immovable property, however—land and houses
and trees—it is clear that the mother of the girl (the original holder)

---

[9] Property that has been maternally inherited by one's mother.

and the father of the girl (the original manager) give up only a minimum of their rights when, in the marriage *majlis* (meeting) they agree
to transfer these to the name of their daughter, and to allow the
son-in-law to manage them.

The son-in-law is then allowed to cultivate these lands, in cooperation with the father-in-law, but would certainly not be allowed to sell
any of the immovables without the full consent of the other persons
concerned. As for cash dowry, it is true that I did learn of instances
where the full amount had been transferred immediately, but it was
always pointed out to me that only a rash father would do such a
thing and that normally one made only a down payment of about half
the agreed amount, with a promise to pay the rest "later." This, indeed, was described as a trick whereby the family of the woman could
test the dependability of their son-in-law.

There were various possibilities: if all was well, and the son-in-law
proved industrious and helpful, the remainder of the dowry was paid.
If the son-in-law did very well himself, then, it was felt, there was no
need to pay the full sum; if the man did *not* live up to expectations,
then also the money was not paid, and this could be made an excuse
to get rid of the man. I was given many examples illustrating this
shrewd way of holding out on the son-in-law.

Hajji Ibrahim Lebbe, for instance, had been promised that his wife
would get about three acres of paddy land, but ten years had passed
and his mother-in-law still had not arranged the transfer to her daughter. Ibrahim's wife's two brothers had been married, but when one of
the wife's sisters was about to be married, Ibrahim was asked if he
would allow one acre of the three promised him to be given to his
sahalappadi (sister-in-law's husband). He told me jocularly that there
was nothing to be done—after all, he had always known there was a
chance of losing the remainder of the dowry lands. He said himself
that his mother-in-law was afraid that once she made the transfer
final, Ibrahim would be under no compulsion to help her: as it was,
she was living with her daughter and Ibrahim, and her fears were
probably justified.

The payment of dowry transfers the obligations of labor a man
has toward his father, and authority over his children, to the matrilocal matrilineal *kudampam*. This is the purpose of dowry: after its
payment, the man virtually becomes—or is expected to become—an
adopted son of the wife's family. He is given milk as if he were a son
of the family; he is fed for six months not by his wife but by his
wife's mother. His father-in-law works lands for him for a season: all
this points to his status as replacing the sons who are allowed to go
out. And after all, it was said, he is a *maru mahan:* the word *mahan*
means "son" and *maru mahan* is "unborn son" (i.e., a "son" by mar-

riage). This cuts both ways, of course, and the Muslims think this to be a great joke: when all is well, it is the man's *mahan*-ness which is remarked upon, but when tensions rise, then, after all, he is a *maru*, an unborn, *mahan*.[10]

The obligations to the house a man marries into are considerable. He helps to make the household prosper; he gives his wife's sisters in marriage, and takes an active interest in this. The new husbands are persons with whom he has to cooperate: eventually, the trust of the father-in-law in his son-in-law (especially the first one) may become so great that he may be allowed to carry on the negotiations with regard to the marriages of his wife's sisters even during the life of their father.

There is, however, another side to the picture: frequently there are persons who cannot get on with the family of their wives, who shirk their obligations and eventually divorce their wives (and pay back the dowry). Because a man's character is usually known to the rest of the villagers, a divorce has disastrous effects on the reputation of the son-in-law: a man who has been involved in a number of divorces cannot hope again to find a wife with a good dowry. His worth as a *maru mahan* becomes too well known.

It must be pointed out, though, that despite all this significant element of adoption in marriages, a man does not cut off his ties with his natal *kudampam*: his position in the sibling group cannot be renounced. The ties of the *kudampam* with the Muslims are many and complex, and thus, odd though it may seem, the debts of the father— who is a stranger—fall upon the sons as full members of the succeeding generation of the *kudampam*: if there are debts of dowry to be paid to the *maru mahan*, these devolve upon the sons, and it is through relationships of this nature that the mother's brother remains an extremely important member of the *kudampam*, though married outside, and continues to have jurisdiction over his sister's children. When they come to be married, the first claims of the mother's brothers upon them are recognized, and this is in the background of the negotiations of marriage.[11]

In the relationship between siblings the existence of a certain amount of undivided property has most remarkable effects. The rules of intestate succession were extremely unclear among the Muslims, and although some professed that the Koranic rule, whereby female siblings get one share less than male siblings, ought to apply, clearly most people tended to think of the rights of the siblings of different

---

[10] The etymology of *maru mahan* has intrigued other writers on South Indian kinship. See the discussions in Karve (1953, p. 213) and in Dumont (1957a).

[11] Even so, the incidence of cross-cousin marriages did not prove to be so great as might be expected: all cross-cousin marriages recorded turned out to be MBD-FZS, although there are no such rules formulated.

sexes as equal in undivided property. At least in some cases, this was of importance in the arrangement of cross-cousin marriages.

By way of example, figure 27 shows a case in which A had transferred some land to B as her dowry. The transfer was complete, but

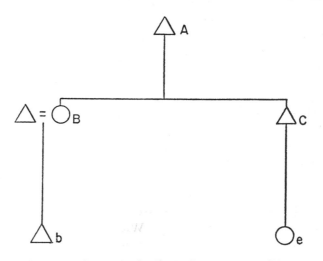

Figure 27. An example of Muslim property rights.

there was in addition a certain amount which had been promised but not transferred, and in this C, too, had rights. All these lands were, however, being worked by B and her husband. As the time for the marriage of C's daughter, *e*, approached, tension rose in this family, which I knew quite well, and eventually C demanded that *b* should marry *e*. The marriage took place, and the mechanics were explained to me. Some of the undivided property was passed on to *b* by his mother; *c* did not have to give any dowry in cash to *b*, though he got some of his lands back through *b*. Clearly, *b* would have preferred to marry out and since he was one of two sons with property he could have got a considerable dowry; but this was obviously impossible, since C would then immediately have made a great deal of trouble over the undivided property which existed between him and B. The property involved was of considerable extent: six acres of paddy land, of which all except two acres was being enjoyed by B, and four acres of highland under coconut and areca nut, also in the hands of B. Half of this—corresponding to C's rights—was eventually passed on to *b*.

THE IMPLICATIONS OF MATRILOCALITY

The transfer of rights and obligations in the arrangements of matrilocal marriages, with dowry, among the Muslims has been considered.

What are the differences between all this and the *binna* of the Kandyans? There are two main differences in the advantages for the husbands of these matrilocal marriages: in the first place, a cash dowry is paid by the Muslims, but not paid in matrilocal unions by the Kandyans; second, the share of landed property which the daughter will receive is fixed from the start among the Muslims, whereas it is only the daughter's share in the estate with the Kandyans.

Obviously, among Kandyans, the share of the *binna*-married daughter will be affected if there are more siblings born, and in any case, the property that is left to daughters among the Muslims—with the brothers leaving the household—is greater in proportion than the property that eventually comes to the *binna* daughter in the Kandyan village.

There is no doubt that all this has significant effects on the kind of son-in-law who comes in matrilocal marriage as well as on the status of the son-in-law in the household of his wife. With the Muslims there is negotiation about the payment and size and kind of dowry, and this is clearly adjusted, as we have just seen, to the position, ability, and wealth of the prospective son-in-law. With the Kandyans, there is no such negotiation: the property belongs to the wife, and the son-in-law accepts the position from the start, and works on his wife's lands. Among the Muslims, the husband is intended to be the manager of the property; among the Kandyans it is the woman who manages it. Thus, among the Kandyans the *binna* husband is of lower status than his wife. With the Muslims, the husband is at least of equal status, and may well be of higher status.

That the matrilocal union among the Muslims is considered a definite contract is made even clearer in the arrangements of divorce. Under Muslim law, a marriage is intended to be permanent and is not dissolved even by the death of the husband. This does not mean that the family of the husband is obliged to furnish another husband to replace the dead one, but it does mean that the widow has special obligations. The funeral, too, serves to bring out highly interesting aspects of the Muslim family.[12]

The payment of *mahar* which must be paid by the son-in-law in case of divorce has been mentioned earlier. Upon the death of the father, the whole sibling group and the mother gather around the deathbed. The son asks his mother whether his father has been a good husband and whether she has any grievances against him. He has to ask especially, "Shall I pay his *mahar* back to you?" (which would

---

[12] It is impossible to go into the subject in this context, but, for example, all the persons who stand in the category *maru mahan* are supposed not to attend the funeral of their *mama* and *mami;* the sibling group, on the other hand, gather in force for the occasion. The role of the son at the funeral is described above.

divorce them), and the mother replies, "No, he has been a good husband, let the *mahar* be *halal*." [13] She thus releases the deceased of his
debts to her. The widow is secluded for a period of 130 days, which is
called *iddah*.

Upon death only the *mahar* is offered in payment, but in case of
an actual divorce, which has to be formalized and accepted by the
Jamaat the sum of money that the son-in-law has to pay back is equivalent to the *mahar* plus the cash dowry that he received from his wife's
family. Payment of this sum formally cuts his bonds with the family
of his wife. His children, however, belong to her and cannot be taken
away by him.

OTHER FORMS OF MARRIAGE

There were occasions when Muslim men did not move into the houses
of their wives but brought their wives to their own homes. It will be
seen that this is contrary to their ideology and cuts across the accepted
rights and obligations of the son-in-law. Nevertheless, such cases do
take place, and they call for explanations.

I noted that there were essentially two reasons for the preference of
matrilocal marriage: (1) it was claimed that one could get a good *maru
mahan* to help one by paying dowry, and (2) that if the daughter
were allowed to go to the house of her husband, her in-laws would
treat her badly and she would be little better than a servant. These
two ideas are indeed associated with the rareness of patrilocal unions
among the Muslims. They occur with great infrequency, and when
they do occur there is always some particular reason behind them. In
every case the woman is of much lower status than the husband, and
often there are some definite mercenary advantages accruing to the
woman and her family.

H. I. Marikkar had two sons; the elder was in bad health, obviously
weak, and it was feared in the village that he might also be sterile.
When the time came for the marriage of these young men some offers
were made to H. I. Marikkar, who was an important member of the
Jamaat as well as influential and rich. However, although the custom
is that the eldest son must marry first and be followed by his younger
brothers, all the offers were made for the younger of the two brothers.

Eventually, rather secretively, a dowry of 500 rupees and lands was
given to the younger brother, and he married the daughter of Ismail
Marikkar. The rumor then went around the village that Ismail Marikkar had "bought" the younger brother with the temptation of the
dowry and had induced him to marry before his elder brother. H. I.

---

[13] An Islamic concept. He has fulfilled his obligations and she foregoes her right
to the *mahar*.

Marikkar was furious. He denied the accusations and told me that Ismail Marikkar had promised 500 and only paid 250, and that any way he had paid it all back to Ismail to save his son's reputation. The latter statement, at least, proved to be mere boasting, for the marriage of the younger son was not annulled.

On the other hand, it became impossible to get a woman for the elder son in the village, and father and son eventually decided to bring a wife from one of the distant tea estates "to look after both of them in the village." This they did; they paid all her expenses, and all the expenses of the wedding, and brought this woman into the village. She was much looked down upon, and it was felt that she had obviously made a match above her station, which had cost the loss of a daughter to her father.[14]

The nonexistence of polygyny in a group of people professing Islam should also be noted. In all discussions of this subject I was told that this was never a custom among the Muslims: it would be allowed by religion, but it was not done. Indeed, the villagers tended to think of it as rather immoral, and unacceptable. The real reasons are, however, fairly evident: the son-in-law falls under definite obligations toward his father-in-law by the very fact of his marriage and his acceptance of dowry. It would be quite impossible for him to be a dowried son-in-law in two different households, with obligations toward two different fathers-in-law: so there were no cases of polygynous unions among the Muslims, nor did I hear of any in past times.

THE HOUSEHOLD

As table 39 shows, in the village of Kotabowe Vidiya, apart from a few notable exceptions, all the men married matrilocally. The preceding discussion of kinship should have made clear how important affinal relations are, not only for men—though these are especially so—but also for women. These relations, in particular those that are confined within a household, as for example the relationship between the son-in-law and the mother-in-law, are highly charged with tension.

Normally, Muslim families try to alleviate such trouble by passing on the house, after a certain time, to their daughter and establishing another house either in the same garden or somewhere else in the

---

[14] A similar example from the Hindu Tamils of the east coast: Wannisingham's first marriage had been with dowry. That wife died and Wannisingham grew extremely rich. He married five women, after his first wife, and all of them he brought to his house. When asked about dowry, he said, "What dowry from these women? They are poor—but they are beautiful!" Asked about his obligations to his fathers-in-law, he said, "No dowry, no obligation. When they annoy me, I can send the women away." This he does seem to have done, but the children, except those of his first marriage, have remained with him, or returned to him.

TABLE 39

Membership of Households, Kotabowe Vidiya
(31 Households Considered)

Relationship of Occupants to Eldest Male in Matrilocal Marriage—22 Households

---

Wife..	17
Unmarried children..	16
Wife's children..	1
Married daughters...	9
Daughters' husbands...	9
Daughters' children..	8
Wife's sister..	1
Wife's sister's husband..	1
Wife's sister's children..	1
Wife's sister's daughter's daughter.................................	1
Wife's sister's daughter's daughter's husband.......................	1
Wife's sister's daughter's daughter's children.......................	1
Son...	1
Son's wife..	1
Son's children..	—

Relationship of Occupants to Eldest Female in Matrilocal Marriage—6 Households
(husband deceased or divorced)

Unmarried children..	1
Daughters...	4
Daughter's husbands...	3
Daughters' children..	4
Daughter's daughter...	1
Daughter's daughter's husband.....................................	1
Daughter's daughter's children.....................................	1
Daughter's daughter's daughter....................................	1
Daughter's daughter's daughter's husband..........................	1
*Son..	1
*Son's wife...	1
*Son's children...	1

* Temporary

Relationship of Occupants to Eldest Male in Patrilocal Marriage—3 Households

---

Wife..	2
Children unmarried..	2
Brother...	1
Brother's wife...	1
Brother's child..	1

village. The obligations still continue, but the villagers realize that at any rate the main source of everyday irritations has been eliminated. Nevertheless, it is remarkable that precisely the relationships that one would expect to be marked by greatest tension, such as the relation between mother-in-law and son-in-law (fraught with difficulty when both live in the same household and the mother-in-law holds the property and controls the son-in-law), are marked by obligatory avoidance. Specifically, the mother-in-law and the son-in-law are not allowed to speak to each other, and they may not look at each other face to face. Their personal names are taboo. Upon the approach of one the other slinks away. Whenever the mother-in-law sees the son-in-law, she is obliged to put up her *mokkada*, which is the end of the sari taken over the head.

A similar situation is said to obtain between the father-in-law and the daughter-in-law, and it is extremely rare indeed that a man visits the house of his son's wife. Both these avoidances are strongest when the relationships are real in the above categories: they are not binding when only classificatory mothers-in-law or fathers-in-law are involved.

It will be noted, however, that the term for mother-in-law and father's sister, and mother's brother's wife (real and classificatory) are all the same: *mami*. Similarly, the terms for father-in-law, mother's brother, and father's sister's husband are also all the same: *mama*. It is admitted that the strongest avoidances lie only between actual affines, and with the father's sister, in the case of a man, and the mother's brother, in the case of a girl, before marriages take place.

The relationship between the son-in-law and the father-in-law is marked by great respect, but there are no special avoidances between them, and they are allowed to speak to each other. I did not observe any striking differences in this particular relationship between the Kandyans and the Muslims. I cannot speak with authority on the relations between a man and his mother's brother: there were no definite formulations on the subject, apart from the necessity for respect, and there were no avoidances that I noticed.

Clearly one of the relationships with the greatest inherent tension, in this context, was the relation of mother-in-law and daughter-in-law, and it was said to be second only to that between the mother-in-law and son-in-law. The two women were, however, allowed to speak, and even to visit each other formally, giving notice weeks beforehand. But since these two persons were in the same village, a great many quarrels took place between them. The daughter-in-law would accuse her husband of going to "help his mother and father unduly" and would charge him with taking his mother food and money which rightfully belonged to his wife and children.

As with the Kandyans, the cross-cousin relationship was thought by the Muslims to be a joking relationship, though among males only. I have no material as to what happened between the females, but in keeping with the great care and preparation lavished on the marriages of daughters, they were extremely well guarded, and their male cross-cousins were not allowed to approach them even though they were the potential mates. The relations between the sibling group, marked quite definitely by gradations of seniority, seemed to be much as they were for Kandyan sibling groups.

Perhaps one of the most significant features of Muslim kinship, and one which is difficult to account for, is the element of respect and avoidance between husband and wife. I described earlier how the Muslims think of the marital relationship as a permanent one, dissolved only by the death of one of the spouses. It is remarkable, therefore, that husband and wife must strictly avoid each other's names, and normally their persons. The feeling is so strong that working in Kotabowe Vidiya this became a great irritation, and it was only possible to get at the names of spouses through other persons—who often did not know them—or by elaborate circumlocutions.

It is interesting to think of this as a way of symbolizing the fact that the husband is a "stranger," but perhaps Islamic belief is here a factor to be considered. The Muslim Tamils are of the Shafi sect, to whom all females are to a greater or lesser extent polluting, and who, in any case, have to avoid even touching females after taking their daily ablutions.

THE MUSLIMS AND THE KANDYANS

We have been concerned with the singular features of Muslim kinship which stand in contrast to the practices of the Kandyans. But the underlying similarities should not be overlooked. These are of two kinds: first, the terminology of kinship, incest, and the marriage rules are identical among the Kandyan Sinhalese and the Muslims; and second, there is a definite tendency to spread the idea of kinship on both the maternal and paternal sides, and to include among one's kin all persons to whom any links at all can be traced by even remote connections.

The use of the terminology is remarkable. With all the differences in the detailed organization of the family, it is clear that both communities use exactly the same terminology, and the same rule of marriage: only classificatory cross-cousins are allowed to marry, and all other kin are forbidden. The terminology which has been described for the Sinhalese can be used word for word for the Muslims. The actual terms are, of course, Sinhalese in one case and Tamil in the other, but the formal structure is identical. Parallel cousins are distinguished in every generation from cross-cousins, and in this case, too, the terminology itself has embedded in it the idea of cross-cousin marriage.

So far as the laws of Islam are concerned, this is a noteworthy situation. In Islam there would be no hindrance to the marriage of the children of brothers and of sisters. Furthermore, even the Muslims who live in villages in the heart of the jungle are well aware of this fact, and when it is in their interest to bring about an irregular marriage, they may introduce Islamic considerations into the argument, and may even attempt to get away with disapproved unions.

There is an important theoretical question here. We have the evidence from two communities, the Kandyans and the Muslims, which are different; why, then, do they utilize the same kinship terminology? The reason is, I think, that there are in fact profound similarities between the kinship concepts of the two peoples, who are related both culturally and historically.

This observation leads to the second similarity between the two communities. Although among the Muslim the residential unit and the family are formed around women who are related, nevertheless kinship through all known links is considered to be important, as indeed it is among the Kandyans as well. We may speak of bilateral kinship among the Muslims of Ceylon, for, though property descends in the female line, the relationships established through the father tend to provide a lateral spread to the rules of kinship and affinity.

If the transfer of the son-in-law to the family of the bride had been complete, if the man had no other interests in common with his sisters, then, perhaps, kinship through affinity might have been less important in this system. In fact, the man's situation is akin to the position of the father which Malinowski described for the Trobriand Islanders: among the Muslims, too, a man's obligations as a brother and husband are in delicate balance. He is the mother's brother to the family of his sisters; he is interested in the future of his sisters and their children, and he may have undivided property with them; at the same time, he is also interested in his own family, including his children.

Therefore, even in this matricentral family organization, the men and the relations established through them cannot be minimized. For this reason, therefore, kinship is spread by affinal links much as it is among the Kandyans. Indeed, it can be argued that the similarity of the terminology reflects this over-all similarity in the general categories of kinship. It is as if the model of Kandyan kinship in which the position of men and women, matrilocal and patrilocal marriage, appears as evenly balanced, has been turned on its side: property pushed through the female line, marriage made matrilocal, the organi-

zation of the family and residence changed, but still in the wider relations the basic similarity retained.

If this point of view is adopted—and it is not an unreasonable one
—then the specific differences between the Kandyan Sinhalese and the
Muslims become even more sharply defined and comprehensible. The
special food customs, the avoidances, the usages of the kinship terms,
the late marriages for the men and early marriages for the women can
all be directly related to this reorientation of family relations: this is
why the Sinhalese do not have them, and why the Muslims do. These
are, in other words, the variations upon a similar theme of kinship.

Take, for instance, the terminology of the Muslims which I said was
exactly the same as the Kandyan. One additional term is in use among
the Muslims: *sahalappadi*. In Sinhalese there is no special term to
describe the relationship of two men who have married two sisters.
Quite often they will live in different places and will not see each
other very frequently. Among the Muslims, however, there is a special
term, *sahalappadi*, for the bond between men who have married sisters, and it is eminently useful, for they will be expected to cooperate
closely in agricultural work, often to live in the same house, and to be
concerned with all questions related to the matrilineal family.

A similar observation may be made about the food customs of the
Muslims. Here again the greater elaboration of formalities is related
to the structure of the family, less clearly defined among the Kandyans,
but consistently matrilocal among the Muslims. Consider the customs
regarding the feeding of the son-in-law when he moves into the household upon marriage. For six months, we noticed, it is not his wife but
his mother-in-law who cooks for him. Only after this feeding process
is the new wife allowed to cook for her husband. On the marriage day,
as we have seen, he drinks milk handed him by his mother-in-law,
and he is expected to exclaim that the milk was just like the milk he
had from his own mother. Later, clearly, the situation changes and
the son-in-law becomes obligated to give his father- and mother-in-law
a meal of rice every day. I have already observed that the particular
family organization of the Muslims is also related to a marked tendency for men to marry late and for women to marry early. These differences, too, should be seen in contrast to the practices of the Kandyans. I need hardly juxtapose the formality of the avoidances among
the Muslims against the informality and the relatively undefined nature of the relations between in-laws among Kandyans.

One distinct feature appears to subsume the similarities and differences between the two systems with special clarity. I have already
underlined this distinction between the terms of address and the terms
of reference. The systematic aspects of the terminology are associated
with the terms of reference, whereas the terms of address may some-

times be different. Note in this context the use of the word *tambi* (younger brother) among the Muslims. Many of the matrilineal Tamil communities on the east coast of Ceylon appear to use the word *tambi* for the "son." A Sinhalese father in speaking to his son and daughter will invariably refer to them as "son" and "daughter," and the terms carry the implications of respect and careful avoidance. The Sinhalese, therefore, were always amazed to hear that a father among the Muslims will address his son as *tambi* (younger brother) and his daughter as *tangacchi* (younger sister). These are obviously terms which denote much greater familiarity than the words "son" and "daughter." Of course, even among the Muslims when the father is in a bad mood and wishes to discipline his children he will shout *"mahan* [son]!" and will refrain from using the more familiar "younger brother."

Such explanations take us back again to the structure of the family. It is clear that among the Muslims the position of the father is quite different from what it is among the Kandyan Sinhalese. Since the father is said to be a "stranger" in the house, his children may speak of their mother's brother as their "real" relative. In terms of property, too, the son of a Muslim may expect much less from his father than a Kandyan son. He will, after all, receive a large dowry with his wife, and if all goes according to plan he will spend the rest of his life working for a different household from that in which his father lives. The position of the Muslim father on the periphery of the family makes it easier to understand why it should be possible for him to call his children "younger brother" and "younger sister."

Many of the differences between the Muslims and the Kandyans turn around the fact that among the Muslims all marriages are, or should be, matrilocal, and that a payment of dowry is necessary to ensure the allegiance of the son-in-law. From this it follows that the dowry payment among the Muslims has two special distinctions which apply to two different kinds of situations. There is, for one, the dowry that is necessary to transfer the attentions of a man of equal standing to the family of the wife, the locality of marriage thus being merely an expression of this change in allegiance; and, second, there is the dowry that is demanded if the son-in-law is superior in standing to the family of the bride.

In both respects, variously emphasized by the Sinhalese and the Muslims, the dowry stands in radical contrast to bride-wealth. It is curious that the learned discussions on bride-wealth in Africa and elsewhere have not served to focus more attention on dowry. In fact, the differences between the kinship systems that utilize one or the other type of payment are fundamental, and systems differentiated in this way stand in quite as direct a contrast to each other as patrilineal and matrilineal societies. If our observation that dowry serves to bind the allegiance of the son-in-law to the family of the bride is accurate, it would seem likely that the contrary payment, bride-wealth, serves to *sever* the connection between the bride and her family. Anthropologists have recoiled from the "sale" theory of bride-wealth, but there is clear evidence that in many societies bride-wealth was very explicitly associated with the "sale" of women. In the Ottoman Empire it appears to have been quite an ordinary practice for some impoverished aristocrats to adopt daughters, educate them and introduce them to the fine arts of various kinds, and then "sell" them as concubines to elegant households.[15] It would seem, then, that there are certain fundamental differences in kinship systems related to the position and transfer of women which have hardly been examined.

Finally, in connection with the customary difference between the Sinhalese and the Muslims, we should observe that the question of residence in marriage, whether patrilocal or matrilocal, is of consequence only in agricultural surroundings, where additional labor in the household is an important consideration. In towns it is not the actual labor so much as the undefined forms of association which are at stake. The word "help" is used by all communities to describe the special obligations of the son-in-law toward the father-in-law. What is meant by "help" is not specified, but the term implies the readiness to stand by the other family in times of trouble, symbolized by the many gifts which pass between them. Such obligations can be met in a number of ways in towns, to a degree that living in the same household is immaterial. It is interesting, therefore, that the marriage customs of the various communities that we have described fall into the same kind of pattern in the towns and even in the bazaar areas. Though residence is no longer considered to be an important criterion of difference, dowry payments are still *de rigueur* for all communities. This preference for dowry and hypergamy, uniform in the various communal groups, takes us back again to the fundamental similarities between the Kandyans and the Muslims.

CONCLUSION: THE GENERAL STRUCTURE

We have now concluded our examination of the kinship structure of the Ceylon Moors as this appears in the practices of Kotabowe Vidiya. For the purpose of generalization the similarities and differences between them and the Kandyan Sinhalese may be subsumed in a more general model. For the material discussed in book two, we may disregard the question of "descent." The important common element in the Muslim and Kandyan systems is simply that both brothers and sisters have equal rights in all property. The critical difference is that

---

[15] See Tugay (1963). Leach (1940) makes similar observations about the Kurds.

in the case of the Muslims it is the brothers who leave their natal households to establish residence elsewhere, without, however, forfeiting their claims on the original household, whereas in the Kandyan case, it is usually—but certainly not invariably—the women who go out, but again retain claims on the parental household and property.

These, then, can be regarded as structural variations on a common theme. Within the confines of a bilateral system in which both men and women have equal rights, the patterns chosen by the Muslims and Kandyans are diacritical indices which set off one community from the other. In Ceylon such signs indicating a person's status are well developed. Most of these are related to the sumptuary laws of the Kandyan kingdom, but Hindu and Muslim Tamils and the Sinhalese are further distinguished by idiosyncracies in dress, manner of wearing ornaments, facial marks, and the like. The structural rules distinguishing the two systems may be regarded as an extension of the indices to deeper levels of social life.

A further point to which attention should be drawn here concerns the so-called "matrilineal puzzle." We have become so accustomed to think in the categories of the matrilineal and patrilineal dichotomy that we often forget that the problem of men dividing their attention between their conjugal household and that of their sisters is by no means confined to matrilineal systems. Indeed, we have seen that the formal structure linking the conjugal family of the brother and the sister—always dividing the attention of both for each other's nuclear family—holds true for the Sinhalese as well as for the Muslim Tamils. In this sense then, the matrilineal puzzle is not matrilineal at all, but rather a question of relative obligations of siblings toward one another and toward their in-laws—obligations that are variously handled in different social systems.

In the case we have been discussing the relations between certain key persons have received formal ceremonial definition. The father or MB especially has certain symbolic duties to perform at *rites de passage*. The duties are not in themselves particularly important, but they serve to establish a symbolic and ceremonial connection between the persons concerned. The total list of persons selected for such formal exchange is the same in the Muslim Tamil and Sinhalese cases. Indeed, the occasions and the rights and obligations are also so similar that we are justified in isolating the common structural elements in the two systems and speaking of this underlying pattern as the general structure. In the following chapters, it will be seen that the general structure has applicability in other parts of Ceylon as well as on a wide scale in South India.

Let us be quite clear about this general structure. It is a model of the interconnected roles of certain key kinsmen. The kinsmen con-

cerned are F-S, MB-ZS, and cross-cousins; the female counterparts of
these dyads; and the mixed-sex counterparts of the same dyads. The
positions are terminologically specific, and the roles have been given
formal ceremonial definition. Thus they are associated with formal
claims on cross-cousins for sex and marriage, and all kinds of related
rites and obligations at all *rites de passage* between these persons. As
we shall see later, this formal structure is used as a way of ordering social relations in many parts of Ceylon and South India. Each community, however, stresses different aspects of this general structure,
as table 40 shows.

TABLE 40

Sinhalese–Muslim Tamil Ceremonial Customs

	MOTHER'S BROTHER–SISTER'S SON	FATHER–SON
	a) MB–ZS and D	*aa*) F–S and D
Sinhalese	Birth: MB present	Birth: ceremonial recognition by father
	Naming: MB ceremonial role	
		Death: ceremonial duties for the son
	Puberty: MB important ceremonial role	
	Marriage: MB important ceremonial role	
	Death: MB ceremonial role	
	ZS ceremonial role	
	ZS claims on MB's personal belonging, lands	
	I.e., asymmetrical reciprocal formal claims, and culturally defined ceremonial roles at every life-crisis	I.e., asymmetrical avoidance relationship; ceremonial duties at birth and death
Muslims	As above	Life crises: as above, but special food customs especially between father and daughter
	I.e., asymmetrical reciprocal formal claims and stressed ceremonial roles	
		Informal warm relationship between father and son
	Death: MB–ZS ceremonial avoidance	Reciprocal elder brother– younger brother terms between F and S
	After marriage + Special avoidance in household taboo on names, facing, etc.	
	+ Ceremonial feeding of son-in-law in matrilocal household	

TABLE 40 (*Continued*)

	FATHER'S SISTER (MOTHER-IN-LAW) *b*) FZ–BS and D	MOTHER *bb*) M–S and D
Sinhalese	Same as *a* I.e., both MB and FZ have direct claims and these are expressed in ceremonial formal relations	No formally defined ceremonial roles; respect assumed
Muslims	As in *a*, formal ceremonial roles greatly emphasized Ceremonial avoidance at funerals *After marriage* + Special avoidance in household taboos on names, facing, etc. + Ceremonial feeding of son-in-law in matrilocal households	No formal ceremonial roles; respect assumed

	CROSS-COUSINS *c*) Same Sex	SIBLINGS *cc*) Elder–Younger, Same Sex
Sinhalese	Joking Reciprocal Friendship	Avoidance Asymmetrical Respect assumed
Muslims	Same	Same

	CROSS-COUSINS *d*) Male–Female	ELDER–YOUNGER SIBLINGS *dd*) Opposite Sex
Sinhalese	Direct claims upon each other for sex and play. Ceremonial recognition to claims, especially at birth, puberty, and marriage	As above, *cc*
Muslims	Ceremonial recognition given to claims, especially at birth, puberty, and marriage	As above, *cc*

The differences between the left-hand and right-hand columns immediately spring to the eye. It is precisely in these relations of ritual affinity (which may or may not be turned into actual affinity) that we find the greatest elaboration of ceremonial customs, special roles at all *rites de passage,* and so on, described in earlier chapters. Merely to give an example, the MB has an important role to play in the puberty and marriage ceremonies of his sisters' children. He must lend them at least his moral support, for he has claims on them, and his presence clearly indicates that he approves of the proceedings and is not cutting his ties in disapproval. He can, of course, actually claim the sisters' children for his own and vice versa.

At death, the body is carried by a son and a sister's son; both must be present. The sister's son is given further ceremonial recognition in that he has the right to all the personal belongings of his mother's brother quite apart from his other legitimate claim.

There can be little doubt that all these ceremonial customs are intended to buttress a danger point in the structure. Hence the correct model for proper behavior is presented in bold and clear-cut lines. All the customs reiterate the point that "ritual affinity" is part of "real kinship."

Note also that there are some important features in the right-hand column. There can be no mistake about maternity: hence there are no ceremonial features designed to give recognition to the mother as a kinswoman. But the Sinhalese are fond of saying "Who knows the father? Can't be sure of that." The comment is indeed true for this part of Ceylon—hence note the specific ceremonial functions given to the father at the birth of a child (he formally takes the child in his arms and returns it to the mother). The son as well as the sister's son (son-in-law) must act as the pallbearer of the coffin at the death of the father.

The point is made more emphatic when we recall that in the Nayar situation in Malabar (as we shall see, culturally as well as structurally related to Ceylon) it is not the MB at all but the father who is singled out for elaborate ritual attention. In these matrilineal castes there are many formal occasions when paternity is given special recognition. Thus the entire pseudo-marriage ceremony *Tāli-kettu kalyanam*, on which much ink has been spent, may be said to be directed solely to this purpose (see Gough, 1955a; Dumont, 1961a; Yalman, 1963). Gough's views have undergone some alteration on this important point, but the facts are not in doubt. Furthermore, not only is the father ceremonially indicated during the pseudo-marriage but the children he has begotten, as well as others symbolically attributed to him, must observed death pollution upon his decease. As in Ceylon, the son in particular has special obligations at the funeral of a Nayar man (see Thurston, 1906). These customs again serve merely to provide correct models for thought and behavior at these relatively weak points in the general structure.

The same concern can be detected in the special food customs directed to the father in matrilocal Muslim households in Ceylon. They can only be understood in the context of their statement that "The father is a stranger." The culture is apparently striving to make him more of a kinsman instead of a mere ritual-affine.

My argument in this chapter has been that Kandyan Sinhalese and Muslim Tamil kin structures represent variations upon the same theme. We have drawn attention to the structural similarities in the two systems as well as to the points of differentiation between them. In fact, I believe that although the communities speak different languages, we are not simply in the presence of structurally homologous systems. The similarity is close to an identity with slight variations. Obviously, the best possible demonstration of this point would be a community where the two systems have merged into each other. I was fortunate indeed in Ceylon to discover such a community. In the village of Panama, and elsewhere on the eastern littoral of Ceylon, it is possible to observe the articulation of two formally separate and distinct kin structures. The village of Panama thus presents important evidence to demonstrate the continuous transformation, in space but not in time, of one structure into another. This is the subject matter of the next chapter.

14

The Articulation of Structures: Panama

"Paoneme contains sixty inhabitants, who cultivate seventy-three ammonams, of paddee ground."—From a Report of William Orr, Esq. on a Journey from Tengalle to Batticaloe, 25th of September 1800, in J. Cordiner, *A Description of Ceylon* (1807), p. 123

Most anthropological work is concerned with the analysis of particular social systems which are regarded as theoretically distinct from other systems. It is well known, however, that there are communities all over the world which are not only bilingual but also bicultural: they exist on the borderlines between two cultures. Such communities have been rarely described, much less analyzed. In this chapter a bicultural community of this kind is examined. The people concerned are the inhabitants of a village in eastern Ceylon where Hindu Tamils and Buddhist Sinhalese have produced a mixed community. The Sinhalese–Tamil intermarriage is all the more surprising since we are accustomed to think of the two peoples as quite separate and now extremely hostile communities. Indeed, the race riots and other tragic events in Ceylon underline the deep cleavages that exist between them. But aside from Tamil–Sinhalese unions, it is well known that the respective castes of both communities remain extremely conservative even about intercaste connections. How is it that members of two communal groups, who will not even think of marrying outside their castes, can successfully intermarry with persons of alien linguistic and religious communities? On a more theoretical plane, how is it possible for two systems to be merged into one? Is this possible with all systems or only with those already fairly similar?

The Panama system described in this chapter appears to be the result of special local conditions in the "shatter zone" between two cultures; apparently as a result of its long isolation, the community has gradually developed an amalgamated social system that is halfway between the Sinhalese and Tamil patterns. This was possible—as I argued in the last chapter—because the systems were already similar in basic essentials. I should note, however, that all intermarriages took place with Hindu Tamils and none with Muslim Tamils. At the present time, with greater mobility and lessened isolation, the community has been faced with the choice of becoming either Sinhalese or Tamil. Thus there is today a cleavage in the community which promises to become even deeper.

In the following pages I begin by examining the type of amalgam that was produced in the village, in terms of kinship, caste, and religion. I then discuss the separation of the village into two camps and the implications of the separation.

THE VILLAGE

The village of Panama, near the Indian Ocean on the east coast of Ceylon, falls between the large Muslim and Hindu Tamil conglomerations like Pottuvil, Tirrukkovil, Kalmunai, and Batticaloa to the north and the small Sinhalese jungle communities to the west. The village, one of the most isolated in all Ceylon, lies in an economically backward area. For miles around, there is nothing but scrub jungle, sparsely populated by tiny Sinhalese communities that barely survive on shifting cultivation. To the north, along the shore, starting with Tirukkovil are large populations of Tamil-speaking people (H. W. Tambiah, 1954). They are separated from the Jaffna area, where again one finds a heavy population of Tamils (H. W. Tambiah, 1956; Banks, 1960). This Tamil-speaking population on the east coast is divided into many subgroups, first by religion—Hindus, Muslims, Roman Catholics, Protestants—and second, especially among the Hindus, by caste.

The communities nearest Panama are Pottuvil, a town of some 7,000 population, almost all Muslims much like those described in the preceding chapter, with the exception of developed matrilineages, and, to the south, Kumane, a tiny village of 67 persons belonging to one of the lowest Sinhalese castes, the Padu (see Ryan, 1953, p. 127 and index). The population of Panama is about 987, according to the census carried out by the village authorities. Historically, Panama is said to have been the center of a feudal state only indirectly connected with the Kandyan kings. (It is apparently mentioned in the Chronicle of Ceylon Kings, the *Mahawansa.*) Certainly, until recently, the lands of the village—hundreds of acres of valuable rice land—seem to have been owned exclusively by the family of the feudal lord, the manor of Miangoda Kotagaha Valawwa, which also had traditional jurisdiction over the famous shrine of Kataragama, one of the foremost sacred pilgrimage centers of Ceylon.

The land of Panama is worked on the *mullekaran* (or *munnilaik-karan*) system described by J. P. Lewis (Codrington, 1938, p. 58), and to my knowledge not used by the Sinhalese in other areas.[1] The huge tracts of land are often owned by a few persons, and the villagers themselves fall into a special category of landless laborers.

The full details of the arrangements for land tenure are not essential to the discussion. Nevertheless, it is worth noting that out of the 707 acres of the ancient lands of the village, 575 belong to the family of a businessman in Jaffna, Marakanda Mudalali, and his children. Of the remaining 132 acres, 68 have been bought and distributed on the Land Development Ordinance by the government. The other 64 acres are held by the descendants of the feudal lord, who in fact were the people who sold the lands mentioned above to Marakanda Mudalali.[2]

MISCEGENATION IN PANAMA

The myths of origin of the village are intriguing. Some say that they are descended from the incestuous union of four brothers with four sisters. Others say that some men came to the area and had intercourse with wild Vedda women who could only mutter meaningless sounds. The former is a reflection of the uniqueness and difference of Panama from other Sinhalese villages in the area. The latter is probably associated with the many individual Tamil men who come and settle with Panama (or Sinhalese) women in these parts. There is little doubt that the Sinhalese–Tamil mixture has been in existence for a long time.

Since the villagers are bilingual and use both Sinhalese and Tamil names it is difficult to make a differentiation into Tamil or Sinhalese between those whose parents are both from Panama. The only people whose positions are quite clear are the new arrivals in the village.

---

[1] The system is based on thirty-acre portions of land, divided into two; one half is worked by four laborers for themselves, and the other half is cultivated by them for the owner of the land. They pay ground rent for the acreage that they work for themselves, as well as interest on the loans of seed and buffaloes from the owner. Not surprisingly, the workers are always in debt to the landlord—so far, indeed, that the landlord has to provide them with rice for food, on which he charges interest at 50 percent per annum. If after all this the workers manage to save anything, it is but a trifling amount, and so the next year they must again cultivate the landlord's fields and borrow rice in order to feed their families.

[2] Apart from the 68 acres of "traditional" lands, new areas of rice lands in the village have been distributed by the government again on the above ordinance: 170 acres (Wadagama) were distributed in 1902, and 405 acres (Elakatuva) were distributed in 1944; but in the latter case, the lands do not have a water supply and the crop is completely at the mercy of the flood waters in the rainy season

These fall into three categories: the Tamils from the north, who are distinguished by their lack of Sinhalese, their dress and ornaments, and their names; the Sinhalese who have settled down with Panama women; and those who have come from the Sinhalese Low Country, also distinguished by their names and very likely of Roman Catholic origin, though this has not led to any social separation (see fig. 28).

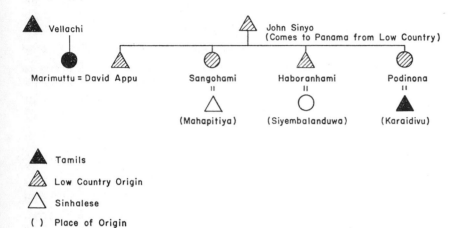

Figure 28. Marriage in Panama.

With all this mixture, it is certainly striking that there have been no intermarriages with Muslims. It will be noted that of the children of John Sinyo (fig. 28), David Appu has married a Tamil woman, Sangohami has settled with a man from Mahapitiya (Sinhalese), Haboranhami has brought a Sinhalese woman from Siyembalanduwa, and Podinona has taken a Tamil man from Karaidivu in the north.

I made a study of the types of names utilized in the village to indicate the balance of Tamil–Sinhalese mixture. It is interesting that the percentages with two separate indices—house names and personal names—agree almost completely. Of 52 houses in Panama, 16 were named in Tamil, 35 in Sinhalese, and 1 in Low Country (in percentages, 30.7 percent, 67.3 percent, and 2 percent of the total house names). Of 558 personal names (that is, names in my genealogical charts), 175 were Tamil, 376 were Sinhalese, and 7 were Low Country (in percentages, 31.3 percent, 67.3 percent, and 1.4 percent of the total number of personal names).

There are two important differences between the Tamils of the east coast and the Sinhalese of the Kandyan areas. In terms of descent, the Tamils of the east coast, both Muslim and Hindu, consider themselves to be matrilineal, and are formed into matrilineages called *kudi*, which are supposedly exogamous. The *kudi* are divided into smaller, more restricted lineages called *vaittu var* (womb tie). In arrangements of marriage, both the Hindu and Muslim Tamil communities almost always pay large dowries; and the marriages, with rare and special exceptions, are always matrilocal.

All east coast Tamils, both Hindu and Muslim, have much the same names for their matrilineages. This is explained by the myth of seven Hindus and seven Muslims described in the preceding chapter. The lineages are highly varied in status and have formal hypergamous relations between them. The highest matrilineage among Hindus is Kurakkal *kudi* which consists of "priests." The *Kurakkal* is the officiator in Shivaite temples. He carries the Shiva *lingam* (phallus) as an emblem of office in a chain around his neck. On the east coast, both the custodianship of temples and the *lingam* descend from the man to his sister's sons in the female line. The Kurakkal lineages in these particular communities are part of a wider community of Kurakkals who exist in other localities in Ceylon and also in India. The principles of hypergamy are carefully observed (as we shall see in chap. 15). The men of Kurakkal *kudi* are allowed to settle down with women from any *kudi*. With suitable dowries they may marry into Karayyar (Fisherman—Tamil) or even Mukkuva (also Fishermen) *kudi*. The children are affiliated to their castes through the mother, and since they also inherit property and social position in the female line, no problem arises. Considerable freedom of choice is thus allowed the men who settle in the village with local women, often coming from places well to the north of Panama. The women, on the other hand, are protected. Women of Kurakkal lineages may only marry men of other equal-ranking Kurakkal lineages, and women of other *kudi* must in the same way marry equals or superiors.

As in Kotabowe, the dowry system is linked to matrilocal residence. Normally, titles to land rest with women, and by promising a daughter a certain amount of land and a proportion of cash dowry during the marriage negotiations a family may acquire a "good" son-in-law. All descriptions of family relations begin and end with the fact that the mother's brother is the "real" relative and the father something of a "stranger." Thus, the pattern of kinship is identical to that described for the Muslims in the previous chapter.

It is felt, for example, that the homes of men are not really with their wives but with their sisters. Accordingly, brothers may always visit their sisters for meals, or may stay with them, but they cannot go into the houses of their brothers, which, under this system, are said to be the houses of "strangers." The same is true of the parents:

a man's mother will continually visit his sisters, and sometimes live in the same house with them, but she will not come into the house into which he was married. The system is, as we have seen, not categorically different from the Sinhalese; on the contrary, it should be regarded as essentially a variation on the same general theme.

PANAMA KINSHIP

The Panama kinship pattern is an extraordinary amalgam of the Sinhalese and Tamil systems. Sinhalese and Tamil terms are used interchangeably. They practice matrilocal marriage, but the majority of the population has little in the way of property for an entry into the dowry system. What little they do have, however—houses, buffaloes, seed in the granaries—they duly pass on to the sons-in-law, who are obliged to come and live in the household with the parents of their wives. Thus a Tamil pattern is followed in the early years of marriage.

On the other hand, most of the people do live on the income from their labor rather than on returns from capital. Therefore, after a few years have passed, the sons-in-law move out of the house to another site, and although relations are kept up, they are never so close or so binding as those I observed in Kotabowe Vidiya or in proper Tamil districts. In the later years of marriage, in fact, the pattern of kinship resembles the Sinhalese.

With the system thus open at both ends to Tamil and Sinhalese, it evidently has been easy for many persons (mainly men) from the Tamil districts of the north as well as others from the Sinhalese areas to come and settle in Panama, and for both groups to merge in this melting pot. It should be noted, however, that although Panama has the pattern of matrilocal residence, it does not have the elaborate lineage organization evident in the east coast districts.

CASTE

Panama does not have its own low castes, but it is not considered very high in status by the small villages in the surrounding jungle, most of which, contrary to their historical antecedents, claim and are accorded high-class status. (Under the Kandyan kingdom they would mostly have belonged to the lower ranks of the high caste.) People in the neighboring villages would say that Panama blood and kinship was *kavalam*, "mixed up." Mixture with the Tamils in particular could not be looked upon as permissible by the villages nearer the central Sinhalese districts. Only in contrast to the Padu caste of the village of

Kumane nearby, which everyone acknowledged as very low status, were the people of Panama ranked as high caste.[3]

The names of the people in Panama, when they use Sinhalese names, are all of the high caste. The family of the ancient feudal over-lord of the district, the Kotagaha Valawwa, had intermarried very closely with the less distinguished members of the village; under normal circumstances in the ordinary Sinhalese village they would have been accorded high status.

In 1955 there was no intermarriage with the Tamil low castes of the east coast by the people of Panama, who, being fluent in both languages, were quite as aware of the status of Tamil castes as they were of the Sinhalese.

A new group of people had arrived in the village from Pottuvil in the preceding decade, and had settled down on the edge of the village. They were extremely closely related among themselves. These people were Tamil Washermen: they spoke only Tamil, and they were accorded the status that Washermen would hold in any locality, either Sinhalese or Tamil, on the island.

The castes, in other words, had remained unmixed in Panama. The only deviation from this rigidity had to do with the people from the Low Country, who were members of the *Karava* caste and who, as elsewhere, had in moving simply elevated themselves to the Sinhalese high castes.

RELIGION

It is well known that popular Buddhism among the Sinhalese contains many elements of Hinduism, one of the most obvious of which is the similarity between the pantheon of gods and goddesses around the Buddha and the pantheon of the Hindu Tamils. Thus, Vishnu, Kali, Pulleyar, and Supramanyar of the Hindus are represented among the Buddhist Sinhalese as Vishnu, Pattini, Ganesha, and Kataragama (Cartman, 1957, chap. 5). The interpretations of the personalities of local deities can be very diverse. The local deity may simply be called Alut Deva (New Deity), or he may be associated with one or another of the well-known deities like Ganesha. The same deity may also be propitiated as Pulleyar by Tamils who have come into the locality.

---

[3] The Padu of Kumane are also bilingual in Tamil and Sinhalese. They claim to be Sinhalese but appear to intermarry with both Sinhalese and Tamil districts. Their paddy lands once belonged to the Kotagaha Manor and later to the Tamil businessman of Jaffna, but recently the land was acquired by the government and given to the village. In 1955 the villagers were a poor and tradition-minded lot, which made it all the more remarkable to find among them one Low Country man from Colombo, who spoke English and wore trousers. He had "married" and settled in the village and was carrying on a profitable business exporting alligator skins to Colombo.

Nonetheless, the Sinhalese Buddhists maintain a clear institutional distinction between the pure Buddhist faith and the religious admixture with Hinduism. The Buddhist temples, *vihara*, are looked after by orders of saffron-robed Buddhist monks. The temples dedicated to the "Hindu" deities—whom the Sinhalese simple call *devaya*—are called by a different name, *devale*, and are looked after by functionaries known as *kapurala*. An established and famous *devale* may have a permanent *kapurala*, but usually the *kapurala* is an ordinary villager whose esoteric specialty happens to be the propitiation of the gods. Unlike the Buddhist priesthood (*Sangha*), the *kapurala* wear special attire only during rituals. They are not supposed to shave their hair, and they are allowed to raise families.

The local *devale* cult of Panama is specially suited to a mixed population of Tamils and Sinhalese. It consists of the well-known "game of the deities" (*devayage sellama*) referred to as *An keliya* (Hook Play). There are excellent accounts of this "game" in Le Mesurier (1884), Raghavan (1951c), and Meerworth-Levina (1916). The myth is that the goddess Pattini went out into the jungle with her husband Palanga to pick flowers off the temple trees. The flowers were high up in the trees and though the couple climbed the branches— Pattini always on the lower branch and Palanga on the higher—they could not reach the beautiful flowers. After a time they found some long branches with hooks at the end and tried using them, but they only succeeded in getting their hooks entangled. So they climbed down from the tree and pulled hard, but still they could not separate the hooks. Finally they traveled to Madura, a famous city in South India, and appealed to the entire populace to help them pull the hooks apart. In the end Palanga's hook broke. Pattini was delighted, and in commemoration of the event ordered the city henceforth to propitiate her in this fashion.

An keliya was one of the annual rituals of Terutenne. In Panama the names of the deities were different. The goddess there is called Valli Amma (she is better known as the mistress of the god Kataragama), and the male deity is simply Alut Deva (New Deity). There were two small *devale* in Panama, in the corner of a field, dedicated to the pair.

The ritual of the Panama *devale* follows the myth closely and uses two hooks, of huge dimension; these are elaborately locked together to the singing of hymns as well as obscene songs. The village takes sides, known as *Uda Pila* and *Yata Pila* (Upper Side and Lower Side), said to be on a hereditary basis but in fact somewhat informal. One of the hooks is tied to a large tree. The other is tied to an immense tree trunk which swings back and forth in a trench especially dug for the purpose. The two sides both pull on the same side on two long ropes tied to the moving trunk. By repeatedly pulling on these ropes, the two hooks, which have been locked into each other, are strained. One of them eventually breaks, to the great joy of the opposing teams. The ceremony goes on for two weeks, with larger and larger hooks being used in the pulling. In the end the last winning hook is taken in a great procession (*perahera*) to the sea, where a special water-cutting ceremony (*diya kapavana*) takes place.

The ritual is admittedly associated with fertility. It is observed at the end of the dry season and is intended to enhance the fertility of the fields, the animals, and human beings. The significance of the ritual in the context of Panama is that the "game" is equally meaningful to both the Tamils and the Sinhalese. It is performed in many Sinhalese districts as well as in the Tamil areas of the east coast, as, for instance, at the annual festivals of Tirukkovil. The game has both a Tamil and a Sinhalese terminology.[4]

The ritual of Panama is timed to coincide with the annual festival of the famous jungle shrine of Kataragama. The celebrations at the end of August in Kataragama bring pilgrims to the area from as far away as South India. Here Hindu Tamils and Buddhist Sinhalese join in the worship of the great enigmatic deity. Panama is on the main pilgrimage route from Jaffna through Trincomalee and Batticaloa to the shrine of Kataragama, and the pilgrims who throng the roads attend the Panama festival as well. By making money offerings (*panduru*) they also have their future foretold by the *kapurala* of Panama, who are in a state of possession throughout much of the ritual.

In the eastern provinces some of the rituals appear to symbolize Tamil–Sinhalese unions on a religious plane. I do not know quite how to interpret this aspect of the annual festivals of this area, but the ritual of Kataragama consists of the famous South Indian god visiting his love Valli Amma, who is said to be a Sinhalese–Vedda girl. The myth tells of the arrival of Kataragama in Ceylon on a hunting trip from South India. He has a wife and family in Madura, but while in Ceylon he falls in love with the Sinhalese–Vedda girl he meets in the jungle. He does not return to South India and his wife sends messengers, Ganesha the elephant-headed, and Vishnu, to induce Kataragama to return home. (It is explained that there are temples to all these deities at this pilgrimage center because these "deities" are still trying to persuade Kataragama to go home. In particular, the Hindu Tamils explain the existence of a mosque at the shrine in this fashion.)

---

[4] In Sinhalese the teams are called *Uda Pila* and *Yata Pila* (upper and lower) and the officials are *Basnayaka Nilama, Kapurala,* and *Betmerala;* in Tamil the teams are *Wada Seri* and *Sen Seri* and the officials *Wannaker, Kattandiya,* and *Wattandiya.*

The annual ritual consists of the enacting of the Kataragama myth. For fifteen nights every year, two times each night, Kataragama is symbolically taken to visit Valli Amma at her temple—which is opposite his—by his priest. Although the exquisite nocturnal procession is watched by thousands in the light of flares, the visit is considered secret. Kataragama must not be seen by anyone. His symbol—an arrow—is taken from his *devale* and is carried by a priest who conceals himself under the crimson cloak of the head *kapurala*. The two men—one hidden from view—one under the cloak of the other—mount a great elephant and ride in splendor to the *devale* of Valli Amma. Thus Kataragama visits Valli Amma secretly and incognito. His arrow is put beside her necklace and the two objects are ritually anointed with oil from the Kataragama *devale*.[5]

It is difficult to say to what extent this ritual is associated with the pattern of Tamil–Sinhalese relations in the Eastern Province. It may also be noted that the Kotagaha Valawwa, which claims to have had jurisdiction over Panama and until recently, owned all the land of the village, also claims to have had jurisdiction over the shrine of Kataragama.[6]

The ritual pattern of a male deity visiting a female deity in procession at the annual festivals is also known from other areas (e.g., Kotabowe Vidiya) but it is by no means always associated with unions between the Tamils and the Sinhalese.

THE SEPARATION OF COMMUNITIES

It is clear that up to a point there was a complete merging of the Sinhalese and Tamil social systems in Panama: a halfway mark had been reached in kinship terms; in terms of caste the two systems had been merged without difficulty; and even in worship an excellent solution had been found. Why, then, are the Sinhalese and Tamils moving apart from each other, and in what ways is this alienation manifested?

In terms of kinship two separate groups have emerged and are moving in opposite directions. Consider the family in figure 29, for instance. They think of themselves as Sinhalese, and claim descent from

---

[5] For further descriptions of the Kataragama ceremony, see Wirz (1954b), pp. 145ff.

[6] Kottagaha Miangoda Valawwa is said to have provided the lay officials (*Basnayaka Nilame*) of the Kataragama shrine. The contributions made to the temples by the pilgrims are quite large, and this is understandably the reason why members of this Valawwa might wish to press their claims. But the shrine has been taken over by the Ceylon government and a member of the famous Kandyan Radala (aristocratic) families has been appointed as *Basnayaka Nilame* to look after the financial affairs of Kataragama.

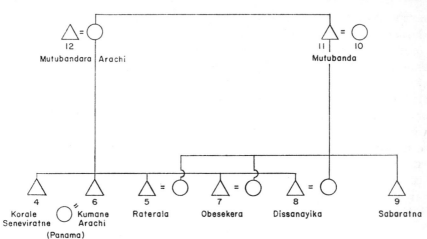

Figure 29. A Sinhalese family in Panama.

the feudal overlords: all their names are Sinhalese—though they
pay dowry—and they have not intermarried with the Tamil areas
for some time now, although they have relatives in Lahugala and
Siyambalanduwa, both inhabited only by Sinhalese. And, in figure 30,
consider these other people who think they are Tamils, who certainly

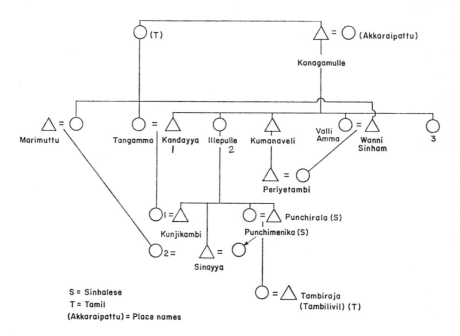

Figure 30. A Tamil family in Panama.

attempt to dress the same way as the Tamils, and who wear the sacred ash which the Hindus wear and the Buddhists do not.

The second family is the more interesting of the two. The desire to become Tamil is not simply an influence of Tamil culture and epic poetry but is associated with economic factors. It was pointed out that the family of a Tamil businessman from Jaffna owned most of the ancient lands in the village. This landlord keeps a permanent agent in Panama, who is himself a Tamil. Following the traditional system, the Tamil agent, in turn, chooses a number of subagents (*mullekaran*), and all these are also Tamils. The *mullekaran* then hire workers from Panama with whom they actually cooperate in cultivating the fields. It is obvious that Tamil names predominate among those chosen to work on the lands of the Jaffna businessman (see table 41). The im-

TABLE 41

Names of Workers on Marakanda Mudalali's Lands, Panama

Subagents (*mullekaran*) (all Tamil)	"Ancestry" of Agricultural Workers Hired by Agents			
	Tamil	Sinhalese	Mixed	Low Country
Sinayya...................	4	7		
Kunjitambi...............	2	1	3	
Periyatambi..............	4	4	2	
Sirivedi..................	4	1		1
K V M...................	6	1		
Total................	20	14	5	1

pression is even stronger in view of the percentage of Tamil names in Panama—only 31.3 percent as against 67.3 percent Sinhalese.

It must not be imagined that these two families—one "Sinhalese" and the other "Tamil"—are unrelated. Figure 31 shows the many

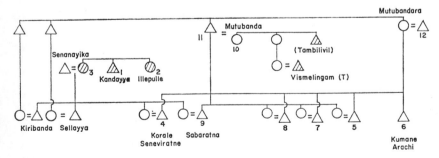

Figure 31. Kinship connections between Figures 29 and 30.

kinship connections between the persons shown in figures 29 and 30. But nowadays the previous connections are no longer emphasized.

SCHOOLS

Faced with this kind of change, the baffled government in Panama has had to set up two schools—a Tamil school with a Tamil teacher and a Sinhalese school with a Sinhalese teacher of the Salagama caste from the Low Country. In 1955 the Tamil school was almost empty except for the children of the people mentioned above (fig. 30). The rest of the villagers seem to have chosen the Sinhalese school—it is, after all, the Sinhalese who are in power today in Ceylon. Though no doubt well intended, the two schools are slowly driving the wedge further into the community; already it is apparent that children of the Sinhalese school are unable to speak as fluent Tamil as their parents, and they will no doubt become more and more Sinhalese as time goes on, barely able to speak Tamil, let alone read it, since the script is quite different from their own.

TEMPLES

With the background of the traditional *devale* ritual, certain new developments in the village of Panama indicate an increased separation of the two elements in the population. A new Buddhist temple was built in Panama in 1927 or thereabouts. It is an elaborate *vihara*, containing the traditional *dagoba* and *pansala* (residence) for the Bhikku. The *vihara* is regularly attended by certain of the villagers, but the "Tamils" tend to avoid it.

When I was in the village in 1955, a bitter dispute broke out over the question of a new Hindu temple for those who were now identified with the Tamils. This was going to be a *Pulleyar Kovil* and the *Kurakkal* from Tirukkovil who was married into Panama was intended to become its incumbent.[7] The reason for the excitement was that the site chosen for the *kovil* was opposite the Buddhist temple. The Sinhalese group, led by the Buddhist monk, vehemently opposed the project. Part of their strong opposition was the fact that there

---

[7] This was not the first Hindu temple in the region, but it was the first in Panama. There is another *kovil* ten miles south of Panama in a deserted place called Okande. The *Kurakkal* who is intended to be the incumbent of the new temple is the priest of Okande. He inherited this from his maternal uncle, since the incumbency of Hindu temples in the East Coast descends in the maternal line. It is significant that the *Kurakkal* of Okande is not allowed to participate in the rites of *An keliya*, though the villagers do ask for his help in agricultural rites to safeguard the crop. Okande, too, is on the main pilgrimage road to Kataragama and this is one of the reasons for keeping up a temple, with a Kurakkal, in the middle of the uninhabited jungle.

was a Bo tree—sacred to Buddhists—very near the site proposed for
the *kovil,* and it would have been necessary to cut down the tree in
order to build the temple. Eventually the Tamil supporters gave way
and agreed to build their temple elsewhere.

Hardly to anyone's surprise, those who supported the building of
the *kovil* on the original site opposite the Buddhist temple were
mainly the subagents of the Tamil landlord and their relatives, with
a few others. The full list (of heads of households) was as follows:

Periyatambi Sinayya Kunjitambi	Subagents of the Tamil landlord
Tambiraja Wannisinham	Close relatives of the subagents
Punchirala Wattevidani*	Also an agent of the landlord
Sinayya	Tamil schoolteacher
Murikesi	New immigrant Tamil mason
4 households	Entire community of Tamil Washermen

* Sinhalese name—an agricultural officer.

The new developments in the ritual life of the community are part
of the social separation of the two groups. The heightened importance
of the Buddhist *vihara* and the Hindu *kovil* indicates that the division
is now centered around the temples and religious functionaries, who,
though no longer common to Sinhalese and Tamils (such as the
kapurala of the *devale*), are indicative of their differences.

I have described here the separation of the population of the village
into two camps. On the Tamil side the incentive to become Tamil
seems closely associated with the magnetism provided by the great
Tamil landlord. Certainly all those who took the lead in the setting
up of the *kovil* were closely associated with this person.

On the Sinhalese side the matter does not seem so simple. The
question appears to be related to an ideological development which
in Ceylon has popularly been called the resurgence of Buddhism. This
is a well-known phenomenon in the towns, but in rural areas it is most
clearly indicated in the dying out of local *devale* rituals. In the villages
where I worked they had become diluted if not abandoned altogether
and were yielding their place to the more purely Buddhist rites and
ceremonies, in which the *vihara* and the monks had a prominent part.
In Vilawa, the *devale* ceremony had not been performed for ten years
and the people attended a new Buddhist *vihara* in the vicinity. In
the Monaragala area *devale* ceremonies had not taken place for fifteen
years, yet there were two very new Buddhist temples. Of course, this
does not mean that the local cults have been given up everywhere. In

Kotabowe Vidiya I attended a very elaborate annual rite on the Kataragama pattern. The *An keliya* was performed in Panama in 1955. Also, I feel sure that in villages where the cults had seemingly died out, the rituals would be revived if contagious disease or some other danger threatened the community.

The development of high Buddhism in Dry Zone villages seems related to the fact that these villages which appear to have been isolated, not only physically but economically, now have closer ties with the outside world. Second, as the language issue has shown, Sinhalese nationalism has now become a formidable ideology in Ceylon. It is noteworthy that Sinhalese nationalism has focused on two indices which differentiate the Sinhalese from the Tamils. One is language— hence the banners reading *Sinhala Pamanay* (Sinhalese Only) in the riots. The other is Buddhism, which has meant that the Buddhist monks have become involved in the Tamil–Sinhalese disputes.[8]

We may now sum up the structural implications of the material from Panama. It is noteworthy that by a slight rearrangement of some of the basic elements in what we have referred to as the general structure, a transformation of the system to what appears to be the first intermediate stage of an entirely different system can be achieved. That this is not merely a demonstration on a theoretical plane on the basis of abstract argumentation but is empirically observable in the field gives more effect to our comments in concluding the Sinhalese system. It is obvious also that just as such transformations can be seen today in a number of different places at the same time, it is quite possible to argue that similar transformations may take place in the history of the same society.

---

[8] This description of Panama related to the state of affairs in 1955. After the race riots and after the recent (1960) breakdown of government functions in the Northern and Eastern Provinces, we may expect the process of separation to be speeded up.

15

On the Eastern Littoral:
The Matrilineal Hypergamous Variant

"Far less frequented by Singhalese and Europeans than any other portion of Ceylon, the Eastern Province has retained many ancient habits, and presents more frequent instances of curious social peculiarities than are to be noticed in the rest of the island."—Sir James Emerson Tennent, *Ceylon* (1859), II, 458

"Tricoil is a considerable village, at which there is a Hindoo pagoda of very great antiquity. . . . We were amused here by the dancing of the girls belonging to the pagoda, who, though neither young, handsome, nor well dressed, danced, I thought, more in cadence, than any professed dancers I had before seen in India."—Notes from a Journey made in 1802, in J. Cordiner, *A Description of Ceylon* (1807), p. 137

We have now discussed the matrilocal systems of the Tamils both in the Dry Zone and on the east coast. We also noted that the fundamental principles of kinship were shared with the Kandyan Sinhalese. The same terminology, the same interest in cross-cousin marriage, the same reciprocal claims between *avassa* (Sinhalese) relations (*sonda* in Tamil) rendered the Tamil and Sinhalese structure not merely intelligible but perfectly compatible in the same community. Panama is important for this reason: the interconnection of the structures is not merely logical, but is empirically demonstrated.

We must now draw attention to further parallels between the Sinhalese and Tamil systems. We noted earlier that hypergamy in the Low Country is associated with unilineal pedigrees which in the Sinhalese case are conceptualized as patrilineal. It is rewarding to find that on the east coast of Ceylon the same situation is reversed: that is, hypergamy is associated with a developed ideology of matrilineal units and pedigrees. The facts are so interesting, and the symmetry of the situation so unusual, that I shall report the facts as I know them even though I do not speak Tamil and was obliged to rely on Tamil interpreters and on bilingual speakers of Sinhalese and Tamil.

Tambiraja was one of my neighbors in Panama. He was a Tamil from Tambilivil, a few miles north on the coast. He had lost large coconut estates and had left his village and settled in Panama. He had not given up his Tamil ways and would come into my hut bearing streaks of holy ash and sporting a single gold earring. We also went to visit his natal village and to discuss the information with others.

According to Tambiraja, there were eight *kudi* in Tambilivil. These were ranked as follows: (1) Kurakkal *kudi,* (2) Kantan *kudi,* (3) Kattapattan *kudi,* (4) Sariveli *kudi,* (5) Singala *kudi,* (6) Vedda *kudi,* (7) Chetti *kudi,* and (8) Karayyar *kudi.* In principle, *kudi* affiliation was strictly matrilineal. A woman of any of these *kudi* could marry a man belonging to a higher *kudi* but never one of a lower *kudi.* The men, on the other hand, were obliged to marry women of lower *kudi,* and they expected large dowries. Tambiraja's mother was Kattapattan *kudi* and his father Kurakkal *kudi.* He had arranged a careful marriage for his sister to a man of Kurakkal *kudi,* but he had himself come down to marry in Panama, which had no *kudi* at all.

In some cases it was possible to marry into the same *kudi* and in others not. Kurakkal *kudi* is the priestly line; it is found in many localities and is subdivided into smaller *kudi.* Tambiraja claimed that he had no right to marry into Kattapattan *kudi* in his own village (the *kudi* is also found elsewhere), but if his mother had been of Kurakkal *kudi* it would have been possible to do so. Tambiraja said that some people married into the same *kudi* even in Tambilivil, but this was disapproved of and such people were excommunicated.

There is little doubt that the system was fully understood by my various informants. I was told, for instance, that only the Kurakkal was allowed into the interior of the temples. A Kurakkal's son could not enter, but his sister's son could accompany him into the sacred enclosure. The son would belong to another *kudi.* Tambiraja also claimed that in Tambilivil he could not marry into his own *kudi:* but enduring connections between *kudi* were recognized, so there were *machang kudi* (male cross-cousin *kudi*) and *machi kudi* (female cross-cousin *kudi*). For him (Kattapattan) the former was Kurakkal *kudi,* and the latter Kantan *kudi.*

The *kudi* has an internal organization in such localities as Tambilivil, Tirukkovil, and Addhalachena on the east coast. It often has elected officers (*Wannaker* and *Maha Makkaran*), and it may have other functionaries. The function of the *kudi* in Tambilivil appears particularly related to the temple (*kovil*). In June every year there is a ceremony held in the temples referred to as *kudi kuradal* (calling the *kudi*). At this time the *kudi* names are recited in the correct order of precedence and the head of the *kudi* receive ritual food (*ufayam*) from the officiating Kurakkal. In 1955 "*kudi* calling" was reported for the Kanda Swami *kovil* (Tirukkovil) and Kannachi Amma *kovil* (Tambilivil).

The role of the *Maha Makkaran* is that of an honored elder. He is said to mediate in disputes concerning the *kudi*. Such issues as a man's refusing to give permission for his son to marry his sister's daughter, or vice versa, would be brought before the *Maha Makkaran*. Or again, if the children were orphaned and an older relative denied their rights, the *Maha Makkaran* would use his influence to obtain justice.

Besides mediating in disputes the *kudi* officials collect contributions from each household for the performance of *kovil* rituals. There is special interest in the rite of "*kudi* calling," which occurs before the famous Kataragama pilgrimage and must be organized by the *kudi* officials.[1]

The differences in status between *kudi* were marked at the temple ceremonies (*puja*) in other aspects as well. The Kurakkal would perform the *puja*, aided by the various *kudi* heads who had specific tasks: the image of the deity would be touched by one *kudi*; others would carry flags and other paraphernalia. In formal marriage ceremonies, too, the *kudi* pattern was recognized. Separate mats would be laid out for the different *kudi*, and the heads of the *kudi* would be seated on these, with the invited guests seated at random. The Kurakkal priest—expressed as the man with the *lingam*—would be specially honored. It was evidently important not to make mistakes in *kudi* precedence, for clashes could occur and women in particular were said to be very sensitive to the question.

The *kudi* were divided into smaller sections called *vahatta var* (one

---

[1] I am grateful to Mr. Arulpragasam, C.C.S., AGA Batticaloa in 1955, for bringing the following case to my notice.

The *kovil* in the Batticaloa district are owned by *kudi*. Each *kudi* has an official (*Wannaker*) and the temple society formed by the *Wannaker* has a chairman referred to as *Maha Makkaran*. In the disputed case, the temple lands were given on a deed (*dapu*) to the *Maha Makkaran*, who in turn would lease out the lands to cultivators and administer the temple. Trouble arose when a group of people from the neighborhood called a meeting and ousted the *Maha Makkaran* and proceeded to elect a new chairman for the temple. The resolutions of this meeting were approved by the authorities and the officials issued a new deed in the name of the new chairman. The deposed chairman claimed that the group which deposed him had no jurisdiction, since the temple belongs to particular *kudi* and the lands also belong to the *kudi* by hereditary right. If the new group is recognized and permitted to depose him, he argued, then any group anywhere in Ceylon could do the same!

The case is noteworthy since it brings into attention customary claims based on *kudi* principles which are no longer recognized as legally binding.

vagina)—that is, persons descended from one named ancestress. Katta-pattan *kudi* in Tambilivil was said to be divided into twelve such subgroups. Each *kudi* even had a special insignia for branding their cattle (fig. 32). Supposedly these insignia had been granted by Kandyan kings.

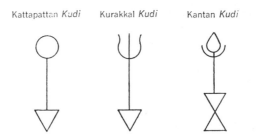

Figure 32. *Kudi* cattle brands, Panama.

The material on east coast hypergamy and *kudi* systems was care-fully checked in Tambilivil, Tambattai, Tirikkovil, and elsewhere, as well as by the reports of numerous other informants from Tamil districts in Panama. These included not only the Kurakkal priest of the Hindu *kovil* in Kumane, but also a Tamil woman from Tiruk-kovil who was a schoolteacher in Panama. The matrilineal *kudi,* the role of the *kudi* in temple ceremonies (*trivala*), marriage, puberty, death, the intense concern with the issue of status—all were repeatedly emphasized. There was not always complete agreement on the precise ranking of *kudi* in different local communities, but that it was the backbone of hypergamy, that women had to marry men of higher *kudi,* and that men could form connections with lower *kudi* were taken for granted.

Given this noteworthy background of the matrilineal *kudi* and the explicit rules of hypergamy, the question of caste becomes a matter of considerable importance. What becomes of all the arguments re-garding endogamous castes? Are there merely hundreds of small *kudi,* each unique in status, mere fragments of caste? And finally, is kinship established by the marriage of men into low *kudi?*

The detailed answer to these questions must await further field work. Here, I shall merely suggest the outlines of an answer permitted by the data I collected.

Tambiraja and the Kurakkal of Panama made a clear distinction between the Vellalar (Cultivators) and the other low "professional" groups such as the Ambattar (Barbers), Mannar (Washermen), and Kallar (see Dumont, 1957a). The latter were said to be further sub-divided into the Tattar (or Kammalar: Blacksmiths) and Kannar (Makers of Lamps and Brass Pots). All these groups were present in

Tambilivil. In Akkaraipattu, farther north, there were Nallavar (or Santar: Toddy Tappers), Kadayar (Lime Burners), and Parayar (Funeral Drummers). These were all colloquially referred to as *kudi*. The term *jati* (caste) was reserved for such larger groups as Sinhalese, Tamils, Moors; and the term *kulam* (*kulaya:* color, i.e., "caste") was also used in a general way.

The difficulty arose with such groups as *Mukkuva* and *Karayyar* (both said to be of the Fisher castes), which some informants included in the internal hierarchy of the *Vellalar* (Cultivator) *kudi*. Thus the lowest section of the Vellalar *kudi* was said to be in order of preference: Saravela *kudi,* Mukkuva Vellalar *kudi,* Mukkuva *kudi,* Karayyar *kudi.* Tambiraja claimed that the Karayyar were part of the hypergamous system: there were occasions, in other words, when a rich Karayyar man would marry a poor Kattapattan woman (hypogamy). He could not expect any dowry, of course, though when a Kattapattan man married a Karayyar woman, he could claim and receive a large dowry. Others said that, although the Karayyar were not acceptable, they had grown rich and educated men had begun to accept dowry offers from them.

At the higher end of the scale, Kurakkal *kudi* was claimed to be a part of Vellalar *kudi.* It was again internally divided into ranked subgroups: Vira Sangamar Kurakkal, Thesandaram Kurakkal, Saiva Kurakkal, Pondari Kurakkal. These, too, were marriageable.

When I first came across the Kurakkal, I inquired whether the term Brahman would be applicable. The answer was No: the Kurakkal claimed unique status. They were not Brahman by origin or appellation, but different (cf. Gough, 1960, p. 16). The men could intermarry with the various sub-*kudi* of the Vellalar, but the women had to marry Kurakkal to remain pure. In fact, I did collect much material to suggest that the rules of hypergamy were not always followed and that a poor Kurakkal family would allow its women to marry such *kudi* as Chetti Vellalar or Kattapattan *kudi,* but these unions were regarded as contrary to the correct principles of the east coast. Their incidence and significance should be investigated in detail.

Students of South India will immediately recognize that this picture of matrilineal *kudi,* in hypergamous connections with other similar groups, and the ambiguity of "caste," is not unique. In many respects it appears to resemble the hypergamous situation on the Malabar coast, the principles of which have been so vividly defined by Karve and Gough. We again have matrilineal lineages (*taravad*) who tend to claim unique ritual status. Their men seek partners from lesser lineages, while their women pride themselves on their husbands of superior status. Thus, all writers report that the concept of endogamous castes becomes highly flexible, involving many gradations of

status from the Kshatriya to the Sudra Nayar. Some are royal lineages
with all the symbols of power; others are merely servant lineages.

Both in Malabar and on the east coast of Ceylon, hypergamy and
unilineal descent are definitely associated. Since ritual status is inherited in one line alone—the female line in the case of the Nayar
groups and the east coast of Ceylon—unions with other status groups
become quite acceptable. These interconnections tend to blur the
clear boundaries of caste which we are accustomed to see in endogamous systems elsewhere, but there is no contradiction in principle.
When the system is bilateral, we find stricter methods to establish
"boundaries"; when one or the other principle of unilineal descent is
dominant, ritual status can be perpetuated without the strict boundaries of endogamy and we find ourselves in the Malabar or Ceylon east
coast situation.

PATRILATERAL KINSHIP?

Readers will note that I have avoided the term exogamy in the above
description. In the field it was extremely difficult to utilize the concept
of exogamy. There were times when informants volunteered the observation that all members of a *kudi* are brothers and sisters(!) and
that you cannot marry within the *kudi*. On the other hand, it was
always agreed that if by whatever reason there were cross-cousins in
the *kudi*, they were marriageable. Hence, the principles inherent in
the structure of kinship always took precedence. Furthermore, even
though the gradation of ritual status was outlined by the *kudi* system,
the relations through the father were considered very important. The
kindred cut across all unilineal boundaries. The principles of cross-
cousin marriage inherent in the terminology were extended to the
kin of the father.

The reason for this situation is that whatever the principle of *kudi*
descent (and there are many interesting suggestions that *kudi* membership can be altered by a simple payment of fees), the principles of
kinship operate in essentially similar terms among the patrilineal
Sinhalese of the Low Country, the bilateral Kandyans, the people of
Panama, and the matrilineal Tamils of the east coast. Descent is a
matter of ritual status; it is certainly important, but it is evident that
it may vary to a large extent independently of kinship structures.

The main principles of the general structure, the reciprocal claims
on the offspring of brothers and sisters, the formal rights of the cross-
cousins upon one another as marriage and sexual partners are re-
iterated whether in the patrilineal or matrilineal end of the logical
spectrum. In both cases an important and continuing connection is
established between a man and his brother-in-law; and the claims on

each other's children, the statement that they "own" the children, is a culturally recognized formal expression of this enduring connection. Hence we find that the term *avassa* used in these contexts by the Sinhalese is replaced by *sonda* in Tamil. This is not to assert that there are no differences between the kinship systems of the matrilineal and the patrilineal peoples in Ceylon, but only to say that the primary classification into patrilineal and matrilineal is misleading. We are dealing with one structural theme and the variations upon it.[2]

[2] Nothing has been said here about the religious traditions of the Kurakkal. The possible connections between them and the Lingayat (*Vira Shaiva*) of Mysore (see Thurston, 1909) should be investigated.

16

The Cross-Cousin in South India

"Indeed he was once guilty of an Act, that seemed to argue him a man of most unbridled lust. For he had a Daughter that was with Child by himself, but in Childbed both dyed. But this manner of *Incest* is allowable in Kings, if it be only to beget a *right Royal Issue*, which can only be begotten that way. But in all other, 'tis held abominable, and severely punished."—Robert Knox, *An Historical Relation of Ceylon* (1681), p. 38

"The Singhalese kings frequently married their sisters . . ."—Sir James Emerson Tennent, *Ceylon* (1859), II, 459

THE TRANSFORMATION OF MODELS

We have now considered what has often appeared to be a bewildering variety of customs concerning marriage and family relations in Ceylon. We have also moved, much as the anthropologist has to during field work, from the known to the unknown. Thus we were at pains to understand the complex kinship behavior and concepts in the village of Terutenne. The fact that these were not completely uniform and that we had to struggle to understand in what sense they were not uniform was an important element in our understanding of the process whereby one "structure" can by almost imperceptible stages turn into another. I do not mean to suggest that Terutenne is turning into another system, but I would underline both the static and the dynamic factors involved.

From Terutenne we moved rapidly to two more Dry Zone Sinhalese communities to examine the distribution of the kin structures we studied in Terutenne. It was then possible to go further afield down to the complex regions of the south coast and attempt to understand the extent to which the structure could be transformed but still remain recognizable. We noted that what were mere tendencies in the Terutenne structure, dowry and hypergamy, were to be seen full-blown in Kottegoda. We noted also that the transformation took place concomitantly with the great insistence on patrilineal ideals.

We then returned to the eastern jungle regions. A slight shift in perspective brought us face to face with an ostensibly alien and in some respects very different marriage and family system. But a closer analysis demonstrated that, with all the externals of Islam, of bilinguality, of cultural differences, only a single feature—matrilocal residence—and its associated complex of ideas and behavior patterns distinguished the Muslims from the Sinhalese. In Kotabowe there was no concept of unilineal descent, and the identical economy, ecology, and basic culture which they shared with their neighbors gave us a valuable test situation. We noted that the fundamental principles of organization in the family, cross-cousin marriage, the insistence on the mutual claims of the brother and the sister on one another's children remained identical in the Sinhalese and Muslim Tamil context. Indeed, the structures were so close that there would have been little to differentiate between an ordinary Muslim Tamil family and a Kandyan Sinhalese family with *binna* marriage. It is precisely for this reason that the general Kandyan structure could be regarded as the fulcrum for the transformation from a patrilocal-patrilineal structures to the variety of possible matrilineal structures.

We then went farther east to the coast. Our sojourn in Panama gave more conclusive evidence than Kotabowe of the structural identity of the Kandyan Sinhalese kin structure and the east coast Tamil kin structure, an example of which was provided by the Muslims. In Panama, we were not only left with an assertion of the very close similarity of these structures but were provided with an empirical articulation of the two.

Further investigations on the east coast brought an important factor to light. With the greater development of dowry, there were associated matrilineal pedigrees—"lineages" of short span and the general hypergamy complexes of the south coast. Here, indeed, was the closure of the system. We were given a complete demonstration of the transformation from a patrilineal-patrilocal to a bilateral-bilocal and a matrilineal-matrilocal system, but always with the underlying marriage structure held as constant.

We must agree with Lévi-Strauss (1962, pp. 339ff.) that if history depicts stages of a society in a time dimension, anthropology lays them out in a space dimension. One can, however, study transformations of structures (or structural change) in both dimensions. In the historical case there is the further element of continuity, but for purposes of structural analysis, as long as the comparative work is undertaken with care and precision, the lack of an element of temporal continuity need not be of fundamental significance.

We are here writing about the fundamental principles of organization in kinship behavior and thought in Ceylon. Our investigations
suggest that the principles are coherent. Even when faced with an
especially complex situation, as at Terutenne, they are not confused.
It is simply that the anthropologist cannot detect what is obviously
going on around him until he has fully immersed himself in the
categories of the new culture and until he has faced and solved all the
complexities which remain even after many years' work. We may call
this "understanding" a culture, but it is certainly possible to begin to
live and think in terms of another culture quite successfully without
discerning its "principles," just as one may be fluent in a language
without understanding its principles. But until the anthropologist has
brought to the surface of consciousness the principles on which a
culture is based, he is not really finished with his task.

The results of our investigation in Ceylon may be condensed into a
simpler model (fig. 33). Take the fundamental categories of cross-

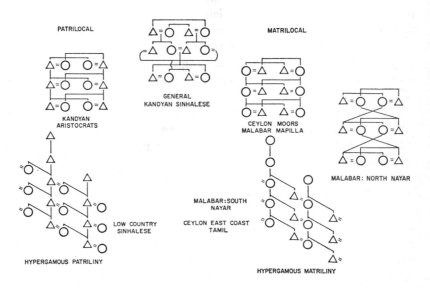

Figure 33. The transformation of models.

cousin marriage and their basic principle whereby sexual relations,
marriage, joking behavior, avoidance, and so on can be organized in
the family: this is the general structure. It carries the implication that
family units may be self-sufficient for kinship and marriage purposes.
The family circle has a unique status which can be preserved since it
may sever its relation with the persons of the same caste-name out-

side it. If it has no kin connection with the outside, it can even claim a unique ritual position within the named caste segment.

In this position concepts of descent are redundant. The family unit is coterminus with a micro-caste. It can be given a special name which will fix its ritual position in the larger hierarchy. The low castes in Ceylon in any locality for the most part fit this description. There is usually no concept of unilineal descent: names refer to localities (top field house, etc.). But there is a definite insistence that marriage can take place only between people already inside the micro-caste; the previous marriage must be demonstrated. Small endogamous groups which are self-sufficient in terms of their women are perhaps the most effective bearers of specific ritual status—so much so that wherever we see small group endogamy we must look for problems of ritual status. The limiting case is brother-sister connections—powerful concepts which were used to breed the supersacred line of pharaohs in Egypt and the royal lines in Hawaii, and perhaps even in Ceylon.

The general structure we have described can be taken in the patri-lateral direction. Patrilocal marriage within the micro-caste will produce "patri-lines" which can be named. If further developed, they can have "unilineal pedigrees" or even "unilineages." Once there are developed unilineal appellations which signify the "patri-line," these can and do take over the ritual status. Ritual status then descends in the male line and it becomes possible to engage in hypergamy and dowry. The general structure is still operative. The marriage partners will be very close kinsmen, hence the insistence on taking and giving women to groups standing adjacent or at any rate nearby in the hierarchy. Furthermore, the connection must be hypergamy and not its opposite, since marriage is the gift of a woman which reaffirms (or establishes) a lasting connection of formal prestations. This is what we find in the Low Country of Ceylon.

Take, then, the general structure in the matri-lateral direction. Matrilocal marriage within the micro-caste will then produce "matri-lines," which again can be named. If these can be further developed, ritual status can be effectively taken over by the matrilineage. Hence each matrilineage is both a line which arranges superior marriages for its women and permits its men to form connections of various kinds with women of lower lines. Arriving from the central parts of Ceylon where endogamy was the dominant mode, I was baffled by the situation on the east coast where each *kudi* (matrilineage) was called *jati* (caste) and *varna*. It was quite clear, however, that there was nothing extraordinary in all this for the people who used the system: they had simply stressed certain features of the same underlying pattern. As far as they were concerned, the ritual status of their own "caste" was protected and that was the matter of importance. We have then a model, logical in its structure, which is applicable with precision to the material from Ceylon. We must now turn to test our model in the conditions of South India.

After these lines were written, I came across the observation by Lévi-Strauss in his remarkable work *Les Structures élémentaires de la parenté* where similar but reversed developments are postulated for the genesis of Indian castes: that is, castes arise from the merging of unilineages which exchange women between themselves. We are not concerned here with the evolution of the castes in India, but it is greatly to Lévi-Strauss's credit to have seen these theoretical and structural possibilities in the confusing masses of evidence in Indian history. I should admit that it is entirely in the spirit of his work that historical developments in structure, which he writes about, should also be observable laid out in space.

Though admiring Lévi-Strauss' a priori models, I must at the same time disagree in particulars. In connection with the marriage of cross-cousins in South India, he has commended Emeneau's brilliant discovery of a "double-descent" system among the Todas. Lévi-Strauss does this because Rivers, in his extraordinary monograph *The Todas* (1906) has described the Todas as patrilineal. Lévi-Strauss knows that the Todas have bilateral cross-cousin marriage. If the Todas are patrilineal, why then are the mother's sisters' children tabooed for Ego? Why only cross-cousin marriage? Is there no "extra" principle? Emeneau's observations are intended to fill this gap: mother's sisters' children and other maternal parallel cousins are tabooed because they are members of a matrilineal descent group (*puliol*). Hence there are patrilineal groups (*mad*) and matrilineal groups (*puliol*) cross-cutting each other; taboos on both sides are taken care of, and we are left with cross-cousin marriage as the only solution possible.

The idea is certainly ingenious, but is this really so? Was Rivers wrong? Against the deep insight demonstrated in Rivers' 700-page work, the brevity of Emeneau's few articles makes such radical "correction" dubious, especially since Rivers himself inclined toward the view that the confrontation of patrilineal and matrilineal features was responsible for the South Indian patterns; and he most certainly would have detected the matrilineal groups in the course of his meticulous work.[1]

The controversy is important, for it exemplifies the profound confusion which assumptions about exogamy have confounded in the literature on South India and Ceylon. The matter must be considered

---

[1] Rivers' article, "The Marriage of Cousins in India," where such sentiments are expressed, appeared in 1907, a year after the monograph.

carefully, because it provides an excellent example of how linguistic marriage categories systematic among themselves can be used in the organization of sexual and marital relations in a community. This has already been amply demonstrated for Ceylon. I shall argue that the Todas are in the same position. To put it quite directly, in these systems marriage and sexual relations are organized by linguistic kinship categories and not by any kind of exogamous lineages. Lineages and unilineal descent are secondary features and may or may not be found in conjunction with cross-cousin marriage rules.

In the remainder of this chapter I shall be concerned with an examination of the structural model constructed on the basis of Ceylonese evidence in certain South Indian contexts. I intend to demonstrate, first, that the same general structure applies in a large number of documented cases in South India irrespective of the patrilineal or matrilineal descent rules. Second, I shall attempt to demonstrate that special developments of unilineal descent have the same effect as in Ceylon—that is, they lead into hypergamy. In the limiting case, each unilineage turns into a ritual status group. Since the material, though abundant, is extremely uneven and at first sight quite confusing, I hope to further our understanding of these interesting structures. Let us now consider the Toda evidence.

THE TODAS

The Todas, though one of the classic tribes of anthropology, have been neglected in recent years. They inhabit the Nilgiri Hills, and from the first arrival of the Portuguese in the East Indies have excited curiosity and speculation. They inhabit a region populated by the Badaga (Cultivators), Kota (Funeral Musicians), and Kurumba (Sorcerers?). The largest section of the population is Badaga. The Toda numbered only 800 individuals at the time of Rivers' field work.

Rivers suggested that they were divided into two moieties; they could also be said to have two ritual groups: the Toda proper (to:rdas, see Emeneau) and the section of their priest, the deva (god) people (pronounced as tevaliol).[2]

They are pastoralists, and buffalo milk, apart from being very sacred, is one of the mainstays of their diet. All their lives and important institutions revolve around the buffalo. In their emergence myths, they come out of a hole in the ground holding onto buffalo tails! The Todas are created with their buffaloes, and the buffaloes, like

---

[2] See also D. Mandelbaum (1938). Mandelbaum describes how among the Kotas the priests do not belong to a separate division but are treated in such a way as to be cut off from the rest of Kota society. The Todas appear to have carried the distinction one step further.

the Toda themselves, have separate ritual categories. Some herds are kept in very sacred dairies and are handled by the most highly purified priests (*palol*). The milking of the sacred buffaloes and the preparation of the various milk products are also relegated to the special priests. All the buffaloes have human names.

The most important ritual institution is the "sacred dairy," which is a temple (*palli*). Entrance or even approach to the temple is severely restricted and in the highest "dairies" there is a division between the especially sacred inner chamber where a sacred cowbell (*mani*) and the various milk-churning utensils are kept and the outer chamber which holds the utensils in which milk products are given to ordinary people. The division between the sacred and the ordinary is so fundamental that when the *palol* drinks water his right hand, used in churning, may not come near his mouth: he pours the water from the right to the left and drinks it from the left hand. The *palli* is in certain respects the model for the ordinary dwelling, where again a division between the sacred inner chamber and the ordinary women's quarters is maintained. In the inner chamber, the men handle milk products; in the outer chamber the women prepare grain for food. Milk is so sacred, according to Rivers, that women are not allowed to cook with it. The household, too, has a sacred bell like the "dairy"—so that, just as the model human society is applied to the buffaloes, the model of the sacred temples is carried over to ordinary dwellings.

In terms of social organization, Rivers observes that they have a territorial organization into *mad* (hamlets), which he deliberately calls "patrilineal clans." They are patrilineal only in the sense that the child belongs to the *mad* of his *pater*. Paternity is fixed in the much-celebrated bow-and-arrow ritual which takes place before the birth of the child and, as Rivers observes, has important similarities to the *tali*-tying ceremony of the matrilineal Nayar. The ceremony gives a public answer to the question, "Whose bow shot the arrow?"

It is important to fix paternity, because sexual and marital relations are almost entirely free from restraints, and all kinds of polyandry, polygyny, wife exchange, and so on are permitted. Without the "public" statement of paternity, the *mad* position of the child could be uncertain. On the other hand, Rivers also makes it quite clear that the Todas are not interested in retaining patrilineal genealogies as such.

The question of matrilineal descent is raised quite specifically by Rivers both as it pertains to human beings and as it pertains to the sacred buffalo. He rejects it in both cases, though it would have been useful for his arguments to have found it with the Todas: "The Toda show few traces of mother-right. . . . If the duties of the man towards his sister's son among the Todas be a relic of mother-right, there can be little doubt that this condition must have been very remote" (Rivers, 1906, p. 547).

How, then, does Emeneau discover matrilineal clans? To answer this question, let us consider the marriage rules. First, the terminology: it is not reproduced here, but there is agreement among all writers that it is of the usual Dravidian type and identical in structure to those we have described for Ceylon. As Emeneau notes, it turns around the proposition that "spouse = cross-cousin." Hence the MB is also father-in-law and FZH, and so on. Again, it is quite clear that all marriages must take place between the persons in the categories of *matchuni* (cross-cousins). Both Rivers and Emeneau note that mistakes occur and that they are disapproved of; and Emeneau provides important examples of how the kinship terminology must be altered after a mistake has taken place.

Even though there are mistakes, the correct union is the marriage of *matchuni*. Rivers (1906) states the rule unequivocally: "While marriage with the daughter of a father's brother and a mother's sister is prohibited, the daughter of a father's sister or a mother's brother is the natural wife of a man" (p. 512). The clearest recognition of the rule is to be seen in the funeral ceremonies of an unmarried girl. Like the Nambudiri Brahman in Malabar, the Toda do not risk letting women out of their control unmarried. The system must be closed and hence the girl even in death must be firmly married. In the final funereal and tragic bow-and-arrow ritual, "the husband always stands in the relation of matchuni to the wife" (p. 514).

The position seems to us clear enough, but Rivers does not always follow his own logic. He goes astray in trying to translate the matter into English: "While marriages between *matchuni* are the rule and marriages between the children of *matchuni* [1] certainly not unlawful, we have seen that marriage with the child of a *matchuni* [2] is prohibited. From our point of view, this means that while marriage with a first cousin is orthodox, marriage with a first cousin once removed is unlawful, while again it seems that marriage with a first cousin twice removed may be lawful" (1906, p. 513; my numerals).

We need hardly point out that in these categorical systems persons in situation (1) are again directly *matchuni* to each other, whereas those in situation (2) are in the position of son or daughter. Rivers' ethnography is so detailed that the basic pattern comes through very clearly, even though many further questions may be raised. Emeneau has much greater difficulty. He seems to think simply in terms of exogamy. The patrilineal clan is "exogamous." What, then, of the children of the sisters of the mother? It is here that he reifies the *puliol* into a matrilineal "sib": "One of the *functions* of the matrilineal sib has appeared in this discussion of the *kinship terminology*. The *primary function* was shown . . . to be that of *regulating marriage;* no Toda may marry a person who is a co-member of a matrilineal sib" (Emeneau, 1941, p. 167; my italics).

Note also how the terminology operates: ". . . even when the lines of a pedigree have been lost to memory the correct terminology based on the lost pedigree is maintained. Each male and female born to the sib is addressed with the appropriate term by every other member of the sib, and persons related by marriage to and descent from the sib members are also addressed with the appropriate terms" (p. 165).

It is clear that the terminology is operating in the same way as the categories of marriage we have seen in Ceylon, but even though this is a particularly impressive use of language in channeling social behavior, Emeneau wants to link the prohibitions to "exogamy" of one kind or another.

The entire case turns around the use of an admittedly difficult key word, *puliol*. Rivers is quite specific about the use of this term. To him it implies certain "prohibited relations": (1) FBD, (2) MZD, (3) FZ, ZD, (4) FFZD (1906, p. 509), and he notes in an important passage p. 509): ". . . if a man thought of a given woman, he thought of her as one, or not one of his puliol, and it seemed to me in several cases as if it came almost as a new idea to some of the Todas that his puliol included all the people of his own clan."

It is a compliment to River's perceptiveness as an ethnographer that he has here detected a subtle matter which gives a good indication to the kin structure of the Toda. He is not really mistaken; it is just that the Toda do not think of the *mad* as exogamous, just as the Sinhalese simply do not think in terms of exogomy, but of prohibited and enjoined "categories."

To Emeneau this passage merely means that Rivers mistakenly includes the clansmen in the puliol who are only the matri-sib members. In trying to fit the recalcitrant facts into his argument he gives many examples which indicate that he has misunderstood this classificatory system:

[Rivers' fourth category (above)] . . . the daughters of the sisters of his father's father gave him trouble because of the two cases of marriage to such persons found in the genealogies. *The truth is that such marriages are not forbidden.* The sisters of a man's paternal grandfather are not poljo:l to him, but urd mort kva:dvoj; they cannot have married his urd mort kva:dvoj; and their daughters will not be related to him in any prohibited way. The rule given that a person must not marry the child of his . . . matchuni, i.e., cross-cousin . . . is incorrect. His cross-cousin may have married a man of his own mod, in which case the daughter will be forbidden to him, [other-wise] there are no objections. (Emeneau, 1937, p. 105)

Emeneau's examples are clear enough. In fact, he also provides internal and conclusive evidence that the Toda disagree with him. About the use of the term *puliol* he says, in a later work (1941, p. 171): "Dare we read in the interpretation that the woman and her daughter belonged to one matrilineal sib and this branch of it is now going to fail, so that the woman feels shame before the matrilineal sib on that account? The Todas certainly seem not to interpret in this way." And, he goes on, "we feel that the püliol (Rivers' spelling) relation between mother and daughter is perhaps is point, though the Todas do not make such an interpretation and the context is decidedly against it." In fact, the Toda merely say that *puliol* includes all the relatives without reference to matri-sib.

The matter is not really very complicated. Emeneau comes surpris-ingly near but entirely misses the point. He notes (1937, p. 106) that the semantics of the word *puliol* means "man of the puli or palli," but, saying that "will not explain our word," he goes off in an entirely different direction trying to find exogamous "houses." In fact, the semantics are quite eloquent: *puliol* are the people who are sacred like the *palli* (dairy)—that is, no "entrance" is permitted.[3] They are precisely all the prohibited categories of kin; hence the term appears to stand opposed to *paiol* or "affines." Rivers does not juxtapose the two but makes the meaning of *paiol* abundantly clear in his treatment of Toda funerals (e.g., 1906, p. 358). The *paiol* (pp. 450, 459) are precisely the persons such as MB (or father-in-law), cross-cousins, ZS (or son-in-law) whom Dumont (1957b) has singled out as "affines."

Hence we see in the Toda case that Dumont's highly interesting structural juxtaposition of "kin vs. affine" is noted and culturally recognized by the Toda themselves in the opposition of *puliol* or *paliol* vs. *paiol*, or kin/affine.

It seems clear that what Rivers wrote in 1906 accords well with some of the best recent analyses of South Indian kin structures. What-ever we finally arrive at as the real meaning of the term *puliol*, we

---

[3] Prince Peter of Greece in a very interesting paper also notes these semantics and links the *puliol* with prohibited categories of kin which he describes, following Emeneau, as "matrilineal sibs." Yet the line of argument from the prohibition of sexual relations between children suckled by one mother to "matrilineal sib" is by no means clear. The Sinhalese, too, have similar ideas on milk kinship" (see above, p. 139) without corporate matrilineages. The evidence for "sibs" such as names which connote obscenity, joking, and simple myths seems curiously meager. This case, too, really rests on the sexual prohibitions which, as we have argued, permit interpretations of a nonlineal kind. I came across this material too late to in-corporate it into the chapter. See Peter, Prince of Greece (1951).

cannot assume that wherever we have marriage prohibitions we must also find exogamous lineages.

In fact, on the basis of Rivers' evidence, the Toda can be established as a particular instance of the general structure described for Ceylon. The crucial indices are present: (1) Cross-cousin categories associated with the systematic Dravidian terminology and marriage rules; and (2) the formally recognized rights and obligations between (MB-ZS) (FZ-BD) and between cross-cousins of either type. The tabulation of Toda requirements will establish them as using the same general structure described above.

MB-ZS	F-S
ZS named by MB (Rivers, 1906, p. 332) (BD named by FZ p. 332)	Handburning (p. 315)
Hair cutting and naming by MB (p. 333)	Bow-and-arrow ritual (pp. 319 f.) before birth to establish paternity
Ear-piercing by MB (p. 334)	Uncover boy's face (p. 331)
Funeral: ZS to supply buffalo; for child MB (also S-in-L)	F chief mourner at funeral
	S chief fourner at funeral
Name of MB and F-in-L tabooed to ZS (and S-in-L) (p. 494)	Cutting of lock of hair at funeral by "son, brother, or father"
ZS gives cord tied around corpse of MB	
Special ceremonial exchanges at funeral	

Matchuni (Cross-cousins)	Brothers
Important role in funerals (p. 499)	No special ceremonial obligations outstanding
Special ceremonial acts while eating together, crossing rivers, etc.	
Special role of male *matchuni* at funeral of female *matchuni*	
Male and female *matchuni* proper sexual mates	

The similarities between the Toda kin structure and the Kandyan Sinhalese go far beyond the superficial. Emeneau rightly observed, for instance, that "these fundamental rules [i.e., the prohibitions inherent in the terminology] govern not only marriage but also all sexual relationships" (1937, p. 104). The same is, of course, true of the Kandyans. It is because the rules of mating are clearly established that the actual connection between the husband and wife can be extremely tenuous. And since paternity is legally and publicly established at the bow-

and-arrow ceremony of the Todas, the position of the child in the kin group is not in any doubt. We cannot argue that wherever we have the general structure we shall also find a loose or easily alterable connection between the spouses, but we can argue that the orderliness of marriageable and nonmarriageable kin categories permits a wide definition of the connection between the spouses: it can mean simply "intercourse," or, as in southern Ceylon, it can create a unique estate and a lasting bond between the pair. The open possibility of the loose connection clearly makes both polyandry and polygyny possible among people who utilize some version of the general structure. We shall look at further examples later on.

The similarity between the kin structure of the Toda and the peoples discussed in Ceylon is hardly surprising. There have been many close contacts between Ceylon and the mainland. Not only does the culture give an impression of underlying similarity but the similarity sometimes persists when pursued to the particulars of ceremonies. Thus the gift of a cloth at the union of a man and woman is a custom found among the Toda, the Sinhalese, and many castes on the Malabar coast. Again, the white cloths which are placed on the corpse by the Kandyan Sinhalese are found among the Toda (and Nayar) though each community puts this cloth to different use.

The further similarity, too, in such key words as *ichchil* (pollution) in Toda and *kili* in Sinhalese, or *matchuni* (Toda for cross-cousin) and *massina* (Sinhalese), and many others increases the impression that we are dealing with variations on a common theme.[4] It is the fundamental features common to both systems which have engaged our attention: it could certainly not be claimed that structural similarity goes beyond the fundamentals. But that is the point: each community in this region uses a variety of special customs to set itself off from others. The manner of wearing clothes, different types of sari and dress, bodily marks—all these are well known. But it appears that the process has been carried even into matters of structural importance, so that one community will have a certain kind of marriage simply in order to distinguish itself even more from another community.

TANJORE ADI DRAVIDA AND BRAHMAN

Although many books have been written by scholars and others on the multifold aspects of Southeast India, those that deal with kinship are few, and of recent date. Our conclusions must, of necessity, be limited

---

[4] The intriguing similarity between the manner of wearing their robes by the Toda priests (who handle the sacred milk) and by Buddhist monks elsewhere is obviously hardly an accident.

and tentative. Let us first consider the material provided by Gough on Adi Dravida low castes and Brahman high castes in a community near Tanjore. The evidence shows close similarities to the conditions encountered in Terutenne in connection with kin structure. Gough (1956) describes a Tamil community divided into small caste groups and in this respect much more fragmented than Sinhalese communities; she also (1960) describes the Tanjore village of Kumbapettai, a population of 962 which is divided into more than twenty-five separate endogamous groups. For our specific purposes it is significant that the kinship structure of the Adi Dravida, who occupy one of the lowest positions in the ritual hierarchy, is largely bilateral and similar in essentials to what I found among the lower groups in Terutenne. The Brahman system, however, is patrilocal-patrilineal, with dowry and hypergamy. It is evident from Gough's description that the practice of hypergamy is associated among the Brahman with religious matters and appears to be defined with great precision. The low status of wife-givers is culturally recognized in a variety of customs, in comparison with which the pattern we described for the Low Country Sinhalese seems to be a rather watered-down version of the South Indian original. It is to be noted, however, that the South Indian structures described by Gough pertain to two different castes, whereas the Sinhalese have been described as different "stages" on a continuum that can stretch from bilateral endogamy to patrilineal hypergamy in the same caste. Although the Brahman and Adi Dravida structures are contrasted in Gough's work, there are numerous suggestions, in both the text and the evidence, that these patterns are also on a continuum and that it would be possible to find in the kinship practices of the castes intervening positions lying somewhere between the Brahman and Adi Dravida. In fact, she suggests that we are dealing not with two separate systems but with subsystems within the same general framework.

Gough discerns important common features between the castes: (1) "bilateral cross-cousin marriage and marriage to the elder sister's or classificatory elder sister's daughter are preferred"; (2) all follow patrilineal descent; (3) marriages are confined to small endogamous groups (1956, p. 826). Against this common background, she goes on to isolate "two main subtypes of kinship systems," and she lists the major differences: (1) the size and generation depth of the patrilineal group, (2) the composition of the dwelling group, (3) rules regulating marriage and divorce, (4) marriage payments, (5) range of incest prohibitions, (6) adoption, (7) patterns of kinship terms, and (8) difference in the rights and obligations, emotional content, and etiquette of behavior between kin.

It is greatly to the credit of Gough as a field worker that she does not reify the two systems as entirely separate or choose to take the simple way out and collapse them into one regular structure. She notes indeed (p. 827) that "the kinship systems of some of the castes of Tanjore combine features of the Brahmanical and the Adi Dravida types. . . . The caste of peasants, artisans, traders and other specialists, who rank between Brahmans and Adi Dravidas and who collectively call themselves non-Brahmans, have a kinship system closely approximating the Adi Dravida type." The Vellalar, on the other hand, approximate those of the Brahman.

Gough is attempting in her article to explain the differences between the Brahman and Adi Dravida, but this distracts her from detecting the important structural problems of "transformation" latent in a context such as this. Surely it is clear that the Adi Dravida structure when emphasized in certain directions can be "transformed" into the Brahman structure. These possibilities are similar to the conditions described from Ceylon, except that in the village of Kumbapettai we have the Kandyan highlands and the coastal lowlands of Ceylon compressed into a single community.

Let us now examine the main features of the Adi Dravida system. This will permit us to see whether it belongs to the same general category as the general structure we described for Ceylon. First note the terminology, which is described as being "bifurcate merging" (p. 844), that is, structurally identical to those of the Sinhalese and Tamils in Ceylon: ". . . father's sister's husband is equated with mother's brother (*mama*), sister's husband with wife's brother and with cross-cousins of both types (*maccunan*), and daughter's husband with son's wife's brother and with sister's son (*marumakan*)" (pp. 845–846).

Again, as in Ceylon, the terminology is extended in all lines to all persons who are considered to be kinsmen: "Comparable lateral extensions take place through all affinal relationships in each generation" (p. 846). But this is not all. In a key sentence, the significance of which is almost lost in the general discussion, the structural implications of these "terms" is suddenly revealed: "Moreover incest prohibitions are extended to all those who, in this wide lateral extension of terms, fall into the same *terminological category* as do members of Ego's immediate patrilineal group" (p. 846; my italics).

We must pause at this juncture. We have been told that the terminology operates in such a fashion as to distinguish those who can be marital and sexual partners from those who are prohibited. This places the Adi Dravida squarely in the same category as all the other peoples in this region who not merely practice "preferential" cross-cousin marriage but who permit sexual and marital connections only with the category of cross-cousins. We also know that the terminology and the incest rules in themselves carry no particular implication of

lineal exogamy. The question then arises as to the roles of these "exogamous" patrilineages. Are they of structural importance? In fact
the author does not appear to be unduly concerned with patrilineal
descent in these low castes. It is not merely that the patrilineal group
is "very shallow, having a depth of only three to four generations,"
but there is not even any insistence on patrilocal residence: "A high
proportion of men in each generation go to live in the . . . villages of
their mothers, their sister's husbands, or their wives." Given these
circumstances, the nature of "patrilineal groups" becomes questionable. There may well be patronymics in use among these castes, but
their social role calls for precise explanations and they can certainly
not be taken for granted as conducive to exogamy.

The question is of some interest, for Gough explains the incest
prohibitions among patrilateral parallel cousins by recourse to the
"patrilineage." She also goes on to find highly specific and very doubtful explanations for the prohibitions on the maternal side. She relates
the matter to the "equivalence of sisters," to the fact that sisters frequently visit each other and have common interests, and so on. In
other words, she tries in various ways to "explain" the marriage rules
on mere utilitarian grounds, dependent on the particular everyday
circumstances which the anthropologist finds around him. In view
of the wide dispersal of the general structure, such explanations are
hardly acceptable, and they weaken other arguments which are found
in conjunction with them.

It is possible, however, to reformulate the Adi Dravida structure
without doing injustice to the material. It appears as yet another
instance of the general structure described for Terutenne. Further
examination of the evidence may bring out the significance of the bias
in the patrilateral direction, but with the evidence on hand the reported "structural relevance" of "exogamous" groups is open to doubt.

What sort of kin groups are to be found in that case? Gough mentions the existence of unnamed "endogamous" groups in various contexts. These are clearly small circles of kin whose internal structure
must resemble the micro-caste in the Kandyan highlands. I would
argue that it is because kinship is particularly important only within
this circle of kin that the rules of incest embedded in the terminology
are extended in all directions inside it.

Let me be quite clear in my reformulation, for I wish to minimize
the role of unilineal descent groups in this system and to emphasize the
significance of these "unnamed circles of kin." In the case of the Adi
Dravida the lineal emphasis is supplied by the ethnographer. I would
suggest that relations of affinity probably overshadow other kin connections in such groups as these.

These small circles are also directly reported by Karve, who calls them *curru,* though she does not discuss their significance much further. But again, let us note, first, the curious fact that although Karve is a very sensitive observer, and well trained for the examination of kinship systems, she too appears to take "patrilineal exogamy" for granted, and then has to fall back on far-fetched explanations for the prohibitions on the relatives on the maternal side.[5] In fact, her own observations (1953, p. 185) make it abundantly clear that the smallest endogamous circles contain both maternal and paternal relatives and are one of the most important structural units in this region: "These smaller endogamous circles are not as absolutely endogamous as the caste or the subcaste, but great dislike is shown by people to marry outside the smaller units. These smaller units which we may call Curram or Curru . . . are not made up of exogamous clans but a few families from some exogamous clans. The endogamous caste is thus divided further into smaller units which, for all practical purposes, are mutually exclusive."

There is, furthermore, little doubt that kinship is confined to this smallest endogamous circle (micro-caste) and that even though clan names are to be found outside the circle the concern is with immediate kin and not clansmen. This fact, too, brings the question of the categorical rules associated with the terminology into better focus: sexual and marital prohibitions are incumbent upon all kinsmen essentially within the circle. Consider indeed what Karve has to say about marriages outside this group (pp. 184–185): "In a southern family the question of bringing a bride from a family of a new clan arises only after all the obligations due to previous marriages have been fulfilled. The new family wishing to give a daughter must first establish to the satisfaction of the caste elders that it had either given or received a bride from the family in question, or that it has given or received a bride from a family which in turn has received or given a bride to the family in question." [6]

Although the existence of these micro-castes has been reported from as far south as the Tamils of Jaffna (Banks, 1960), we are not yet in a position to clarify their role in connection with caste and kinship. One point, however, can be made: we are not dealing with simple patrilineal systems in which men may bring wives from anywhere. By

---

[5] For example (Karve, 1953, p. 186): "The types of marriage allowed in South India conform to the rule of clan exogamy. There is one exception and that is that there is a general prejudice against the marriage of the children of two sisters. . . . In South India a man can . . . marry his wife's younger sister; two sisters sometimes marry two brothers and this possibility may have resulted in the prejudice against the marriage of maternal parallel cousins." It would appear that, much as Gough brings West African concepts to her material, Karve is looking at South India with North Indian spectacles.

[6] Compare this with D'Oyly as quoted earlier (p. 203, n. 10).

virtue of micro-caste endogamy, these are basically bilateral systems, and the terminology, together with the marriage categories, is an excellent device to specify marriageable and prohibited kin without causing permanent rents in the fabric. Thus we should expect all the elaborate rights and obligations indicative of the general structure to be present in this context as well. Further material would probably show that the interconnections between cross-cousins of both sexes, between MB and ZS and between FZ and BD, are probably as highly formalized as those between the similar kinsmen in Ceylon.

Tanjore Brahman

The Tanjore Brahman utilize a special version of the general structure which we have detected in Gough's description of the Adi Dravida system. The most direct evidence is, first, the categorical distinction between parallel and cross-cousins; second, the claims of the brother and sister upon each other's offspring; and, third, the strict allocation of all marriages within a small, unnamed endogamous group. Stated in these terms, the importance of affinal relations as against patrilineal kinsmen becomes more understandable. We can understand also why Dumont (1957b) has so carefully insisted on the matter of affinity for this area. It is not simply a question of formal categories of kinship; the description of the behavior immediately brings out the fact that affines cooperate and are generally involved with each other's personal matters. We hear little about kinship cooperation, for instance, among FB's children, let alone among FFB's children. Such kinsmen are located in "sibling" categories, and they may hold land in common, but immediate affines would probably be considered nearer and more important kinsmen than such "distant" parallel relatives. In this sense, then, the formal patrilineal genealogy provided for the Brahman could be very misleading. It could give rise to a conception of a patrilineal local group united in action against others—which is hardly the case. As Gough notes, the genealogy is more important for residual land claims than for immediate group action in the village. The picture is rounded out by the fact that the MB and cross-cousins, the wife's brother, and the sister's husband all have conspicuous and formal roles to play at the *rites de passage*.

We are, I think, back once more at a conception of a small kin group formed, like the Sinhalese *pavula,* on the double axes of descent and marriage. We can regard this unit as the smallest cell of a caste. We see the same centripetal principles operating inside this cell as at higher and higher levels of more inclusive categories, for which we use the shorthand term "caste."

I think that Gough's analysis of Brahman kinship needs the further emphasis to bring out the importance of affinity. Dumont, in his usual intense style, puts the issue succinctly: 'Effectively we are dealing with two theories. The theory of lineages or descent groups . . . [and the theory of affinity]" (1960, p. 77).

Though not minimizing the importance of the Brahman patri-lines, which are patriarchal, patrilocal land-owning families, I must draw attention to the curious and complicated customs that surround Brahman conceptions of marriage. This intense preoccupation with marriage alone would be enough to suggest that here we have an important structural feature counterbalancing the interest of the Brahman in unilineal pedigrees.

I shall accordingly first discuss the marriage issue. Brahman marriage is a sacrament in which, just as Shiva must have his female consort to be complete as a deity, the Brahman must have his wife. It is noteworthy that in the ceremonies undertaken by the Brahman the presence of the wife is imperative. Gough writes of the customs whereby the wife is "assimilated" to the husband. Not only does she worship him in the morning, but in the past was expected to immolate herself on his funeral pyre. To this day the widow remains, in theory, a being more in the other world than in this world. I would go further to say that the intense formal connection established between husband and wife in the Brahman caste is the structural equivalent of the union of the pure male and female principles which is behind both the caste system and much of Hindu theology on these subjects. An endogamous ritual status group must be based on the union of the male and female principles. We see this principle at work in the Brahman man and wife who form the nuclear family, in the larger circle of kin which is always concerned with marriage with pure persons, in the preoccupations with the purity of women, in the question of early marriage (when both partners are pure), and finally in the formal endogamy of all categories of caste. Hence from the center of the nuclear family in ever widening circles of concentric kin groups and more inclusive caste categories the concern is to make the marriage partners partake of the same ritual essence.

The greater widening of the endogamous circle increases the threat of impurity entering the circle by way of persons whose ancestry may contain blemishes. Among the most pure and sacred groups, therefore, the tendency must be in the direction of closer and closer marriage. The final logical limit of endogamy, the closest union possible, is brother-sister marriage, and it should be recalled that (though unreliable in details) brother-sister and other incestuous unions have been reported in special cases such as the Hawaiian royal lines, the dynasties of Egypt, and even the Kandyan Kingdom, where we have reason to suppose that a special ritual quality was associated with the royal line. The practice of endogamy preserved and in such very close kin marriages probably enhanced this special divine quality.

Close-kin endogamy in South India and Ceylon seems to me to serve the same purpose—to preserve and enhance the ritual quality of the smallest circle—and it is therefore natural to look for the greatest interest in close-kin endogamy in the highest castes of the system.

The case is made even more intriguing by the fact that some of the ideas which we have arrived at by deduction are echoed quite directly in traditional Hinduism. Karve (1953, p. 43) writes:

In the marriage hymn of Rigveda we have the expression "May you be 'Grahapatni.' " The bride should become . . . the partner of her husband in all ritual. . . . The Indian grammarian Panini (7th century B.C.) enunciates the rule that the feminine of the word *Pati* can be effected by suffixing the syllable *ni* only when the wife takes part with the husband in the performance of a sacrifice. . . . The early expression of Grahapatni and the later expression of Dharmapatni may well refer to this ritual function of a wife. . . . Among Hindus there are two types of ritual . . . For both of these it was necessary that a man and wife acted together. A widower could not perform most of these religious acts."

The husband-wife pair is an aspect of the eternal pair in Hinduism. These ideas are repeated in the myths of creation (Danielou, 1964, p. 243, quoting from the *Taittiriya Upanishad*):

He desired: would that I were many! Let me procreate myself! He warmed himself. Having warmed himself, he created this world, whatever there is here. Having created it, he entered it. Having entered it, he became both the perceptible and what is beyond, both the defined and the undefined . . . both knowledge and unknowing, both the true and the false.

and again (quoting, p. 245, from the *Brhad-aranyaka Upanishad*):

Once the creator became separated into a male and female. "The female thought: 'How can he copulate with me when he has just created me out of himself? Come let me hide.' She became a cow. He became a bull and copulated with her. Thus cattle were born. She became a mare; he a stallion . . . Thus, indeed, he created all, whatever pairs there are, even down to the ants."

In this way Shiva created the goddess Sakti out of himself. The relations of the Brahman husband and wife are modeled on the unity and duality of the god and the goddess.

Such is the theological background of marriage in the Brahman caste. I noted earlier that the Tanjore Brahman have basically the same kinship terminology and marriage rules as do the lower castes. Both insist on cross-cousin marriage: in both cases brothers and sisters have claims upon each other's offspring for purposes of marriage, with one difference—that among the Brahman a man can claim his own sister's daughter not for his son but for himself.

First, let us note that this brings about an even tighter circle of endogamy: it is, after all, the nearest equivalent to the marriage of the sister. The marriage of the sister being carefully arranged to an honored person, the purity of the sister's daughter is assured. Second, note that consistent sister's daughter marriage is structurally identical

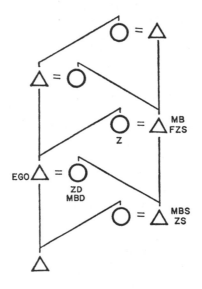

MBD + ZD MARRIAGE

Figure 34. MBD + ZD marriage (Brahman).

with cross-cousin marriage. Third, it expresses the desired asymmetry between the god-husband and the consort-wife: the husband is a MB as well as a cross-cousin. Lastly, observe that it is quite in keeping with hypergamy, dowry, the gift of a virgin, and the other cultural preferances associated with the marriage of pure women. Thus, a sister's daughter marriage, far from being antithetical to cross-cousin marriage, appears as a superb logical extension of the principles inherent in cross-cousin marriage. This kinship system is a special development of the general structure: we are still dealing with a main theme and its variations (see fig. 34).

There are, of course, structural difficulties and contradictions exhibited by a cross-cousin terminology associated with a sister-daughter marriage pattern. These have been discussed by Dumont (1961a), but the material is inconclusive and I shall not be further concerned with it.

The differences between the Adi Dravida and the Brahman appear in sharpest outlines in connection with hypergamy. Among the Brahman we find again the dowry complex associated with the great insistence on patriliny and the unique claims to ritual purity on the part of the lineage. Gough does not stress this difference, but it seems central. Among the low castes, she says, "brothers-in-law have equal status and almost equally balanced rights in the woman who links them" (Gough, 1953, p. 846): this is the usual state of affairs in communities using the general structure. But when the model is taken in the patrilateral direction, as with the Brahman, we find that the relations between the in-laws are marked by a deep asymmetry. The differences of status are associated with the complex of "the gift of a virgin" and hypergamy. The father of the girl enhances her value with the dowry and then transfers her "as a personal gift" (Gough, 1953, p. 841) to the husband, who must be of superior status. The brother of the bride, however, far from being enhanced by his sister's status, is scorned by the husband and his kin. He is treated casually, made fun of, and thought of as a "fool."

The MB (father-in-law), too, is placed in a low position (Gough, 1953, p. 843)—indeed, the asymmetrical relations between in-laws is the most striking feature of Brahman kinship. If consistent MBD marriage were practiced, there would be nothing surprising in these differences of status (Leach, 1951). Yet we have here a curious contradiction: for even though ZD marriage can be harmoniously connected with cross-cousin marriage (see fig. 34), this carries the implication that the differences of status between patri-lines must be reversed at each marriage.

Of course, given a system of extreme hypergamy associated with MBD marriage, ZD marriage may well be favored precisely because it does reverse the status positions of the in-laws. It would allow Ego to partake in the heightened status of his sister and to make a claim on the dowry given with her, because of his own marriage to her daughter. Such a union would still be asymmetrical since the girl would be marrying up one generation to her own MB. This is not the case in FZD marriage (fig. 35), which is evidently permitted but not favored (Gough, 1953, p. 844).

Here, then, we find once again the association of the dowry gift and hypergamy with unilineal descent and status differentiation which we observed in Ceylon. In the case of the Brahman, the "gift" also concerns the religious ideal of the "gift of the virgin."

This association of dowry, hypergamy, and patrilineal descent invites one further comment. As we shall see, hypergamy may be combined with matrilineal descent in a harmonious fashion. This is the pattern on the east coast of Ceylon and in Malabar. Indeed, with descent taken in the female line, each lineage acquires unique ritual status and may enhance this quite directly by the superior quality of the seed received from high-status husbands acquired for the women. The endogamous castes may then turn into a collection of hypergamous ranked matrilineages.

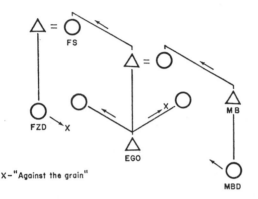

X – "Against the grain"

Figure 35. FZD marriage (Brahman).

But patrilineal descent does not combine harmoniously with hypergamy. For if a man gives his sister with dowry to a superior patrilineage, it has no immediate effect on the status of his own children or patrilineage. For a return on capital expended, he must wait until the next generation and then claim his ZD either for himself or for his own son. This appears to be the picture among the Brahman of Tanjore. The status differences implied by the first marriage are either short circuited by a ZD marriage or are completely reversed by a FZD marriage. In this latter case, therefore, hypergamy has an inherent tendency to turn into symmetrical exchanges, which in turn carry the implication of endogamy. It is noteworthy that this is precisely what we do find among Tanjore Brahman, where the patrilineages exist within the confines of small endogamous circles.

I have argued elsewhere that so far as ritual status is concerned, either kind of unilineal descent or endogamy can serve the purpose of clearly delimiting a category of people. The Brahman evidence suggests that the use of the principles of endogamy does not render the unilineal principle entirely redundant. Given an endogamous circle, patrilineal descent within it, for instance, may enhance one's own status, but again a few patrilineal descent groups can combine to form a smaller endogamous circle within the larger to claim extraordinary

status. The possibilities of these Chinese-box principles are not ex-
hausted until we reach the divine husband-wife pair.

These analytic remarks have a close bearing on the empirical data.
They suggest that where we have particular interest in high status and
ritual purity, we may expect great interest shown in contrapuntal
fashion both in endogamy and in unilineal descent—so much so, indeed, that patronymics and patrilineal pedigrees may be preserved for
many generations and greatly elaborated even when such categories of
people do not necessarily form property-owning or otherwise corporate
groups.

Granted that this question of the role of unilineal descent within
endogamous castes has been analyzed with limited empirical evidence,
the description of Kumbapettai appears to be in line with the above
remarks.

In Kumbapettai, the local Brahman caste segment was divided into
four named "patri-lineages" called *kuttam*. In the past, perhaps fifty
years ago, these lineages had a basis for lineage unity in the fact that
they held joint landed estates (Gough, 1956, p. 829). Today, however,
land is divided and Gough makes it clear that the patronymic group
is not "corporate" in the usual sense of that term (p. 831) even among
Brahman. In so far as the analysis relates to the present position,
Gough's reason for making the "patrilineage" (the unity of the lineage, etc.) the keystone for the kinship system appears to be that
the people have a name and that the group so formed is "exogamous."

We have questioned the "exogamy" of the patronymics elsewhere,
and in this case also it would help analysis to distinguish the systematic marriage rule (and prohibitions) from the issue of "exogamy."
But even if the patronymic units do have sufficient self-awareness to
be "exogamous," it is clear that we are not dealing with a simple case
of corporate and independent patrilineages. In the first place, affinity
is emphasized at the expense of lineal relations, and second, the
patrilineages exist within the framework of a "marriage circle." Gough
reports (1956, p. 829) that Brahman marriages must be confined to an
unnamed endogamous local group—like the Ceylon *variga*—consisting of a small number of villages (ideally eighteen) within a radius of
thirty miles.

The endogamous circle of Kumbapettai Brahman is part of a more
inclusive category called Brahacaranam which in turn is a section of
the broad sect of Smartha Brahman, who in turn are distinguished by
certain criteria from the Ayyangar Brahman. These inclusive endogamous categories are cross-cut by *gotra* clan patronymics. The four
patronymics found in the village are branches of the same clans that
are found among both Smartha and Ayyangar Brahman, even though
effective kinship is confined to the local marriage circle.

We find confirmation, then, both for the underlying pattern of the general structure and for the logical transformations which have been discussed in the previous pages. In the limiting case, we have the patrilineal Brahman using dowry and hypergamy for ritual status within the group, but again operating within the confines of small endogamous kin groups.

FURTHER TAMIL EVIDENCE

Dumont in his important "Hierarchy and Marriage Alliance in South Indian Kinship" (1957b) is concerned mainly with three questions: (1) an examination of Lévi-Strauss's rule on harmonic systems; (2) the description of inherent categories in the Dravidian terminology; (3) the establishment of formal gift exchanges as a reflection of affinity and their diachronic aspect, that is, the inheritance of affinal obligations. Dumont's description is so condensed and the ideas so complicated and novel that it is hardly surprising that this work has not had the recognition it deserves. In fact, it is one of the most original and ambitious attempts to analyze South Indian kinship. It is also one of the very few attempts that have been made to apply comparative data to South Indian kinship. It will be seen that I am in sympathy with Dumont's general position. The analysis of the Ceylon material seems to lead in the same direction. It is all the more important, therefore, to acknowledge the originality of Dumont's views and to stress the significant convergence in our findings.

Perhaps the most important issue is his feeling, pulled out of a skein of tangled evidence, that there is some kind of underlying unity behind all the complex manifestations of patrilineal, matrilineal, bilateral features associated with all kinds of marriage rules. He sees this unity, which he calls the "principle of alliance," as a counterweight to unilineal descent. I call this unity the general structure and go further to say that the feature of descent is not a primary variable at all. The evidence shows that it has a shifting character. Where we have small, fully endogamous groups, it is relegated to a secondary position in the system. Where, however, we have complex groups with hypergamous relations, then the unilineal feature comes to the surface and dominates the nature of the kinship groups, as we have just seen.

Dumont's main line of argument is as follows: he describes some closely related groups in South India; they have in common the fact that they speak the same language and use the same terminology (Dravidian); in all of them, authority in the household goes from father to son; they all disapprove of exchanging sisters in bilateral cross-cousin marriage and they do not permit ZD marriages which are practiced by the higher castes. In our terminology, they all use variants of the general structure.

But despite these common features, they are quite different:

(1) Nangudi Vellalla, a relatively high caste, are matrilocal and matrilineal. The matrilineal exogamous groups are named, and they are subdivided into smaller groups (*pidir*). These latter are sometimes claimed to be patrilineal, but are according to Dumont smaller sections of the exogamous groups. They divide their property into male and female shares: half of it goes from mother to daughter and the other half from father to son. They prefer the patrilateral form of cross-cousin marriage.

(2) Kondaiyam Kottai Maravar are a low caste considered to be killers and dangerous. They are matrilineal, but patrilocal. The matrilineages are recognized to be exogamous, but the local patri-lines are not formulated in exogamy terms. The terminological categories (i.e., parallel cousin sibling terms) forbid marriage inside the local patri-line in de facto fashion, even though there is no de jure formulation of "boundaries" for the group. Dumont distinguishes two subgroups and notes that the marriage rule shifts from patrilateral to bilateral.

(3) Ambalakkarar are also a low caste, probably part of the Kallar. They appear to have no exogamous groups, but they do have patrilocal units called *karei*. Both patrilateral and matrilateral cross-cousin marriage rules are accepted.

(4) Pramalai Kallar are another low caste (Thieves), but at the opposite end of the scale from the Nangudi Vellalla. They are patrilineal and patrilocal and among them we again find clear preferences for matrilateral cross-cousin marriage.

From this complex material Dumont concludes that, with certain important reservations (pp. 22–23), the broad view of Lévi-Strauss regarding unilateral marriage rules in "harmonic systems" tends to be vindicated. It should be observed that Dumont reaches this tentative conclusion after discarding much of the original hypothesis concerning the relations between lineages as such, and that he has had to restrict his conclusions to tiny foci of two or three generations. Even then it is clear that we are provided only the most general "preferences," with no "rules." Moreover, much of Lévi-Strauss's argument regarding status differentiation between bride-givers and receivers on which Leach has laid much stress is hardly brought into the discussion.

From this base, Dumont moves on to an extended analysis regarding the similarities of the various groups he has described. He notes that all use the same kinship terminology. He analyzes the terminology to show the importance of the category of "affines" and how this "affinity" is transmitted from generation to generation. Finally, he demonstrates how the affinity is expressed in the complex customs of gift exchanges.

In one of the most significant passages he demonstrates how in a patrilineal patrilocal context the primary affine is recognized as the MB and the formal gift exchanges are in that direction; in the matrilineal matrilocal context, however, there is no need to reaffirm the bonds with the MB, and it is instead the FS who is singled out for formal attention. (The reader will recall that a similar phenomenon has been described earlier in this book in connection with the Sinhalese and the Muslim Tamils.)

Dumont's conclusion is important: "Whereas the principle of descent and the other features shift and change, the principle of alliance is found everywhere in slightly different forms" (p. 44).

In my opinion, though this is certainly a brilliant analysis, it is not pursued far enough. Dumont never states the direct interconnections between the kinship terms as categories, the cross-cousin marriage rule, the question of alliance and the gift-giving, and so on. The reason for this is that he is still operating with the concept of "exogamous" lineages, which are primary units in the system. It is important to understand that the features of South Indian kinship to which he draws our attention are not intrinsically associated with any lineages at all. On the contrary, the functioning of the system is most clear in systems such as the Sinhalese where the categories of kinship are not submerged in lineal groupings.

We need not return to earlier descriptions. Suffice it to recall that it is the systematic linguistic categories of kinship (the terms of reference) which structure the entire kin circle and specify in an orderly manner marriageable and unmarriageable persons in that universe. What we call cross-cousin marriage is simply a restatement of the rights and obligations inherent in certain categories. There is no lineal emphasis at all, but only rules regarding the interconnections between categories; and it should be noted also that the affines of affines can be distinguished by brother-sister or crossed categories and the rules of the terminology as well as those of behavior also apply to them.

It is precisely on this issue of the effects of the systematic terminology upon kinship behavior that Dumont seems unclear. In a kinship universe without lineal descent rules and without locality restrictions such as the Kandyan, the distinctions of sex and generation may perhaps be made by common-sense impressions, but the systematic differentiation of cross- and parallel-cousins, can only be made and systematically maintained by the reference terminology. Language fully determines these categories and defines those that are marriageable and those that are forbidden. Therefore the complex distinction that Dumont wishes to maintain between "terminological kin" and "terminological affines" is not really necessary. The entire structure is "terminological." We should say simply that the categories of the kinship system define one another. Those other distinctions between "kin" (ourselves) and "affines" (those people) only arise in unilineal contexts.

For this reason again, even though Dumont has sensed the unity of South Indian kinship, I find it difficult to follow his statement that "affinity" is transmitted from generation to generation on the same principles as membership in a "lineage" (1957b, p. 24). There is here a reification of affinity that is confusing. A lineage is a corporate group; affinity consists of relations between persons or groups of persons. What can be transmitted under the guise of "affinity" is again rights and obligations.

What Dumont calls "affinity" I would translate as rights and obligations between brothers and sisters. This permits us to see the mechanism of transfer more clearly. If we consider the claim of the cross-cousins upon each other as marriage partners, we can detect that these claims are part of the claims that a man has over his sister's children and the counterclaims of the sister upon her brother's children. It is the previous claims of the parents which the offspring reiterate as their rights upon each other. Let us further observe that in the South Indian context the claims of the brother on the children of his sister are simply a further statement of his claims upon her person. The brother has an important voice in the marriage of the sister, because her marriage has important side effects upon his status; it also brings in as part of the closed endogamous circle a person (cross-cousin) with whom he will have to cooperate.

In figure 36, for example, the claims of X upon Y do not arise out of the "transmission of affinity" from X's father, B. They are the claims of a upon A and A's children, which are being restated. Similarly, the claims of Y upon X do not concern the previous connection

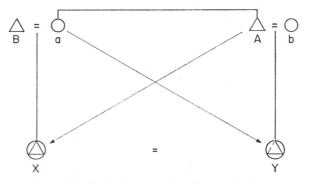

Figure 36. Claims between brothers and sisters.

of the group with B; they are the claims A has upon *a* and her children being expressed by A's children. It is these claims of the brothers and sisters upon each other which are the fundamental principle Dumont has detected as the common background in South Indian kinship. I am concerned neither with debunking the role of the "alliance" nor with defending the "principle of the unity of siblings," but merely with examining this idea of the "transfer of affinity" from generation to generation. Notice, however, that this formulation permits us to understand the formal customary background of a sister's daughter marriage mentioned in connection with the Brahman. That type of marriage is simply a tightening of the claims in accordance with the emphasis on endogamy and hypergamy in the Brahman caste. A description of the claims between brothers and sisters explains what appears to be a curious phenomenon much more adequately than Dumont's recourse to the "inheritance" of affinity.

To return to general issues: Dumont must be given credit for having detected the uniformity in some fundamental features of South Indian kinship systems, but he has expressed the matter still in lineal terms as an opposition between "kin" and "affines." I suggest that uniformity is better explained in terms of kin categories and the fundamental claims of the brothers and sisters upon each other. This is the reason why we find a centripetal tendency so clearly at work in South India. Smaller and smaller circles of endogamy form purer and purer circles of kin who may be permitted to claim—at least in their own minds—higher ritual status. This also explains the curious aversion, even among the humblest caste, against "mixtures" in their pedigrees.

Our formulation of South Indian kinship draws attention to the shifting character of descent. On the basis of a very similar kin structure, different groups operate various descent preferences: even within the same caste we find some who choose patrilineal descent and some who choose matrilineal descent as distinctive characteristics. It should be clear that the important kin groups are the circles—*curru*—noted by Karve, Banks ("sondakara castes"), and others. Descent is sometimes so secondary that, as Dumont observes, succession and inheritance run counter to descent ideas in numerous castes (1957*b*, p. 20). I would suggest that we have in these low castes a Kandyan preference based on endogamy and bilateral kinship. We shall see, when we turn toward the Malabar coast, that with the development of matrilineal descent, hypergamy again makes its unmistakable appearance.

THE MALABAR COAST

In our consideration of South Indian kinship systems we have been concerned, first, to detect an underlying pattern for the bewilderingly complex, contradictory, and difficult material collected by many authors, and, second, to test the Ceylon model of the association of hypergamy with unilineal descent. It will be recalled that Gough's Kumbapettai village seemed to include the variations in kinship found dispersed over a large area in Ceylon. On the Malabar coast, the situation is, if possible, made even more complicated: in this famous region we find every possible variation of our model, from matrilineal hypergamous systems to endogamous and patrilineal hypergamous systems, all existing pell-mell in the same area. In general, it seems clear that these various features are used as structural indices to distinguish communities from one another. The over-all pattern, by contrast, seems uncluttered: in lower levels of social rank we find, on the whole, endogamous castes which so far as the material goes exhibit the fundamental characteristics of the general structure. In the higher levels of Hindu and Muslim society we find an intense preoccupation with status and social rank, and unilineal descent systems are built out of the general structure. Then, in the limiting cases, each matrilineage behaves as if it were a single unique caste having only hypergamous connections with the outside world.

In this section, I shall first attempt to establish the existence of the general structure in castes in both North and South Malabar, and I shall then go on to examine the questions of descent and hypergamy. Before we come to specific cases, I should observe that the region exhibits an impressive general cultural uniformity: the language, Malayalam, is very closely related to Tamil; the details of the customs find immediate echoes not only in the material from the rest of South India but among Buddhists in Ceylon as well. Quite apart from structural matters, there is an intuitive appreciation of the fact that we are in a civilization with a distinctive style of its own in which the different customs of discrete groups appear as permutations and combinations of the same set of general ideas.

The term Nayar covers a motley collection of categories of people. Primarily, they are aristocratic Nayar descended from the important royal houses of Cochin and Travancore. There are also people of servant castes who have allegedly taken on the Nayar title in the last century and are only Nayar by courtesy. Some of these categories may be fully endogamous and others, at the higher levels, hypergamous. Though there are again uniformities, it is important to specify which group of Nayar are being considered. The word *taravad*, used by various castes in Malabar, denotes a group of matrilineally related persons with the same name who observe rules of exogamy. The *taravad* may be split into smaller property-holding groups, each with a head *Karanavan*.[7]

---

[7] "One who 'acts' ": comp. *Karanava,* "to do" in Sinhalese.

NORTH NAYAR

Anthropological investigations in Malabar have usually gone straight
to the most spectacular cases: the matrilineal Nayar *taravad* of
Cochin and Travancore. This tendency, though understandable, is
hardly justified, since the matrilineal *taravad* achieves its greatest
elaboration among the aristocratic ranks of the ruling families and
can hardly be accepted as a typical feature of the landscape.

It should be clear that today there is great variation in practice
among the Nayar groups in Malabar, not only from the aristocrats to
the low-caste menials (who like to call themselves Nayar) but also
within the same Nayar "subcastes." In an illuminating passage, Karve
(1953), for example, notes how many individual Nayar feel that they
should lay the foundations for a new *taravad* in their sister's name as
soon as they can afford to do so, for a named matrilineal *taravad* is
clearly an important aspect of status for Nayar men. Gough (1952a)
has used a historical model to deal with the variations. She argues, in
effect, that the past was orderly and the present is confused. Theory
and practice were harmonious in the past but are now breaking down.
The tempo of new developments, political, economic, social, can
hardly be denied, but we can suggest that the past idealized by Gough
may well have been as diverse (in terms of the structure of matrilineal
taravad) as the present. It is likely that there always were nascent,
medium-sized, and fully developed *taravad* based on the same principles.

We shall examine the aristocratic Nayar lineages in a moment. In
North Malabar, the *taravad* is significantly different from the region
around the Cochin kingdoms. In the North, there was apparently less
political centralization and a relatively limited development of subcategories of Nayar castes with special duties. Most of the Nayar were
called Nambiar and were small landowners who lived in villages.
They recognized dispersed matrilineal clans, and the property group
in the locality was regarded as a segment of such a clan.

At marriage the girl moved to the household of her husband, but
she returned temporarily to her natal household to bear her children
(a custom still followed among the Sinhalese). The children when
grown went to their MB; the males stayed with the MB as members of
matri-lines and the females were married off from that house.

Here, clearly, are the complex claims on the sister and her children.
I need hardly point out that all aspects of the general structure are
to be seen in their organization. First, the usual Dravidian terminology
was used for reference (Schneider and Gough, 1961, p. 404). A clear
distinction was made between the categories for reference and the

terms of address. Related to this Dravidian terminology we find, as might be expected, that all parallel cousins on both sides are forbidden as sexual partners and consequently there is categorical cross-cousin marriage (p. 397). We are not given any details regarding the circle of kin which we have called the micro-caste, for Gough is again more concerned with "lineages." However, it is quite clear that all the kinship customs, especially the obligations between the various categories of kin, appear very similar to the Sinhalese.

The categories of the terminology are widely extended and relations with paternal kin are formally defined. The son, for instance, must make annual offerings to his dead father's spirit. "Paternal kin are known and accorded kinship terms within a range of three to five generations" (Gough, 1955a, p. 55). The father's sister's son was considered to have special claims on the girl (Schneider and Gough, 1961, p. 398).

It is noteworthy that with the residence pattern in which men live on lineage land with their MB, it is precisely the rights of the paternal kin that are emphasized in customary rituals. Thus paternal kin have an important place in all *rites de passage:* first pregnancy, naming, first rice feeding, *tali*-tying, marriage, first menstruation, and death. At the naming ceremony, for instance, the infant's father's mother chooses the name, the father's father confers it, and the father gives a gold gift (Schneider and Gough, 1961, p. 401).

These rights and obligations are of interest in contrast to the Sinhalese, where residence tends to be patrilocal and where it is, in fact, the claims of the maternal kin that are given the most prominence in the various life-cycle ceremonies.

We should observe that even the joking relationship, which is an interesting feature of the Sinhalese cross-cousin relationship, is duplicated in North Malabar: "Male and female cross cousins had a joking relationship with implicit sexual privileges." And, of course, marriage was initiated with the "gift of the cloth."

So far as the general structure is concerned, there is little doubt as to where we are. However, we are not given much information regarding endogamy and hypergamy. Gough notes only incidentally that "ordinary" Nambiars . . . married exclusively with each other" (1955a, p. 56), which suggests kin group endogamy with a likely diminution of unilineal descent ideology in such groups. Gough elsewhere also observes in passing that there were "hypergamous marriages in aristocratic lineages" (1961, p. 400), which conforms to the idea expressed above. Since the pattern can be seen with greater clarity in the evidence regarding the Cochin aristocrats, I refrain from discussing the question of hypergamy here.

NORTH TIYYAR

The organization of kinship among the Tiyyar is so similar to the Nayar castes that an extended discussion is unnecessary. Gough observes a difference of degree in the question of the locality of marriage: whereas Nayar men may return to the lands of their MB and marry there, the Tiyyar tend to be grouped together in patrilocal clusters, except that there are some among them who also return to live with their MB (1961, p. 409). These slight differences are unlikely to be of great significance, for the reader should recall that many of these marriages take place in the same village or area, that in this region houses and huts are easy to build and that Nayar men tend to build houses for their wives and children as well.

In Gough's writings the similarity of the kin structure between the Tiyyar and the Sinhalese is particularly evident. The claims of the cross-cousins upon each other, the categorical Dravidian terminology, the nature of the marriage tie, and the various details of custom clearly indicate that we are dealing with the same cultural idiom.

The claims of the MB and FZ are manifested in *rites de passage*. In the *tali* ceremony (which is the well-known prepuberty rite in this area) both these persons appear, and the FZ (or MB wife) ties the *tali* as a "potential mother-in-law" (Gough, 1955a, p. 58).

The role of the cross-cousins is perhaps more revealing. "The cross-cousin's claim to become a girl's husband . . . must be met at the . . . marriage ceremony if the girl marries some other man. As the couple leave the house, the girl's cross-cousin steps forward in mock attack . . . He is bought off by the bridegroom with a nominal fee and the couple then pass unmolested" (Gough, 1955a, p. 59).[8] This symbolic statement is identical to the Sinhalese, where the cross-cousin stops the bridal couple at the gate and demands his rights. He is given one hundred betel leaves and the couple moves on.

The Tiyyar of Cochin

It is intriguing to study the kin structure of the Tiyyar caste South Malabar and Cochin—the same term as in North Malabar—which

---

[8] There is an interesting contradiction in Gough's materal: though she writes of the similarity of the Nayar and the Tiyyar, she notes that with the Tiyyar the MBS (i.e., FZD) is the correct marriage partner (1955a, p. 57), whereas with the Nayar the FZS (i.e., MBD) is considered the rightful claimant (1961, p. 398). In view of Dumont's discussion, it would be interesting to know whether significant preferences are involved. Gough does not pursue the matter, but given the contradictions involved in patrilateral cross-cousin marriage (e.g., it cannot be combined with hypergamy rules) it is likely that Gough is merely using a shorthand formula for symmetrical cross-cousin marriage.

here turns out to be patrilineal and patrilocal. We shall see that, as usual, the question of descent is attached to the same general structures as elsewhere.

We first note that the "patrilineage" of the South is called a *taravad* like the matrilineal units of the Nayar. The patrilineage is reported to be exogamous with a depth of five to seven generations united by the worship of lineage gods, ancestors, and snakes. Marriage tends to be patrilocal, and one of the interesting features of the Tiyyar of this area is that, as with the Sinhalese, polyandrous marriages are freely permitted. A woman is married to a group of brothers who have access to her, it is said, by order of seniority. The ceremony of marriage again involves the gift of the cloth, and we note the custom of feeding the groom or grooms and the bride with porridge and milk as with various groups in Ceylon.

Inheritance is in the male line, but women retain rights in their natal household. Indeed, this right is expressed in the customary relations between brothers and sisters. At divorce, the woman returns to her brother. Her eldest brother is considered her guardian. At the death of a married woman, her brothers and their children observe ritual pollution. At the death of a man, his sister's sons observe pollution and perform mourning offerings to his spirit.

The customary claim of the MB and the FZ are given recognition in numerous ceremonies. In the prepuberty rituals, a girl goes through a mock-marriage ceremony with a boy from a "lineage" into which she might marry, who clearly stands to her in the relation of cross-cousin. Her "mother's brother's wife" (FZ?) parts her hair in certain pregnancy ceremonies. The ritual husband-boy is brought by his MB, and the girl by her MB. The boy places the *tali* necklace—indicative of married status—on her neck, where it is tied by her FZ.

Gough notes that cross-cousin marriage is "preferential," though with the observation that it is not "enjoined to the extent" that it is in the North (1955*a*, p. 62). It is clear that this statement refers to actual cross-cousin, not categorical cross-cousin, marriage. We are informed that parallel cousins on both sides are tabooed and must conclude that here again we have the Dravidian pattern of categorical cross-cousin marriage.

I have no information about the terminology of reference or address, though it seems likely that terms of reference, at least, are identical to those of the North Tiyyar.

I think that all the elements of the general structure can be detected in this system. There is categorical cross-cousin marriage, and the various claims of the MB and FZ upon Ego are indicated in ritual terms. This is quite in accordance, as we noted before, with the strong claim of the brothers and sisters upon one another, a point which is indeed specifically made by Gough (1955a, p. 61).

In view of all this evidence, it is somewhat disconcerting to discover that Gough finds it necessary to identify "residual matrilineages" to explain the role of maternal kin as well as the taboos on maternal parallel cousins in this caste. We are faced once more with the inexplicable bias in the direction of "lineage" explanations to the exclusion of others even in so sophisticated an observer as Dr. Gough.

She notes (1957a, p. 61) that "the former existence of exogamous matrilineal clans underlines this persistence of the bond between women and their natal kinfolk, especially their brothers." But the evidence she gives (p. 60) to show even the former existence of such clans is hardly convincing: "My informants knew nothing about these clans except that they were once exogamous. They are not so today, since some people do not remember their clan names. Though the clans have died out, marriage is prohibited between known matrilineal kin."

Although the general structure is verified in this group as well, we have no information regarding hypergamy. We can only say with certainty that the comparison of the Tiyyar in North and South Malabar shows quite directly that slight variations permit the general structure to be linked to a patrilineal as well as a matrilineal descent ideology. The underlying theme is general, and the variations in descent, in residence, in inheritance are local and highly specific.

THE MATRILINEAL CASTES OF COCHIN AND HYPERGAMY

Before we turn to an examination of the aristocratic matrilineages of Cochin which have fascinated many anthropologists by their perfectly logical but highly exotic solutions to sex and marriage, I wish to underline some of the principles of endogamy and hypergamy.

First, the purpose of endogamy is to cut off the unit from kinship connections with other units. A complete severance of all intercourse (food and sex are usually chosen as symbols) renders the unit unique, but it will not in itself establish hierarchical superiority. To express hierarchy (as well as separation) some asymmetrical relations are logically necessary. In endogamous castes this takes the form of asymmetrical forms of address, dress symbolism, and, significantly, a rule such as "They will take food from us (A), but we will not take food from them (B)—A, in other words, is superior to B.

Second, when the groups are placed on an interlocking hierarchy, more subtle expressions can be used. "A will not accept food from B, but *B* will from *A*; furthermore, *A* will not 'give' women to *B*, but will 'take' women from *B*." The second method (hypergamy), though only a logical development of the first, and a very precise way of manifesting superior status, has complex implications. In effect, a progressive distinction of status is made between the children of the sister (superior) and the children of the brother (inferior). Hence not merely the caste but the entire network of kinship is placed on a gradient of ritual status. Furthermore, if hypergamy is to be combined with lineages, it should be clear that, although the matter can be harmoniously combined with matrilineages (i.e., the brother partaking of the superior ritual connections of his sister), the patrilineal principles raise difficult problems, since the sister is given "away" to a superior group and the brothers can partake in the increase in ritual status only by reason of their claims on her children or in some other indirect fashion. Also, since the position of the woman affects the status of her children in both matrilineal and patrilineal contexts, it appears difficult to combine intracaste hypergamy with patrilineal descent at least in South India. Thus we get ZD marriage (i.e., symmetrical exchange) coupled with Brahman caste endogamy in Tanjore, but an entire scale of hypergamous matrilineages all the way from Kshatriya to Sudra status in Malabar. A similar feature was observed in eastern Ceylon.

The first method (endogamy) permits the ethnographer to make simple statements about discrete categories of people; the second (hypergamy) is more complex, since the status-bearing unit can be a single lineage with hypergamous connections and it may be difficult in the continuous descending steps of status to say exactly where one "caste" category ends and the next begins (see fig. 37).

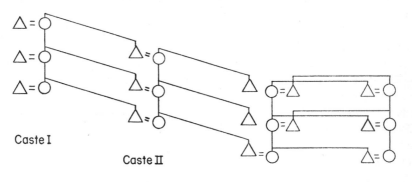

Caste I

Caste II

Caste III

Patrilineal   Matrilineal

Figure 37. Patrilineal and matrilineal hypergamy.

Let us now return to the facts:

The Nayar family in Cochin and South Malabar (also referred to as Central Kerala) is also organized on the principles of the matrilineal *taravad*. Among ordinary people, matrilineal groups beyond the household are barely recognized for most intents and purposes, but among the wealthy and aristocratic classes, the *taravad* finds an impressive elaboration. Gough presents the ideal model as a matrilineal clan with localized matri-lines all of which are exogamous. The women have equal or hypergamous connections with men of other *taravad* or castes, whereas the men visit women of lower *taravad*. The residential pattern is that brothers and sisters live in the same household and men visit their "wives" in their own households. This contrasts with the North Nayar picture in which women join their husbands in their houses, and with the Mapilla picture (their Muslim neighbors) in which the men join their wives in the houses as in Ceylon. Of course, in a climate and region where houses are easily built and where the kin of both the husband and the wife are quite likely to be in the near vicinity of the married couple, if not in the same community, these residential arrangements may be looked upon primarily as symbolic statements of "difference" rather than fundamental differences in kinship systems and sentiments.

We may now raise further questions:

First: to what extent does our previous discussion of the general structure help us to understand the Nayar situation? A careful examination of the data makes it clear that the Nayar family in Cochin and South Malabar presents a further elaboration upon the Dravidian theme. It should be emphasized that this is hardly the impression one would have received from the earlier work of Gough. It is curious to observe, as Dumont (1961a) does, to what extent Gough's picture of the Nayar situation has progressively altered from one in which there were matrilineages with hardly any recognition of the role of the *pater,* to one in which the father and his kin are recognized and "preferential" cross-cousin marriage is at least observed. The change in point of view is a sobering thought as far as "objective" anthropology is concerned: for a perusal of the writings of this highly observant and careful author shows that she is using an African model (including concepts of clanship and ties of ritual collaboration) in her earlier work. It is only very gradually that she comes around to consider her material in its context in South India.

As far as we can observe, the kin terminology of the high-caste Nayar of Cochin and South Malabar is structurally identical to that of North Malabar and hence to the Dravidian terminology of cross-cousin marriage, with one significant difference: there appears to be no term for actual cross-cousins. It is true that Gough does not provide

a consistent terminology of reference—which is important in South
India and Ceylon—but since the language and indeed all the rest of
the terms themselves are identical to those of North Malabar, the lack
of terms precisely for cross-cousins may be significant. The matter is
all the more curious since such terms as, for example, *maru mahan*
(son "by marriage"!)[9] which Ego uses for ZS in the same *taravad*
and which reciprocates with MB (*mama*) also carry the implication
"son-in-law" and "father-in-law."

However we may wish to interpret this intriguing lacuna (could it
be an aspect of Nambudiri–Nayar hypergamy?), it appears that there
is, first, a prohibition on sexual and marital connections with parallel
cousins and also a "preference" for cross-cousin marriage. Both rules
are clearly present, though they do not carry the categorical implication which is attached to them elsewhere.

Gough's account of this matter is not very clear. She notes first
(1961, p. 365): "Bilateral cross-cousin marriage was freely permitted,
with some preference for marriage to the mother's brother's daughter
or step-daughter." A little further on she notes the "preference" in
passing: "It may seem strange that preferred cross-cousin marriage
should have existed side by side with group marriage, for cross-cousin
marriage . . . suggests an interest in prolonging the ties brought
about both by paternity and by matrilineal kinship."

It seems to me that even in her most recent publication Gough is
trying to minimize the role of paternity among the Nayar when the
facts are palpably otherwise. She notes, "Many men, presumably,
entered marriage relations with cross-cousins only incidentally—often,
presumably, without being fully aware of the blood relationship"
(1961, p. 365)—a presumption which seems extremely unlikely even
in the Malabar conditions she describes.

We should perhaps stress that Gough's data suggest much closer
similarities to a South Indian pattern than her theoretical framework
permits. Consider the customary relations between cross-cousins:
"Cross-cousins of the same sex and caste had a familiar, mildly joking
relationship if they maintained contact . . . cross-cousins of the opposite sex might talk to each other with rather more freedom than to
unrelated persons. In his role of enangan a boy sometimes tied the
tali for his maternal uncle's daughter . . ." (1961, pp. 364–365).

We should note this last sentence particularly: the role of *enangan*
as a cross-cousin and hence a perpetual affine on the Dravidian pattern
is a new development in the work of Gough. It confirms our impression that even in Cochin where the *taravad* reaches its greatest development, a version of the general structure is still visible. The question
of "perpetual affinity" has been discussed extensively by Dumont

---

[9] See the discussions of *maru* by Karve (1953, p. 213) and by Dumont (1957a).

(1961*b*, pp. 20 ff.), and it is important in tying the Nayar material into the South Indian picture.

With all these similarities, in what sense, then, is this system a logical elaboration of the general structure? What makes the structure of kinship among the aristocratic Nayar a special case is that in it we find again the combination of hypergamy and unilineal descent.

As we noted above, extensive hypergamy in the context of matrilineage results in a consistent differentiation of status between lineages, and it allows special ritual status to be claimed by each autonomous matrilineage. It will be observed that matrilateral cross-cousin marriage is the only consistent pattern that can be associated with the hypergamous and matrilineal kin structure described above.

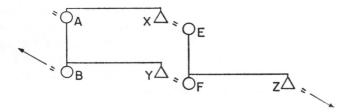

Figure 38. Matrilateral cross-cousin marriage.

In figure 38, sister A establishes a *sambandam* connection with a person of superior status. Her children, B and Y (members of the matrilineage), are themselves superior in status to the children of their MB (X), who has a *sambandam* with a woman of equal or lower status to himself (E). Hence if cross-cousin marriage is to take place, the MBD (F) may be hypergamously connected with Y (i.e., matrilateral cross-cousin marriage), but B, like her mother A, will be given further up the hierarchy and cannot be permitted to have *sambandam* with Z (i.e., patrilateral cross-cousin marriage).

We should note in passing that this association of MBD marriage and hypergamy in these castes is a remarkable corroboration of Leach's hypothesis regarding the structural implications of matrilateral cross-cousin marriage systems. Leach (1951) writes of patrilineal systems associated with hypogamy (women go down) among the Kachin. It is certainly salutary to find that this mirror-image of Leach's model, that is, matrilateral cross-cousin marriage in a matrilineal context, is associated with hypergamy, asymmetry, and distinctions of status.

To return to Malabar, the combination of matrilineal descent together with the rules of hypergamy is consistent with great differentiation of status between the descent groups—so much so that in the proliferation of descent groups it appears to be difficult, indeed impossible, to say where one caste ends and the other begins. Some descent groups may be generally placed in the highest categories and still be connected by a chain of descending unions with such categories as the Sudra. To recall the situation in Ceylon, such groups as the Karava (Fishers), who are usually seen as a "separate" caste in other parts of the island, are associated with the hierarchy of Vellalar matrilineal descent groups on the eastern littoral. Thus, in the Malabar context, too, a category such as Nayar covers a wide spectrum of ranked descent groups. Gough suggests that apart from the royal matrilineages of the various kingdoms, it is possible to detect five subcategories of Nayar groups (1961, pp. 308–309): *(a)* Kiriattil and Vellayma Nayar, *(b)* Puratta Charna (Outdoor Retainers) Nayar (but these have subdivisions such as Pariccha Menon (Leaders of the Shield), *(c)* Agatta Charna (Indoor Retainers) Nayar, *(d)* Pallichan Nayar, and *(e)* Sudra Nayar. This is not a hard and fast hierarchy and we are told (p. 309) that "In some districts they ranked in the order given and men of the higher [category] might marry women of the lower [category]; the reverse was in theory forbidden. In other districts the [categories] seem to have disputed for precedence and *not to have regularly intermarried*" (my italics).

It is clear that in this system it is possible, for instance, to have at the top a single matrilineage whose men may be connected to a small group of matrilineages who are equals and who marry among themselves. They in turn may be connected with a larger group of matrilineages of a still lower caste, and so on. Furthermore, actual *sambandam* connections may or may not be systematically established between the levels. As long as the principles are clear, it hardly matters what the status-bearing groups are called: in widening circles we have the matrilineage, which may be part of a hypergamous cluster (category), which in turn may be part of a more inclusive "subcaste" or indeed an endogamous caste.

Also in the Cochin region, according to Gough (1961, p. 319), hypergamy is a custom of the aristocratic matrilineages and is associated with the prestige of unilineal descent, whereas in the levels "below the Nayar temple menials" the categories were endogamous "as is usual in the caste system throughout India."

Why hypergamy at the aristocratic levels? Gough in answer to this question has taken a curious combination of materialist-psychoanalytic arguments: it is her theory that hypergamy accords with the power structure of the political system and with the special reasons why virgins must be deflowered by powerful men before they are safe for ordinary mortals (see Gough 1955a and 1961, *passim*).

Dumont has proposed an important, but very different, answer. He notes rightly that the most powerful and superior Nayar lineage still had hypergamous connections with Brahman who were ritually superior but politically inferior to the royal lineages. This would indicate that the arguments emanating from the power structure are of limited value. Nor does the psychoanalytic argument carry conviction (see Yalman, 1963).

Dumont further suggests that the Nayar position has significant cultural affinities to certain practices of the Basavi. Among the Basavi, a girl is given in marriage to a god. She may then be approached by all kinds of men, and the children she may bear belong to her own family. Thus by virtue of her marriage to a god, her children are freed from the constraints of the rule of patrilineal descent and follow matrilineal descent. In the same fashion, Dumont thinks the girls of aristocratic matrilineages are married to Nambudiri Brahman, who are referred to as "Gods of the Earth."

Dumont's point is worth making, for it shows the element of piety involved in these customs which have been severely misunderstood in India and elsewhere. The man of the matrilineage sacrifices his own children (who belong to others) in order to give his sister to a god and keep her children.

This may indeed be one of the cultural dimensions of hypergamy in this region, but the system is so clearly and effectively associated with the fundamental structural principles of matrilineal descent groups in a caste context that the specific cultural features (piety, etc.) do not need to be treated as a necessary part of the picture. A similar set of structural circumstances gives rise to an essentially similar picture in Ceylon.

The general principles of status differentiation in Cochin have been subsumed under the following ideal formula by Karve (1953, p. 269):

Nambudiri m.	marries	Nambudiri f.	Children	become	Nambudiri
Nambudiri m.	=	Ksatriya f.	Children	=	Kshatriya
Ksatriya m.	=	Ksatriya f.	Children	=	non-Kshatriya [sic.]
Nambudiri m.	=	Nayar f.	Children	=	Nayar, status 1
Ksatriya m.	=	Nayar f.	Children	=	Nayar, status 2
Nayar m.	=	Nayar f.	Children	=	Nayar, status 3

It is quite clear that we find the matrilineal *taravad* in its most impressive development as a corporation precisely at the highest levels of society. At the other end of the scale we have only the desire for prestige:

The Tharvad is always named after an ancestress and referred to as the Tharvad of so and so (woman). If a man does not belong to a Tharvad he is not respected and I was told by an officer in a mill that though he was well educated and a salaried man he had not the requisite social position as

they were landless orphans. If he bought land, built a house and settled there
with his sister, bringing up her children, he would gain social status. He said
he knew of many a poor labourer serving in the mill, saving money to establish a Tharvad in his sister's name and become "somebody" in his caste.
(Karve, 1953, p. 267)

The problem of finding suitable husbands for the women of aristocratic matrilineal Tharvads has been solved by the Nambudiri Brahman connection in Cochin. The situation is not very different with
North Malabar aristocrats. We are told that the Kolattiri lineage had
difficulty in getting accepted as of high status among the ancient
"Kshatriya" lineages of Kottayam and Kurumbranad, so the Kolattiri
Rajas brought a caste called Koil Tamburan from Travancore. "Kolattiri women married Koil Tamburan or Nambudiri men and Kolattiri
men Samantan Nambiar or Nambiar women" (Gough, 1955a, p. 56).

Karve with her usual insight and evocative examples puts the issue
simply (1953, pp. 258–259): "The Kshatriyas claim descent from the
sun-family of the ancient Hindu Kshatriyas of the north—the house
of Rama. All the sons born in Kshatriya families, i.e., ruling houses
of Travancore and Cochin have Sanskrit names of the Sun-god with
the suffix varmā . . . We have already seen that in olden times as a
rule and even now generally the Kshatriya women have Nambudiri
Brahmins as husbands. . . . There is a village near Cochin belonging
to a rich Nayar Thārvad . . . which is called the 'village of evening
visits of the Nambudris.' " And this accurate and colorful picture is
rounded up with the direct statement, "Among poorer Nayars cross-
cousin marriage is favoured."

Other Evidence from Malabar

We have considered the evidence from Malabar from the point of
view of other South Indian systems and have, I believe, been able to
establish both the principles of the general structure and the association of systems of hypergamy with unilineal descent. A further point
to note is that systems of descent, at least in this region, could be
considered as a secondary feature to a large extent independent of
the specific forms of kinship and marriage. Very similar groups appear
to follow different forms of descent in various regions. We should
recall that even the Sinhalese, who are regarded as being "patrilineal"
by many authors today, followed "matrilineal" descent at least among
the royal family in the seventeenth century. And conversely one author
has noted that in some parts of Kerala "the Nairs also follow the
father right social system" (D'Souza, 1959, p. 493).

There is a vast body of literature, especially in connection with

Malabar, in which patrilineal and matrilineal castes who are similar in their kinship customs are described, and again we find that other sections of the same casts are patrilineal or matrilineal in different localities. In parts of Ceylon I would hear villagers suggest that sons took their "names" from their father and daughters from their mother, a reflection not so much of descent (for these ideas were not applied in practice) but of the difference between the sexes.

Even the Muslims are not very different. On the Malabar coast the diversity of origins in the Muslim community can be easily traced in the complex body of customs, appellations, different signs, and practice whereby subgroups appear to distinguish one another. Gough (1961) has discussed some features of the matrilineal Muslims (Mapilla); D'Souza (1959) in a carefully documented article observes that, leaving aside a special group who call themselves *Arabi* and attempt to follow traditional Islam, Muslims in general conform to the patterns of kinship usual in Malabar and are divided into patrilineal and matrilineal *taravads* (p. 492). Moreover, in the case of patrilineal *taravads*, several of them again come together to form an *endogamous* group; hence in any locality there are several endogamous Moplah groups (p. 493). He goes on to make the following observation (p. 498):

In the coastal North Malabar, as one proceeds southwards to places like Quilandy and Badagara, the mother right social organization undergoes a change. The change becomes quite distinct in the coastal region of South Malabar. The change in mother right traits . . . may be primarily attributed to the fact that whereas in North Malabar the ancestral property is inherited exclusively in the female line, in the south it is inherited . . . in the male line. But the social organization is essentially mother right and the modifications are such as suit the change in the principle of inheritance.

It is not merely this shifting picture of descent and inheritance which strikes one as being entirely in line with the material collected by Iyer (1909, 1912, 1937) in all kinds of small caste groups, for D'Souza (1959, p. 502) firmly establishes that the Muslim Mapilla also follow the Nambudiri–Nayar model of hypergamy with considerable dedication: "For instance, the Thangal males can marry women from any other groups of Moplahs [Mapilla] but Thangal women cannot marry any man other than a Thangal. An Arabi male can marry any [Mapilla] woman other than a Thangal, but the Arabi woman can marry, besides an Arabi male, only a Thangal male, and so on."

There is little doubt that the marriage customs recorded by D'Souza bear a close similarity to those recorded for the Moors of Ceylon earlier in this volume. D'Souza's evidence on names is not directed to the question of hypergamy and prestige, but it does appear that names are perpetuated as indices of status—to the extent, indeed, that with the matrilineal Thangal group, who also claim patrilineal descent from the Prophet, an elaborate combination of patronymics and matronymics has been developed (1959, p. 501).

CONCLUSION

In view of the great number of communities that have remained untouched, the evidence considered in detail may seem to offer only a very narrow theoretical base. This is not so. We have attempted to show that the general structural model may be connected to a great variety of descent patterns. Only a few cases would be sufficient to demonstrate the point. We have found many more. We have also noted the interesting balance in the customary recognition given to the formal claims of the paternal and maternal relatives upon the children of the marriage. In structures such as the Tanjore Brahman, where the father-son relationship is assured by common residence and inheritance, it is precisely the rights of the MB which are elaborated at all *rites de passage,* and the ZS has formal obligations at this man's funeral.

In the matrilineal structure of Malabar and Ceylon we find in contrast that the great proliferation of ceremonial is concerned with the rights and obligations of the father. Quite apart from the entire complex of *Tali kettu kalyanam* in Malabar, we may note that the obligations of the son at this father's funeral receive special emphasis, particularly among the Nayar. As Fawcett notes in connection with Nayar funerals: "The deceased's younger brother, or, if there is none surviving, his nephew (his sister's eldest son) sets fire to the pyre at the head of the corpse. If the deceased left a son, this son sets fire at the same time to the pyre at the foot of the corpse" (Thurston, 1906, p. 209). At this most solemn occasion the Nayar and the Kandyan Sinhalese agree on balancing the obligations of the offspring of brother and sister, for with the Sinhalese, too, the ZS as well as the son must partake in the final rites of a man.

There is always the emphasis on the connections between the children of the brother and the sister. Brother and sister must be separated, but their offspring must also be united. Dumont writes of the double principles of consanguinity and affinity, but it seems that the two must be intermeshed to protect and perpetuate the purity of the family. Perhaps this is an aspect of the union of those divine creative principles which one hears so much about in Indian philosophy: male and female, man and wife, the Brahman Lord and his consort, Shiva and Shakti. These are two, but they are also one.

Even the terminology of kinship exemplifies the idea of the union of the two principles in one. Thus, such terms as *massina* (Sinh. and Tamil) and its variants *maittunan* or *maccinan* (Tamil) and *maiduna* (Kannada), all of which carry the implication of cross-cousins who are expected to unite, appear to be derived from the Sanskrit *maiduna* or *mithuna* which also refers to the sexual intercourse between the god Shiva and the goddess Shakti, who are both one and two.[10] The depiction of them in the very act of union (*mithuna*) is one of the intriguing motifs in Indian religious sculpture, a form of art which in its formal beauty and religious expressiveness is almost unmatched.

These ideas are not intended to be mysterious. They are simply the logical implications of caste principles carried to their very limit in the highest caste. There should be no doubt at all that Indian thinkers, great logicians and great mystics, should have been concerned with the ultimate origin of purity.[11]

A conception such as this, the union of man and wife, who are also the children of a brother and sister, allows us to observe the principle of *jati* ("caste," but also birth, category) from the inside. The narrowest circle is the individual. Then the couple, ideally cross-cousins. Then the small circle of kin who intermarry with one another. And going on from this, wider and wider concentric circles and the more inclusive categories of caste. The patterns of North India are likely to be different, but the principles of caste endogamy are intimately related to the family in South India and Ceylon.

Our itinerary has now been completed. We started from a mountain village in Ceylon and widening our investigations have ended up in South India. Behind the great differences in thought and behavior, we have found that the general principles of kinship appear to have considerable uniformity in this region. Ostensibly, kinship systems can be classified as matrilineal, patrilineal, hypergamous, and bilateral in Ceylon: a rapid journey through the Tamil-speaking parts, the Nilgiri Hills, and the Malabar coast has made us aware that a similar classification is possible in South India. But all these variations appear to exist within the framework of principles common to all the groups we have considered.

It is to be hoped that it will be possible in the future to carry the work farther north in order to learn whether South Indian structures are transformed into North Indian structures. In the realm of kin structure in South India and Ceylon, we appear to be dealing with

---

[10] On the etymology of the terms see Karve (1953), p. 209.

[11] It seems possible that one of the simplest and most frequent ritual acts in Ceylon and South India—the splitting of a coconut into two and allowing the liquid inside to run out—may be a part of *mithuna* symbolism. For the coconut has a *male* and a *female* end: in the act the male and the female are split. This is an idea of wide prevalence in Ceylonese ritual; see Yalman (1966).

the dialects of a common language. It is curious that principles of social organization should take us back to systems of communication.

I do not wish to reify the principles of South Indian kinship into something distinct from certain categories of thought and certain patterns of behavior. In all our work there is always this curious dialectic between the fact and the idea, between action and thought, between constructs of the mind and the activities of men. But both sides of the dialectic can be regarded as emanating from the same traditional "structure" behind both the thought and the act. It is noteworthy to observe how the form of the "structure" varies in a given region like the dialects of a language. Yet the variations appear as logical permutations of a limited set of principles. Again like language, the principles are clearly not embedded in the utilitarian particularities of specific social systems. They appear to be certain fundamental principles of organization which are behind the various manifestations of specific social patterns. In this sense what we call "social structure" corresponds to a grammar which relates the activities of individuals to one another and makes communication and order possible in social life.

Glossary, Bibliography, and Index

Glossary

[Note: The words and phrases are Sinhalese except when indicated to be otherwise in parentheses. T stands for Tamil. Whole sentences are not included here, as those given in the text are always accompanied by their translations. For Sinhalese kinship terms, see page 211.]

Achari, Blacksmith caste

Adi Dravida, "Dravidians," low castes (T)

adukka, special food offering for Hindu deities

ahanta balaya, "the strength to demand"

ahara, food

Ahikuntakiyo, Snake Charmer caste

almayra, cupboard

Alut Deva, New Deity

Amarapura Nikaya, an order of Buddhist monks named after a town in Burma

Ambattar, Barber caste (T)

amunam, 4 pale, a variable measure of land, often held to be 2 acres

amunu, main dams in rice fields

An keliya, annual ritual dedicated to the goddess Pattini

ande, a traditional sharecropping arrangement on rice lands, one-half generally going to the landlord

anuloma, "with the hair or grain," hypergamous marriage

apata ne, "not of us"

ape kande, "our mound"

apele, period of difficulty in the horoscope

api apata, "ourselves"

api e gollanta sambandha ne, "We those people intermarriage no," "We do not intermarry with those people"

api pavula ekkenek, "one of our kindred"

api tatvaya ne, "not of our status"

apirisithu, polluted

appochila dennai, "two fathers," reference to polyandry

astom, "at home," a celebration

atta, seeds

attang, a form of labor exchange

ava magul gedara, house where death has occurred

avanambu, dishonorable

avassa, own, rightful

avassa massina, real or own cross-cousin, male

avassa massinagen samava illima, the pardon of the cross-cousin at marriage

avassa nana, real or own cross-cousin, female

avassa pavula, own kindred

avurudda maruvata, worked year by year

ayin karala, separated

bada, stomach

Badaga, Cultivator caste (Toda)

Badde minissu, polite local term for Tom-Tom Beater caste

Baddegama, Tom-Tom Beaters' village

bambu, fathom

bana, Buddhist sermon

Banda, "Lord," Cultivators' personal name

bara denava, transfer of responsibility

Basnayaka Nilame, lay officials of a temple

bat bulat kanava, "rice–betel eating," preliminaries to marriage discussions

Beravaya or *Bera Karaya,* "drum people," Tom-Tom Beater caste

bethma, the reduction of the irrigable field into a half, a third, or two-thirds of the total

Bhikku, lit. "beggar," Buddhist monk

bima giya vi, "amount of rice sown," the portion of a crop given to the landlord

binna, matrilocal form of Kandyan marriage

bisniss kariyo, businessmen

bittara, eggs

boru, lies (n.)

boru konde, "false bun" (hairpiece), bridal gift

Brahman, priestly caste among Hindus

bulat puwak siyak denava, "hundred betel-leaf giving," one part of the marriage ritual

butti vindinava, living off the land

chanchala badu, movable property

Chee, chee e golle enni ne, enni ne, "Those people will not come"

(chee, an expression of disgust used against filth or filthy animals)

chena, highlands used for shifting cultivation

curru, small circles of kin in South India

dagoba, also *stupa,* sacred memorial mound built over the relics of the Buddha (shortened form of *dhatu garbhaya,* "dhatu in the womb," sacred tomb and monument)

dalada, tooth-relic of the Buddha

dalupata, small new tanks

dapu, deed

dayade lestuva, gift list

dayakaya, benefactors of a Buddhist temple

Dayakaya Samitiya, Law Benefactor's Society

deega, patrilocal form of Kandyan marriage

Deng api ata hodanta puluvan, "Well, now we can all wash our hands"

denu mutta, wise elders

deva, Hindu deity

devala gama, temple estates dedicated to Hindu deities

devale, temple of the local Hindu deities

devaya, Hindu deities

devayage sellama, game of the deities

devedde or *dayade,* dowry

dhatu, relics of the Buddha; also semen, seed

dhoties, Tamil male dress

diya kapavana, water-cutting ceremony

diyawadana nilame, the watcher of the royal bath

dos, sin

duka, pain, sorrow

dura, distant

Durava, Toddy Tapper caste

e golle, those fellows

egoda gama, "that side village"

eka ge kanava, "eating in the same *ge*," polyandry

eka gedara kattiya, "one house people," people inhabiting one house

eka le, one blood

eka minissu, one people

eka pavul kattiya, one family

eka sahaya inni, "living in one peace," polyandry

eka yataliya, "one roof," people who inhabit the same house

ekata, united

ekata kanava, "to eat together," polyandry

ela, irrigation line

enangan, also *enangar,* ritual affines (Malayalam)

gabini, pregnant woman

gam ande, "landlord's share," one-fourth of the total

gam kariya, landlord

Gam Maduva, "village hut," an annual ritual

gam nila, lands which were perquisites of feudal office

gama, village, hamlet, estate, or landholding of one person

gama kata, village lore

gamata poda, land common to the village

ganan kariyo, "calculators," referring to shopkeepers

gani urumaya tibbe, illanni ne, lit. "Women had rights, did not claim them"

ganiyek tiyegannava, "taking a woman"

ganja, a mild narcotic

ganu pakse, lit. "female side"; kinship connections through women

garu, respect

gati guni, character

ge, see *gedara*

ge atulaya, interior of a dwelling

gedara or *geyak,* house

gedara inni ekkenek, "the one in the house," wife

gedara kariyo, owner of the house

gedara kattiya, household

geniyek henata geniyanava, "taking a girl to the chena," marriage

gireya, "areca-nut cutters," traditional marriage gift

goda idam, highland

goma gahanta, application of cow dung

gotra, clan patronymics, lineage

Goyigama, High Cultivator caste

grahayo, planets and supernatural beings that influence men's lives

gu, feces

Ha! Hondai! "Yes, it is good"

haal, uncooked rice

hada gatta, adopted

Hak gedi Amma, "conch shell matron," Tom-Tom Beater's name for Blacksmith woman

hakku dhatu, jawbone, relic of the Buddha

havul idam tieni minissu, holders of undivided land

helueng denava vagei, "as if giving her naked"

hen or *hen yaya,* see *chena*

Henea, Washerman caste

Henea Mama, "Washer F-in-L"

Henea Nenda, "Washer M-in-L"

hetti, blouse

hira ganu denu karanni ne, "There is no give and take of women between us"

honda, good

honda le, good blood

honda minissu, good people

honda velava, auspicious times

huniyam, sorcery

hura, see *massina*

ichchil, pollution (Toda)

idam kadam venas kirima, separation of land

idam karaya, landlords

illasitima, request

irishiya, jealousy

ismatta, highland strip associated with paddy lands

issara, strips of paddy fields

janmaya, "pedigrees," a term with feudal associations implying land grants to specific groups

jataka, stories of the Buddha's different births

jati, birth; descent, race; rank, genealogy; a sort of, a kind of

Kadayar, Lime Burner caste

kadei karaya, shopkeepers

kadulu bulat, gate betel

Kallar, Thief caste (T)

kamaraya, room

Kammal Kariyo, Blacksmith caste

kanava, to eat

Kanda Uda Pas Rata, "Five Counties Above the Mountains," the Kingdom of Kandy

Kannar, caste of Makers of Lamps and Brass Pots (T)

kannit bonnit ne, "no eating and drinking"

Kano a paito, the bilateral kindred (Tikopia)

kantankudatan, "give and take" (T)

kapu mahatmaya, marriage broker

Kapurala, the priest of the *devale,* also the Sinhalese marriage broker

Karanavan, chief of the joint family (cf. *karanava,* to do, in Sinhalese) (Malayalam)

Karava, Fisher caste

Karayyar, also *Mukkuva,* Fisher caste (T)

karei, patrilocal units of the Ambalakkarar low caste (South India)

karma, a particular configuration of the *grahayo* at birth, personal fate

kassada bandinava, marriage

kat, ceremonial food parcel

Kataragama, the ritual center in the Eastern Province; also the name of the god known to Tamils as Supramanyar

katti, a measurement of earth used for the upkeep of the bund: 12 ft. long, 6 ft. wide, 1½ ft. deep

kattiya, groups, factions

kavalam, "mixed-up"

kavum, sweet cakes

kayya, a form of labor association

kele, spittle

keliya, play

kere, semen

khesa dhatu, hair, relic of the Buddha

kili or *kilutu, killa,* pollution

kiligedara, house polluted by death or menstruation

killote, "silver betel box," traditional marriage gift

Kinnarayo, Mat Weaver caste

kiri, milk

kiri gaha, milk-exuding trees

kiri päni, curd and treacle

kiribat, milk-rice, a favorite food

kolomba, a low stool

koraha, water basin

Korale, Kandyan title associated with a feudal estate

Kota, Funeral Musicians caste (Toda)

kovil, Sinhalese village shrine dedicated to Hindu deities, also Tamil temple

kudampam, family (T)

kudi, house, matrilineage, caste (East Coast Tamil, Ceylon)

kudi kuradal, "calling the *kudi,*" a ceremony in Hindu temples

kula bedimak, caste divisions

kula sirit, caste custom

kulam or *kulaya,* color; also caste

Kumbalu, Potter caste

kumbura, rice lands

kurakkan, finger-millet

kurakkan attuva, finger-millet granary

kurakkan kapana kali, finger-millet reaping time

Kurukkal, Hindu Tamil priest

Kurumba, Sorcerer caste (Toda)

kuruni, Sinhalese measurement re-

ferring to rice land which can be
sown with a certain size of basket
full of seed, $\frac{1}{10}$ of one *pale*

kusiya, cooking place

kuttam, patrilineages (South India)

ladjai, ashamed

laha, $\frac{1}{10}$ of one *pale,* see *kuruni*

lajjai-bayai, "ashamed and afraid"

lalata dhatu, frontal bone, relic of
the Buddha

langa langa, very near

le, blood

le kavalam venava, "blood would get
mixed"

le nedeyo, blood relatives

le urumaya, blood claim, blood kinship

Lebbe, an Islamic religious functionary (Muslim Tamil)

leda, illness

lekam mahatmaya, marriage registrars

lekam miti, registers of persons liable
to regular public service

lensuvak, handkerchief

lingam, phallus

maccunan, cross-cousin (T)

machang, see *massina*

machang kudi, male cross-cousin lineage (T)

machi kudi, female cross-cousin lineage (T)

mad, patrilineal groups (Toda)

mada idama, paddy land, the low
irrigable rice lands

madane machi, "seven female cross-
cousins" (T)

magul gedara, house of ceremonies

magul kapurala, marriage broker

magul poruva, cagelike structure used
at weddings

maha bulat adukku, "grand betel offering," one part of the marriage
ritual

Maha Makkaran, elected officers of
Tamil temple communities

mahan, son (T)

mahar, a payment agreed to be made
in case of an Islamic divorce (Muslim Tamil)

Mahavansa, "The Great Dynasty,"
the chronicle of the kings of Ceylon

majlis, council (Muslim Tamil)

malan kumburu, rain-fed rice fields

mama uyanaekkenek, "the one I
cook for," husband

Mangalla Davasa, Festive Day

mani, sacred cowbell (Toda)

Mannar, Washerman caste (T)

mapilla tolergar, special name among
Muslim Tamils for cross-cousin

marikkar, elected representatives of
the laity in Muslim Tamil temple
communities

maru mahan, ZS (male speaking), BS
(female speaking), son in-law

massina, male cross-cousin [also, *maittunan* or *maccinan* (Tamil) or *maiduna* (Kannada)]; derivation from
Sanskrit, *maiduna* or *mithuna*

massina-nana, male-female cross-cousins, marriage partners

matchuni, cross-cousin (Toda), see
massina

Matticham, lit. "mediator," chairman
(T)

mayang, trance state

Me lamayek mata one, "I want this
child for me"

megoda gama, "this side village"

Menika, "jewel," Cultivator's personal name for females

mohottala, feudal chief

mokkada, the end of the sari taken
over the head and used to cover
the face (Muslim Tamil)

molgaha, pestle

mu, urine

muaddin, mosque servant who calls
the faithful to prayer (Muslim
Tamil)

Mudali, subcaste of Goyigama

mudianse nama, aristocratic name,
Kandyan title

mul gedara, the family seat, **original** house

mullekaran or *munnilaikkaran,* a form of sharecropping in the Eastern Province (T)

muthusom, inherited property (T)

nädäya, kinsman

naginava, climbing

näkam, kinship

näkam kavalam venava, "kinship is confused"

Nallavar or *Santar,* Toddy Tapper caste (T)

nama gama, name and estate

nambu, honor

naraka, bad

naraka minissu, bad people

naya polanga vagei, "like the cobra and the Russell's viper," referring to innate enmity

nayaka thero, head Buddhist monk of the region, charged with ordination and appointment of incumbents to the local temple

nedekam venas kirima, separation of kinship

nekam kedila, "kinship is broken"

nikang innava, "nothing being," living together without formal marriage

ninde, a class of land or its proprietor not subject to feudal service during the Kandyan kingdom

niyachala, immovable property

nyaknya kirima, to beg

nyepata dhatu, fingernail, relic of the Buddha

okka, Coorg lineage (South India)

Ooliyakkareya, demeaning feudal service

padenchi gedara, settlement house

padenchi nama, settlement name

pahata rata minissu, Low Country people

paiol, affines (Toda)

paito, patrilineal house (Tikopia)

palata, districts in a division of the Kandyan region

pale, Sinhalese measurement referring to an amount of land that can be sown by a certain amount of seed measured in a basket called a *pale;* often held to be ½ acre, but actually a variable measure

palli, dairy (Toda)

palli or *palliya,* church or temple

Palliya Jamaat, mosque council (T)

palol, priests (Toda)

Pandita, Potter caste

pandura, large torch

panduru, money offerings

pangu, a share

pangu karaya, shareholders

pansala, Buddhist temple; specifically, residence of monks

parampara, ancestry, descent, rank, status (also *pelapata, pelentiya, peruve, janme, gotraya, wamsa, jati*)

parampara nama, ancestral name

parana deval, "old stuff," customs

Parayar, Funeral Drummer caste (T)

pava panga, father's share (T)

pavada, white cloths which decorate the house of the bride

pavul ganu denu, "exchange of families," intermarriage

pavul venava, "becoming," setting up a family

pavula, family, kindred (*palaveni pavula,* first wife; *deveni pavula,* second wife)

pelapata, pedigree

perahera, annual processions of temples

pettak, side, group

pettak, pettak, "side, side," split into two

pevatigenima, position, generation, birth

pidir, segment of a matrilineage (Nangudi Vellalar)

pinarawa, the stream of merit

pirimi gani vagei, "like man and woman"

pirisithu, purity

pirit, ceremonial Buddhist chanting

pol kiri, coconut milk

polj, see *palli*

poljol, see *puliol*

Polova denta be, "Land cannot be given"

poruva, ceremonial structure used at marriage

poya days, Buddhist "Sundays" on four quarters of the moon

pratiloma, "against the hair or grain," hypogamous marriages

puja, temple ceremonies

puliol, matrilineal groups, the people who are sacred (Toda)

Radala, aristocratic subcaste

rajakariya, "King's duty," feudal services

rata keliya, night sex play

redi, female loincloth

Rodiya, Beggar caste

sahalappadi, the term for the bond between men who have married sisters (T)

sambandha, lit. "tied together," marriage, intermarriage, equality; also respectable word for sexual intercourse

sambandha gama, "marriage villages"; also equal, connected

sambandham, Nayar marriage or union (Malayalam)

sampata, fertility

Sangha, the Buddhist community of monks

Sannyasi, Hindu holy men

sarai, powerful

sarui, fecund

sastra karaya, astrologers

sellam karanava, play, joke

Serendip, ancient name of Ceylon

Siam Nikaya, the Siamese order of Buddhist monks

Sinhala Pamanay, "Sinhalese Only," the national language movement

siura, monk's garments stitched from pieces of cloth

sonda, own (T); see *avassa*

Sri Lanka, Ceylon in Sinhalese

tai vali, "mother's way" (T)

tali or *thali,* a necklace, symbol of marriage in South India

Tali kettu kalyanam, "tying the *tali* festivity," marriage (T)

tambi, younger brother (T)

tangacchi, younger sister (T)

Tapasa Bhikku, ascetic Buddhist monks

Taprobane, ancient name of Ceylon

taravad, lineage; term used by various castes in Malabar denoting a group of matrilineally related persons

tatta, father

Tattar or *Kammalar,* Blacksmith caste (T)

tatvaya, level

tauma, town

tavalam, bullock transport

tevaliol, a section of the Toda tribe, probably meaning "god-people"

timbay, see *kuruni*

trivala, Hindu temple ceremonies (T)

tulana, a section of a village in Wanni Hat Pattuva

Uda Pila, "Upper Side team"

Uda rata minissu, Up Country people

udav, help

ufayam, ritual food in Hindu temples

ukas, mortgage

ure mama, rightful, actual MB, F-in-L; see *urumaya*

ure massina, rightful, actual cross-cousin

urumaya, rights, inheritance claims

vahalu, serfs, slaves

vahatta var or *vaittu var,* "one vagina," persons descended from one

named ancestress, smaller segments
of the matrilineal *kudi*

Vahumpura, Jaggery Makers' caste

Vala Vidane, Irrigation Headmen

valala, "bangles," bridal gift

Valan Karayo, Potters' caste

Valaw karaya, "mansion owner," high
caste

valawa, mansion

vandinava, worship

vangedi, mortar

yapa saraya, sowing extent of land

varada kassada, wrong marriages

variga, descent, subcaste, family

varna, color; ancient fourfold division of Hindu society: Brahman
(priests), Kshatriya (warriors),
Vaishya (traders), Sudra (farmers)

vas, rainy season in traditional Buddhism, a period when Buddhist
monks stay at one place and refrain from wandering

vasagama, lit. "dwelling village,"
used as aristocratic title

veda karani minissu or *veda kariya,*
lit. "working people," service castes

veda mahatmaya, native physicians

Vellalar, Cultivator caste (T)

vi, unhusked rice

vi attuva, paddy granary

vi badu lekam, tax collector

vidi kari, "owner of the house," wife
(T)

vihara, Buddhist temple; specifically,
chamber with the Buddha image

vihara gam, temple estates dedicated
to the Buddha

visiriyena or *kirikada hale,* "twenty
yards of cloth," traditional marriage gift

wamsa, pedigree, lineage, rank

Wannekar, elected officers of Tamil
matrilineages

wasama, Village Headman's area in
Walapane

watte, gardens (sometimes *gedara
watte,* house-gardens planted with
fruit trees)

wela, field

wewa, tank

wewa bendala, lit. "tied the tanks,"
constructed the bund

yakka or *yaksha,* he-demons

yakka vedarala, devil dancer, medicine man

yakkini, she-demons

yanni enni ne, "no visiting"

yantram, charmed figures

Yata Pila, "Lower Side team"

Bibliography

The following abbreviations are used:

Amer. Anthrop. *American Anthropologist*
JRAI *Journal of the Royal Anthropological Institute*
JRAS (CB) *Journal of the Royal Asiatic Society* (Ceylon Branch)

Administration Report of the Director of Rural Development (1950). Colombo.
Aiyappan, A.
  1937 *Social and Physical Anthropology of the Nayadis of Malabar.* Bulletin of the Madras Government Museum, N.S., General Section, Vol. II, No. 4. Madras.
  1944 *Iravas and Culture Change.* Bulletin of the Madras Government Museum, N.S. General Section, Vol. V., No. 1. Madras.
Aiyar, P. Jagadisa
  1925 *Some South Indian Customs.* Madras.
Aiyar, S. Subbarama
  1925 *Economic Life in a Malabar Village.* Bangalore.
Ali, Muhammad
  1929 *The Moplahs of Malabar.* Madras.
Altekar, A. S.
  1938 *The Position of Women in Hindu Civilization from Pre-Historic Times to the Present Day.* London.
Ames, M.
  1961 "Ideological and Social Change in Ceylon," *Human Organization,* 22(1):45–53.
  1964a "Buddha and the Dancing Goblins: A Theory of Magic and Religion," *Amer. Anthrop.,* 66(1):75–82.
  1964b "Sinhalese Magical-Animism and Theravada Buddhism," in E. B. Harper (ed.), *Religion in South Asia* (Seattle: Asian Society).
Archer, W. G.
  1957 *The Loves of Krishna.* London.
Ariyapala, M. B.
  1956 *Society in Medieval Ceylon.* Colombo.
Armour, John
  1842 "A Grammar of Kandyan Law," *The Ceylon Miscellany.*

Baden-Powell, B. H.
  1892   *Land Systems of British India.* Oxford.
Bailey, F. G.
  1958   *Caste and the Economic Frontier.* Manchester.
  1963   "Closed Social Stratification in India," *Archives Européens de So-
         ciologie,* 4:107–124.
Banks, M.
  1960   "Caste in Jaffna," E. R. Leach (ed.), *Aspects of Caste in South In-
         dia, Ceylon, and North West Pakistan* (Cambridge Papers in Social
         Anthropology, No. 2).
Barnett, L. P.
  1916–
  1917   "Alphabetical Guide to Sinhalese Folklore from Ballad Sources,"
         Indian Antiquary (Supplement), 55–56:1–120.
Barth, F.
  1959   *Political Leadership among Swat Pathans.* London.
Bell, R.
  1953   *Introduction to the Quran.* Edinburgh.
Bergson, Henri
  1935   *The Two Sources of Morality and Religion.* New York. (Original
         French edition, 1932.)
Berreman, G. D.
  1962   "Pahari Polyandry: A Comparison," *Amer. Anthrop.,* 64(1):60–75.
  1963   *Hindus of the Himalayas.* Berkeley and Los Angeles.
Bleichsteiner, Robert
  1937   *Die Gelbe Kirche.* Vienna.
Brown, W.
  n.d.   "Water Supply of Ceylon Villages," *Transactions of the English As-
         sociation of Ceylon.*
Burling, R.
  1963   *Rengasanggri; Family and Kinship in a Garo Village.* Philadelphia.
Callaway, J., trans.
  1829   *Yakkun Natanava: A Singalese Poem, Descriptive of the Ceylon
         System of Demonology.* London.
Carstairs, G. M.
  1956   "The Hinjra and Jiryan," *British Journal of Medical Psychology,*
         (29):128–138.
  1957   *The Twice Born.* London.
Carter, C.
  1924   *A Sinhalese–English Dictionary.* Colombo.
Cartman, J.
  1957   *Hinduism in Ceylon.* Colombo.
Codrington, H. W.
  1926   *A Short History of Ceylon.* London.
  1938   *Ancient Land Tenure and Revenue in Ceylon.* Colombo.
Coomaraswamy, A. K.
  1905   "Notes on Some Paddy Cultivation Ceremonies in the Ratnapura
         District, *JRAS* (CB), 18:413–428.

1956   *Medieval Sinhalese Art.* New York.

Coomaraswamy, K. Ananda
  1931   *Yakshas.* Washington, D.C.

Copleston, Reginald S.
  1892   *Buddhism—Primitive and Present in Magadha and in Ceylon.* London.

Danielou, A.
  1964   *Hindu Polytheism.* New York.

Davy, John
  1821   *An Account of the Interior of Ceylon and of its Inhabitants, with Travels in That Island.* London.

Deraniyagala, B. E. P.
  1936   "Some Blood Games of the Sinhalese," *Man,* 36(55):46–47.

Dickson, J. F.
  1886   "Daily Religion . . . and Ceremonies before and after Death," *JRAS* (CB), 3(29):203 f.

Denham, E. B.
  1912   *Ceylon at the Census of 1911.* Colombo.

Diehl, Carl Gustav
  1956   *Instrument and Purpose: Studies in Rites and Rituals in South India.* Lund.

Dissawe of Velassa
  1817   *Account of Kandy Perahersa, August 19, 1817.* Colombo.

D'Oyly, Sir John
  1929   *A Sketch of the Constitution of the Kandyan Kingdom.* Colombo.

D'Souza, Victor S.
  1959   "Social Organization and Marriage Customs of the Moplahs of the South-West Coast of India," *Anthropos,* 54(parts 3–4):487–517.

Dube, S. C.
  1953   "Token Pre-Puberty Marriage in Middle India," *Man,* 52:18–19.

Dumont, Louis
  1950   "Kinship and Alliance among the Pramalai Kaller," *Eastern Anthropologist* 4(1):3–26.

  1953   "The Dravidian Kinship Terminology as an Expression of Marriage," *Man,* 54:34–39.

  1957a   *Une sous-caste de l'Inde du Sud: Organisation sociale et religion des Pramalai Kallar.* Paris.

  1957b   "Hierarchy and Marriage Alliance in South Indian Kinship," *Occasional Papers of the Royal Anthropological Institute,* No. 12.

  1961a   "Marriage in India, the Present State of the Question." *Contributions to Indian Sociology,* 5:75–95. The Hague.

  1961b   "Les Marriages Nayars comme faits Indien," *L'Homme.* 1(1):11–36.

International Bank for Reconstruction and Development
  1953   *The Economic Development of Ceylon.* Baltimore.

Ehrenfels, U. R.
  1941   *Mother Right in India.* Hyderabad, Bombay.

  1952   *The Kadar of Cochin.* Madras.

Eickstedt, Dr. Egon Frhr, von.

1927   "Rassengeschichte einer singhalesich-weddaischen Adelsfamilie," in
        Archiv für Rassen-und Gesellschafts-biologie, Band 19, Heft 4.
        Munich.

Eliot, Sir Charles
1921   *Hinduism and Buddhism.* 3 vols. London.

Emeneau, M. B.
1937   "Toda Marriage Regulations and Taboos," *Amer. Anthrop.*, 39:103–
        112.
1938   "Kinship and Marriage among the Coorgs," *JRAS* (Bengal branch),
        4:123–147.
1941   "Language and Social Forms: A Study of Toda Kinship Terms and
        Dual Descent," in *Language, Culture, and Personality*, Sapir Me-
        morial Vol. (Menasha, Wisc.).

Epigraphia Zeylonica, Being Lithic and Other Inscriptions of Ceylon.
1911–
1927   Vol. II, ed. and trans. by Don Martino de Zilva Wickremasinghe.
        London.

1934–
1941   Vol. IV, ed. by S. Paranavitana. London.

Evers, Hans Dieter
1963   "Die Soziale Organisation de Singhalesischen Religion." Unpublished
        MS, Institut für Empirische Soziologie, Mannheim.

Farmer, B.
1944   "Agriculture in Ceylon," *Foreign Agriculture*, 8:3–20.
1957   *Pioneer Peasant Colonization in Ceylon.* London.

Fausböll, V., ed., and T. W. Rhys-Davids, trans.
1880   *Buddhist Birth Stories; or Jataka Tales.* London.

Fawcett, F.
1915   *The Nayars of Malabar.* Bulletin of the Madras Government Mu-
        seum, No. 3. Madras.

Fernando, H. F., and F. A. Fernando
1920   *A Dip into the Past or Matters of Historical Interest Relating to the
        Portion of the Singhalese Known as KA-U-RAWA.* Colombo.

Ferroli, D.
1939   *The Jesuits in Malabar.* Bangalore.

Firth, R.
1936   *We, The Tikopia.* London.
1951   *The Elements of Social Organization.* London.
1954   "Social Organization and Social Change," *JRAI*, 84 (parts 1–2):1–20.
1957   "A Note on Descent Groups in Polynesia," *Man*, 57:4–8.

Fonseka, Lionel de
1921   "The Karave Flag," *Ceylon Antiquary and Literary Register*, 3
        (part 1):1–11.

Fortes, M.
1945   *The Dynamics of Clanship among the Tallensi.* London.
1949a   "Time and Social Structure," in G. P. Murdock (ed.), *Social Struc-
        ture in Southeast Asia* (New York).

1949*b* *The Web of Kinship among the Tallensi.* London.

1959 "Descent, Filiation and Affinity," *Man,* 59:206–212.

Freeman, J. D.

1961 "On the Concept of the Kindred," *JRAI,* 91(part 2):192–220.

Geiger, Wilhelm

1941 *An Etymological Glossary of the Sinhalese Language.* Colombo.

1960 *The Culture in Medieval Times.* Ed. by H. Bechert. Wiesbaden.

Ghurye, S. C.

1932 *Caste and Race in India.* London.

Gilbert, William H., Jr.

1945 "The Sinhalese Caste System of Central and Southern Ceylon," *Journal of the Washington Academy of Sciences,* Vol. 35, Nos. 3–4.

Gluckman, M.

1950 "Kinship and Marriage among the Logi of Northern Rhodesia and the Zulu of Natal," in A. R. Radcliffe-Brown and D. Forde (eds.), *African Systems of Kinship and Marriage* (London).

Gogerly, Rev. D. J.

1853–

1858 "Laws of the Buddhist Priesthood," *JRAS* (CB), No. 6 (1853), pp. 17–31; No. 8 (1855), pp. 123–125; No. 11 (1858), pp. 1–4.

Goody, Jack, ed.

1958 *The Developmental Cycle in Domestic Groups.* Cambridge. (Cambridge Papers in Social Anthropology, No. 1.)

Goonewardena, Dandris de Silva

1865–

1866 "On Demonology and Witchcraft in Ceylon," *JRAS* (CB), 5(13): 1–122.

Gough, E. Kathleen

1952*a* "Changing Kinship Usages in the Setting of Political and Economic Change among the Nayars of Malabar," *JRAI,* 82:71–88.

1952*b* "Incest Prohibitions and Rules of Exogamy in Three Matri-Lineal Groups of the Malabar Coast," *International Archives of Ethnography,* Vol. 46, No. 1.

1955*a* "Female Initiation Rites on the Malabar Coast," *JRAI,* 85:45–78.

1955*b* "The Social Structure of a Tanjore Village," in McKim Marriott (ed.), *Village India* (Chicago).

1956 "Brahmin Kinship in a Tamil Village," *Amer. Anthrop.,* 58(5):826–853.

1958 "Cults of the Dead among the Nayars," *Journal of American Folklore,* 71(281)240–272.

1959 "The Nayars and the Definition of Marriage," *JRAI,* 89:23–34.

1960 "Caste in a Tanjore Village," in E. R. Leach (ed.), *Aspects of Caste in South India, Ceylon, and North West Pakistan* (Cambridge Papers in Social Anthropology, No. 2).

Government of Ceylon

1827 *Return of the Population of the Island of Ceylon.* [Census of 1824.] Colombo.

Grunwedel, Albert
  1893   "Singhalesische Masken," *International Archiv für Ethnographie,* Vol. VI.
Gunasekera, Mudaliyar A. M.
  1914   "The Sinhalese Terms of Relationship," *Ceylon Notes and Queries,* R.A.S. (CB), 67(part 2):xix–xxii.
  1953   "Pūnā Maduva," *Spolia Zeylonica,* 27(part 2):63–75.
Hayley, Frederic Austin
  1923   *A Treatise on the Laws and Customs of the Sinhalese, including the portions still surviving under the name Kandyan Law.* Colombo.
Hettiaratchi, D. E.
  1946   "Two Sinhalese Terms of Kinship," *JRAS* (CB), 37(101):16–23.
Hocart, A. M.
  1923   "Buddha and Devadatta," *Indian Antiquary,* 52:267 ff.
  1924–
  1928   "The Indo-European Kinship System," *Ceylon Journal of Science,* Section G., Vol. 1.
  1925   "The Cousin in Vedic Ritual," *Indian Antiquary,* 54:16–18.
  1931   *Temple of the Tooth in Kandy.* London.
  1950   *Caste in Contemporary Study.* London.
  1952   *The Life Giving Myth.* London.
Hutton, J. H.
  1946   *Caste in India, Its Nature, Function and Origins.* Cambridge.
Ievers, R. W.
  1880   "Customs and Ceremonies Connected with Paddy Cultivation," *JRAS* (CB), 6:46–52.
  1899   *Manual of the North Central Province, Ceylon.* Colombo.
Indra, V. V.
  1955   *The Status of Women in Ancient India.* Benares.
International Bank for Reconstruction and Development
  1953   *The Economic Development of Ceylon.* Baltimore.
Iyer, L. A. K.
  1909,
  1912   *The Cochin Tribes and Castes.* 2 vols. Madras and London.
  1937   *Travancore Caste and Tribes.* Trivandrum.
Jaques, E.
  1953   "On the Dynamics of Social Structure," *Human Relations,* 6(1) 3–23.
Jennings, Sir Ivor
  1951   *The Economy of Ceylon.* Madras.
John, V. K.
  1929   *Land Systems of Malabar.* Madras.
Jouveau-Dubreuil, G.
  1957   *Iconography of Southern India.* Trans. by A. C. Martin. Paris.
Kapuruhami, K. A.
  1948   "Rata Sabhawa," *JRAS* (CB), Vol. 38, No. 106.
Karve, Irawati
  1938   "Kinship Terminology and Usage in Rig Veda and Atharva Veda,"

Annals of the Bhandarkar Oriental Research Institute, 20:60–69, 109–144, 213–234.

1953 *Kinship Organization* in India. Poona.

Kirfel, W.

1920 *Kosmographie der Inder.* Bonn.

Knox, Robert

1681 *An Historical Relation of Ceylon.* London. Reprinted 1911, Glasgow.

Kramrisch, S.

1946 *The Hindu Temple.* Calcutta.

"Land for the People" (n.d.). A Brochure on Crown Land Alienation; Building the Nation Series, No. 2. Colombo.

Lanerolle, J. de

1938 *Review of "Ancient Land Tenure and Revenue in Ceylon," by H. W. Codrington, JRAS* (CB), 34:199–230.

Lawrie, Archibald Campbell

1898 *A Gazetteer of the Central Province of Ceylon (excluding Walapane).* 2 vols. Colombo.

Leach, E. R.

1940 *The Social Organization of the Ruwandez Kurds.* London.

1951 "The Structural Implications of Matrilateral Cross-Cousin Marriage," *JRAI,* 81:23–55.

1953 *The Political Systems of Highland Burma.* London.

1955 "Polyandry, Inheritance and the Definition of Marriage," *Man,* 55: 182–186.

1958 "Magical Hair," *JRAI,* 88(part 2):147–164.

1959 "Hydraulic Society in Ceylon," *Past and Present,* No. 15, pp. 2–25.

1960 "The Sinhalese of the Dry Zone of Northern Ceylon," in G. P. Murdock (ed.), *Social Structure in Southeast Asia* (New York).

1961a *Rethinking Anthropology.* London.

1961b *Pul Eliya, A Village in Ceylon: A Study of Land Tenure and Kinship.* Cambridge.

Le Mesurier, C. J. R.

1860 *Niti Nighanduwa or The Vocabulary of Law as it existed in the Last Days of the Kandyan Kingdom.* Trans. by C. J. R. Le Mesurier and T. B. Panabokke. Colombo.

1884 "An-Keliya," *JRAS* (CB), 8(29):369 ff.

1898 *Manual of the Nuwara Eliya District.* Colombo.

Lévi-Strauss, Claude

1949 *Les Structures élémentaires de la parenté.* Paris.

1953 "Social Structure," in Sol Tax (ed.), *Anthropology Today* (Chicago).

1960 "On Manipulated Sociological Models," *Bijdragen tot de taal-, Land-, en Volkenkunde,* No. 116, pp. 45–54.

1962 *La Pensée sauvage.* Paris.

Lewis, F.

1916 "Notes on an Exploration in Eastern Uva," *JRAS* (CB), 23(67):276–293.

Lewis, J. P.

1884a "The Language of the Threshing Floor," *JRAS* (CB), 8(29):237 f.

1884*b* "On the Terms of Relationship in Sinhalese and Tamil," *Orientalist*,
   1:217–223; 2:64–69.
1921   "Kandyan Notes," *Ceylon Antiquary and Literary Register*, 6(part
   4):181–190; 7:139 f.
Ludowyk, E. F. C.
1958   *The Footprint of the Buddha*. London.
The Mahavamsa or the Great Chronicle of Ceylon (1934). Trans. by Wilhelm
   Geiger. London.
Maine, Sir Henry
1950   *Ancient Law*. Oxford.
Mandelbaum, D. G.
1938   "Polyandry in Kota Society," *Amer. Anthrop.*, 40(4):574–583.
Marriott, McKim
1955   (ed.) *Village India*. Chicago.
1959   "Interactional and Attributional Theories of Caste Ranking," *Man
   in India*, 39(2):92–107.
Marshall, H.
1846   *Ceylon: A Description of the Island and Its Inhabitants*. London.
Matar, S.
1883   *Native Life in Travancore*. London.
Mauss, M.
1923   "Essai sur le Don," *Année Sociologique*, N.S., No. I.
Maybury-Lewis, D.
1960   "The Analysis of Dual Organisations: A Methodological Critique,"
   Bijdragen tot de taal-, Land-, en Volkenkunde, pp. 18–44.
Mayer, Adrian C.
1952   *Land and Society in Malabar*. Bombay.
1958   "The Dominant Caste in a Region of Central India," *Southwestern
   Journal of Anthropology*, 14:407–427.
1960   *Caste and Kinship in Central India*. Berkeley and Los Angeles.
McCormack, W.
1958   "Sister's Daughter Marriage in a Mysore Village," *Man in India*,
   38(1):34–48.
Meerworth-Levina, Ludmilla
1916   "The Hindu Goddess Pattini in the Buddhist Popular Beliefs in
   Ceylon," *Ceylon Antiquary and Literary Register*, Vol. 1.
Menon, K. P.
1924   *History of Kerala*. Emakulom.
Menzies, I. E. P.
1960   "A Case-Study of the Functioning of Social Systems as a Defense
   against Anxiety," *Human Relations*, 13(2):95–121.
Miller, E.
1954   "Caste and Territory in Malabar," *Amer. Anthrop.*, 56:410–420.
Molegode, W.
1943   "Paddy Cultivation in Kandy," *Tropical Agriculturist*, 99:152–156.
Moore, Lewis
1905   *Malabar Law and Customs*. Madras.

Mulla, D. F.
  1919 *Principles of Hindu Law.* Bombay.
Munasinghe, Martin Edward
  1928 *Supplementary Memorandum Submitted at the Request of the Commissioners on the Reform of the Constitution with Reference to the History of the Wahumpera Caste of the Singhalese Race.* Colombo.
Nadel, S. F.
  1951a *Black Byzantium.* London.
  1951b *The Theory of Social Structure.* London.
Nair, K. M.
  1922 *Malabar Tenancy Agitation.* Calcutta.
Needham, R.
  1959 "The Formal Analysis of Prescriptive Patrilateral Cross-Cousin Marriage," *Southwestern Journal of Anthropology*, 14:199–219.
  1960 "Patrilateral Prescriptive Alliance and the Ungarinyin," *Southwestern Journal of Anthropology*, 16:274–291.
  1961 "Notes on the Analysis of Asymmetric Alliance," *Bijdragen tot de taal-, Land-, en Volkenkunde*, 117:93–117.
  1962 *Structure and Sentiment.* Chicago.
Nell, L. A.
  1881–
  1882 "A Huniyam Image," *JRAS* (CB), 7:116–124.
Neville, Hugh
  n.d. "Notes," in British Museum Collection of Neville Manuscripts, Vol. I.
  1885–
  1888 (ed.) *The Taprobanian.* Vols. 1–3. London.
  1885 (trans.) *Janawamsa,* in *The Taprobanian.* Also "Notes on the Janawamsa" (1886).
  1887 "Social Rites of the Sinhalese," in *The Taprobanian.*
Obeyesekera, G.
  1963a "Pregnancy Cravings in Relation to Social Structure and Personality in a Sinhalese Village," *Amer. Anthrop.* 65(2):323–342.
  1963b "The Great Tradition and the Little in the Perspective of Sinhalese Buddhism," *Journal of Asian Studies*, 22(2):139–153.
Overseas Economic Surveys: Ceylon (1959). London.
Pannikkar, K. M.
  1901 *Malabar and Its Folk.* Madras.
  1929 *Malabar and the Portuguese.* Bombay.
  1931 *Malabar and the Dutch.* Bombay.
Paranavitana, S.
  1933 "Matrilineal Descent in the Sinhalese Royal Family," *Ceylon Journal of Science,* Section G, 2(part 3):235–240.
Parker, H.
  1887 "The Wannias," in Hugh Neville (ed.), *The Taprobanian.*
  1909 *Ancient Ceylon.* London.

Percival, Robert
    1803   *An Account of the Island of Ceylon.* London.
Perera, Arthur A.
    1917   *Sinhalese Folklore Notes.* Bombay.
Perera, A. B.
    1951   "Plantation Economy and Colonial Policy in Ceylon," *Ceylon His-torical Journal,* Vol. I, No. 1.
Pertold, O.
    1922   "A Study in Sinhalese Magic," *Journal of the Anthropological So-ciety of Bombay,* Vol. XII, No. 5.
    1925   "Inquiries into the Popular Religions of Ceylon, Part I: Sinhalese Amulets, Talismans and Spells," *Facultes Philosophica Universitatis Carolinea Pragensis* (Prague).
    1929   "The Conception of Soul in Sinhalese Demon Worship," *Archiv Orientalium,* 1:312–322.
    1930   "The Ceremonial Dances of the Singhalese," *Journal of the Czecho-slovak Oriental Institute,* 2:108–426.
Peter, Prince of Greece and Denmark
    1951   "The Mother Sibs of the Todas of the Nilgiris," *Eastern Anthropolo-gist,* 5(2–3):65–73.
    1955a "The Todas: Some Additions and Corrections to W. H. R. Rivers' Book as Observed in the Feld," *Man,* 55:89–93.
    1955b "Polyandry and the Kinship Group," *Man,* 55:179–181.
Peters, E. L.
    1963   "Aspects of Rank and Status among Muslims in a Lebanese Village," in J. Pitt-Rivers (ed.), *Mediterranean Countrymen* (Paris).
Phear, Sir John B.
    1880   *The Aryan Village in India and Ceylon.* London.
Philalathes
    1817   *The History of Ceylon to the Year 1815.* London.
Pieris, P. E.
    1939   *Tri Sinhala: The Last Phase.* Colombo.
    1949   *The Ceylon Littoral.* Colombo.
    1950   *Sinhale and the Patriots, 1815–1818.* Colombo.
Pieris, Ralph
    1953   "The Brodie Papers on Sinhalese Folk Religion," *University of Ceylon Review,* 2:110–128.
    1956   *Sinhalese Social Organisation. The Kandyan Period.* Colombo.
Pocock, D. F.
    1957   "Inclusion and Exclusion: A Process in the Caste System of Gujerat," *Southwestern Journal of Anthropology,* 13(1):19–31.
Pridham, Charles
    1849   *An Historical, Political, Statistical Account of Ceylon and Depend-encies.* London.
Queyroz, Fernao de
    1930   *The Conquest (Temporal and Spiritual) of Ceylon.* Trans. by S. G. Perera. Colombo.
Raghavan, M. D.

1951*a* "Cultural Anthropolgy of the Rodiyas," *Spolia Zeylonica,* 26(1):77–116.

1951*b* "The Kinnaraya," *Spolia Zeylonica,* 26(2):217–249.

1951*c* "The Pattini Cult as a Socio-Religious Institution," *Spolia Zeylonica,* 26(2):251–261.

1953*a* "Traditions and Legends of Nagarcoil," *Spolia Zeylonica,* 27(1):179–185.

1953*b* "The Ahikuntakaya," *Spolia Zeylonica,* 27(1):141–169.

1953*c* "A Kalvettu of the Seerpadam in the Eastern Province," *Spolia Zeylonica,* 27(1):187–193.

1953*d* "Folk Sports," *Spolia Zeylonica,* 27(1):171–177.

1953*e* "The Sinhalese Social System: A Sociological Review," *Spolia Zeylonica,* 27(1):195–211.

1957 *Handsome Beggars: The Rodiyas of Ceylon.* Colombo.

1961 *The Karava of Ceylon.* Colombo.

Raja, P. K. S.

1953 *Medieval Kerala.* Annamalai University, Chidambaram.

Ranasinha, A. G.

1950 *Census of Ceylon, 1946. General Report.* Colombo.

Rao, M. S. A.

1957 *Social Change in Malabar.* Bombay.

Rao, P. Kodanda

1924 *Malabar Tenancy Problems.*

Report of the Commission on Marriage and Divorce, October 1956–July 1959 (1959). Colombo.

Report of the Kandyan Law Commission (1935). Colombo.

Report of the Kandyan Peasantry Commission (1951). Colombo.

Report of the Land Commission (1958). Colombo.

Report of the Temple Land Commissions on the Progress and Results of the Commission (1857). Colombo.

Reimers, E.

1928 "Feudalism in Ceylon," *JRAS* (CB), 31(81):17–54.

Rhys-Davids, Mrs. T. W

1934 *Outline of Buddhism.* London.

Rhys-Davids, T. W., and William Stede

1925 *Pali-English Dictionary.* Chipstead.

Ribeiro, Joao

n.d. *History of Ceilao.* Trans. by P. E. Pieris. Galle.

Richards, A. I.

1950 "Some Types of Family Structures amongst the Bantu," in A. R. Radcliffe-Brown and D. Forde (eds.), *African Systems of Kinship and Marriage* (London).

Rivers, W. H. R.

1906 *The Todas.* London.

1907 "The Marriage of Cousins in India," *JRAS* (Great Britain and Ireland), 611–640.

Ryan, Bryce

1950 "Socio-Cultural Regions of Ceylon," *Rural Sociology,* 17(1):8–28.

1952   "The Ceylonese Village and the New Value Systems," *Rural Sociology*, 17(1):9–28.

1953   *Caste in Modern Ceylon: The Sinhalese System in Transition.* New Brunswick, N.J.

Ryan, Bryce, and Sylvia Fernando

1951   "The Female Factory Worker in Ceylon," *International Labour Review*, 64(5–6):438–461.

Ryan, Bryce, with C. Arulpragasam and C. Bibile

1955   "The Agricultural System of a Ceylon Jungle Village," *Eastern Anthropologist*, 8:151–160.

Sampson Rajapakse, Mudiliyar

1912   *A Memoir with a Sketch of the Salagama Sinhalese, Their Chiefs and Clans.* Colombo.

Sarasin, F.

1939   *Reisen und Forschungen in Ceylon.* Basel.

Sarathchandra, E. R.

1953   *The Sinhalese Folk Play.* Colombo.

Sastri, K. A. N.

1955   *History of South India.* Oxford.

Sawers, Simon

1826   "Memoranda and Notes on the Kandyan Law of Inheritance, Marriage, Slavery, Etc.," in F. A. Hayley, *A Treatise on the Laws and Customs of the Sinhalese* (Colombo, 1923).

Schmidt, E.

1897   *Ceylon.* Berlin.

Schneider, D. M., and E. K. Gough, eds.

1961   *Matrilineal Kinship.* Berkeley and Los Angeles.

Seligman, C. G., and B. Z. Seligman

1911   *The Veddas.* Cambridge.

Silva, Hon. W. A. de

1927   "Sinhalese Vitti Pot (Book of Incidents) and Kadaim Pot (Book of Division Boundaries)," *JRAS* (CB), 30(80):303–325.

Sirr, Henry Charles

1850   *Ceylon and the Cingalese.* 2 vols. London.

Sivaswami, K. D., ed.

1945   *Exodus from Travancore to Malabar Jungles.* Coimbatore.

Slater, G.

1924   *The Dravidian Element in Indian Culture.* London.

1936   *Southern India: Its Political and Economic Problems.* London.

Slater, G., ed.

1918   *Some South Indian Villages.* London.

Spittel, R. L.

1928   *Wild Ceylon.* Colombo.

1933   *Far Off Things.* Colombo.

Srinivas, M. N.

1952   *Religion and Society among the Coorgs in South India.* Oxford.

1955   (ed.) *India's Villages.* Bengal.

Stevenson, H. N. C.

1954 "Status Evaluation in the Hindu Caste System," *JRAI*, 84(parts 1–2):45–65.

Straus, M. A.

1951 "Mental Ability and Cultural Needs: A Psycho-cultural Interpretation of the Intelligence Test Performance of Ceylon University Entrants," *American Sociological Review*, 6(3):371–375.

Tambiah, H. W.

1954 *The Laws and Customs of the Tamils of Ceylon*. Colombo.

1956 *The Laws and Customs of the Tamils of Jaffna*. Colombo.

Tambiah, S. J.

1958 "The Structure of Kinship and Its Relationship to Land Possession and Residence in Pata Dumbara, Central Ceylon," *JRAI*, 88(part 1):21–44.

Tambiah, S. J., and N. K. Sarkar

1957 *The Disintegrating Village*. Colombo.

Tennent, Sir James Emerson

1850 *Christianity in Ceylon*. London.

1859 *Ceylon: An Account of the Island*. London.

Thomas, P. J.

1940a *Some South Indian Villages: A Re-Survey*. Madras.

1940b *Commodity Prices in South India (1918–38)*. Madras University Economics Bulletin No. 3.

Thurston, E.

1906 *Ethnographic Notes on South India*. Madras.

1909 *Castes and Tribes of Southern India*. Madras.

1912 *Omens and Superstitions of India*. London, Leipzig.

Trautz, Friedrich M.

1926 *Ceylon*. Munich.

Tugay, E. F.

1963 *Three Centuries: Family Chronicles of Turkey and Egypt*. London.

Turner, J. L. B.

1923 *Report on the Census of Ceylon, 1921*, Vol. I, Part I. Colombo.

Vittachi, T.

1958 *Emergency '58*. London.

White, H.

1893 *Manual of Uva*. Colombo.

White, J. S. L.

1945 "Notes on the Opening of Manual Labour of Land in the Dry Zone of Ceylon," *Tropical Agriculturalist*, 101:148–152.

Whitehead, Henry

n.d. *The Village Deities of South India*. Bulletin of the Madras Government Museum, Vol. 26, Part II.

Wijayasekara, D. P. DeAlwis, re. and trans.

1914 *The Ruwanmal Nighantuwa or Narmaratna Malawa: A Poetical Lexicon of the Sinhalese Language, by his Majesty Sri Parakrama Bahu VI*.

Wijesekera, N. D.

1949 *The People of Ceylon*. Colombo.

Wirz, Paul

 1940*a* "Ton figuren auf Ceylon," *Verhandlungen der Naturforschenden Gesellschaft Basel,* Band LI.

 1940*b* "Die kultische Bedentung der Kokosnuss bei den Singhalesen," *Verh.. d. Naturf. Ges. Basel,* Band LI.

 1941 *Exorgismus und Heilkunde auf Ceylon.* Bern.

 1949 "Die Tier und Menschen darstellungen in der Sinhalesichen Kunst," *Verh. d. Naturf. Ges. Basel,* Band LI.

 1954*a* *Exorcism and the Art of Healing in Ceylon.* Leiden.

 1954*b* "Kataragama, die Heiligste Stätte Ceylon," *Verh. d. Naturf. Ges. Basel,* Band LV, No. 2.

Wood, A. L.

 1961 "Crime and Aggression in Changing Ceylon," *Transactions of the American Philosophical Society,* Vol. 51, Part 8.

Woolf, Leonard

 1913 *The Village in the Jungle.* London.

Wriggins, W. Howard

 1960 *Ceylon: The Dilemmas of a New Nation.* Princeton.

Yalman, Nur

 1960 "The Flexibility of Caste Principles in a Kandyan Community," in E. R. Leach (ed.), *Aspects of Caste in South India, Ceylon, and North West Pakistan* (Cambridge Papers in Social Anthropology, No. 2).

 1962*a* "The Ascetic Buddhist Monks of Ceylon," *Ethnology,* 1(3):315–328.

 1962*b* The Structure of the Sinhalese Kindred: A Re-examination of the Dravidian Terminology," *Amer. Anthrop.,* 64(3):548–575.

 1963 "On the Purity of Women in the Castes of Ceylon and Malabar," *JRAI,* 93(part 1):25–58.

 1964 "The Structure of Sinhalese Healing Rituals," in E. B. Harper (ed.), *Religion in South Asia* (Seattle: Asian Society).

 1966 "Dual Organisation in Central Ceylon? or The Goddess in the Tree-top," *Journal of Asian Studies,* 24(3):441–447.

Zimmer, Heinrich

 1926 *Kunstform und Yoga im Indischen Kulturbild.* Berlin.

Addenda

Three important articles which could not be discussed in the text should be mentioned: (1) L. Dumont, "Marriage in India: The Present State of the Question," *Contributions to Indian Sociology,* No. VII (March, 1964), pp. 77–102; and (2) S. J. Tambiah, "Kinship Fact and Fiction in Relation to the Kandyan Sinhalese," *JRAI* (1965), 95(part 2), pp. 131–173; and (3) E. R. Leach, "Did the Wild Veddahs Have Matrilineal Clans?" *Studies in Kinship and Marriage: Essays Dedicated to Brenda Z. Seligman on Her 80th Birthday,* I. Schapera (ed.), London: R.A.I. (1963), pp. 68–78.

Index

Achari, Blacksmiths, 29, 55, 62, 69, 70, 90

administration: district and village, 29–31; Village Headman, 30, 64, 147, 156–158; Village Committee, 31

affines, 155, 185, 358. See also kinship

agricultural settlements, types of, 21–22

agriculture, 48. See also chena; land tenure; paddy cultivation

Ahikuntakiyo, Snake Charmers, 60, 90

Akkaraipattu, 329

Ambattar, Barbers, 328

An keliya, 28, 34, 317–318, 322n. See also annual ritual

annual ritual, 29, 68, 319; procession, 11, 17, 38; *vihara* or *devale,* 72. See also Kataragama

Anuradhapura, 13, 15

Arulpragasam, Mr. (AGA Batticaloa), 327n.

ascetic monks, 61n.

avoidance, 182, 184, 299

Badaga, Cultivators, 337

Baddegama, 62–63. See also *Beravaya*

Bailey, F. G., 52

Bandaranaike, S. W. R. D., 14

Banks, M., 207, 311, 347, 359

Barth, F., 151

Batticaloa, 272, 311

Beals, A., 208n.

Bell, R., 290n.

Beravaya, Tom-Tom Beaters, 27, 29, 47, 55, 60–64, 68, 90; ancestral names of, 63, 66; cross-cousin marriage, 66, 171

Bergson, H., 5

Berreman, G. D., 111

Bhikku, 34, 61

Bibile, 11, 142n.

binna, 65, 122–132, 136, 176, 263, 265, 295

Brahman, 61, 172; in Tanjore, 343, 348, 350–351; role of wife, 349; marital relations, 350; sister's daughter marriage, 351; hypergamy, 352–353

bridewealth, 95, 176; in India, 176; Sinhalese and Muslim compared, 303; sale theory, 304

British rule in Ceylon, 14, 20, 29, 109

Buddha, 12, 34, 138; relics of, 137n.

Buddhism in Ceylon, 12, 15; sects, 33; Amarapura order, 33, 69; Siam Nikaya order, 33, 69; resurgence of, 323. See also annual ritual; *vihara*

Burma, 4

Buttala, 17

Carstairs, G. M., 137n.

Cartman, J., 316

caste, 58; services, 16, 54n., 62, 71, 165; in Kandy kingdom, 58–60; in Terutenne, 60; of Buddhist Sinhalese, 61; of Hindu Tamils, 61; low, 62; marriage across, 65, 69, 71–73, 87; names, 74, 91; changes, 82, 185; known in Galpitiya, 88–89; symbols of, 89, 92, 94–95; myth of, 89; prohibitions of, 95; etiquette, 206; in Makulle Watta, 233–234; in Panama, 315

categories: of kinship in Ceylon, 152–154, 171, 209–210, 243; of Dravidian kinship, 169, 209–221; of cross-cousins, 169–170; confusion of, 221

Ceylon: Eastern Province, 7, 310–331;

Walapane Division, 10, 19, 21, 24–35; North Central Province, 10, 207, 252, 269; population of, 12–14; independence of, 14; history of, 14–16; ecology of, 18–23; exports, 19; Uva Province, 227–246, 282–309; Northwest Province, 247–270; Low Country, 271–281

change, structural, 7, 121

chena, 19–20, 23, 40–41, 46, 82, 100, 232, 237

Christians, 233; population, 12

Codrington, H. W., 29, 101, 249, 252, 312

Colombo, 3, 13

colonization scheme, 9

color-bar complex, 59

commensality, 102, 115, 204–205

communication. See language

contractual relations, 100

Cordiner, J., 310, 325

cross-cousins, 181, 211, 213; marriage of, 66, 71, 139, 151–152, 169–172, 217, 367–368; joking behavior of, 181; avoidance of, 182; MBD marriage, 352, 369; etymology, 375

culture, as system of communication, 4

dagoba, 15

Danielou, A., 350

Davy, J., 58, 96, 121, 276

deega, 122–132, 136–138, 173, 263, 265

descent, 121, 138, 140–141, 335–336; dogma of, 136–140. See also matrilineal descent; patrilineal descent

devale, 33, 34, 317

disputes: of inheritance, 134–135; in Terutenne, 155–158; in Panama, 322; kudi, 327

divorce, 187; in Kotabowe Vidiya, 295; among Muslims, 296

Dondra, 271

dowry, 95, 132, 136, 149, 172–176, 180–182, 291–292; 297n.; in Vilawa, 266; in Low Country, 271–275; in Kotabowe Vidiya, 295; Sinhalese and Muslim compared, 303

D'Oyly, Sir John, 11, 16, 17nn., 18, 30, 74, 96, 130, 132, 133n., 144, 168

D'Souza, V. S., 207, 372, 373

Dravidians, 217, 219, 339, 343; and kinship categories, 169, 209–221;

Ceylon and Adi Dravida compared, 345

Dry Zone, 15, 18–19, 36

dual organization, 28

Dumont, L., 29, 210, 217, 219, 308, 328, 341, 348–359 passim, 367, 370, 371, 374

Durava, Toddy Tappers, 60, 86, 272

Dutch in Ceylon, 14

East India Company, 20n.

economy, 49, 56; incomes, 36, 97–98; capital, 56; subsistence, 56; black market, 57; entrepreneurs, 57

Eikstedt, E., von, 142n.

Emeneau, M. B., 139n., 217, 218, 336–342 passim

endogamy, 59, 64–65, 74, 169, 200, 202, 349, 365–366, 370

excommunication, 184, 256, 326

exogamy, 218, 220, 330, 354; Toda, 339; Tanjore, 346

exports, 19

family. See nuclear family

Farmer, B., 19

Fawcett, F., 374

feudal services, 16–18

Firth, R., 222n.

food. See household

Fortes, M., 4, 169

Freeman, J. D., 208

functionalism, 9

Gal Oya colonization scheme, 8–9, 229

Galle, 13

Galpitiya, 77, 82, 88–89; schools in, 54n.; Low Country settlers in, 86–87

garden lands, 47

ge. See nuclear family

Geiger, W., 15n.

gifts: exchange of, 163; dowry, 274; of a virgin, 352

Gluckman, M., 187n.

gods, 316. See also annual ritual; Kataragama; Pattini

Gough, E. K., 60, 178n., 179, 206, 217, 218, 308, 344, 345, 346, 348, 352, 354, 361–370 passim, 373; and D. M. Schneider, 283, 361, 362

Goyigama, Cultivators, 28, 35, 59, 60, 62, 74, 77, 89, 117; Radala subcaste of, 16, 73; names, 142

Hayley, F. A., 221
Henea, Washermen, 29, 55, 60–62, 65, 68, 89
Hindu. See Tamils
horoscope, 162
household, 117, 119, 297, 299; cooking and eating, 108, 287, 302; rights and obligations, 114
hypergamy, 95, 149, 172–173, 176–178, 183, 329, 352, 365–366; among Nayar, 178; and caste, 179; in Low Country, 271, 277; matrilineal, 325, 365, 369; patrilineal, 352–353; Brahman, 352–353; among Muslims in Malabar, 373

illness, 162n.
incest, 346; in Tanjore, 345; brother-sister, 349; rules against, 356–357
inheritance, 121–123, 133–135, 136, 139, 174–175; and polyandry, 112; and descent, 121; patterns of, 121, 130, 132; in Makulle Watta, 237–238; in Kotabowe Vidiya, 291
irrigation systems, 15, 20, 37. See paddy cultivation
Iyer, L. A. K., 283n., 373

Jaques, E., 8n.
Johnstone, Sir Alexander, 283
joint family, 101
joking behavior, 181

Kachin, 4
Kadayar, Lime Burners, 329
Kallar, Thieves, 328, 356
Kalmunai, 311
Kandy, 13
Kandyan Kingdom, 15–16, 58–60, 74
Kandyan Law Commission, 60, 132, 133n.
Kandyan Peasantry Commission, 17, 20nn.
Kandyan Sinhalese: population of, 14
Kannar, 328
Kapurala, 34, 35, 170
Karava, Fishermen, 53, 59, 86, 88, 272
Karayyar, Fishermen, 314, 329
Karve, 347n., 350, 359, 361, 372; on Nayar hypergamy, 371
Kataragama, 17, 318; *Valli Amma,* 318; myth of, 319
kindred, 60, 97, 203, 330; at weddings,

164, 166; boundaries of, 189–190; in Helagama hamlet, 190–194; co-operation and identity, 195–197; stresses in, 197–199; and caste, 205–206; and land, 257–260
Kinegolle, 83, 125
Kinnarayo, Mat Weavers, 60, 90
kinship, 10, 138; structure of, 6; rules of, 96; categories of, 152–154, 171, 209–210, 343; terms of, 210–212, 216–217, 221–222; Dravidian, 219; in Makulle Watta, 238, 246; in Vilawa, 255, 256; general structure of, 279, 304, 330, 334, 342–343, 352, 355, 362, 364–365, 368, 372; milk, 290n.; in Kotabowe Vidiya, 299; in Panama, 315; Toda terms, 340; comparisons of, 342; in Tanjore, 345; in Malabar, 360
Knox, Robert, 12, 16n., 150, 189, 227, 271, 332
Kota, Musicians, 337
Kotabowe Vidiya, 11, 286; marriage in, 287–290, 296; inheritance in, 291; divorce in, 295; kinship terms in, 299
Kottegoda, 272
kovil, 33, 284n., 322
kudi, 314; internal organization of, 326; in Tambilivil, 326, 327, 328; in Tirukkovil, 327; disputes in, 327; divisions of, 327; Malabar and Ceylon compared, 329
Kumane, 311, 316
Kumbapettai, 354
Kurakkal, 61, 314, 326
Kurumba, Sorcerers, 337
Kurunegala, 11

land: classification of, in Terutenne, 21, 39; in Dry Zone, 36; measurements of, 37–38; as dowry in Terutenne, 175; classification of, in Vilawa, 254–255
land tenure: in Kandyan Kingdom, 16, 18n.; and service tenures, 17, 18; and temple organization in South India, 18n.; and shares, 98–99, 102; and kinship in Vilawa, 255–263; in Panama, 312, 321, 323
Lanerolle, J. de, 29
language, 3, 5; as communication, 5, 6; and bilingual population, 8, 284, 310, 316n.; national, 13, 32, 324;

Sinhalese, 15n.; and incest rules, 357

law: Mitakshara, 101; Dayabhaga, 101; Roman Dutch, 273. See also Kandyan Law Commission

Leach, E. R., 4, 7, 9, 21, 61n., 149, 207, 208n., 210, 269, 304n., 352, 356, 369

Le Mesurier, C. J. R., 50, 317

Lévi-Strauss, C., 4, 8, 217, 333, 336, 355, 356

Lewis, F., 312

Low Country, 7, 9, 14, 88, 271–278; settlers, 86–87, 234–236, 271, 313

Ludowyk, E. F. C., 12

Mahavansa, 15n.

Maho, 11, 50n.

Maine, Sir Henry, 131

maittunan or mithuna, 350, 375n.; etymology, 375

Makulle Watta, 11, 40–41, 50, 228–230; economy in, 51–53, 231; temples in, 85; caste in, 233–234; town composition of, 234; kinship and marriage in, 236–246

Malabar coast, kinship systems of, 359–369 passim; compared with Ceylon, 329

Malinowski, B. K., 301

Mandelbaum, D. G., 337n.

Mannar, Washermen, 328

Maravar, 356

marriage, 63, 104, 130, 150–154, 184, 355; rules of, 9, 96, 209–210, 216; Sinhalese–Tamil, 11, 310–315; cross-caste, 65, 69–73, 87; marital obligations, 107, 114, 124; patterns of, 121, 127, 130; concepts of, 134, 159–169; and weddings, 159–169; negotiations for, 161–162; and elimination of weddings, 168; traditional, 168; payments, 172–173; stability of, 185–187; remarriage, 188; denials of, 190–191; wrong, 213–216; in Makulle Watta, 236–246; in Vilawa, 266–268; in Low Country, 276; among Karava, 276–277; in Kotabowe Vidiya, 287–296; sister's daughter (Brahman), 351. See also binna; deega; cross-cousins; dowry; matrilocal system

Marshall, H., 112n.

matrilineal descent, 6; and hyper-gamy, 7, 325, 365, 369; Muslim, 283–284; a puzzle, 305; in Ceylon and Malabar, 329, 369; Toda, 336, 341n.; Cochin, 365–367

matrilocal system, 7, 130, 286, 294–295. See also binna

Mauss, M., 274

Maybury-Lewis, D., 5

Meerworth-Levina, L., 317

Menzies, I. E. P., 8n.

micro-castes, 335, 347; in South India, 306; in Ceylon, 206–207; of Tamils in Tanjore, 207; of Islamic Moplah community, 207; endogamy in, 349

models. See structure

Monaragala, 11, 50n.

Mukkuva, Fishermen, 283, 314, 329

Mulla, 101, 102

Muslims: Marakkala, 272n.; in Ceylon and South India, 283; role of Jamaat, 284, 289–290, 296; food customs of, 285n., 302; kudampam, 286–287; mahar, 290, 295–296; matrilocal, 294; and Kandyans, 300–304; kinship of, 300–307; Mapilla, 373; hypergamy among, 373

myth: of castes, 89; of names, 145–147; of Muslims, 283; of Panama, 312; of Kataragama, 319

Nadel, S. F., 4

Nallavar, Toddy Tappers, 329

names, 63, 66, 142, 148; of castes, 74, 91; personal, 91; J. Davy on, 91; in Terutenne, 143–145; myths of, 145–147; in Makulle Watta, 237; in Vilawa, 269; in Low Country, 278; in Panama, 313

national language issue, 13, 32, 324

nationalism, 14, 19, 41

nature, social order an imitation of, 5

Nayar, 7, 171, 178–179, 360–361, 367; paternity among, 308; cross-cousin marriage among, 367–368; Ceylon compared with, 369

Needham, R., 210

Nildandahinna, 26, 50n.

nuclear family, 40, 46, 96–97, 101–115

Okande, 322

Overseas Economic Survey (Ceylon), 20

paddy cultivation, 20–23, 37, 44, 55, 97–98; cooperative, 196–197; in Makulle Watta, 231; yields of, 254; in Vilawa, 257; in Panama, 312, 321

Padu, 311, 316

Panama, 8, 310–312; land tenure in, 312, 321, 323; names, 313; caste in, 315; kinship in, 315; disputes in, 322

pangu, 252

Parayar, Funeral Drummers, 329

Pathans, 54*n*., 151

patrilineal descent, 6, 7, 139, 144–145, 223, 271, 278, 280, 336, 348, 353, 369, 371, 372

patrilocal system. See *deega*

Pattini (goddess), 28, 33, 316, 317

Peradeniya, 3

Percival, R., 36, 96

Peter of Greece, Prince, 109, 341*n*.

Peters, E. L., 222*n*.

Pieris, R., 15

political institutions, 6

pollution, 59, 63, 68, 81, 107*n*., 137, 138*n*., 177, 200, 343

Polonnaruwa, 15

polyandry, 11, 96, 108, 110–112, 241, 245; frequency of, 109

polygamy, 96

polygyny, 112–113, 245

populations. See Ceylon

Portuguese, 14–15

Pottuvil, 311

puberty, 161

Pul Eliya, 207, 252, 269

purity. See pollution

Queyroz, F. de, 24

Radala, 16, 73

Radcliffe-Brown, A. R., 111

Raghavan, M. D., 142*n*., 276*n*., 317

religion. See Buddhism in Ceylon; Christians; Muslims; Tamils

Richards, A. I., 288

rites de passage, 163, 362

ritual: offering of food, 93–94; village, 138*n*. See also annual ritual

Rivers, W. H. R., 217, 336–341 *passim*

Rodiya, Beggars, 60, 90

Rural Development Society, 31

Ryan, B., 60, 74, 88, 103*n*., 311

Sannyasi, 61

Sarkar, N. K., 135*n*.

Sastri, K. A. N., 15*n*.

Schneider, D. M., 283, 361, 362

schools, 54

Seligman, C. G., and B. Z., 23, 229

settlements, agricultural, types of, 21–22

sex. See cross-cousins; pollution; women

Shah, A., 208*n*.

shifting cultivation. See chena

siblings, 335, 359

Sinhalese language, 13, 32, 324

slaves, 79*n*.

sorcery, 125

South India, 60, 151–152, 171. See also Dravidians; Malabar coast; Tanjore

Srinivas, M. N., 60, 217, 218

status, 30, 140, 172–173, 184, 200–202. See also caste; dowry; hypergamy

Stevenson, H. N. C., 137*n*., 177

structure, 5, 6, 8, 9, 305, 334; social, 3, 4, 5, 9, 121, 163, 168, 200; linguistic, 3; models of, 4, 8, 332; change of, 7; merging of, 310; transformations of, 8, 324, 332–333, 345, 355

suicides, 9

symbolism: of food and women, 93, 116; of caste, 89, 92, 94, 95

systems. See structure

taboos, 139, 179

Talensi, 4, 169

Tambattai, 328

Tambiah, H. W., 283*n*., 291, 311

Tambiah, S. J., 135*n*.

Tambilivil, 326–328

Tamils, 11, 61; population of, 12; of Jaffna, 13, 15, 347; micro-castes among, 207; Muslim, 282–309; of East Coast, 310–331; of South India, 344–359

tank villages, 21. See also Vilawa

Tangalla, 271

Tanjore, 207; Dravida and Brahman of, 343, 348, 350–351; incest in, 345; exogamy in, 346

Tattar or *Kammalar*, Blacksmiths, 328

tea estates, 19

temples: in South India, 18*n*.; Toda, 338. See also *devale; kovil; vihara*

Tennent, Sir James E., 20*n.*, 24, 247, 282, 325, 332

Terutenne, 10–11, 24–28, 62; dual organization of, 28; land tenure in, 39, 175; caste in, 60; names in, 143–145; disputes in, 155–158

thought. See categories; structure

Thurston, E., 308, 374

Tikopia, 222

Tirukkovil, 311, 318, 327, 328

Tiyyar, 363–364

Toda, 336–341

Tolfrey, comments on D'Oyly, 130

traders, 88

trances, 35

Trincomalee, 272

Tugay, E. F., 304*n.*

urumaya, 133*n.;* in Vilawa, 264, 265

Vahumpura, Jaggery Makers, 60, 62, 93

Valan Karayo, Potters, 29, 60, 62, 70, 71, 73

Valli Amma, 318

vas, 29, 34

Veddas, 23, 227

Vellalar, Cultivators, 328, 329, 356

vihara, 33, 34, 72, 317. See also annual ritual

Vilawa, 40, 50, 248, 250, 251; land tenure in, 41, 250–251, 257–263; households in, 240–241; kinship and marriage in, 242–245, 255–256, 263–265; returns on land in, 254; mobility in, 268–269

Vittachi, T., 41*n.*

wasama, 31

Wekumbura, 27

Wet Zone, 18, 19

Wirz, P., 33

Wittgenstein, L., 3

women: position of, 122, 131, 133, 141, 180, 223; purity of, 107, 176, 177, 180; and land, 223, 263, 265

Woolf, L., 229